South
SEAS

VIKINGS OF THE PACIFIC

The Discovery of New Zealand

SOUTH SEAS

MYTHS AND LEGENDS

DONALD A. MACKENZIE

SENATE

South Seas – Myths & Legends

First published in 1930 as *Myths & Traditions of the South Sea Islands* by The Gresham Publishing Company Ltd, London.

This edition first published in 1996 by Senate, an imprint of Random House UK Ltd, Random House, 20 Vauxhall Bridge Road, London SW1V 2SA

Copyright © Donald A. Mackenzie 1930

ISBN 0 09 185040 1

Printed and bound in Guernsey by The Guernsey Press Co. Ltd

CONTENTS

CONTENTS

MYTHS AND TRADITIONS OF THE SOUTH SEA ISLANDS

CHAPTER I

The Coral Islands of the Pacific

Beginnings of Navigation—Cultivating the "Sea Sense"—Island Paradises of the Egyptians, Sumerians, Greeks, Celts, Hindus, Chinese, Japanese, Polynesians, and pre-Columbian Americans—European Explorers in Oceania—Robert Louis Stevenson's "Isles of Longevity"—Polynesians as Lotos-Eaters—Decline of Sea-faring—Lost Continent Theory—Ethnics of Oceania—Ancient Mariners and Colonists—Skilled Neolithic Artisans—Polynesian Astronomers—Priestly Scholars resembled Druids—Four Divisions of Oceania: Indonesia, Melanesia, Micronesia, and Polynesia—Script and Memory Training—Maori Colleges—Great Migrations.

The glamour of the isles of the sea, which stirs us when mention is made of Polynesia, pervades the poetry of all maritime peoples, and appears to be of great antiquity. We can detect it in certain ancient inscriptions and in immemorial folk-tales that echo of early experiences. When the pioneer sea-farers, who first ventured upon the uncharted waters of the Mediterranean, were beginning to cultivate what we know as the "sea sense", they had experience of that glamour, for they were enticed from mainland coasts by the mysterious and alluring Cyclades:

> "the sprinkled isles,
> Lily on lily that o'erlace the sea,
> And laugh their pride when the light wave lisps 'Greece'."

The farther they sailed the more the marvels grew. On

reaching what had seemed to be an ultimate isle, they saw with wondering eyes still more distant islands dimly pencilled on the far horizon; and when driven far to sea by contrary winds and currents, they caught glimpses of strange blue capes and mountains rising like " sea-shouldering whales " out of the wilderness of waves. In their dreams of a virgin world these early mariners visioned the distant islands of an Earthly Paradise.

The mystery of the sea haunts some of the Pyramid Texts of Ancient Egypt. There are in these significant references to the " Outer Ocean " which was supposed to flow round the world, and it is crossed by Horus. As the rescuer and guide of disembodied souls, that god leads the Pharaohs after death across Celestial waters to an island Paradise on which are to be found an ever-flourishing Tree of Life and an everlasting Well of Life. The papyrus story of " The Shipwrecked Sailor " tells of a mysterious floating island, peopled by supernatural beings, which sinks beneath the sea, or is " changed into waves ".

Early maritime experiences can similarly be detected in the literature of Ancient Mesopotamian civilization. The Sumerian legends make mention of the Paradise of Dilmun in the Persian Gulf. When that epic hero, Gilgamesh, who dreads to die, makes search for his ancestor Ut-napishtim, to whom the gods have revealed the secret of longevity, he crosses the strange and perilous sea called " Waters of Death ", and reaches an island on which dwells Ut-napishtim and his wife. Gilgamesh is directed by Ut-napishtim to another island, and he visits it and finds there the " Plant of Life ", but as the hero stoops to drink from a brook, the plant is snatched from him by a supernatural monster, the guardian serpent-dragon.

The Greeks had dreams of the " Isles of the Blest ":

" those Hesperian gardens famed of old,
Fortunate fields and groves and flowery vales."

Golden, life-giving apples grew there and were protected by dragon-serpents. Celtic songs and stories tell
of a western island paradise called " Apple Land " with
its " Isle of Women ", " Land of the Ever-Young ",
" Happy Plain ", &c.:

> " a lovely land
> On which the many blossoms drop, . . .
> Without grief, without sorrow, without death,
> Without sickness, without debility."

There are wonderful Hindu folk-stories of floating
and vanishing islands of the deep; and Sanskrit literature contains descriptions of islands peopled by immortals, which are situated far beyond " Jambu dvipa ",
the central island of the world of which India is a part.
The Chinese possess many stories of the floating islands
of Paradise with their " white saints ", the " fungus of
immortality ", and " Wells of Life ". Ancient Emperors
fitted out expeditions to search for those mysterious
islands. Japanese legends tell of an island Paradise,
named Horaizan, with its longevity tree and life-giving
fountain, and a similar island is met with in the folk
literature of Polynesia. Even among the pre-Columbian
Americans there existed a haunting belief in an island
Paradise known as " The Land of Souls ".[1]

The legends of distant isles inhabited by immortals
were perpetuated in Europe into mediæval and later
times. When, therefore, European navigators first discovered the coral islands of the Pacific, it seemed as if
reality had been imparted to the sailor-tales of old
Romance—that the daring explorers of the Deep had
actually made discovery of the " Fortunate Isles ":

> " the island valley of Avilion;
> Where falls not hail, or rain, or any snow,
> Nor ever wind blows loudly; but it lies
> Deep-meadowed, happy, fair with orchard lawns
> And bowery hollows crowned with summer sea."

---

[1] *Lafitau sur les Mœurs des Sauvages Ameriquains*, tome I, p. 401, and my *Myths of China and Japan*, p. 106, for various references to authorities.

Like the ancient mariners of East and West who had searched for the fabled longevity islands with their " Wells of Life " and " Plants of Life ", Robert Louis Stevenson set forth upon his voyage to the South Seas in the hope of being able to prolong his days. " I believed," he tells us, " I was come to the afterpiece of life, and had only the nurse and undertaker to expect. It was suggested I should try the South Seas; and I was not unwilling to visit like a ghost, and be carried like a bale, among scenes that had attracted me in youth and health." He was, as he makes confession, caught in spell by the glamour of Oceania:

" Few men who come to the islands leave them; they grow grey where they alighted; the palm shades and the trade wind fans them till they die. . . . No part of the world exerts the same attractive power upon the visitor. . . . The first love, the first sunrise, the first South Sea island, are memories apart and touched a virginity of sense. . . .

" I was now escaped out of the shadow of the Roman Empire, under whose toppling monuments we were all cradled, whose laws and letters are on every hand of us, constraining and preventing. I was now to see what men might be whose fathers had never studied Virgil, had never been conquered by Cæsar, and never been ruled by the wisdom of Gaius or Papinian." [1]

Long centuries before Europe had first come to hear of the wonderful coral islands of the Pacific, they had been discovered and peopled by bold and enterprising sea-farers, and the descendants of those men are known to us as the Polynesians. In their isolated island homes the Polynesians became veritable Lotos-Eaters. They gradually abandoned their habit of making long voyages of exploration, they built smaller and smaller vessels to suit local needs, and they discarded certain crafts which had ceased to be absolutely necessary for their existence.

Some writers, misled by the decadent condition of

[1] *In the South Seas*, Chapter I.

Polynesian civilization, and ignoring Polynesian traditions which are so eloquent of former great achievements in navigation, have refused to believe that the ancestors of the islanders were the greatest known mariners of the ancient world. They have therefore found it necessary to imagine that there once existed in the Pacific a great Continent which was shattered and engulfed during a comparatively recent seismic disturbance, leaving the widely-scattered islands and their inhabitants as memorials of its former existence. Like the "lost Atlantis", the lost Pacific continent is, however, a myth. It has never had existence since the Ice Age, except in the imaginations of writers untrained in scientific method.

Ethnologists have found that the Polynesians are a people of mixed descent. Professor Elliot Smith has detected the Polynesian type in Indonesia, the Malay Archipelago, round the coasts of Ceylon and India, on the shores of the Persian Gulf, and on the island of Madagascar. Skulls revealing "the same distinctive traits" as those of Polynesia, are not rare even "on the Pacific coast of Central and South America". This authority considers that the original homeland of the Polynesian wanderers was North Syria, where the early blending of broad-headed people of the Armenoid race, with sections of the long-headed Mediterranean race, imparted to skulls certain unmistakable characters. As the earliest specimens of these skulls have been found in the ancient Giza necropolis in Egypt, Elliot Smith refers to them as the "Giza type".

During Egypt's Late Pre-dynastic and Early Dynastic periods, representatives of the Giza type entered the Delta and Nile valley. They were a heavier and more muscular people than the proto-Egyptians, and had larger and loftier skulls with broader foreheads. There was, however, "a very wide range of variation amongst them as regards the form of the skull and face". Elliot

Smith tells us that he has "found skulls of this type widespread in Polynesia ".[1]

The sea-farers of the Giza type who, during the course of many long centuries, migrated from North Syria into Mesopotamia, from the shores of the Persian Gulf to India and from India to Indonesia were originally acquainted with the use of metals. When, however, they reached Polynesia, they possessed neither metal weapons nor metal implements. From the archæologist's viewpoint they were, therefore, in the "Neolithic Age". They constructed their boats with stone tools; their weapons were of stone and wood, as were also their agricultural implements; they also made use of shells, bones, &c.

It should not be assumed, however, that the Polynesian craftsmen were greatly hampered because they possessed no metal tools. A writer who has made a special study of Hawaiian stone implements writes in this connexion:

"In watching the shaping of a canoe I have seen the old canoe-maker use for the rough shaping and excavating an ordinary foreign steel adze; but for the finishing touches he dropped the foreign tool and returned to the adze of his ancestors, and the blunt-looking stone cut off a delicate shaving from the very hard *Koa* wood, and never seemed to take too much wood, as the foreign adze was apt to do. That skill was an important element in the use I was convinced, for, with all the teaching of the native, I could only make a dent where I tried to raise a shaving."

Another writer, telling of canoe-making at Tahiti says:

"This work, difficult as it would be to a European with his iron tools, they perform without iron, and with amazing dexterity. They hollow out with their stone axes as fast, at least, as our carpenters could do, and dubb, though slowly, with prodigious nicety. I have seen them take off the skin of an angular plank

---

[1] *The Ancient Egyptians* (Second Edition), pp. 116 *et seq*. and 160 *et seq*.

without missing a stroke, the skin itself scarce one-sixteenth part of an inch in thickness."

In his "Journal", Sir Joseph Banks writes of the Tahitians:

"A stone axe in the shape of an adze, a chisel or gouge made of human bone, a file or rasp of coral, the skin of stingrays and coral sand to polish with, are a sufficient set of tools for building a house. Their axes (adzes) are made of black stone, not very hard, but tolerably tough; they are of different sizes; some, intended for felling, weigh 3 lb. or 4 lb.; others, which are used only for carving, not as many ounces. . . . Felling a tree is their greatest labour; a large one requires many hands to assist, and some days before it can be finished, but when once it is down they manage it with far greater dexterity than is credible to a European. If it is to be made into boards they put wedges into it, and drive them with such dexterity that they divide it into slabs of three or four inches in thickness. These slabs they very soon dubb down with their axes (adzes) to any given thinness, and in this work they certainly excel; indeed, their tools are better adapted for this than for any other labour. I have seen them dubb off the first rough coat of a plank at least as fast as one of our carpenters could have done it; and in hollowing, where they were able to raise large slabs of the wood, they certainly work more quickly, owing to the weight of their tools. Those who are masters of this business will take off a surprisingly thin coat from a whole plank without missing a stroke. They can also work upon wood of any shape as well as upon a flat piece." [1]

"Neolithic culture", when studied in a museum, is often referred to as "primitive" and "savage", or "semi-savage". The evidence afforded by Polynesia, however, makes us revise our former views and regard the early stone-using peoples with more respect than some of us have hitherto been wont to do. These men were skilled artisans who accomplished wonderful work with "primitive" tools which would be of little use in the hands of modern European artisans.

[1] E. Best, *The Stone Implements of the Maori*, Bulletin No. 4, Dominion Museum, Wellington (N.Z.) 1912, pp. 154 *et seq.*

Certain archæologists incline to doubt if boat-building and navigation were much advanced before metals came into use. They assume that planks could not be cut from trees before copper saws were invented, but, as is shown above, the Polynesians split the wood with the aid of wedges and dressed the planks with stone adzes. We have no reason for assuming that the Neolithic carpenters of Europe were in ancient times less skilled than were the Polynesians of the South Sea islands before the introduction into the Pacific islands of metal tools by European sailors and traders.

The Polynesians are not the only Neolithic sea-farers of whom we have of late years acquired considerable knowledge. Dr. Laufer tells us of the Neolithic Su-shên of North-eastern Asia, whom he refers to as the " Vikings of the East ". They had in the seventh century of our era become notorious both in Japan and China on account of their persistent sea-raids and battles. For a thousand years before that time they were known as daring mariners on the Chinese coasts. " From Chinese records," says Laufer, " we can establish the fact that the Su-shên lived through a Stone Age for at least fifteen hundred years down to the Middle Ages, when they became merged in the great flood of roaming Tungusian tribes." While still making use of stone tools, the Su-shên were the carriers to China of iron armour manufactured somewhere in Siberia. Their own arrow-heads were made of hard greenstone, and were quite as effective as those of copper, bronze, or iron.[1]

The " Neolithic " Polynesian mariners had a wonderful knowledge of astronomy, and they were able to steer their vessels across the ocean guided by the heavenly bodies; they were expert navigators and could battle successfully with wind and tide. They had learned by experience how to preserve food, and carried in their

[1] Laufer, *Chinese Clay Figures*, pp. 271–2, and E. H. Parker in the *Transactions of the Asiatic Society of Japan*, Vol. XVIII, pp. 157 *et seq.*

ships sufficient supplies for long voyages; they could even store and keep sweet enough water to last for weeks on end. Their vessels were eminently seaworthy, and the crews were well disciplined.

We have no written records of the long voyages accomplished by the ancient Polynesian Columbuses and Cooks. Some of these voyages, however, are found to be immortalized in oral traditions. Among the Polynesians, as among the ancient Gauls and other peoples, there were groups of professional priestly scholars and historians who devoted their lives to the preservation of family and tribal lore. Happily, a considerable amount of the Polynesian oral literature has been collected and placed on record by British Empire and other collectors, and has been made available for anthropologists and historians. It is now possible, owing especially to the researches of New Zealand scholars, to trace with a wonderful degree of accuracy some of the migrations from Indonesia into Polynesia, and certain of the migrations from one part of Polynesia to another. It has even become possible to arrange a system of chronology for Polynesian civilization.

One of the old Polynesian mariners, whose fame has come down the centuries, is known to have voyaged from Tahiti to Samoa and back, a distance of 2640 miles, from Fiji to Paumotu and back, a distance of 2400 miles, and from Fiji to Easter Island and back, a distance of 4200 miles. Earlier Polynesian mariners who sailed from Borneo to the Hawaiian group of islands covered between 6000 and 7000 miles, and we must regard them as among the most famous explorers in the history of navigation. To appreciate fully their wonderful achievements, one should give heed to the wise suggestion of the late Lord Salisbury, which was addressed to those who failed to realize the extent of the British Empire—that is, to study large maps. Easter Island received its early settlers from the Solomons and New Zealand from Tahiti, but the great lengths of these voyages are rarely fully realized. The American continent is nearer to Hawaii than Hawaii is to either Easter Island or New Zealand. Easter Island is about 2000 miles distant from the South American coast, but it is about 7000 miles distant from the island of Nukuoro to the south of the Carolines, and yet the same language is spoken on Nukuoro and on Easter Island. Mr. Elsdon Best reminds us that the Polynesian language is spoken " over a great oceanic area of four thousand by five thousand miles in extent, flecked by many isles. . . . Members of a common race, speaking dialects of a common tongue, these units in far-sundered lands not only held undisputed possession of the central and eastern Pacific, but also heard dim echoes of their racial tongue from their outposts in Melanesia and Micronesia."[1]

There are four main ethnographic divisions of the vast area of scattered islands which has been given the collective name of Oceania. The first is Indonesia, and includes Sumatra, Java, the Celebes, Borneo, the Philippines and Formosa; the second is Micronesia, and includes the Pelew Islands, the Carolines, the Mariane group, the Marshall Islands, the Gilbert Islands, and the Ellice Islands; the third is Melanesia, and includes New Guinea, the Bismarck Archipelago, the Solomon Islands, the New Hebrides, New Caledonia, and the Fiji Islands; the fourth, and by far the most extensive group, is Polynesia which extends from the Hawaiian Islands (called by Captain Cook the Sandwich Islands) in the north to New Zealand in the south, and eastward from the Union group and the Samoan and Tonga Islands to beyond the Marquesas Islands, the Tuamotu Archipelago, and the Gambier Islands, as far as lonely Easter Island. The Polynesian area is about four times larger than that of Indonesia, yet the southern part of Indonesia is so extensive that if the Dutch East Indies (Sumatra, Java,

---

[1] *Transactions and Proceedings of the New Zealand Institute*, Vol. XLVIII, p. 447.

&c.), are placed across a map of Europe of similar scale, it will be found that they reach from Iceland almost to Asia Minor. A liner's voyage from end to end of the Dutch East Indies occupies a full week.

Before the cultural influence of Europe swept through Polynesia and its people were suddenly " transported " from the archæological " Neolithic Age " to the modern Age of Steel, its inhabitants were, as has been indicated, a people with " long memories ". Their priestly scholars were systematically trained from youth to perpetuate the lore of their ancestors—the oral traditions, the pedigrees of great families, and religious myths and practices. The " wise men " of Polynesia formed as exclusive a caste as did the Brahmans of India, the Magi of Persia, the Galli of Syria, and the Druids of Gaul and the British Isles. There is evidence, as in the wooden tablets carved with figures which the missionaries found in Easter Island, that a system of hieroglyphic writing was known and practised. Mrs. Routledge [1] tells that the men who were acquainted with this art of writing have all perished:

" The natives said that they burnt the tablets in compliance with the orders of the missionaries, though such suggestion would hardly be needed in a country where wood is scarce; the Fathers, on the contrary, state that it was due to them that any were preserved. Some certainly were saved by their means and through the interest shown in them by Bishop Janssen of Tahiti, while two or three found their way to museums after the natives became aware of their value; but some or all of these existing tablets are merely fragments of the original."

The Maori of New Zealand, on the other hand, are not known to have had any form of script. " It has been suggested," writes Elsdon Best,[2] " that in olden days some form of written characters was employed, but that

---

[1] *The Mystery of Easter Island*, p. 207.
[2] *The Maori*, Wellington, New Zealand, 1924, Vol. II, p. 201.

the art was lost." Mr. Best is sceptical in this connexion and writes:

" There is no reliable evidence to support such statements or
theories, and the best negative evidence is that the Maori formerly
used the quipus or knotted cord for recording tallies. We do not
know that this system was actually used here, but it certainly was
in Polynesia, and the Takitumu natives have preserved a memory
of it, a traditional knowledge of the *aho ponapona*, as they term it.
This name means ' knotted cord ',[1] and the local tradition tells
us that it was employed in sending messages to distant places, a
statement that it is not easy to accept. Had the Polynesians, or
their isolated offshoot in New Zealand, been acquainted with any
form of written language, then why should they have anything
to do with the cumbrous quipus?"

Staves with knobs were, however, used as "aids to
memory" in reciting genealogies.

It may be that the use of a script had been dropped
before the Maori section of Polynesians migrated to
New Zealand. The Druids, according to Julius Cæsar
(*De Bello Gallico*, Book VI, 15), used the Greek alphabet
in both their public and private accounts, but retained
a superstitious objection to committing their doctrines
to writing. It was also feared by those Gaulish Druids
that if the pupils were to depend on written texts, they
might relax the cultivation of memory. Cæsar himself
remarks in this connexion that constant dependence on
manuscripts weakens the powers of mental application
and retention. In our own day it is no uncommon thing
to find University-trained men complaining of their poor
memories, and men who have never studied in univer-
sities possessed of prodigious memories.

The Maori of New Zealand had, until comparatively
recently, their Schools of Learning which were known
by various names, including " whare wanaga " (" high-
class knowledge house "), and " whare purakau "
(" legend house "). The aim of the education system in

[1] The " Knotted Cord " was known in China and in pre-Columbian America.

Photo A. J. Iles

MAORI MOTHER AND BABY

The cloak in which the baby is carried is made of flax and kiwi feathers. The mother is
tattooed on the lips and chin

LONG-VOYAGE SAILING-BOAT, WITH OUTRIGGER, HERMIT ISLANDS

(2)

these " Colleges " was the preservation and transmission from generation to generation of Maori lore " without any change by interpolation, omission or deterioration. . . . Any form of change in olden teachings," says Mr. Elsdon Best, " met with strong disapproval; any questionings of ancient teachings was held to be a grievous insult to Tane (the god), the origin and patron of knowledge." Indeed, " any deviation from olden teaching was black treason ".

In the various classes the pupils listened to and memorized, in the ideal Freemason fashion, the recitals of the elderly instructors. From time to time severe and exacting examinations were held. Pupils had to be " word perfect " if they were to pass. " Each scholar who successfully underwent the examination," says Best, " took his seat on the right of the house; those who failed had to go on the left side. The latter might be granted another opportunity to memorize the lectures." When after the British occupation of New Zealand, the young Maori learned to read and write, the students of the native colleges began to use notebooks. Their teachers disliked the innovation, and frowned at it, but their power over the young was slipping away.

The New Zealand scholars who have collected and studied Maori lore have found evidence of three great migrations from Indonesia to the islands of the Pacific. The first brought the Samoans, Tongans and others, the second the branch which included the Rarotongans, Tahitians, Marquesans, the Maoris, &c., and the third the Hawaiians, and the east-coast Maoris.

Before dealing with these and other data regarding Polynesian sea-faring activities, it would be well to gain some knowledge of the vessels which were built and navigated by the South Sea islanders. Some modern writers are constantly asserting that it was impossible for the Polynesians to migrate far in their " frail canoes ", assuming, apparently, that the canoes of the Pacific were as frail as those used on the rivers and lakes of North America.   Others appear to imagine that the vessels possessed by the ancient Polynesians were no larger than those nowadays constructed by natives for fishing and for short voyages.   The fact is overlooked that after the introduction of European vessels, the South Sea islanders ceased to build war canoes.   When European control of the isles was established, native wars were suppressed, and " war canoes " went completely out of use.   As is shown in the next chapter, it is necessary to glean evidence regarding Polynesian vessels from various sources.   The available records are far from being as full and detailed as we should have liked them to be.   There are, however, sufficient data to emphasize that the writers who usually refer to great migrations across the Pacific in early times have not done so without good cause.   These writers have been accused of " rashness " and " bold speculation ", but their critics have not themselves been lacking in " rashness ", for they have been prone to attach a positive value to negative evidence, and even to formulate views without first studying the mass of important evidence which is condensed in the next chapter.

CHAPTER II

Ancient Polynesian Boats

Captain Cook's Evidence—War and Sea-going Canoes—Maori Vessels—
Swiftness of Canoes—The Sacred Canoe—Large Fleets of Tahiti—Transports
accompanied Battle Fleets—Homeric Spectacle—The Chief's Canoe—Fishing
and Trading Vessels—The Outrigger—Triangular and Lateen Sails—Long
Canoes—Bonito Boats—Maori Single Canoes—Samoan and Malayan Vessels
compared—Moriori of Chatham Islands—Long Voyages—Supplies of Water
and Food—Priests on Polynesian and Phœnician Vessels—Astronomers who
set Courses—Fleets in Crescent Form—Indonesian Connexions—Antarctic
visited — Hawaiki — Hawaii and Java — Original Polynesian Homeland —
Memories of Dutch East Indies and India—Irrigation Clue—Long Voyages
cease.

When during his first voyage Captain Cook visited
Tahiti in 1769, he became interested in two particular
types of native canoes. In the record compiled from his
diary we read:

" Some of the smaller boats are made of the bread-fruit tree,
which is wrought without much difficulty, being of a light spongy
nature. Instead of planes, they used their adzes with great dexterity. Their canoes are all shaped with the hand, the Indians
(Polynesians) not being acquainted with the method of warping
a plank.

" Of these (canoes) they have two kinds, one used for short
trips, and the other for longer voyages. These boats are in no
degree proportionate, being from 60 to 70 feet in length, and not
more than a thirtieth part in breadth. The ivahahs, or war-boats,
are fastened together side by side when they go to sea, at the distance of a few feet, by strong wooden poles, which are laid across
them and joined to each side. A stage or platform is raised on the
forepart, about 10 or 12 feet long, upon which stand the fighting
men whose missile weapons are slings and spears. Beneath these

15

stages the rowers sit, who supply the place of those who are wounded. The pahies (*pa'i*), or sea-going boats, in going from one island to another, are out sometimes a month, and often a fortnight or twenty days, and if they had convenience to stow more provisions, they could keep the sea much longer. These vessels are very useful in landing, and putting off from the shore in a surf, for by their great length and high stern they land dry, when the *Endeavour's* [1] boats could scarcely land at all."

Cook saw similar canoes in New Zealand:

" The canoes of this country are long and narrow; the larger sort seem built for war, and will hold from 30 to 100 men. One of those of Tolaga measured nearly 70 feet in length, 6 in width, and 4 in depth. It was sharp at the bottom, and consisted of three lengths, about 2 or 3 inches thick, and tied firmly together with strong plaiting; each side was formed of one entire plank, about 12 inches broad, and about 1½ inches thick, which was fitted to the bottom part with equal strength and ingenuity. Several thwarts were laid from one side to the other, to which they were securely fastened, in order to strengthen the canoes.

" Some few of their canoes at Mercury Bay and Opoorage, were all made entirely of one trunk of a tree, which is made hollow by fire; but by far the greater part are built after the manner above described."

Cook goes on to say that:

" these vessels are rowed by paddles, between 5 and 6 feet in length, the blade of which is a long oval, gradually decreasing till it reaches the handle; and the velocity with which they row with these paddles is very surprising.

" Their sails are composed of a kind of mat or netting, which is extended between two upright poles, one of which is fixed on each side; two ropes, fastened to the top of each pole, serve instead of sheets.

" The vessels are steered by two men, each having a paddle, and sitting in the stern; but they can only sail before the wind, in which direction they move with considerable swiftness."

William Lockerby, who was a prisoner on board one

[1] Cook's ship.

of the double war canoes which carried 200 men, wrote that " Captain Cook's account of the swift sailing of these vessels is quite correct, however incredible it may appear to those who have not seen them. With a moderate wind they will sail twenty miles an hour." [1]

William Ellis, the missionary, describes a variety of Polynesian vessels.[2] He was once a passenger in a double canoe which was named *Tiaitoerau* (" Wait for the West Wind "). " It was between thirty and forty feet in length " and well built. The keel, or bottom, was formed with a number of pieces of tough Tamanu wood, twelve or sixteen inches broad, and two inches thick, hollowed on the inside and rounded without, so as to form a convex angle along the bottom of the canoe." The planks were laced with tough elastic cinet made with the fibres of coco-nut husk.

" The joints or seams were not grooved together, but the edge of one simply laid on that of the other, and fitted with remarkable exactness by the adze of the workman, guided only by his eye: they never use line or rule. The edges of their planks were usually covered with a kind of pitch or gum from the bread-fruit tree, and a thin layer of coco-nut husk spread between them. The husk of the coco-nut swelling when in contact with the water, fills any apertures that may exist, and considering the manner in which they are put together, the canoes are often remarkably dry."

Ellis and his friend sat on the platform between the bowsprits under an awning of platted coco-nut leaves which " afforded a grateful shade ". His description of the " rowers " is worth quoting:

" Their paddles, being made of the tough wood of the hibiscus, were not heavy; yet, having no pins in the sides of the canoe, against which the handles of the paddles could bear, but leaning the whole body over the canoe, first on one side, and then on the

---

[1] *The Journal of William Lockerby, Sandalwood Trader in the Fijian Islands*, 1808–1809 (Hakluyt Society Works, second series, No. LII, p. 41).

[2] *Polynesian Researches* (First Edition), London, 1829, Vol. I, pp. 163 *et seq.*

other, and working the paddle with one hand near the blade, and the other at the upper end of the handle, and shovelling, as it were, the water, appeared a great waste of strength. They often, however, paddle for a time with remarkable swiftness, keeping time with the greatest regularity. The steersman stands or sits in the stern, with a large paddle; the rowers sit in each canoe two or three feet apart, the leader sits next, the steersman gives the signal to start, by striking his paddle violently against the side of the canoe, every paddle is then put in and taken out of the water with every stroke at the same moment; and after they have thus continued on one side for five or six minutes, the leader strikes his paddle, and the rowers instantly and simultaneously turn to the other side, and thus alternately working on each side of the canoe, they go along at a considerable rate."

Captain Cook refers to canoes 108 feet long, but Ellis never saw one more than 70 feet in length. The latter says that the chief's canoes had " sterns remarkably high, sometimes fifteen or eighteen feet above the water, and frequently ornamented with rudely carved hollow cylinders, square pieces or grotesque figures ". One type of war canoe had a low stern with a shelter to give protection against the stones of assailants; other types had elevated sterns " curved like the neck of a swan ". The " sacred canoe was always strong and large, more highly ornamented with carvings and feathers than any of the others. Small houses were erected in each, and the image of the god, sometimes in the shape of a large bird, at other times resembling a hollow cylinder ornamented with various coloured feathers, was kept in these houses. Here the prayers were frequently preferred, and the sacrifices offered."

Ellis tells that the Tahitians formerly possessed " large and magnificent fleets of war canoes " and held regattas and naval reviews, when the vessels " ornamented with carved images, and decorated with flags and streamers of various native coloured cloths, went through the different tactics with great precision ". The sacred canoes " formed part of every fleet, and were generally the most imposing in appearance and attractive in their decorations ".

Captain Cook, when on his second voyage, saw at Tahiti a fleet of 160 large double canoes " very well equipped, manned and armed ", the warriors wearing breast-plates and helmets.

" The vessels were decorated with flags and streamers, so that the whole made a grand and noble appearance. . . . Besides the vessels of war, there were 170 sail of smaller double canoes, all with a little house upon them, and rigged with mast and sail, which the war canoes had not. These were designed for transports and victuallers—for in the war canoes was no sort of provisions whatever. In these 330 vessels there were no less than 7760 men."

The fleet departed on an expedition to some distant island.

Captain Cook and a party when on shore saw at a later date a fleet of war canoes making for the shore.

" When they got before the landing place, they formed themselves into divisions, and then each division, one after the other, paddled in for the shore with all their might, in the most exact and regular manner. All their motions were observed with such quickness as clearly showed them to be expert in their business."

Ellis was reminded by such a spectacle of the descriptions and pictures of Homeric vessels:

" The peculiar and almost classical shape of the large Tahitian canoes, the elevated prow and stern, the rude figures, carving and other ornaments, the loose folding drapery of the natives on board, and the maritime aspect of their general places of abode, are all adapted to produce a singular effect on the mind of the beholder. I have often thought, when I have seen a fleet of thirty or forty approaching the shore, that they exhibited no faint representation of the ships in which the Argonauts sailed, or the vessels that conveyed the heroes of Homer to the siege of Troy."

A chief's double canoe, Ellis informs us, was always named " The Rainbow ", and it was usually from 20 to 30 feet long. A type of neat double canoe, called " The Twins ", was made out of the hollowed trunks of trees. Single canoes used by fishermen seldom carried more than two persons and were suitable for shallow water. The trading vessel, with mast and sail, which was favoured for long voyages, had an outrigger, and planks were fixed along its sides " after the manner of wash-boards in a European boat ". Ellis gives an interesting description of the outrigger:

" This is always placed on the left side, and fastened to the canoe by two horizontal poles, from five to eight feet long; the front one is straight and firm, the other curved and elastic; it is so fixed that the bark, when empty, does not float upright, being rather inclined to the left; but, when sunk into the water, on being laden, &c., it is generally erect, while the outrigger, which is firmly and ingeniously fastened to the sides by repeated bands of strong cinets, floats on the surface.

" In addition to this, the island-canoes have a strong plank, twelve or fourteen feet long, fastened horizontally across the centre, in an inclined position, one end attached to the outrigger, and the other extending five or six feet over the opposite side, and perhaps elevated four or five feet above the sea. A small railing of rods is fastened along the sides of this plank, and it is designed to assist the navigators in balancing the keel, as a native takes his station on the one side or the other, to counteract the inclination which the wind or sea might give to the vessel. Sometimes they approach the shore with a native standing or sitting on the extremity of the plank, and presenting a singular appearance, which it is impossible to behold without expecting every undulation of the sea will detach him from his apparently insecure situation, and precipitate him into the water."

Ellis goes on to say that in navigating their double canoes, the natives frequently used two sails (the tri-angular and the lateen). In their single vessels, however, they had only one sail. Like the ancient Egyptian

mariners those of Polynesia lowered their masts when
sails were not in use. Sails were made " with the leaves
of the pandanus ", which were " split into thin slips "
and " neatly woven into a kind of matting ". Ropes
" from the corners of the sails are not usually fastened,
but held in the hands of the natives ". These and other
ropes were manufactured from the twisted bark of the
hibiscus and from the fibres of the coco-nut husk.

Turner, the missionary, tells that in Samoa the width
of a canoe was only about eighteen to thirty inches, while
the length was from fifteen to fifty feet. " But for an
outrigger," he says, " it would be impossible to keep
such a long, narrow thing steady in the water." [1] Mr.
S. Percy Smith saw in Samoa " several vessels of from
forty to fifty feet in length; some were double-banked
like the old Roman trireme ". At Upōlu he was greatly
interested in a boat which was a hundred and forty-seven
feet long with sixty-five oars on each side. Ordinary
outrigger canoes, from fifteen to twenty feet long were
used for fishing. A special type of outrigger canoe still
favoured for fishing that beautiful blue-backed silver-
bellied member of the mackerel family, the tropical
Bonito which preys largely on flying fishes, and is good
although rather dry eating. As it is a " running fish " the
Bonito canoes are drawn many miles to sea in chase of it.
The Samoan name for this type of canoe is *va'a-alu-atu*,
and it is usually " from twenty-five to thirty feet in length,
eighteen inches deep, and twelve inches broad ", with
about eight to ten feet at bow and stern decked over.
The outrigger is a sharp, pointed log with two arms.
Mr. Percy Smith gives us a vivid impression of a Bonito
canoe which is a speedy and sea-worthy vessel. He writes:

" When coasting along the north shore of Upōlu in the well-
manned consular boat with Mr. Churchill, we were once struggling
against a heavy tide rip and a strong north-west wind. We were
outside the reef, and to leeward of us was an ugly black lava point

[1] Rev. George Turner, *Nineteen Years in Polynesia*, London, 1861, p. 267.

against which the mountainous waves were dashing with thunderous noise. We could barely hold our own against the great seas. Right ahead of us suddenly appeared one of those beautiful *va'a-alu-atu*, flying before the gale, urged along by a man and a boy. They flew past us in almost less time than it takes to write this, apparently quite dry and comfortable. They passed quite close, but barely looked at us (Samoan fashion), so different from Maoris, who would have stopped and not departed until they had learned all about us. From this incident I formed a high opinion of the sea-going qualities of the *va'a-alu-atu* which probably was the class of canoe that came out in such numbers to reconnoitre Bougainville when he discovered the Samoan group, and which occurrence caused him to give it the name of ' Navigation Group '. This was in May 1786." [1]

Captain Cook saw single canoes with no outriggers on the coasts of the North Island of New Zealand, but on the coasts of the South Island single canoes were rare, outriggers and double canoes being the commonest. Mr. Elsdon Best says that in the Auckland museum there is a fine specimen of the old-time Maori canoe.

" It is 83 feet in length, and has a width of seven feet. The hull is of one piece, with a top strake attached. If provided with an outrigger, and rigged with either the lateen or triangular upright sail she would sail with surprising swiftness. Shallow draft meant little hold on the water and the greater necessity for an outrigger. When necessary, paddles were employed. Cruise mentions seeing a fleet of Maori canoes in 1820, many of which were 70 to 80 feet long, and few less than 60. One of a length of 84 feet was 6 feet wide and 5 deep, hewn from a single log. With ninety paddles and three fuglemen she moved with astonishing rapidity, causing the water to foam on either side." [2]

Mr. S. Percy Smith tells of two examples of the great sea-going double canoes, called *alia* (in Rarotonga *karika*) which he saw in Samoa, one at Manu'a, the most easterly island of the group, and the other at Savāi'i. He gives in one of his many papers, the following

[1] S. Percy Smith in *Journal of the Polynesian Society*, Vol. VII, pp. 155 *et seq.*
[2] *The Maori*, Wellington, New Zealand, 1924, Vol. I. pp. 29-30.

description of the *alia* by Mr. Kennison, a boat-builder in Savāi-i:

"The biggest canoe of the two is sometimes as much as 150 feet in length; each end tapers out to nothing: the second canoe is not nearly so long as the first. They sail fast, and like the Malay proas, do not go about in beating, but the sheet of the sail is shifted from bow to stern instead. There is a platform built between the two canoes, and both ends are decked over for some distance. On the platform a house is usually erected. These double canoes will turn to windward very well.

"The canoes are built up of many slabs joined together with great neatness, and each plank is sewn to the next with sinnet, which passes through holes bored in a raised edge on the inside of each plank." [1]

When sails were not hoisted the Polynesian vessels were propelled by paddles. The Moriori folk of the Chatham Isles, however, did not paddle their canoes, but rowed as did the ancient Phœnicians, using a thole pin and strap.

Before they were able to undertake long voyages the ancestors of the Polynesians had to solve the problem of supplies. It was necessary that sufficient quantities of food and water should be carried to last for several days and even for the weeks occupied in passing from one island group to another. Water was carried in Polynesian canoes in bamboos and in seaweed bags, and during the day the latter were, as is gathered from the stories of voyages, immersed in the sea over the sides of vessels, to keep the water cool and prevent evaporation. Green coco-nuts were also carried, and these provided a sweet and refreshing fluid. The Rev. J. B. Stair [2] questioned the Samoans regarding their experiences on long voyages and states:

"In reply to my enquiry whether they did not often run short of water, they have astonished me by telling me that the early

[1] *Journal of Polynesian Society*, Vol. VII, p. 157.
[2] *Ibid.*, Vol. IV, p. 109.

voyagers always took a supply of leaves of a certain kind of herb
or plant, as a means of lessening thirst. . . . By chewing the
leaves of this plant they declared that, to a certain extent, they
could drink salt water with some kind of impunity and thus
assuage thirst. I made very many unsuccessful attempts to obtain
the name of this shrub and ascertain its character. . . . They themselves said that they did not now (1838–40) know it, as the custom
had fallen into disuse, but they were confident it had prevailed
in the past when voyages were more frequently made by their
ancestors."

Bread fruit, cooked in the form of a paste, could be
used for several months. Mr. S. Percy Smith tells that
other preserved foods, mentioned in the stories, included
the *kumara*, or " sweet potato ", dried fish, cakes made
of fern root and a food called in the stories *arai-toto-kore*
which, he suggests, may have been rice, sago, or preserved bananas. Dr. Kramer [1] saw on the Marshall
Islands rolls of preserved pandanus-nuts, about eight
feet in length, and six feet in circumference, which were
carried on long sea voyages. The nuts had been
cooked and then scraped with sea shells into a paste
which was exposed in hot sunshine. The paste thickened
into cakes, and these were laid on end to form rolls of
sausage shape. These rolls were wrapped in leaves and
bound tightly like hams with strong twine. Pieces were
cut off during a voyage as desired. This nut food is said
to be very sustaining.

In the *Periplus* (circumnavigation) of Hanno, the
Carthaginian, mention is made of the prophet who
accompanied the explorers of the African coast. When
a landing had been effected on an island, supposed to be
in the Gulf of Bissagos, they heard the natives shouting
in the darkness and the sounds of flutes, cymbals, and
drums. Great fear came upon them, and the prophet
bade them leave the place. The Polynesians had likewise
tohunga or priests on their vessels, who sat in the

[1] *Hawaii, Ostmikronesien und Samoa.*

stern, where the gods were kept. These priests were really the navigators who advised the commander or chief how his vessel should be steered. When storms arose they recited invocations, and with the aid of their sacred symbols they were supposed to ensure safe voyages. It was these men who studied the stars and set the courses by night. In the *Hawaiian Annual* for 1891, Professor W. D. Alexander translates a paper written by a learned native, named S. M. Kamakau, in which he states:

" If you sail for Kahiki (Tahiti), you will discover new constellations and strange stars over the deep ocean. When you arrive at the Piko-o-wakea, the equator, you will lose sight of Hoku-paa (the North Star) and then Newe will be the southern guiding star, and the constellation of Humu will stand as a guide to you."

In a Maori account of an early settlement in New Zealand translated by Mr. H. Beattie, and quoted by Mr. S. Percy Smith,[1] it is told that Matiti visited Tokopa to obtain information from him regarding the propitious and non-propitious stars, and that he subsequently steered by the stars named " Wero-i-te-ninihi" and " Wero-i-te-Kokota ".

Mr. S. Percy Smith informs us that the Polynesians were in the habit of setting out on voyages in fleets. When they expected to make land at some small island a fleet " spread out in the form of a crescent to distances of about five miles apart on each side, so as to extend their view. Whichever crew saw the land first, signalled their neighbours, who passed the signal on, and so on, till the whole fleet were enabled to steer for the expected land. A fleet of ten canoes would thus have a view of over fifty miles on their front." [2]

Mr. Smith gives the following voyages of a celebrated Rarotongan sea-farer named Tangiia:

[1] *Hawaiki* (Fourth Edition), pp. 219–20.
[2] *Ibid.*, p. 188.

					Miles
From Tahiti to Mauke and back	...	...	...	...	960
„ Tahiti to Samoa and back	...	...	...	...	2640
„ Tahiti to Savāi'i	...	...	...	...	1380
„ Savāi'i to Avaiki and back	...	...	...	...	?
„ Uvea to Upolu, Samoa	...	...	...	...	270
„ Upolu to Uvea and back	...	...	...	...	540
„ Upolu to Fiji	...	...	...	...	480
„ Fiji to Easter Island	...	...	...	...	4200
„ Easter Island to Moorea	...	...	...	...	2400
„ Moorea to Porapora	...	...	...	...	150
„ Porapora to Fiji	...	...	...	...	1680
„ Fiji to Paumotu	...	...	...	...	2400
„ Paumotu to Tahaa	...	...	...	...	720
„ Tahaa to Rarotonga	...	...	...	...	540
					18,360

Mr. Smith was of opinion that Avaiki was in Indonesia, but as he could not locate it, he could not give the distance traversed. He found in the old Polynesian stories references to the Antarctic, where the sea was covered with what seemed to be scraped arrow-root which, Mr. Smith notes, " is exactly like snow ". The Maoris depicted in their ancient carvings and remembered in their traditions a tusked sea-monster which appears to be the walrus, or the sea-lion, or the sea-elephant. " Long before our ancestors had learnt to venture out of sight of land," wrote Mr. Smith, " these bold sailors had explored the Antarctic seas and traversed the Pacific Ocean from end to end." [1]

The migrations into Polynesia, according to the traditions, took place from the Fatherland called by the Maoris Hawaiki. As " h " and " s " and " w " and " v " are convertible letters in the Polynesian language, and there is a tendency in some areas to drop consonants, we find Hawaiki rendered in different areas as Havaiki, Avaiki, Savaiki, Hawai'i, Sava-i, Savai-i, &c.

---

[1] *Hawaiki* (Fourth Edition), pp. 175 *et seq.*

Mr. J. R. Logan [1] says that the names " Java, Jaba, Saba, Zaba, Jawa, Hawa is the same word " and that it is in Indonesia " used for rice-fields which are irrigated. The word is primarily connected with the flowing of water." He says further that " Sawa, Jawa, Saba, Jaba, &c., has evidently in all times been the capital local name in Indonesia ", and adds that " the Bugis apply the name Jawa, Jawaka to the Molukas ". It is possible, as has been suggested, that the original Hawa, Jawa, Java or Sawa was an area in India. The Polynesians who settled on the islands of the Pacific were not only acquainted with agriculture, but in some cases irrigated large areas. In Hawaii it is said that the term *Kanawai*, which is used for laws in general, originally referred to the ancient irrigation laws.

Mr. S. Percy Smith tells [2] that on Kauai Island in the Hawaiian group, Mr. Wilcox " pointed out to me the remains of two water-races (auwai) which in design and magnitude surprised me. That in the Lihue district is several miles in length. It formerly brought down the water from the Wai-aleale mountains, 4000 feet high, to the fertile but dry lands of Lihue. It is related that a modern water-race laid out by engineers follows it closely and frequently comes to the old Hawaiian water-channel. Again, when steaming along the north coast of Kauai, at the Kalalau valley, we saw, at least 500 feet up on the precipitous sides of the mountains, following the sinuosities of the steep hills, the distinct line of an old Hawaiian water-race. It was very surprising to see it there; its appearance was just the same as one of the many water-races that are seen on our gold-fields."

According to Maori tradition Hawaiki-nui (old or great Hawaiki) was situated in a land called Irihia, which the New Zealand scholars identify with India, as has been indicated. Mr. Elsdon Best says that, according

---

[1] *Journal of the Indian Archipelago*, Vol. IV, p. 338.
[2] *Journal of Polynesian Society*, Vol. VII, p. 164.

to the Maoris, Irihia was " an extremely hot land,
wherein grew the prized food called *ari* [1]—a land inhabited by many dark-skinned peoples, a land of great
extent ".[2]   From Irihia the sea-farers migrated to the
Dutch East Indies about 65 B.C. and about the fifth
century A.D. Samoa was reached.   New Zealand appears
to have been first visited about the seventh century. " It
is fairly clear, as shown by many traditions of many
isles," says Mr. Best, " that for a period of at least eight
centuries the Polynesians must have made many voyages
in the Pacific, some of great length, traversing vast areas,
peopling and repeopling many lands.   In later times
long sea voyages of set purpose to outlying lands were of
much rarer occurrence, those to New Zealand and the
Hawaiian Isles apparently ceasing altogether." [3]

[1] ? rice.
[2] *Transactions and Proceedings of the New Zealand Institute*, Vol. XLVIII, p. 457.
[3] *Ibid.*, p. 157.

CHAPTER III

Searches for Jade

New Zealand discovered by Searchers for Jade—Dark Green Jade of New Guinea—Jade Axes the Standard of Currency—White and Green Jade of New Caledonia—Traces of Ancient Workings—Battles for Jade—How Jade was worked—New Caledonian Green and Brown Jade in New Zealand—Maori Ceremonial Jade Axes or Adzes—Natives refuse to sell Jade Necklaces—Yellow and Green Jade of New Hebrides—Green Jade of Louisiade Archipelago—Jade and Gold—Captain Cook on Maori Jade Symbolism—Discovery of New Zealand Jade—Voyage of Kupe and Ngahue—Ancient Jade Trade—Religious Rites connected with Search for Jade—Myth of Ngahue—The Jade God and the "Lady of Obsidian"—Flight and Return of Ngahue—Migrations from Tahiti to New Zealand, the Land of Jade—Motives for Long Voyages—Colonists, Explorers, Tourists, &c.—The *Moa* Bird of New Zealand.

When the Polynesians were migrating to the South Sea islands some groups had knowledge of jade, to which, indeed, they had attached a religious value; they knew how to work it, and they searched for and found it in Oceania. The discovery of New Zealand was connected with the search for jade, and supplies from that quarter were carried to various islands. At an earlier period than that in which the New Zealand discovery was made the highly-esteemed stone was found in localities less remote from Indonesia. A dark greenstone, which has been identified as jade, was found *in situ* in New Guinea, and there jade-stone axes had long been "the greatest standard of currency". According to Mr. Jack, formerly Government Geologist of Queensland, these New Guinea jade axes were exchanged in important transactions "such as the purchase of a canoe, or a pig, or in obtaining a wife". The Polynesian searchers for jade found it in New

Caledonia. M. Garnier writing in *Océanie* [1] tells that on a mountain in Ouen Island he

" was suddenly attracted to some rocks of peculiar appearance, which, besides presenting the features of novelty, exhibited that of beauty. They were somewhat translucent, of a very pure white, among which ran veins of a delicate green. Their physical character recalled tropical jade. It is of this stone that the New-Caledonians formerly made their finest axes, the *situs* of which I had until now sought in vain. There was ample evidence that this was one of their ancient quarries in the fact that the soil was scattered over with debris, and with splinters which the hand of man alone could have produced. Nevertheless the dull fractures indicated that a long time had elapsed since these heaps had been made; and the young men of Ouen Island, who accompanied me, regarded with as much astonishment as I did, these traces of an ancient work of their ancestors."

An elderly islander to whom Garnier subsequently showed the specimens he had collected said:

" That is the stone which was used for making axes. Formerly people came from as far as the Loyalty Islands to search for pieces. What sanguinary battles my ancestors have fought against strangers who have sought to invade the territory in search of that precious stone!"

The native described the difficult process of working jade—how the axes were cut and the surface polished " with coarse and fine sand ". Much time was consumed in the work of making an adze. " The lifetime of a man was not always sufficient to finish one."

This native, whose name was Zachario, told M. Garnier that " the thinner an axe became the more it was prized ". Such an axe was, as in New Guinea, a standard of currency. With it " peace could be purchased, an alliance secured, great canoes bought—in short ", added Zachario, " it was as gold is to you ".

Mr. S. Percy Smith, who quotes Garnier, [2] says there

---

[1] Paris, 1871.
[2] *Transactions and Proceedings of the New Zealand Institute*, Vol. XXIV, pp. 537-8.

is an axe of this type in the Colonial Museum, Wellington, New Zealand. " It is a disc of greenstone, eight inches long by six inches wide, very thin, and highly polished. . . . It forms a most formidable *casse-tête*, but not a useful tool. It is a dark green, of several shades intermixed, and with a brownish tinge. It is undoubtedly nephrite, and in New Zealand would be regarded as of a rare but not unknown colour."

Elsdon Best refers to the finely worked jades as being highly esteemed for their religious value in New Zealand. " The long thin adzes of greenstone, used much as ceremonial objects, and mounted on handles of wood, elaborately carved, were," he says, " highly prized by the Maori, and are now rare." [1]

He explains that the " highly ornamented form of adze was used more as an insignia of rank or baton than as a weapon or tool. Such forms were much in vogue among the chiefs and men of good family; and when addressing an assembly of people such a person always had in his hand either such an adze or a *patu*, *mere*, or *taiaha*, or some other weapon. . . . These ceremonial implements . . . were usually made of greenstone." [2] When Captain Cook was at Dusky Sound, New Zealand, he was honoured more highly than he realized. " The chief, before he came on board," he relates, " presented me with a piece of cloth and a green talc (jade) hatchet."

M. Garnier emphasizes how highly the jade from New Caledonia was appreciated in the Loyalty Islands. In writing of the people of the Island of Uvea he says:

" Most of them had ornamented their throats with necklaces of the green jade of Ouen Island. We essayed in vain to purchase some of these; our most brilliant offers failed to obtain a single one of the ornaments. It is always thus among the tribes of New Caledonia: if one wishes to possess one of these necklaces, one must purchase them bead by bead."

[1] *Dominion Museum Bulletin*, No. 4. Wellington, 1912, p. 195.
[2] *Ibid.*, p. 119.

Jade was discovered in the New Hebrides. Mr. S. Percy Smith describes a small yellowish adze, a very dark stone adze, and a pale greenstone axe with five transverse seams of black from this group, which are preserved in the Wellington museum. Of the latter he says:

"This is unlike New Zealand stone; it is more like some I have seen from China. Its shape is characteristic of the New Hebrides, not of New Zealand. It is manifestly a jade of a different character from that found in New Zealand."

In his *Cannibals and Convicts* (p. 284) Julian Thomas states that when in Tanna, New Hebrides, he found specimens of a rock he "took to be the same as the New Zealand greenstone. The natives made charms of it, as in Maoriland."

Jade was discovered in the Louisiade Archipelago. Basil H. Thompson, in his account of his explorations in that area,[1] writes:

"We could not ascertain the actual spot whence the 'greenstone' from which the stone adzes were made is brought; but, as the natives of Goodenough Island pointed westward, it is probably to be found in Huon Gulf. In New Zealand the greenstone is generally found associated with gold."

Jade is found on the west coast and the interior of the South Island of New Zealand. Captain Cook, who called it "green talc", found that it was an article of trade throughout the whole North Island. He made inquiries regarding it, and his interesting record sets forth:

"They tell us that there is none of this stone to be found but at a place which bears its name, somewhere about the head of Queen Charlotte Sound, and not above one or two days' journey at most from the station of our ships. I regretted much that I could not spare time sufficient for paying a visit to the place, as

---

[1] *Proceedings of the Royal Geographical Society*, 1889, p. 540.

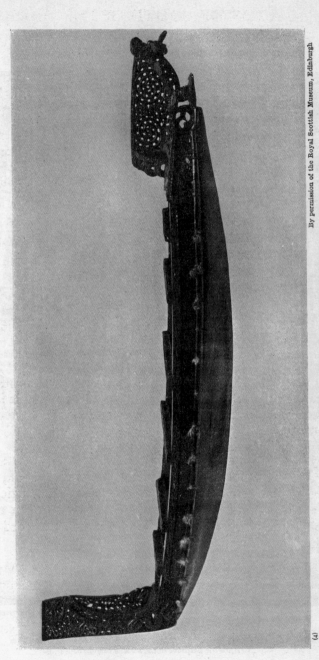

MODEL OF MAORI CANOE

(4)

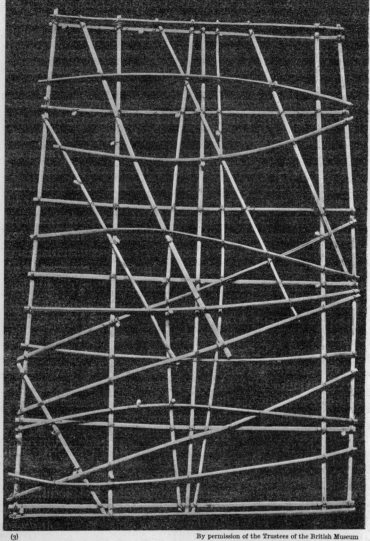

NATIVE CHART FROM MARSHALL ISLANDS

Made of open cane-work to which shells and stones are fastened in different places
to mark the positions of the various islands

we were told a hundred fabulous stories about this stone, not one
of which carried with it the least probability of truth, though
some of their most sensible men would have us believe them.
One of these stories is that this stone is originally a fish, which
they strike with a gig in the water, tie a rope to it, and drag it to
the shore, to which they fasten it, and it afterwards becomes stone.
As they all agree that it is fished out of a large lake, or collection
of waters, the most probable conjecture is that it is brought from
the mountains, and deposited in the water by the torrents. This
lake is called by the natives Tavai Poenammo [1]—that is, the water
of green talc—and it is only the adjoining part of the country, and
not the whole Southern Island of New Zealand, that is known to
them by the name which hath been given to it on my chart."

In another part of his " Journal " Captain Cook says:

" Their greatest branch of trade was the green talc or stone
called by them *poenammo* (*pounamu*), a thing of no great value;
nevertheless, it was so much sought after by our people that there
was hardly a thing they would not give for a piece of it."

The discovery of jade in New Zealand was first
made, according to Maori tradition, by the navigator
Kupe and his companion, Ngahue. Kupe was a native of
the Society Group of islands, and when on a visit to
Rarotonga, set out on a voyage of exploration towards
the south-west. He sighted the North Cape of North
Island, and the new land was named Aotea-roa, which
means " The-long-white-cloud ". Having replenished
their stores, the explorers sailed down the east coast to
Wellington harbour. They afterwards circumnavigated
South Island, sailing along the west coast and returning
by the east coast. Then they proceeded through Cook
Strait up the west coast of the North Island. They returned direct to Society Group, probably to the island of
Ra'iatea where, it is believed, Kupe had his home. In
after time the course from Rarotonga to New Zealand
was memorized by the Maori students as follows:

---

[1] " Te Wai Pounamu," corrects Elsdon Best.

" In sailing from Rarotonga to New Zealand, let the course be to the right hand of the setting sun, moon, or Venus, in the month of February."

S. Percy Smith says that " this course is quite right, as anyone may prove . . . by trying it on a chart ".[1]

The South Island, which has an area of about 55,225 square miles, is traversed from north to south by a mountain chain which averages about 8000 feet in height. The loftiest peak is Mount Cook, on the west coast, which is 13,200 feet high. There are extensive plains on the east coast.

The west coast has steep and forbidding shores. One of its rivers, the Taramakau flows from the mountainous area in which jade is found *in situ*. It carries down boulders of that stone which are found in old gravels and on the sea-beach. Some think this river was the Wai-pounamu ("Water of Jade ") discovered by the early explorers. They may have landed to replenish their supplies of food and water, and found specimens of the highly-prized stone. Jade is also found in a stream called Arahura, nine miles farther south, and there is Maori evidence that this was the " Water of Jade ".

After New Zealand had been occupied by various Maori tribes, the difficult and dangerous mountain passes leading from the east coast to the jade area were discovered. The Rev. J. W. Stack, missionary to the South Island Maoris, writing in 1881, stated:

" Most of the greenstone (jade) worked up in the South Island was carried across the Southern Alps on men's backs in a rough state. The labour of procuring the stone was very great. The tracks across the mountains were most dangerous, and some one skilled in prayers and charms always attended the party of carriers, who led the way, uttering petitions for safety whenever the party reached any particular difficulty. On reaching the coast the *tohunga* performed certain religious rites, and retired to rest alone, and in his dreams a spirit would come and indicate the spot where

[1] *Hawaiki* (Fourth Edition), pp. 216-7.

a stone would be found. On waking he would summon his companions, and, spreading themselves along the river-bed, they would proceed up stream till they reached the spot indicated in the vision, when the stone was sure to be found, and received the name of the spirit who revealed its position. This method of discovery is still adopted; and I have a piece of greenstone in my possession that is known by my name, the finder, an old chief at Ahura, having found it in a place indicated to him by my spirit during the visions of the night."

Another missionary, the Rev. J. F. H. Wohlers, wrote in the same year from Ruapuke, Foveaux Strait:

" I think that the ancestors of the Maori long ago were in possession of some culture, which they had lost during their migrations to the South Sea Islands, where they sank down to what is called the period of stone implements; [1] and that the noble bearing among the chiefs' families and the sense of art are remains of that culture."

Mr. Wohlers goes on to say:

" There is an old tale of a mad Maori woman who long ago wandered from the west coast, where greenstone (jade) is found, into the high mountains, carrying a greenstone axe with her. By good luck she found a passage over and through the mountains, and wandered on to the east coast, where, south of Banks Peninsula, near one of the large rivers, she came upon Maoris who were chipping with axes made of inferior stones. She said to them, ' Your axes are not good: try mine.' Then the woman was questioned about the greenstone place (*wahi pounamu*); and, having listened to her description about the road thereto, it was resolved to visit that place. Two large parties were formed for that purpose. One party perished in the snow and ice on the high mountains; the other reached the west coast, and returned with greenstone. . . .

" When I came among the Maoris here in 1844 there were still some real *tohungas* (wise men) living among them. Some men were learned in old tales; some were skilful in works of art: but

---

[1] Mr. F. R. Chapman, in the *Transactions and Proceedings of the New Zealand Institute*, Vol. XXIV, p. 518, thinks this is " impossible ", but it is a view now shared by not a few anthropologists.

such very high art as has been found in the North was never produced here in the South." [1]

It was quite evidently from the North that Maori culture entered New Zealand. The Rev. Mr. Stack refers to a myth regarding the discovery of jade in the South Island. It tells that at Hawaiki (Tahiti) a woman, named Hine-tua-hoanga, caused a man named Ngahue to be driven away. His god was a sea-monster called Poutini. "He rode on the back of his sea-monster to Tuhua . . . and settled at Arahua, where he discovered the greenstone." [2]

Ngahue appears to have been the same man as Ngake, who accompanied Kupe on his first voyage of exploration from Rarotonga to New Zealand. The traditions of the Kahungunu clans of the Maori credit Kupe with the discovery of New Zealand jade. It is told that during his voyage along the west coast of South Island he put ashore at Arahura. He and his party went up the river. "While engaged in netting *inanga* (a small fish)", says Elsdon Best [3] in his summary of the traditions, "one Hine-te-uira-i-waho took up a stone from the river-bed to serve as a net-weight, and was struck by its peculiar appearance. That stone was the variety of nephrite known as *inanga*, which name was then applied to it. Thus was the *pounamu* (jade) discovered." The jade ornaments were worn by persons of high rank alone. "The Arahura river," Best says, "was so named on account of Kupe making an exploring trip up its valley, from *ara* (a path or way) and *hura* (to discover, explore, uncover, &c.)." The Kahungunu people "assert that Ngahue was another name of Ngake's ". [4]

Sir George Grey, in his *Polynesian Mythology*, gives a version of the Maori myth which tells of the trouble which arose in Hawaiki, and the expulsion of Ngahue.

[1] *Transactions and Proceedings of the New Zealand Institute*, Vol. XXIV, pp. 481 *et seq.*
[2] Quoted by Elsdon Best, *New Zealand Dominion Museum Bulletin* No. 4, p. 186.
[3] *Op. cit.*, p. 180.   [4] Best, *op. cit.*, p. 180.

His god is referred to as the " fish " named Poutini.

This god was a personification of Jade, and the woman Hine-tu-a-hoanga who drove Ngahue out of Hawaiki was " the grindstone-backed woman ", a personification of the grindstone—" a kind of tutelary deity of stone-grinders ", says Elsdon Best. The significance of this myth will be dealt with in the next chapter.

According to the Maori tradition of the discovery of New Zealand, Ngahue fled from Hawaiki to a strange land and was followed by the grindstone lady. He landed on the North Island, but fearing his enemy would come too near, he set out to sea again, taking his precious stone (his god) with him. He coasted along the western side of the South Island, and went ashore at Arahura. There he discovered jade. After exploring the coast still farther, he reached Wairere (apparently in the North Island) and visited Whangaparoa and Tauranga. He afterwards returned to Hawaiki (Tahiti) and told that he had discovered a new country in which were found the bird called the *moa* and jade. He manufactured axes and ear-rings of jade. The tribes at Hawaiki were engaged in war, and when Ngahue told of the new country he had discovered, some of his friends resolved to migrate to it.

The tradition goes on to tell that trees were felled and canoes constructed with the jade axes. The canoes were named Arawa, Tainui, Matatua, Takitumu, Kura-hau-po, Toko-maru and Matawhaorua. The jade axes which were used for making the canoes were named Hauhau-te-Rangi and Tutauru. " These axes," according to Grey's version of the Maori story, " were made from the block of greenstone brought back by Ngahue to Hawaiki, which was called ' the fish of Ngahue '. He had previously come to these islands (of New Zealand) from Hawaiki (Tahiti), when he was driven out from thence by Hine-tu-a-hoango (Lady of the Grindstone), whose fish or stone was Obsidian. From that cause

Ngahue came to these islands; the canoes which afterwards arrived here came in consequence of his discovery."
Mr. S. Percy Smith tells in his *Hawaiki* (fourth edition,
pp. 263 *et seq.*) that at Rarotonga he met with an old
native, named Tamarua, who could tell of " several
migrations from Rarotonga ". He gave a version of
the story of Ngaue (Ngahue), saying:

" The fleet of canoes I have mentioned left here to go in search
of another country for their crews, as Rarotonga was fully occupied
when they came, and they also went to look for the *toka-matie*
(jade). There were two kinds of stone used in making *tokis* (adzes)
in ancient times, the *toka-matie* and *kara*. The *toka-matie* belonged
to Ina.[1] It was Ngaue who hid the *toka-matie* so that Ina should
not find it. Ngaue went to New Zealand to hide the *toka-matie*.
When he was at New Zealand, he saw some great birds there as
high as the wall-plate of this house (about ten feet); they are
called the *moa*. Ngaue brought back part of those birds preserved
in an *ipu* (calabash) as well as the *toka-matie* (jade). These were
the two things he brought back. It was after Ngaue returned
that the fleet of canoes sailed for New Zealand, but I do not know
how long after. It was because of the voyage of Nague to New
Zealand that the fleet went there. Nague called the *toka-matie*
' *e ika no te moana*,' a ' fish of the sea '."

Mr. Percy Smith was puzzled at first by the name
toka-matie, which means " grass-stone ", but when he
showed the old man a piece of New Zealand jade he
exclaimed, " Ah! It is true then what our ancestors told
us of the *toka-matie*—there is such a stone."
Percy Smith adds:

" He was very pleased at this, but his pleasure scarcely equalled
mine in finding that the Rarotongans had a traditional knowledge
of the greenstone, and the fact of their giving it a different name
showed that they did not derive their knowledge from the Maoris
in late years."

The Maori name *pouanamu* apparently referred to the

---

[1] The Grindstone Lady.

colour of the stone, for *namu* is, according to Percy Smith, an old Tahitian word meaning " green ".

Mr. Elsdon Best, commenting upon Mr. Percy Smith's Rarotongan evidence, regarding later voyages, says:

" Here it is shown that the Rarotongans (and doubtless other Polynesians) knew of the existence of nephrite in New Zealand at least as early as the middle of the fourteenth century, and were making voyages here (to New Zealand) to obtain it."

Jade was not the only thing which the Polynesians searched for. Rarotongan traditions, for instance, refer to an ancestor named Ui-te-rangiora, who went on a long voyage from Fiji or from Samoa—it is uncertain which —to a land called Enua-manu, for the purpose of procuring a supply of sacred scarlet feathers. Mr. Percy Smith had little doubt that Enua-manu was New Guinea, and that the feathers were those of the Bird of Paradise.[1]

In one of the stories of the early migrations to New Zealand reference is made to the sanctity of the colour red (kura). The late Sir George Grey's version of the tale in question reads:

" As they drew near to land, they saw with surprise some pohutu-kawa trees of the sea-coast, covered with beautiful red flowers, and the still water reflected back the redness of the trees.

" Then one of the chiefs of the canoe cried out to his messmates: ' See there, red ornaments for the head are much more plentiful in this country than in Hawaiki, so I'll throw my red head-ornaments into the water '; and so saying, he threw them into the sea. The name of that man was Tauninihi; the name of the red head-ornament he threw into the sea was Taiwhakaea. The moment they got on shore they ran to gather the pohutu-kawa flowers, but no sooner did they touch them than the flowers fell to pieces; then they found out that these red head-ornaments were nothing but flowers. All the chiefs on board the Arawa (canoe) were then troubled that they should have been so foolish as to throw away their red head-ornaments into the sea. Very

[1] *Hawaiki* (Fourth Edition), p. 177.

shortly afterwards the ornaments of Tauninihi were found by Mahina on the beach of Mahiti. As soon as Tauninihi heard they had been picked up, he ran to Mahina to get them again, but Mahina would not give them up to him; thence this proverb for anything which has been lost and is found by another person. ' I will not give it up, 'tis the red head-ornament which Mahina found.' "

Some voyages were made simply to found colonies, a particular group of islands having become overpopulated, or rendered uncomfortable for a tribe on account of the prevalence of war. Other voyages were undertaken by adventurous men who wished to visit the distant lands referred to in family and tribal traditions. Mr. S. Percy Smith quotes, in this connexion, from the history of Te Aru-tanga-nuku, a famous navigator:

"The desire of the ariki Te Aru-tanga-nuku and all his people on the completion of a canoe, was to behold all the wonderful things seen by those of the vessel Te Ivi-o-Atea in former times. These were those wonderful things:—the rocks that grow out of the sea in the space (area) beyond Rapa[1]; the monstrous seas; the female that dwells in those mountainous waves, whose tresses wave about in the waters and on the surface of the sea; and the frozen sea of *pia*, with the deceitful animal of that sea who dives to great depths—a foggy, misty and dark place not shone on by the sun. Other things are like rocks, whose summits pierce the skies; they are completely bare and without any vegetation on them."[2]

Apparently the frozen sea was the Antarctic with its whales, sea-elephants, &c., its icebergs and its great waves on which bull kelp floats.

In addition to these voyages of exploration by daring "tourists", there were also drift voyages, owing to sudden storms, in the course of which many islands were discovered.

Reference has been made to the *moa* bird which

---

[1] Rapa or Opara, an island about 1100 miles south-east of Rarotonga.
[2] *Hawaiki* (Fourth Edition), pp. 175-6.

existed in New Zealand when the Maori settled there.
This is the Dinornis, which has been classed with the
ostrich of Africa, the emu and cassowary of Australia
and Melanesia, the kiwi of New Zealand, and the rhea
of South America. It was a running, wingless bird, and
the largest variety attained a height of about 11 feet.
The Maoris hunted and devoured *moas*, and there are
indications that their eggs were sometimes placed in
graves.

CHAPTER IV

Jade Symbolism in Various Lands

Polynesians and Su-shên—Egyptian Type of Vessels in Far East—Indonesian Jade Searchers—Indonesian Links with Japan—Chinese Jade Workers—Jade or Jadeite in Ancient Egypt, Mesopotamia, and Troy—Jades in Malta, Sicily, Brittany, and Ireland—The Glasgow Greenstone Axe—Jade found in Europe—Psychological Motive for Searches for Jade—Myth of Maori Jade God—The Jade-fish God—Maori and Chinese Myths of Liquid Jade and Luminous Jade—Jade Gongs of Maoris and Chinese—Sonorous Stones of Peru—Screes-stones and Fire-making Mirrors in Old and New Worlds—Mexican Gods of Jade and Obsidian—Polynesian Jade and Obsidian Gods and Peoples—Versions of Maori Myths—The Ladies (Goddesses) of Bowenite and Jade—Jade and Obsidian Totems and Gods—Andean Totemism—Stone Totemic Names.

The fact that the Polynesians attached a religious value to jade (nephrite) before it was discovered in New Zealand is one of very special interest and significance. It links their culture, in the first place, with that of the sea-faring Su-shên of the north-eastern Pacific area who, as has been indicated, were known to the Chinese for about 1500 years as a stone-using people. The Su-shên valued red and green jade, and occasionally carried jade to China. Their arrow-heads were " made of green-stone ".[1] It does not follow, however, that the Su-shên and the Polynesians were racially akin. Cultures, like languages, have ever overflowed the barriers of race.

Jade symbolism may have been imported into the Su-shên area in north-eastern Asia by the early mariners who reached the Far East, coasting as far north as the Sea of Okhotsk. These mariners introduced the proto-types of the modern Koryak craft which, according to E. Keble Chatterton, " have at any rate in respect of

[1] *Transactions of the Asiatic Society of Japan*, Vol. XVIII, pp. 157 *et seq*

rigging, several highly important similarities to the Egyptian ship of the Fourth and Fifth Dynasties. . . . Instead of rowlocks they have, like the early Egyptians, thong-loops, through which the oar or paddle is inserted. . . . But it is their (tripod) mast that is especially like the Egyptians and Burmese." [1] Thong loops were, as has been indicated, used by the Moriori of Chatham Island, who were in New Zealand before the arrival of the Maoris. The Moriori appear to have appreciated jade, and it may be that they were the original discoverers of it in the South Island.

It is possible that the Su-shên, the Moriori, the Maori and other Pacific sea-farers learned to appreciate jade in Indonesia. De Visser has detected Indonesian influence in the dragon lore of Japan, which had an intimate connexion with jade symbolism. He refers in this connexion to a dragon myth which is prevalent " on the Kei Islands as in Minahassa " and writes:

" The resemblance of several features of this myth with the Japanese one is so striking, that we may be sure that the latter is of Indonesian origin. Probably the foreign invaders, who in prehistoric times conquered Japan, came from Indonesia and brought this myth with them." [2]

The original carriers of certain cultural elements into different areas were in some instances supplanted in later times by representatives of other races. When the carriers were small although influential minorities, they were absorbed by the peoples among whom they settled. The fact that the Su-shên carried jade to China does not imply that they introduced jade and its symbolism into that country. The Chinese appreciated jade at an early period in their history, and before they had reached the sea coast. Apparently they were influenced by the jade-workers in Chinese Turkestan who were not and could not have been sea-farers. When, about 1700 B.C.,

---

[1] *Sailing Ships and their Story*, pp. 32–3.
[2] *The Dragon in China and Japan*, Amsterdam, 1913, pp. 140–1.

the Chinese settled in Shensi province, they found jade
in situ there, and they worked it until the supply was
exhausted.[1]

The Chinese were certainly not the first of the ancient
peoples who appreciated and worked jade. Both jade and
jadeite reached Egypt at a very early period. " Several
specimens of one or other of these materials," writes Mr.
A. Lucas, " have been found in ancient Egyptian graves,
the principal examples being two axe heads of pre-
dynastic or Archaic date, one now in the Cairo museum
and the other in the Museum of University College,
London." Mr. Lucas suggests that the jade (or jadeite)
which reached Egypt was probably from Turkestan.
The pre-dynastic Egyptian axes date beyond 3400 B.C.[2]

Jade was imported into Mesopotamia also at an early
period, and apparently from Chinese Turkestan. Some
of the Babylonian cylinder-seals were of jade.[3]

Schliemann found votive axes of white and green
jade among the relics of the first city of Troy, and for a
time after his discovery the theory found favour that the
Aryans had been the carriers of jade from the borders of
China to Troy and into Europe. Small jade axes, perforated for suspension, have been brought to light
among the Neolithic relics of Malta, in Sicily, and in
Brittany and Ireland. In Glasgow there was found in
1780, at a depth of 25 feet below the surface of " St.
Enoch's. croft ", an ancient oak canoe in which lay a
polished axe of greenstone which has gone amissing.
It is uncertain whether this axe was of jade, jadeite, or
callais (a variety of turquoise).

The theory that the Aryans were the carriers of jade
into Europe was abandoned after discovery was made
that nephrite and jadeite were to be found *in situ* in

---

[1] B. Laufer, *Jade* (Field Museum of Natural History, Publication 154), Chicago, 1912, p. 23.

[2] A. Lucas, *Ancient Egyptian Materials*, London, 1926, pp. 212, 220-2. Mr. Lucas
says, " Unless the material is examined chemically or microscopically, it is impossible to
distinguish jade from jadeite." To the ancient peoples nephrite and jadeite were therefore
" jade ".

[3] *British Museum Guide to the Babylonian and Assyrian Antiquities*, p. 157.

Switzerland, North Germany, Austria, Italy and Silesia. Near Maurach in Switzerland " a sort of nephrite workshop " was discovered. Apparently the jade artifacts of the Swiss Lake Dwellings were of local manufacture. Some archæologists rather rashly assumed that the " nephrite question " ceased to exist in consequence of these discoveries. They could no longer entertain the view that unworked or worked jade had been imported into Europe from Asia. But although clay is much more widely distributed than is nephrite, they continued and still continue, to trace cultural and racial migrations by means of pottery in a more or less fragmentary state.

The " nephrite question " still remains, however, and must be frankly faced. Before the early settlers in Europe began to search for jade, they must surely have acquired some knowledge of it. Jade is difficult to find and difficult to work. There must have been some very special reason which moved various peoples, widely separated in space and time, to attach a magico-religious value to this rare stone. The Maori mariners who settled in New Zealand, and the unknown mariners who settled in Malta, for instance, regarded jade axes as sacred objects. Was this merely a coincidence? Dr. B. Laufer, dealing with the problem, writes with characteristic force and insight:

" Nothing could induce me to believe that primitive man of Central Europe incidentally and spontaneously embarked on the laborious task of quarrying and working jade. The psychological motive for this act must be supplied, and it can be deduced only from the source of historical facts. From the standpoint of the general development of culture in the Old World, there is absolutely no vestige of originality in the prehistoric cultures of Europe which appear as an appendix to Asia.

" Originality is certainly the rarest thing in this world, and in the history of mankind the original thoughts are appallingly sparse. There is, in the light of historical facts and experiences, no reason to credit the prehistoric and early historic populations of Europe with any spontaneous ideas relative to jade; they received these, as everything else, from an outside source; they gradually learned to appreciate the value of this tough and compact substance, and then set to hunting for natural supplies."

A similar view may be reasonably urged in connexion with the Polynesian jade problem. The mariners and prospectors who discovered, appreciated and proceeded to make use of New Zealand jade, had previously discovered and utilized the jade of the New Hebrides, New Caledonia, the Louisiade Archipelago, and New Guinea. Deep-rooted in their mythology was a belief in the existence of the god Pounamu, who was a personification of jade (*pounamu*), as the Egyptian goddess Hathor was, as Nubt, a personification of gold (*nub*), and was also the goddess of turquoise. Mr. F. R. Chapman, in his paper " On the Working of Greenstone or Nephrite by the Maoris ",[1] explains:

" Pounamu was one of the sons of the great Polynesian deity Tangaroa (Lord of the Ocean), who was the son of Rangi (Heaven) and Papa (Earth). Tangaroa married Anu-matao (The Chilly Cold), who became the mother of four gods, all of the fish class, of whom Pounamu was one. The substance *pounamu* (jade), it is said, was formerly supposed to be generated inside a fish (the shark), and only to become hard on exposure to the air.

" Poutini was the twin brother of Pounamu. He gives the name to the mythical stone brought by Ngahue to New Zealand, commonly called in story the ' Fish of Ngahue '. The stone *pounamu* was by learned Maoris classed with fish. The traditions respecting its discovery at Arahura (in New Zealand) state that Ngahue found it ' in a lifeless state '—that is, unformed."

Captain Cook, when at Queen Charlotte Sound in 1777, ascertained that jade, which he refers to as " green jasper " and " serpent stone ", as well as " green talc ", was " esteemed a precious article " by the Maoris. " They have," he adds, " some superstitious notions about the method of its generation which we could not perfectly understand."

Polack, who wrote about a century ago, tells in his book [1] relating his New Zealand experiences, that jade was found in the lake called " Water of Green Talc ". According to the information he received, it is embedded on the banks. " When first dug from its bed it is found to be of a soft nature, but it hardens on exposure to the air." Pollack found that the natives esteemed very highly their jade artifacts, and especially those of ancestors, and no inducements would cause the owners to part with them. " The natives," he says, " have many superstitions regarding this stone. The priests, to whom I always applied for any information relating to native polemics, always said the *poenamu* (*pounamu*) was originally a fish, who, naturally vexed at being unceremoniously taken out of the water, transformed itself into a stone."

The Chinese believed, as did the Polynesians, that jade existed *in situ* in a liquid state. In one of the stories of the Chinese " Isles of the Blest " it is told that from the rocks of jade " issues a brook like sweet wine; it is called the ' Brook of Jade Must '. If, after drinking some pints out of it, one suddenly feels intoxicated, it will prolong life." A Chinese alchemist of the fourth century says: " Grease of jade is formed inside the mountains which contain jade. It is always to be found in steep and dangerous spots. The jade-juice, after issuing from these mountains, coagulates into such grease after more than 10,000 years. This grease is fresh and limpid like crystal. If you find it, pulverize it and mix it with the juice of herbs that have no pith; it immediately liquifies; drink one pint of it then, and you will live a thousand years. . . . He who swallows gold will exist as long as gold; he who swallows jade will exist as long as jade. Those who swallow the real essence of the dark sphere (the Heavens) will enjoy an everlasting existence. The real essence of the dark sphere is another name for jade." [1]

As stated, jade axes were sacred objects in Polynesia. They were similarly sacred in China, and like jade discs, batons, &c., were symbols of rank. Withal, jade was connected with fish in China as in Polynesia. The Chinese placed in graves and used as symbols of power and rank fish-form jades. Dr. Laufer quotes in this connexion a Chinese writer who explains that the fish design was favoured because a jade, bearing a prophetic inscription, was found in the belly of a carp. [2]

Elsdon Best, who notes that the Maoris " often-speak of nephrite as a fish ", quotes Dr. Shortland's statement that " pounamu (greenstone) was supposed to have been generated inside of a fish (the shark), and at that time was quite soft, only hardening by exposure to the air ". Shortland added, " *Pounamu* was classed with fish, Poutini (brother of Pounamu, the personification of jade) is also called " the fish of Ngahue ". A Maori legend regarding the origin of jade is given by Charles Wilkes [3] who writes:

"Our Consul interpreted to me a singular story that the southern natives had invented relative to these stones (jade)—that they were found in a large fish, somewhat resembling a shark, which they were obliged to capture and kill for the purpose of obtaining them. When first taken from the stomach of the fish the stone is soft, but from exposure becomes hard, and must be wrought in the soft state."

Another link between Chinese and Maori jade symbolism is afforded by the myth about the luminosity of jade. De Groot quotes the Chinese author Wang Kia (probably of the fourth century), who tells that in the time of the Emperor Shen-nung (twenty-eighth century B.C.) " there existed jade which was obtained from agate rocks under the name of ' Light shining at night '. If cast into

[1] De Groot, *The Religious System of China*, Vol. I, pp. 272–3.
[2] *Jade*, pp. 171–2.
[3] *Narrative of the United States Exploring Expedition*, 1838–1842.

the water in the dark, it floated on the surface, without its light being extinguished." [1]

Elsdon Best refers to a Maori song in which " mention is made of searching for nephrite in water: *A ka kitea i reira, e tuhi ana, e rapa ana*, an allusion to its being found by means of its gleaming appearance." He suggests that this is explained by Mr. Chapman's statement regarding jade being brought down by flood-waters:

" On the subsidence of the water the natives wade about searching for it (jade) in the bed of the river (Arahura), and the heightened colour of the stone in the water soon reveals it to them." [2]

It may be, however, that like the myth of the origin of jade in the stomach of a fish, this myth regarding luminous jade was imported into Polynesia and China from a common centre.

Jade gongs were used by the Chinese and the Maoris. The Chinese made ceremonial use of resonant jade. A single " sonorous stone " cut " somewhat in the shape of a carpenter's square", Laufer tells, "is still employed during the ceremonies performed in the Confucian temples and struck with a hammer . . . to give a single note at the end of each verse." Compound stones of different degrees of thickness were used to give different musical notes. In the American Bishop collection of jades there is " a large flat gong of nephrite ", which has a date mark, indicating the period of construction to have been 116–111 B.C. It does not follow, however, that this inscription is to be relied upon, because the Chinese were rather prone to impart a fabulous antiquity to a jade object. Resonant jades were made in dragon and other forms.[3] Bronze imitations of resonant jades include one of " a fish monster with dorsal fins ending in a bird's head ". When struck with a wooden mallet the resonant jade or bronze sounds " like thunder ".[4]

[1] *The Religious System of China*, Vol. I, pp. 277–8.
[2] *Dominion Museum Bulletin*, No. 4, p. 163.
[3] Laufer, *Jade*, pp. 327–30.   [4] *Ibid.*, pp. 177 *et seq.*

Here the Chinese jade fish is connected with the thunder-god—that is, with the dragon.

Elsdon Best quotes in his valuable monograph on *The Stone Implements of the Maori* the following statement by Mr. Fenton regarding a jade gong in New Zealand:

" Much was said of a greenstone slab called *Whakarewha-tahuna*, which it was alleged carried with it the *mana* of Tamaki, and possession of it was evidence of the ownership of the land. It appeared that this greenstone was used as a gong in Kiwi's *pa* (fort) at One Tree Hill." [1]

Laufer gives in his *Jade* (p. 327, Note 1) the following references to sonorous stones in America:

" Sonorous stones from Peru are referred to by C. Engel, *A Descriptive Catalogue of the Musical Instruments in the South Kensington Museum*, p. 81. Professor M. H. Saville (*The Antiquities of Manabi, Ecuador*, p. 67, New York, 1907) relates after Suarez that in Picoaza there was preserved, until a little while ago, a bell of the aborigines of that locality; it was a stone slab of black slate, a metre (little more or less) in height, and some centimetres wide; when this stone was suspended from one of its ends, the striking of it with another stone or with the hand produced a metallic and pleasant sound, which vibrated like that of a bell. . . . A beautiful sonorous stone excavated by Dr. George A. Dorsey in Ecuador is in the collections of the Field Museum."

Black sonorous stones are referred to by Pliny.

The sacred axes, mirrors, &c., of various kinds of stone or polished steel were in various countries used for purposes of divination and for kindling sacred fires. Sir James G. Frazer refers to the virgin priestesses of the Incas of Peru procuring " new fire " at midsummer by means of a hollow mirror which reflected its beams on a tinder of cotton-wool. A similar ceremony was performed by the Greeks who used a crystal. " Nor," Sir James writes, " were the Greeks and Peruvians peculiar in this respect. The Siamese and Chinese have also the habit of kindling a sacred fire by means of a metal mirror or burning glass." [1] The "smoking mirror" of the Mexican god Tezcatlipoca was a "fire-getter", and a "scree stone", which revealed the future and the will of the gods. The Hindus had their "wonder working stones", too, and so had the Chinese.

Tezcatlipoca's "smoking mirror" and the Inca "stone mirror" of Peru appear to have been of black obsidian.[2] Tezcatlipoca was intimately connected with obsidian, and in one of his forms is, indeed, a personification of obsidian (*itzli*). On the other hand, the rival god Quetzalcoatl had a connexion with greenstone (jadeite). Tezcatlipoca is represented as the persecutor of Quetzalcoatl: he drove Quetzalcoatl out of Mexico, and that god set out to sea towards the east on his serpent (dragon) vessel. He was a mild and gentle god who hated war and violence. When he was compelled to depart towards the east, he threw at a tree, or concealed in it, precious stones (apparently jadeite) and this tree was ever afterwards reverenced as "the tree of the old man". Quetzalcoatl was also connected with the morning star.

In Maori myth we find traces of a similar myth. A "Jade people" are persecuted by an "Obsidian people".

Mr. Colenso, who went to New Zealand in 1835, was informed by an elderly native of Tauranga that jade was "both a fish and a god" and that the jade-god "formerly lived at the island of Tuhua, whither the skilled men of all the neighbouring tribes went to obtain it (jade) which was done by diving, accompanied with several superstitious ceremonies in order to appease its wrath and to enable them to seize it without injury to themselves".[3]

Tuhua, or Mayor Island, is "of volcanic origin and abounds in pumice, obsidian, slag lava, pitchstone, and other vitreous and volcanic substances".

---

[1] *The Magic Art* (Golden Bough), Vol. II, pp. 243–5, and Note 1, p. 244 (Third Edition).
[2] My *Myths of Pre-Columbian America*, pp. 272 et seq.
[3] *The Tasmanian Journal of Natural Science*, 1845.

The jade " fish " was not only a god, but had a connexion with the sky. Poutini, brother of Pounamu, is
" a star name ". The " fish " was a shark. It would
appear, therefore, that the " jade people " were the
" shark people ". Ngahue fled from Hawaiki (Tahiti)
from his enemy the Grindstone Lady, whose sacred stone,
as we have seen, was obsidian. He rode across the ocean
on the back of his jade-fish god, as Quetzalcoatl rode on
his sea-serpent, or serpent (dragon) raft.

The oldest version of the myth tells that a dispute
arose in a distant area named Moana-kura (the Red Sea)
between Poutini (the jade and star god) and a fish god
named Tutunui (Great or Old Tutu). We are not informed precisely regarding the nature of this dispute.
Tutunui, it appears, claimed the sea as the home of all
kinds of fish, including shell-fish, and Poutini, the guardian of jade, made some counter-claim. In the war
which ensued the grindstone goddess, Hine-tu-a-hoanga,
marshalled the Sandstone people. Poutini was defeated
and took flight to a distant area.

In what appears to be a later version of the myth,
the war was waged at Tahiti (Hawaiki). Hine-tu-a-
hoanga, supported by the Mataa (also called Waiapu),
the personification of flint, attacked Poutini who fled.
Poutini reached Tuhua (Mayor Island) in the Bay of
Plenty, New Zealand, but there he was attacked by the
Obsidian people. Continuing his flight, Poutini found,
at length, a resting place at Arahura, on the west coast of
the South Island of New Zealand—that is, in the area
in which jade is found.

In one of the versions of this myth a battle takes
place between the Jade people and their pursuers. " The
attack," it states, " is delivered on the Jade people. A
chief is speared and he falls in death. This is Kai-kanohi.
Again the Jade people are attacked, and another chief,
named Kaukaumatua, is slain."

It would appear that the old myth regarding the war

between the Jade people and the Obsidian people became mixed up with the traditions regarding the explorers who discovered in New Zealand both jade and obsidian. On Mayor Island is obsidian " of a beautiful greenish-black colour ". Perhaps the statement that Poutini lingered on that island for a time refers to some prospector's mistaken identification of the obsidian as a variety of jade. Mr. Colenso gives a myth about Mayor Island which tells that the jade-fish deity formerly lived there. Various tribes obtained supplies of the greenstone, but suddenly the god covered the island with " excrementitious substances ", and then fled to the South Island.[1]

In the story of an explorer named Tama-ahua,[2] it is told that he followed Poutini, who had stolen his wives. The names of the wives are those of varieties of jade. Tama-ahua has a slave, named Tuhua (obsidian), and on reaching Arahura River, he slays Tuhua, and then he finds his wives who were, however, changed into stone.

A Taranaki version of this myth makes Poutini a woman (or goddess) who lived on Tuhua Island (Mayor Island), and Tama, her brother. Poutini is said to have " quarrelled with the people there on account of the green jade, and in consequence was driven away, leaving behind her a brother named Tama ". Poutini fled in a canoe with her " jade people " and arrived at a place called Kotore-pi, a bay twenty miles north of Greymouth, where the canoe was made fast to a tree. Water was bailed out, and that is why greenstone is found there now. Continuing their voyage, the party coasted as far south as Arahura, " which river they entered and paddled up to the mountains, stopping at a waterfall just under a peak on the Southern Alps, named Tara-o-tama. . . . The greenstone was also deposited here, and is still to be found in that place."

---

[1] The Tasmanian Journal of Natural History, 1845.
[2] Journal of the Polynesian Society, Vol. V, pp. 233 et seq.

During his pursuit, Tama was guided by throwing a dart, and in one instance it led him to Milford Sound, where on the beaches is found the beautiful stone called bowenite, which is translucent, and usually of shades of green. Chapman, however, refers to a blue variety of it. The Rev. Mr. Stack says that bowenite is so soft that " when first taken from the block it can be worked with an ordinary knife and file ", but that it " hardens on exposure to the air ". The appearance of what looks like water drops in the texture of the stone gave rise to the story that when Tama found his first wife transformed into bowenite as Hine-tangiwai (woman of bowenite) he shed tears. In his work *The Maoris of New Zealand*, Mr. Cowan says that Tama's tears " flowed so copiously that they penetrated the rock, and that is why the clear kind of bowenite found on the slopes and beaches of Mitre Peak in that great sound (Milford Sound) is called *tangiwai*. Marks like teardrops are sometimes seen in this greenstone, hence the name."

At Arahura, where Tama slew Tuhua (obsidian) and he found his other wives transformed into three varieties of nephrite, his weapon fell into a fire. The sparks fell on the *kawa-kawa* jade, and that is why it has black spots.

Although in this Tama story there may be memories of an antique myth, it has evidently been transformed to account for local phenomena. Tama is said by one tribe to have arrived in the Tairea canoe before the arrival of the Arawa, and other canoes, but another tradition makes him a member of the crew of the Kura-hau-po canoe, in which sailed Whatonga when he searched for his grandfather Toi.

It may be that it was due to the persistence of the old myth regarding the wars between the jade people and the obsidian people that " some of the natives living on the west coast of the South Island took Poutini as a tribal name for themselves. This," according to Elsdon

Best, " seems to have occurred in comparatively modern times ".[1]

It may be that originally jade and obsidian were the totems or the symbols of the totems of the jade and obsidian clans who waged periodic wars against one another. Mr. Richard E. Latcham, in an important paper on " The Totemism of the Ancient Andean Peoples ", says that the Andean totem " was only occasionally an animal or other living being; the most common (totems) were chosen from celestial bodies, natural phenomena or forces, geographical features and inanimate objects. . . . On the sea-coast fishes and marine animals were the most frequent. When the totem chosen was some celestial body, natural force, or inanimate object, it was generally represented by a symbol, which was some living creature, which took the place of the totem in many of the rites and ceremonies. Sometimes the totem animal or the animal symbol was considered sacred, and there was a prohibition to kill and eat it. . . . The totem, together with its human ally, the founder of the lineage, were the tutelar beings of the clan, and their duty was to protect and watch over their descendants. . . . In some parts, as among the Incas, the principal national totems as the sun, thunder, moon, &c., had become deified. . . ."[2]

Poutini, as we have seen, was connected with jade, a star, and the shark, and there was a sacred shark which the Polynesians never attacked. In the next chapter it will be found that the jade axe god was connected with thunder, and the dragon-god. It may well be that the resemblances between Mexican and Polynesian jade and obsidian symbolism were due to the original totemic significance of these stones. *Cala* (stone) totemic names are common in the highlands of Peru and Bolivia.

In the Central American Cakchiquel *Annals*, a work which has close affinity with the *Popol Vuh*, but is chiefly

---

concerned with the territorial rights of a particular family, descent is claimed for the family from Xibalbay, " one of the four men from Tulan ". One of these men (gods) was " at the sunrise (east) ", and Xibalbay was " at the sunset (west) ", being apparently cardinal points' deities. Xibalbay was connected with obsidian which was apparently the tribal totemic stone. The mythical narrative, referring to the family's origin, proceeds:

" And now the Obsidian Stone is brought forth by the precious Xibalbay, the glorious Xibalbay; and man is made by the Maker, the Creator. The Obsidian Stone was his sustainer when man was made in misery and when man was formed; he was fed on wood, he was fed on leaves; he wished only the earth; he could not speak, he could not walk; he had no blood, he had no flesh, so say our fathers, our ancestors, O ye my sons. Nothing was found to feed him."

It was when there was brought from " within the sea " the blood of the serpent and the tapir and maize was kneaded with the blood, that " the flesh of man was formed of it by the Maker, the Creator ".[1]

Here the " Obsidian stone " is a " life-giver ". It gave origin to man and it sustained him even before he had flesh and blood.

Obsidian was used for divination by the Cakchiquel people, as it was by the Aztec worshippers of Tezcatlipoca, and as was the " Awhio-rangi " adze by the Maori tribe which has treasured it, regarding it as an inheritance from the beginning of time when the god Tane used it to cut the sky props. The " Obsidian stone " of the Central American tribe came from Tulan, as the New Zealand adze came from the " hidden land of Tane ". Both Tulan and the " hidden land " were Paradises in which man had origin. The serpent from " within the sea " in the American myth is obviously the dragon; the tapir was connected with rain-giving.

---

[1] *The Mythology of all Races: Latin America.* By Hartley B. Alexander. Boston, 1920, pp. 178 *et seq.*

CHAPTER V

The Maori God-axe

Axe or Adze of the God Tane—Shaping the Poles of the Cardinal Points
—Sacred Adzes and the Polynesian Gods—Adze that stilled a Storm—Girl's
Discovery of Hidden God-adze—Thunderstorms caused by Sacred Adze—
Worshipping the God-adze—Lamentations over Adze—Offerings of Green
Branches to Adze—Sacred Maori Adze Reddish and Polished—Reddish Jades
of New Caledonia and China—Sacred Axe of Crete—Offerings of Flowers to
Axe-goddess of Mycenæ—Cretan "Harvester Vase" Ceremony—Greek "Sky-
axe"—Hittite Axe-god—Assyrian Priest venerates Axe—Votive Axes of Pre-
historic Europe—Axe Symbol in Southern Asia—Chinese Axe Emblems of
Emperor and Chief God—The Fiery Axe—Chinese Constellation called "the
Axes"—Jade and Sun Worship.

Sacred or ceremonial axes or adzes of jade were highly
esteemed by the Maoris. The most famous of these is
named Te Awhio-rangi. It is reputed to have been originally in the possession of the great god Tane (the Kane of
Hawaii), who made use of it when the sky was first
separated from the earth and supported by the four poles
of the cardinal points. Tane directed operations, being
the Indra of Polynesia—the elder son of the sky-god
Rangi, and the earth-goddess Papa. Three axes or adzes
were used to cut the sky-poles, their names being
Awhio-rangi (" around the heaven "), Pare-arai-marama
(" diverting the light "), and Motu-whariki ("the cut
weeds to sleep on "); and the lashing of these axes or
adzes was called Kawe-kai-rangi (" carried food of
heaven ").[1]

Elsdon Best [2] says that the Awhio-rangi, " a very
ancient and highly *tapu* stone-axe or adze " may have

[1] John White, *The Ancient History of the Maori*, Vol. I, p. 161.
[2] *Dominion Museum Bulletin*, No. 4, Wellington N.Z., 1912, pp. 215 *et seq.*

been carried into New Zealand by early settlers, " as is affirmed by the Maori people ". It is still treasured by the Nga-Rauru tribe of Wai-totara, and is known traditionally to all the tribes.

"Very few men would dare, or be allowed, to touch it. If handled or even seen by any unauthorized person, we are told on native authority that some convulsion of nature, such as a severe storm, is sure to ensue."

Te Awhio-rangi is said to be a red-looking axe, speckled and so highly polished that it reflects objects.[1] A fuller description of it is given below.

In a Maori newspaper of 31st May, 1902, a native writer named Te Whatahoro, tells that certain jade adzes were carried from Hawaiki (Tahiti) to New Zealand. He proceeds (according to Mr. Best's translation):

"Regarding the *Awhio-rangi* and *Te Whiro-nui*: these two nephrite (jade) adzes were *tapu* adzes that were ' waved ' before, or offered to, the gods; they were not used as tools wherewith to work timber. Those adzes were last used in such a manner when Tane-nui-a-rangi [2] cut the supports of Rangi (the sky), and, secondly, when used to hew a way through the billows that obstructed Takitimu."

The reference to Takitimu is of special interest. It was one of the canoes constructed with the axes made of the jade which Ngahue carried from New Zealand to Tahiti. The first canoe that sailed was the Arawa.

When the Takitimu was approaching New Zealand a great storm came on. The Polynesian priests were, like the Celtic Druids, supposed to be able to control the elements, and the leader in the Takitimu canoe blamed the priest of the Arawa for raising the storm with purpose to prevent them following. The order was given, " Get out the *toki tapu* (sacred axe) *Awhio-rangi*, and recite a *karakia* (invocation), so that we may cut a path through

---

[1] As in the mirrors of the gods referred to above.
[2] Great Tane, the son of the sky-god Rangi.

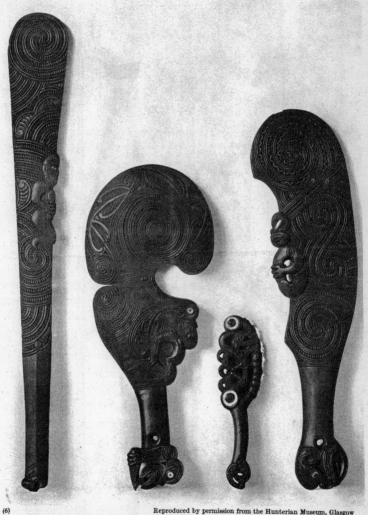

CARVED MAORI WEAPONS AND IMPLEMENTS

The small object is edged with shark teeth and may have been used for ceremonial
self-mutilation as well as the cutting of sacrificial victims

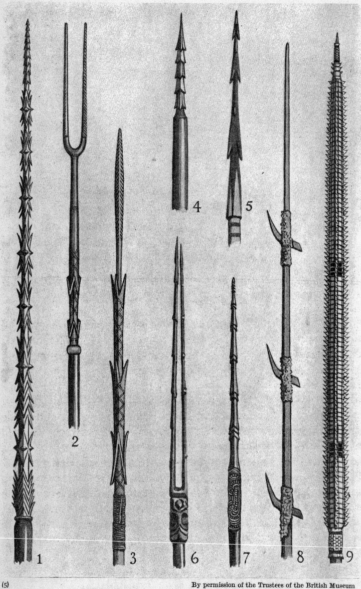

1   2   3   4   5   6   7   8   9

TYPES OF SPEARS FROM POLYNESIA AND MICRONESIA

1, Samoa. 2, 3, Niué. 4, Hawaiian Islands. 5, Caroline Islands. 6, 7, New Zealand. 8, Gilbert Island parrying spear. 9, Gilbert Islands (edged with shark's teeth)

the waves rolling before us." Tamatea added, " I know
who has done this (raised the storm). It was Ngatoro-i-
rangi (of the Arawa vessel). No other priest would dare
to do it." The invocation or charm was then recited, and
soon the sea became quite calm.

When the Takitimu canoe came to shore in New
Zealand, Tamatea and his party were welcomed by Turi
of the Aotea canoe and provided with food. The daughter
of Turi fell in love with the brother of Tamatea, and the
couple were married. As a wedding gift, Tamatea presented to his sister-in-law the sacred adze *Te Awhio-
rangi* " which had cut a path through the storm on the
way from Hawaiki (Tahiti)" [1]

The story of the accidental discovery of the Awhio-
rangi, which had been concealed in a sacred (tabooed)
area, was given by Wiremu Kauika in 1888 in the Maori
newspaper *Te Korimako*, and it has been translated and
abbreviated by Mr. S. Percy Smith [2] as follows:

" All the people of this island have heard of the axe Awhio-
rangi, but hitherto none has seen it, since it was hidden by our
ancestor Rangi-taupea, seven generations ago. It has recently
been found by our people living at Okoutuku. A girl named
Tomai-rangi, who is a stranger here, but married to one of our
tribe, and who was not acquainted with the tribal sacred places,
went out by herself in search of hakekakeke, or fungus, and inside
a hollow *pukatea* tree saw something gleaming which alarmed
her. She rushed away crying out in alarm, whilst at the same
time a fearful thunderstorm burst, with much lightning and a
fall of snow, which made her quite foolish. One of our old men,
named Rangi-whakairi-one, hearing the woman and seeing the
storm, at once knew that someone had trespassed on a *wahi-tapu*,
or sacred place. He therefore lifted up his *karakia*, and the storm
ceased. Presently all the people assembled and the old man asked,
' Which of you has been to Te Tieke?'

" The woman replied, ' Which is Te Tieke?'

" ' Behind there, near the bend in Wai-one.'

---

[1] Quoted by Elsdon Best from a history of the Ngati-Kahunguna tribe by Mr. Downes
of Whanga-nui.
[2] *Journal of the Polynesian Society*, Vol. IX, pp. 229 *et seq.*

"Said Tomai-rangi, ' I have been there, but I did not know it was a *wahi-tapu.* I saw something there, it was like a god, and great was my fear.'

" After this the people went to look at the object, and all recognized it (by description handed down) as Te Awhio-rangi. Moreover, the descendants of the guardians, Tu-tangata-kino and Moko-hiku-aru were there.[1] Rangi-whakairi-one now said a *Karakia,* after which the axe was taken from its hiding-place, and all the people cried over this relic of their great ancestors, after which it was taken to the village.

The place where the axe had been hidden was known traditionally to the Nga-Rauru tribe, because Rangi-taupea—he who concealed it—had informed his people, saying, ' Te Awhio-rangi lies hidden at Tieke on the flat above the cave of sepulchre.' That place has never been trespassed on for these seven generations, until the 10th December, 1887, when Tomai-rangi found the axe.

" The people of Nga-Rauru, Whanganui and Ngati-Apa assembled to the number of 300 on the 11th December to see the axe, which was exhibited at 5 a.m. It was placed on a post so that all might see it. Then the priests, Kapua-Tautahi and Werahiko Taipuhi marching in front reciting their *karakias,* were followed by all the people, each carrying a branch in their hands, to the post, where all cried over Te Awhio-rangi.

" As they approached the spot, the thunder rolled, the lightning flashed, and the fog descended till it was like night. Then the priests repeated the *karakias,* and it cleared up, after which the people all offered to the axe their green branches, besides the following articles: six *parawai,* four *koroai,* four *paratoi,* and two *kahu-waero* cloaks.

" Following the presentation, came a great wailing and crying over the axe, and then some songs were sung in which Te Awhio-rangi is referred to. . . .

" There are a great many songs about Te Awhio-rangi. In appearance this axe is ruddy (kura) like a china cup, but it is also like the breast of the *Pipiwharauroa* (the little cuckoo, i.e. striped); at the same time it is like nothing else. One's likeness can be seen in it. It is eighteen inches long and one inch thick, the edge is six inches broad, and the slope of the sharp edge is two and a half inches, and it is shaped like an European adze."

[1] These are two *makutu,* or wizard gods, in the form of lizards. Probably the people saw one near the place.—S. Percy Smith's note.

The Maori writer goes on to say that " this axe was sought for by our ancient ancestor Rua-titi-pua in the Kahui-kore, and he brought up " the stone of Ngahue, i.e. Te Awhio-rangi ". Mr. Percy Smith considers that this statement shows a " want of historical knowledge, for Ngahue, the discoverer of greenstone, flourished ages after the Kahui-kore, which are some of the early stages of creation ".

The Maori writer continues, " Ngahue devised the axe to Tane at the time that the Heavens embraced the Earth, and with it Tane severed the muscles of Heaven and Earth. When they were separated Tane received the name Tane-toko-rangi (or Tane-who-propped-up-the heavens). Te Awhio-angi hence became the *măna* for all the axes in this world." [1]

The axe was handed down by elder son to elder son through the generations from Tane-toko-rangi to Rakau-maui. Turi, the great-grandson of the latter, carried it across the ocean to New Zealand in the Aotea canoe. It was ultimately concealed by Turi's descendant, Rangi-taupea, " in his sacred mountain of Tieke at Moerangi ".

Mr. Percy Smith states that a sketch of the axe, obtained from a native by the Rev. T. G. Hammond, of Patea, shows that " it is unlike the ordinary Maori axe in shape and size ". He thinks it may turn out to be " one of the great axes made of the giant *Tridacna* shell of Polynesia ". The axe is " looked on as a god ". According to Mr. Smith the sacred axe " is still in possession of the Nga-Rauru tribe, but hidden away in a secret place only known to a few. It is too *tapu* for any white man to see." [2]

As stated above, a learned Maori has referred to the Awhio-rangi as a nephrite adze. Mr. Elsdon Best comments:

---

[1] Percy Smith here suggests that " măna " may in this connexion be probably used to signify " proto-type ". On the other hand it may be that the măna (magic) of all axes was supposed to be derived from Tane's axe.

[2] *Journal of the Polynesian Society*, Vol. IX, p. 220.

" It is strange that Te Whatahoro should refer to the Awhio-rangi as being made of nephrite (*pounamu*), whereas it seems to be quite a different stone, judging from what we have heard of it." [1]

If it is ultimately found that the adze is really of red nephrite (jade), we can conclude without hesitation that it was never fashioned in New Zealand. Red jade was known and used in New Caledonia and in China.

Apparently the sacred axe (or adze) was greatly revered by ancient sea-faring peoples. The greenstone axe found in the pre-historic canoe dug up in Glasgow may have been, like the Awhio-rangi, a god—or " god body " or a totemic symbol. The Minoans of Crete venerated a sacred axe. A great double axe from Hagia Triada is a prominent exhibit in the principal room of the museum at Candia. The axe symbol is found depicted between " the horns of consecration " on Minoan walls, pillars, and seal-stones. On a gold signet from Mycenæ the axe figures beside a goddess who sits under a vine; the sun and moon symbols figure in the upper part, and a god bearing an 8-form shield hovers high on the left. Offerings of flowers are being made to the goddess by votaries.

The Maori ceremony of making offerings of branches of trees to the *Awhio-rangi* axe after it was accidentally discovered by a woman, may throw light on the significance of the so-called " Harvester vase " found at Hagia Triada in Crete. Round this vase marches a procession of young men carrying three-pronged forks and scythe-like blades, which may have been used to cut corn or prune trees. They are led by a priest, who wears a bulging robe. It may be that this ceremony was connected with the veneration of the axe.

The Greeks appear to have venerated the axe in early times. Max Müller, in his *Biographies of Words*, refers to a small jade axe " worn in a necklace by a Greek girl

. . . as a talisman probably "; modern Greeks refer to
lightning flashes as blows of the " sky axe " (*astro peléki*).
The Hittite sky god carried the " double axe ", and this
deity and his symbol were known in North Syria. On
an Assyrian cylinder a priest venerates a double axe. As
has been stated, small jade axes perforated for suspension
were in use in Malta in early times, and also in Cyprus.
Greenstone votive axes have been found in Southern
Spain, and an axe figures on a standing stone in Brittany.
Mosso considers that the axes of friable sandstone found
in various parts of Europe were " votive axes "; they
could have served no practical purpose.[1] In the Congo
the sacred axe is still known.[2] The *neter* (god) sign in
Egyptian hieroglyphs has been referred to as an axe, but
it is really a bundle of linen.

The axe symbol is widespread in Southern Asia. In
China "as early as the Shang dynasty (1766–1122 B.C.)",
says Dr. B. Laufer, " the axe seems to have been the
victorious emblem of the sovereign ", who was the
earthly form of the chief god. An ancient ode [3] describes
a monarch as " the martial king displaying his banner,
and with reverence grasping his axe, like a blazing fire
which no one can repress ". Laufer says:

" The axe was accordingly a sovereign and martial emblem,
and the emperors of the Chou dynasty had a pattern of axes em-
broidered on their robes. . . . Embroideries with representations
of axes (*fu*) were used on the altar of the God *T'ai-i* ' the Supreme
Unity ', the ' most venerable among the gods '. . . .

" There was a constellation called ' the Axes ' which, being
bright, foreshadowed the employment of axes, and, when in
motion, a levy of troops. The axes symbolize the events in the
army and refer to the execution made in times of war."

Laufer goes on to say that " the jade emblems of
sovereign power were made in the shape of hammers,

---

[1] *The Dawn of Mediterranean Civilization*, pp. 132 et seq.
[2] *My Myths of Crete and Pre-Hellenic Europe*, pp. 160 et seq., 310 et seq.
[3] Legge, *Shi King*, Vol. II, p. 642.

knives, and other implements ". These " were connected
with an ancient form of solar worship ". Jade emblems
were placed in graves, because " they shared in the
quality of sunlight ", and " were efficient weapons in
warding off from the dead all evil and demoniacal influences ". [1]

[1] Laufer, *Jade*, pp. 45–6.

CHAPTER VI

The Asiatic Dragon in Polynesia

Turi, the Polynesian Arthur — Sea-monster Myth — Jade Fish-god as Carrier of Ngahue—Greek Legend of Arion—Celtic Dolphin-rider—Indonesian Fish-rider—Japanese Crocodile-rider—Chinese Gods and Kings ride Sea-monsters—The Hindu Makara as Carrier of God—Makaras and Dragons —Polynesian Dragons—Hawaiian Ancestor Gods as Sharks which carry Men —New Zealand Dragon Stories—Spenser's Dragons—Jade as "God Body"— Chinese and Japanese Dragons in Stones—Transformations of Chinese Dragons —Thunder-axe Stones—Japanese and Polynesian Dragons of Hills, Cliffs, Boulders, and Rocks — Hawaiian Dragon Goddess and Family — Hawaiian Pool-dwelling Dragons cause Thunder — Lizards and Eels as Dragons in Oceania, China, and Japan—Polynesian Dragons and Hindu Nagas (Serpent Gods)—Dragons guard Royal Families in China and Hawaii.

Turi, who carried the sacred adze, Awhio-rangi, to New Zealand, is said to have lived to be an old man. Like King Arthur, Thomas the Rhymer, and other famous European "sleepers", he had a mysterious passing. "He departed and died at some other place," Maori tradition tells, "but no one knows where—perhaps he returned to Hawaiki; he did not die in this land (New Zealand); he disappeared totally, and maybe he returned by aid of the taniwhas (sea monsters)." Mr. S. Percy Smith, commenting on this tradition, says:

"It is a remarkable thing that the Ra'iatea people say that whilst Turi never returned to his old home in Eastern Polynesia in the flesh, his spirit did and used to trouble them much. . . . Turi is not singular in being supposed to have made a voyage by aid of a taniwha, or sea-monster; several instances are quoted in tradition. This is simply to say, in other words, that it is not now known, or forgotten, how these taniwha-riders came here." [1]

[1] *Journal of the Polynesian Society*, Vol. IX, p. 227.

The interesting fact is really that the sea-monster-riding myth should be remembered in New Zealand. As will be shown it has a very decided significance, the taniwha being a form of the dragon.

A Maori authority, in a communication to the *Journal of the Polynesian Society* (Vol. VII, pp. 32–4), refers to the canoe of the hero Toi. He says it was named Tutara-kauika, and that " it was a taniwha (sea monster)" —that is, a " dragon-boat ". But in the story of " Kame-Tara and his ogre wife ", the senior wife is prevailed upon by the ogre to dive into the sea. When she did so the ogre wife cut the rope of the anchor and paddled the canoe away. The senior wife invoked the taniwhas to come to her help. " One came, and took her (on his back) and landed her at another end of the island." Here the taniwha is a genuine sea-monster.[1]

Ngahue, the reputed Maori discoverer of New Zealand jade, is said to have crossed the sea on the back of his jade-fish god which carried him away in safety from his enemies, the Obsidian people.

One is reminded, in this connexion, of the Greek legend of Arion, the poet and musician of Lesbos. Arion leapt from a ship into the Mediterranean to escape from the sailors who had plotted to murder him that they might become possessed of the great wealth he had acquired during his sojourn in Italy. Arion, as we learn from Herodotus, Ælian, Plutarch, and others, was carried safely to his island home " on the back of a dolphin ".

On the Gundenstrup bowl, preserved in the Copenhagen museum, which shows the Celtic god Cernunnos squatting like a Buddha, and grasping in his hands the symbols of the Hindu-Buddhist god Virupaksha,[2] a man is seen on the same plaque riding on the back of a dolphin. It is assumed by some that this Celtic fish-riding figure

---

[1] *Journal of the Polynesian Society*, Vol. VI, p. 98.
[2] My *Buddhism in Pre-Christian Britain*, p. 109.

is of Greek origin, but fish-riding gods were commoner in Asia than in Europe. De Visser gives interesting references regarding an Indonesian myth which tells of a man who dives into the sea "and is brought home on the back of a big fish". According to a Japanese version of this myth, the hero returns home "on the back of a crocodile".[1] In a first-century Chinese work saints, kings and gods ride on the backs of dragons, or in cars drawn by dragons,[2] and dragons had an essential connexion with water. When the eighth-century Chinese Emperor Ming "crossed a river" a dragon "appeared in the water and carried the ship forward on its back".[3] Sometimes a dragon-god "appeared at the surface of the sea in the shape of an enormous shark". Shi Hwang, founder of the Ts'in dynasty, who put to sea with a strong force to search for "the island of the blessed" on which grew a life-prolonging herb, had a shark dragon slain at sea.[4]

The Hindu *makara*, the vehicle of the sea-god, Varuna, is a "composite wonder beast" which was taken over by the Buddhists and presented in endless variety, as a "sea elephant", a crocodile, a whale with crocodile's feet, a shark with a lion's head, and so on.[5]

The dragon was well known in Polynesia. In Hawaii it was believed that a corpse which had been flung into the sea became "a shark or an eel, or perhaps a *mo-o*[6] or dragon-god, to be worshipped with other ancestor gods of the same class". W. D. Westervelt writes regarding the aumakuas (ancestor gods) of this class:

"All the aumakuas were supposed to be gentle and ready to help their own families. The old Hawaiians say that the power of the ancestor-gods was very great. . . . Suppose a man would call his shark, ' O Kuhaimoana (the shark god)! O, the One who lives in the Ocean! Take me to the land!' Then perhaps a shark would appear, and the man would get on the back of the shark, hold fast to the fin and say, ' You look ahead. Go on very swiftly

[1] *The Dragon in China and Japan*, p. 141.   [2] *Ibid.*, p. 83 and p. 122.   [3] *Ibid.*, p. 124.
[4] *Ibid.*, pp. 124-5.   [5] Elliot Smith, *Evolution of the Dragon*, pp. 90 et seq.
[6] The Maori *moko*.

without waiting!' Then the shark would swim swiftly to the shore." [1]

The Bishop of Wellington, New Zealand, contributed to *The Journal of the Ethnological Society of London* (new series, Vol. I, Session 1868–69), a paper entitled " Notes on the Maoris of New Zealand and some Melanesians of the South Pacific ", in which he says:

" There are numerous stories of dragons, like our dragon of Wantley, afloat among the natives; and I have just received from New Zealand an account of one such in a freshwater lake: ' it had jaws like a crocodile, and spouted water like a whale '."

Sir George Grey, in a paper " On New Zealand and Polynesian Ethnology " in the same journal (pp. 333 *et seq.*) quotes several passages from Spenser's *Faerie Queene*, together with " corresponding passages from New Zealand dragon legends ". This part of his paper is worth giving in full:

" Eftsoons that dreadful dragon they espied,
Where stretched he lay upon the sunny side
Of a great hill, himself like a great hill."—*Spenser*.

" Hardly had Hotupuku (the dragon) scented a smell like the scent of men ere he came creeping out of his den; the war party were still hidden by the slope of the hill and the bushes from him, and he from them. Before they saw him, alas! alas! he had stolen down upon them; and ere they could break and fly when they did see him, he was so large and near that he looked like a great hill."—*New Zealand Legend*.

" With that they heard a roaring hideous sound,
That all the air with terror fillèd wide,
And seemed un'neath to shake the stedfast ground;
Eftsoons that dreadful dragon they espied!"—*Spenser*.

" Like the crashing and rumbling of thunder was the loud roaring sound made by the dragon in rushing forth from its den."
—*New Zealand Legend*.

[1] *Legends of Gods and Ghosts (Hawaiian Mythology)*, Boston and London, 1915, pp. 248 *et seq.*

" But all so soon as he from far descryed
Those glistering arms that heaven with light did fill,
He roused himself full blythe, and hastened them untill."

—*Spenser.*

" The huge dragon when it saw its favourite food (the warriors)
all ready, as it were a meal prepared for it, joyed exceedingly,
and, opening wide its vast mouth, stretched forth its tongue to
lick them in, and hastened out of its den."—*New Zealand Legend.*

" As for great joyaunce of his new-come guest,
Eftsoons he 'gan advance his haughty crest,
As chaffèd boar his bristles doth uprear,
And shook his scales to battle ready dress'd."

—*Spenser.*

" By the power of these prayers and incantations, the large-
pointed spines of the crest of the dragon sank down flat again
upon its back, although just now they had been all standing erect,
as he joyed to think he should devour the men he smelt."

—*New Zealand Legend.*

" But stings and sharpest steel—did far exceed
The sharpness of his cruel rending claws.

" But his most hideous head to tell
My tongue does tremble.

" And over all with brazen scales was armed
His large long tail, wound up in hundred folds,
Does overspread his long brass-scaly back." —*Spenser.*

" It lay there, in size large as a monstrous whale, in shape like
a hideous lizard; for in its huge head, its limbs, its tail, its scales,
its tough skin, its sharp spines, yes, in all these it resembled a
lizard."—*New Zealand Legend.*

" His blazing eyes, like two bright shining shields,
Did burn with wrath and sparkle living fire.

" So flamed his eyes with rage and ravenous ire.

" But far within, as in a hollow glade,
Those glaring lamps were set that made a dreadful shade."

—*Spenser.*

" They soon saw the terrible monster crouching there, with its fierce large eyes, round and flaming as the full moon, as it shoots up above the horizon. Whilst they watched those eyes they seemed to flash with various colours; and from the sun's bright rays playing through the green leafy places into the creature's covert, its eyes seemed to shine with a fierce green, as if a clear green jadestone had been set for a pupil in the dark black part of each of its eyes."—*New Zealand Legend.*

Sir George Grey concludes:

" Without pursuing this subject into many other similar details, I will add one other quotation from the *Faerie Queene.*

" I wot not whether the revening steel
    Were hardened with that holy-water dew,
    Wherein he fell, or sharper edge did feel,
    Or his baptizèd hands now greater grew,
    Or other secret virtue did ensue,
    Else never could the force of fleshly arm,
    Nor molten metal, in his blood embrue."   —*Spenser.*

" The New Zealand legends regarding dragons generally equally assert that it was only by some secret virtues, obtained by prayers or supernatural means, that their heroes were enabled to destroy dragons."

Lecky, in his *History of Morals,* expresses the view that fairy tales should be considered as natural products of the human mind in a certain stage of development, and that fairy beliefs may be found anywhere in the world among ignorant and rustic peoples. Sir George Grey accepted this theory, adding: " But it is only a partial truth; for it holds good of a belief not only in fairies but in dragons, and of all similar delusive beliefs which the human mind is capable of conceiving." He did not, however, include Spenser among the " ignorant and rustic " dreamers, " the truth being ", he says, " that Spenser has simply recorded images which had their existence given to them long before his time, and in a certain state of civilization in England, and that under similar circumstances in New Zealand the human imagination, giving reins to its fancy, had, of very necessity, fallen upon exactly similar images."

Since 1869 our knowledge of dragon lore and fairy stories has been greatly extended. It can now be said with assurance that many of the " images ", &c., which Spenser made poetic use of, did not originate in England in any stage of its civilization. The poet drew upon ancient romances that were in part not only imported into England but into Europe. Buddhist and other stories were incorporated in mediæval literature.

The Maori story-tellers of New Zealand may have similarly made use of imported " images " and stories. When their ancestors entered Oceania and began to settle on various islands, they appear to have imported from South-eastern Asia dragon stories, and many beliefs about complex dragon-gods, including the " makaras ". These dragon beliefs were intimately connected with jade symbolism. The dragon-fish of Ngahue was, as we have seen, a piece of jade, and he rode on it when he fled from Hawaiki to New Zealand. The jade was a dragon-god body and could assume dragon form as a " carrier " or " vehicle ".

Certain stones were in China and Japan believed to be " dragons' eggs ". A native Japanese writer tells of one which was kept in a Shingon monastery. It was like " a diamond-natured thunder-axe-stone " or " Tengu axe ". Its colour " was red, tinged with bluish grey, just like the thunder-axe-stones, but its lustre was more like that of glass than is the case with the latter. There were some spots on the egg, which Shosan (the author) considered to be dirt left on it by the dragon which produced it." The Japanese had not only " thunder-axes ", but " thunder-knives ", thunder-hammers ", " thunder-blocks ", thunder-rings ", thunder-pearls ", " thunder-pillars ", thunder-ink ", thunder-swords ", and " thunder-pins ".

" They are found in spots struck by lightning. The black ones are thunder-axes, those which are white, tinged with blue, are thunder rings, the purple ones, tinged with red, are thunder pins."

Like the Chinese, the Japanese believed that pre-historic stone weapons and utensils were thunderbolts.[1]
De Visser says of the Chinese dragons:

" They transform themselves into old men, beautiful women, and fishes, or sometimes assume the shapes of trees and objects as, e.g. swords. They have a pearl under their throats or in their mouths. As to their eggs, these are beautiful stones to be found in the mountains or at the river side; water is constantly dripping from these stones till they split and a small snake appears, which in a very short time grows larger and larger and in the form of a dragon ascends to the sky amid thunder, rain, and darkness." [2]

The dragon's connexion with rain and thunder was, however, " supposed to begin long before his birth ".[3] The " egg " or " thunder-axe " might of itself cause a thunderstorm. There are many Chinese and Japanese stories of stones splitting and dragons issuing from them as small worms or lizards. Other stones, although not " dragons' eggs ", were connected with dragons. De Visser refers to a big stone in Omi province, Japan, which lies " in a hollow excavated by a waterfall near Kayao village ". It was supposed to belong to the local dragon-god, and was called " Dragon-god-stone ". It disappeared mysteriously. Another stone, which was black, " lay in a garden and was said to cause even a clear summer sky to become cloudy in a moment when it was touched by somebody ".[4]
Japanese dragons, like those of Polynesia, became rocks, capes and hills. De Visser mentions a tradition of a hill which was supposed to be formed " by the dead body of a dragon ". On this hill " a big rock in the shape of a dragon's head is worshipped in a Shinto temple ".

[1] *The Dragon in China and Japan*, pp. 218–9.   [2] *Ibid.*, p. 233.
[3] *Ibid.*, p. 219.   [4] *Ibid.*, p. 218.

A rock in Tosa province, Hataya district, is called "Dragon skewer", a cliff in Omi province, "Dragon's nose", in Taga district there is "Little dragon-mountain", and elsewhere "Dragon-peaks", "Dragon capes", "Dragon mound", &c.[1]

The dragon lore of Hawaii has, as will be seen, interesting points of resemblance to that of Japan. In the Polynesian legends of that area a prominent part is taken by Mo-o-inanea ("The Self-reliant Dragon"), who was regarded as a powerful goddess—more powerful even than the gods Ku, Kane, and Kanaloa.

The dragon goddess and her brothers, the gods, migrated to the Hawaiian Islands from the "Hidden Land of Kane (Tane)". They all resided for a long period at Waolani, but when the dragons grew very numerous, "it was necessary to distribute them over the islands". The dragon-goddess herself removed to Puunui in the lower part of Nuuanu valley, where she was worshipped. It was believed she had a "dual nature —sometimes appearing as a dragon, sometimes as a woman".

Mr. W. D. Westervelt [2] tells that there is a very rich clayey soil at Puunui, and the natives formerly used it "sometimes eating it, but generally plastering the hair with it". Queen Kaahumanu made this place very taboo (*tapu*).

The dragon-goddess was supposed to dwell in a clay pit called Lua-palolo ("pit of sticky clay"). She distributed her dragon family "over all the islands from Hawaii to Niihau". Mr. Westervelt continues:

"Two of these dragon-women, according to the legends, lived as guardians of the pali (precipice) at the end of Nuuanu valley, above Honolulu. After many years it was supposed that they both assumed the permanent forms of large stones which have never lost their associations with mysterious, miraculous power."

---

[1] *The Dragon in China and Japan*, pp. 225-30.
[2] *Legends of Gods and Ghosts (Hawaiian Mythology)*, pp. 255 et seq.

In his *The Voyage of the Blonde*, Mr. Bloxam, the chaplain of that British man-of-war, writes regarding these dragon stones:

"At the bottom of the Parre (pali) there are two large stones on which even now offerings of fruits and flowers are laid to propitiate the Aku-wahines, or goddesses, who are supposed to have the power of granting a safe passage."

Mr. Bloxam found that these deities were a kind of moo-o or reptile. He could not explain the name because there were no large serpents or reptiles on the islands.

The following native account of the dragon stones is given by Mr. Westervelt:

"There is a large grove of hau-trees in Nuuanu valley, and above these lie the two forest women, Hau-ola and Ha-puu. These are now two large stones, one being about three feet long with a fine smooth back, the other round with some little rough places. The long stone is on the seaward side, and this is the Mo-o woman, Hau-ola; and the other Ha-puu. The leaves of fern cover Hau-ola, being laid on that stone. On the other stone, Ha-puu, are lehua flowers. These are kupuas."

Navel cords were buried under these stones, a custom which was supposed to bring protection against evil to children.

Another dragon-goddess named Ala-muki and her family protected paths on the plains of Waialua. Sometimes travellers were slain by them.

Three dragon-goddesses dwelt in precipices on the northern coast of the island of Kauai.

A great dragon-goddess, named Kihawahine, lived in a large deep pool beside the village of Lahaina on the island of Maui. Mr. Westervelt says that she was "worshipped by the royal family of Maui as their special guardian".

Two dragons lived in the river Wailuku near Hilo, on the island of Hawaii. "They were called 'the moving boards', which made a bridge across the river. Sometimes they accepted offerings and permitted a safe passage and sometimes they tipped the passengers into the water and drowned them. They were destroyed by Hiiaka."

Mr. Westervelt says that the mo-o priests and the sorcerers of the islands were " sacred to these dragons ", and they " propitiated them with offerings and sacrifices, chanting incantations ".

The dragons were called mo-o by the Hawaiians, and mo-ko by the Maoris of New Zealand, and the same name was applied to lizards. " Their use of this word in traditions," says Mr. Westervelt, " showed that they often had in mind animals like crocodiles and alligators, and sometimes they referred the name to any monster of great mythical powers belonging to a man-destroying class." Eels, sharks, big turtles, sharks, and other large fish were likewise called mo-o.

Mr. Westervelt's important summary of Hawaiian dragon-lore should here be given, because it not only throws light on the myth of the jade-fish god of Ngahue and the mysterious " thunder axe ", the Awhio-rangi adze, which caused the thunderstorm, but links up Polynesian dragon-lore as a whole with the dragon-lores of China, Japan, and India. He writes:

" The most ancient dragons of the Hawaiians are spoken of as living in pools or lakes. These dragons were known also as kupuas, or mysterious characters who could appear as animals or human beings according to their wish. The saying was: ' Kupuas have a strange double body.'

" There were many other kupuas besides those of the dragon family. It was sometimes thought that at birth another natural form was added, such as an egg of a fowl or a bird, or the seed of a plant, or the embryo of some animal, which when fully developed made a form which could be used as readily as the human body. These kupuas were always given some great magic power. They were wonderfully strong and wise and skilful.

" Usually the birth of a kupua, like the birth of a high chief, was attended with strange disturbances in the heavens, such as reverberating thunder, flashing lightning and severe storms which

sent the abundant red soil of the islands down the mountain-sides
in blood-red torrents known as *ka-ua-koko* (the blood rain). This
name was also given to misty fine rain when shot through by the
red waves of the sun.

"By far the largest class of kupuas was that of the dragons.
These all belonged to one family. Their ancestor was Mo-o-
inanea (the Self-reliant Dragon) who figured very prominently in
the Hawaiian legends of the most ancient times, such as 'The
Maiden of the Golden Cloud'."

It has been suggested by those who believe the
dragon-lore of Oceania was of spontaneous generation
that the original *mo-o* or *moko* was simply a lizard, or eel,
or shark. Mr. F. W. Christian, on the other hand,
inclines to regard the *mo-o* as fundamentally a memory,
and he writes in this connexion:

"It is very remarkable the horror in which Micronesians and
Polynesians alike hold lizards and eels, and it certainly seems to
point to a traditional recollection of the crocodile and venomous
serpents they left behind them in the great rivers and jungles of
Asia and the larger islands of Indonesia. What proves this so
strongly is the fact that crocodile and snake names in New Guinea
in many instances coincide with lizard and eel designations current
in the dialects embracing all the isles of the Pacific." [1]

Mr. Christian refers to a large pugnacious green eel
which he saw and heard much regarding at Ponape.
The natives of that Caroline island called it *macho* "to
distinguish it from the common river eel". It lives in
salt-water marshes and feeds on crabs, and it climbs
trees. A woman who was bitten by a *macho* while Mr.
Christian was on Ponape "died in less than two days,
probably from shock; the natives said from its venom".
The natives dreaded this eel, believing it was "the incarnation of the spirit of a wicked and cruel chief who
murdered his wife and children and was chased into the
swamps by the avengers and put to death".

---

[1] *The Caroline Islands*, London, 1899, pp. 365-6.

Mr. Christian's theory that lizards and eels were feared and reverenced by the Polynesians as traditional memories of crocodiles and serpents may seem a plausible one, but in China and Japan the many forms assumed by dragons includes, as it happens, those of lizards and eels.

The Japanese " little stone dragon " or " little mountain dragon " is the *tokage* or *imori* (lizard). It is " born between stones in the mountains, and has got the name of ' little dragon ' because it was (or is) believed to cause hail by its breath, and to give rain to those who prayed to it ". The gavial (the crocodile of India and of South and Eastern Asia) was a form assumed by dragons. De Groot refers to gavials acting as demons, and Wells Williams says that in South China rain is foretold or brought on by " a large triton, gavial, or water-lizard ". In a Japanese work the story is told of a man who had in his house a remarkable stone " white as crystal and as big as the palm of the hand ". A cup of water was left beside the stone and was emptied. The owner of the stone placed beside it next day a big bowl filled with water, and " while he was talking with some friends in the next room, they heard a noise as of wind and waters. At once they went to look what the matter was, and discovered a lizard (*tokage* = little stone dragon) running from the bowl to the stone, which it entered ".[1] A Chinese story tells of two dragons visiting the palace of an Emperor of the Hia dynasty. They left foam on a piece of cloth and " the foam changed into a black lizard ".[2]

A ninth-century Chinese author states: " Tradition says that dragons and water-lizards belong to the same species." [3]

Eels and worms were forms assumed by Chinese

---

[1] De Visser, *The Dragon in China and Japan*, pp. 74 *et seq.*, p. 217. De Groot, *The Religious System of China*, Vol. V, pp. 625 *et seq.*

[2] De Visser, *op. cit.*, p. 52.   [3] Quoted by De Visser, *op. cit.* p. 119.

dragons. A dragon as a white reptile wound itself around one of the legs of a horse which entered a river. This reptile was taken away in a box and it subsequently assumed dragon form and caused thunder, rain, and gusts of wind.[1]

Another Chinese story tells of a dragon being caught by villagers when it was in the shape of a white eel. Fishes were believed to become dragons when they ascended the " Dragon gate " which was " apparently a waterfall ".[2]

The history of the Polynesian dragon appears to be rooted in India and South and Eastern Asia. Indian *nagas* (serpent gods), and Chinese and Japanese dragons " lived in pools or lakes " like the Hawaiian dragons and similarly appeared " as animals or human beings ". The Hindu *nāga*, which De Visser shows to have been the prototype of the Chinese and Japanese dragons, dwelt " at the bottom of the sea, or in rivers or lakes ", or " guarded a big tree which stood in a large pond ", and it had three forms. These forms are given by De Visser as follows: " First: fully human; secondly: common serpents, and thirdly: a combination of both, i.e. snakes of which the upper part of the body looks human . . . the lower part of the body entirely snake-like." [3] Chinese and Japanese dragons, as has been indicated, caused at birth thunder and lightning like the Hawaiian newly-born dragons. The dragon-mother of Hawaii recalls the Chinese " dragon-mother ". In one of the stories she is an old woman, and when she washed clothes in the rivers " fishes (the subjects of the dragons) used to dance before her ". She died " and was buried on the eastern bank of the river; but the dragons made a violent storm arise and transferred the grave to the opposite side of the stream ". . . . According to the Chinese work, the *Kwah i chi*, " there is always much

[1] De Groot, *op. cit.*, p. 112.   [2] De Groot, *op. cit.*, p. 128.
[3] De Visser, *op. cit.*, pp. 4, 5.

wind and rain near the dragon-mother's grave; then people say, ' The dragons wash the grave '." In another Chinese work it is told that a dragon-woman " jumped out of a big egg found at the side of a pool. She gave wealth to the house where she lived, but at last she ran away and in the form of a snake disappeared into the crack of a rock in the mountains ".[1]

In China as in Hawaii there were dragon guardians of royal families[2], and dragons which helped one to cross a river or attempted to drown one. A Chinese story tells of two yellow dragons attempting to drown the Emperor Yu; they threatened to upset his vessel by taking it on their backs.[3] The Hawaiian priests, who propitiated dragons " with offerings and sacrifices, chanting incantations ", acted as did the Buddhist priests of India, China and Japan. The sacerdotal dress of the Wu-ist priests of China who controlled dragons and therefore the elements was a magical dress.[4] Offerings and sacrifices to dragons were common in Japan.[5] The pre-Buddhist dragons of Japan " lived in rivers and seas, valleys and mountains ", and in " rivulets, lakes, and ponds ". They were "rain masters ". A dragon river god received offerings of hemp and fibre, and occasionally a black horse was sacrificed " in order to cause him to give rain ". A red horse sacrifice also brought rain, but a white horse sacrifice caused rain to stop falling.[6] Rice and red beans were offered to dragons by Japanese priests.

In view of the comparative notes provided in this chapter, it would appear that the Polynesians imported into their islands, in addition to a religious appreciation of jade, a fairly complete knowledge of the dragon-lore intimately associated with jade in China and Japan. The fish-god riding heroes like Ngahue, Turi, and others,

[1] De Visser, op. cit. p. 89.
[2] De Visser, op. cit., pp. 122 et seq.
[3] De Visser, op. cit., p. 124.
[4] De Visser, op. cit., pp. 102–3 and pp. 113 et seq.
[5] De Visser, op. cit., pp. 152 et seq.
[6] De Visser, op. cit., p. 157.

were local heroes, who displaced the older legendary heroes, and the gods of the imported dragon myths. Their gods had their habitation in jade. The Awhio-rangi adze which brought thunder was, as has been said, a dragon-axe—a habitation of a god, or, as the Maori story of its discovery states plainly, a god in itself.

CHAPTER VII

Mummies as Gods

Burial Customs express Religious Ideas—Samoan Mummies called "Sun-dried" Gods—Mummy Connexions with Stones, Stars, &c.—Powers of Priests—Only Influential Persons Embalmed—The "Corpse-praying" Priest —Methods of Mummification in Society Islands—Offerings of Food, Fruit, and Flowers—Sins of the Dead—Embalmers Unclean—Hereditary Embalmers of Samoa—Magical Mummy Bandages—Face painted Red and Black—New Caledonian, Gilbert Islands, and New Zealand Mummies—Use of Salt—The Drying Process—Bones coloured Red—Marquesan Mummies—Flaying Cere-mony—Stone Platforms of Embalming Houses—The Decorated Biers—Coffins and Canoes—Skulls Preserved—Images of Dead—Cook Islands Customs—Cave Burials—Hawaiian Mummies—The Dead as Guardians of the Living—Tomb houses—Burial Caves—Bones thrown into Volcano—Corpses thrown to Sharks—Dead facing East or West—Cremation in Hawaii and New Zealand—Exposure of Dead—Invalids buried Alive.

The funerary customs of the Polynesians and other South Sea Islanders are of considerable interest and importance because they give indication of the varied cultural influences to which their ancestors were sub-jected at different periods and in different areas during the course of their wanderings. These, as is found, in-cluded mummification (the preservation of the body from decay), cremation (the destruction of the body by fire), and disposal by exposure on platforms, and by burial in the earth, in stone-lined tombs, in caves or crevices of rock, and in water. Behind these customs there were definite beliefs regarding the destiny of the soul.

Some would have it that although the various funerary rites differed so greatly, they should all be considered as perfectly "natural". Dealing with mummification, for instance, Professor J. L. Myres said at the 1914 meeting of the British Association in Melbourne:

" What is more natural than that people should want to pre-serve their dead? Or that in doing so they should remove the more putrescible parts? Would not the flank be the natural place to choose for the purpose? Is it not a common practice for people to paint their dead with red ochre?" [1]

If it is held that it is " natural " to preserve the dead body, can it be contended at the same time that it was " natural " to destroy it by fire, or by throwing it into the water, so that it might be devoured by sharks?

In all parts of the world we find that funerary customs expressed religious ideas. Polynesia does not appear to have been an exception to this rule. It has to be recog-nized, however, that, when its customs have been investi-gated, the religious beliefs of Polynesia were of as com-plex a character as was its social system. The islanders did not believe that all men were equal, or that the same destiny awaited each individual after death.

In his study of the religious beliefs and customs of the old Samoans, " before the natives had had much intercourse with Europeans ", the Rev. John B. Stair has thrown a flood of light upon the significance of the custom of mummification in its relation to religious ideas. He shows that in Samoan mythology there were four classes of " Principal Deities "—the *Atua*, or original gods of the sky and Pulotu (Paradise), the *Tupua*, or deified spirits of chiefs, the descendants of the original gods and the ghosts and apparitions. Of the *Tupua* he writes:

" The deified spirits of chiefs . . . . were supposed to dwell in Pulotu. The embalmed bodies of some chiefs were also wor-shipped under the significant name of *O le Fa'a-Atua-lala-ina* (made into a sun-dried god), as were also certain objects into which they were supposed to have been changed, as blocks of stone, &c., which were also called *tupua*, and held to personate them."

Further on he states:

[1] Quoted by Elliot Smith in *The Migrations of Early Culture*, p. 25.

" The deified spirits of deceased persons of rank appear to have comprised another order of spiritual beings, the more exalted of whom were supposed to become posts in the house or temple of the gods at Pulotu. Many beautiful emblems were chosen to represent their immortality, as some of the constellations, such as *Li'i* (the Pleiades), *Tupua-le-ngase* (Jupiter), also *Nuanua* (the rainbow), and *La'o-ma'o-mao* (the marine rainbow), with many others.

" The embalmed bodies of chiefs of rank, or those who had been *Fa'a-Atua-lala-ina* (made into sun-dried gods), were also reverenced under the name of *Tupua;* which name also, as I have before stated, appears to have been applied to blocks of stone and other objects in various parts of the islands, into which certain chiefs were supposed to have been changed at their death." [1]

It will thus be seen that a mummified chief was a god to whom worship was paid, that he was connected with certain heavenly bodies, and with the worship of stones, wooden pillars, trees, &c. When the embalming process had been completed with due ceremony under the direction of a priest, the mummy was declared to be a " sun-dried god ". Evidently we are dealing, therefore, not with simple natural beliefs and customs, but those of highly complex character—so complex that they must have a very definite history. The arbitrary and unnatural association of embalmed corpses with stars, temple-pillars, and blocks of stone has to be accounted for in the light of comparative evidence. Similar complexes are to be met with outside Polynesia.

The *tupua* (sun-dried kings) were supposed to be very powerful and influential. They directed the activities of the living and, on occasions of crisis, gave important decisions through the medium of the priesthood. The high priest and prophet was known by the name of Tupai.

" He was greatly dreaded. His very look was poison. If he looked at a coco-nut tree it died, and if he glanced at a bread-fruit tree it also withered away." [2]

---

[1] *Journal of the Polynesian Society*, Vol. V, 1896, pp. 33 *et seq.*
[2] Dr. George Turner, *Samoa a Hundred Years Ago*, London, 1884, p. 23.

Mr. William Ellis, the pioneer Polynesian missionary, writing on the burial customs of the South Sea Islands, says that " the bodies of the chiefs, and persons of rank and affluence, were preserved " and " those of the middle and lower orders buried ". These facts, fully confirmed by other recorders, are of vital importance. They indicate in a most conclusive way that the custom of mummifying the dead was not a " natural " but a significant religious custom. " It is singular," remarks Ellis, " that the practice of preserving the bodies of their dead by the process of embalming, which has been thought to indicate a high degree of civilization, and which was carried to such perfection by one of the most celebrated nations of antiquity, some thousands of years ago, should be found to prevail among this people. It is also practised by other distant nations of the Pacific, and on some of the coasts washed by its waters."

Ellis [1] informs us that the process of embalming at Tahiti was conducted under the direction of a priest called the *tahua bure tiapapau*—that is, " the corpse-praying priest ". A temporary house was erected for the treatment of the corpse which was laid on a platform inside it. The intestines, brains, &c., were removed, and all moisture extracted from the body by puncturing and pressing. Then it was dried in the sun in a sitting posture and frequently turned over at night. " The inside was then filled with cloth saturated with perfumed oils, which were also injected into other parts of the body, and carefully rubbed over the outside every day." In a few weeks " the whole body appeared as if covered with a kind of parchment ". Then daily offerings were made to it of fruit, food, and flowers. If after several months the body decayed, the skull was " carefully kept by the family ", while " the other bones were buried within the precincts of the family temple ".

During the embalming process the priest had a hole

---

[1] *Polynesian Researches* (Second London Edition), Vol. I, pp. 400 *et seq.*

dug below the platform on which the body had been placed. He prayed to the god that the dead man's sins should be deposited there and " not attach in any degree to the survivors ". Ellis continues:

" The priest next addressed the corpse, usually saying *Ei ia oe na te hara e vai ai,* ' With you let the guilt now remain '. The pillar or post of the corpse, as it was called, was then planted in the hole, perhaps designed as a personification of the deceased, to exist after his body should have decayed—the earth was thrown over, as they supposed, the guilt of the departed—and the hole filled up.

" At the conclusion of this part of the curious rite, the priest proceeded to the side of the corpse, and, taking a number of small slips of the *fa maia,* plantain leaf-stalk, fixed two or three pieces under each arm, placed a few on the breast, and then addressing the dead body said, ' There are your family, there is your child, there is your wife, there is your father, and there is your mother. Be satisfied yonder (that is, in the world of spirits). Look not towards those who are left in this world.' "

All those who were employed in the embalming were, Ellis tells, regarded as unclean. They were fed by friends lest their food should be defiled by their polluted hands. According to Elsdon Best, the Maoris similarly regarded those persons who handled the bodies of the dead as " extremely *tapu* (taboo) ". The *tapu* had to be lifted when the burial party returned home. Says Best:

" This rite was performed in water, in which the *tapu* persons had to immerse their bodies; they would be absolutely nude at such a time. The officiating priest intoned the necessary ritual formulæ to remove all restrictions. A funeral feast followed this performance." [1]

The ancient Egyptians and the ancient Hindus also removed " uncleanness " by plunging in water. Modern Hindus perpetuate this rite.

Ellis informs us that on some South Sea Islands the

---

[1] *The Maori,* Vol. II, p. 69.

bodies were dried, wrapped in numerous folds of cloth, and then suspended from the roofs of dwelling houses.[1]

Dr. Turner, who had forty years of experience as a Polynesian missionary and anthropologist, states that in Samoa embalming was practised exclusively by the women of one particular family of chiefs. His description of the process is as follows:

"The viscera being removed and buried, they (the women), day after day, anointed the body with a mixture of oil and aromatic juices. To let the fluids escape, they continued to puncture the body all over with fine needles. In about two months the process of desiccation was completed. The hair, which had been cut and laid aside at the commencement of the operation, was now glued carefully on to the scalp by a resin from the bush. The abodmen was filled up with folds of native cloth; the body was wrapped up with the same material, and laid out on a mat, leaving the hands, face, and head exposed. A house was built for the purpose, and there the body was placed with a sheet of native cloth loosely thrown over it. Now and then the face was oiled with a mixture of scented oil and tumeric, and passing strangers were freely admitted to see the remains of the departed. Until about twenty years ago there were four bodies laid out in this way in a house belonging to the family to which we refer, viz. a chief, his wife, and two sons. They were laid on a platform raised on a double canoe. They must have been embalmed upwards of thirty years, and although thus exposed, they were in a remarkable state of preservation. They assigned no particular reason for this embalming, further than that it was the expression of their affection to keep the bodies of the departed still with them as if they were alive. None were allowed to dress them but a particular family of old ladies, who all died off; and, as there was a superstitious fear on the part of some, and an unwillingness on the part of others, to handle them, it was resolved at last to lay them underground."[2]

P. Burzen, quoted by Schmidt[3] says that after the viscera had been removed the Samoan corpse was soaked

[1] *Polynesian Researches* (First Edition), 1829, pp. 519 *et seq.*
[2] *Samoa a Hundred Years Ago*, pp 148–9.
[3] *Jahrbücher der gesammten Medicin*, 1890, Bd. 226, p. 175.

for two months in coco-nut oil mixed with vegetable juices. The cloth with which the body was packed was "soaked in vegetable oil and resinous materials; then the mummy is wrapped up with bandages, the head and hands being left exposed ".[1]

In New Caledonia chiefs alone were mummified. When the body had been punctured to extract the fluids, vegetable juices were introduced to prevent decay. Then the body was dried or smoked, dressed in the chief's clothing, and the face painted red and black. After the mummy had been suspended inside a hut, the place was closed and tabooed.[2]

Mr. A. Grimble was informed by an old native of Maiana in the Gilbert Islands that his adoptive grand-father's corpse had been kept till the abdomen collapsed. It was then placed on a platform to be dried in the sun, fumigated, and anointed. In the end there was nothing left but the bones and the blackened skin. The " mummy " was then placed on a shelf under the northern gable of the house. Relatives anointed the head with oil when they muttered charms, supposed to bring them good luck. On festival days the body was decked with flowers, and it was taken to dances and treated as if it were a guest.[3]

According to Dr. Macmillan Brown, the skeletons of mummified bodies are, in some parts of New Zealand, " found in the crouching or sitting posture ". De-scribing the method of embalming, which was not common, he says that " after the extraction of the softer parts, oil or salt was rubbed into the flesh, and the body was dried in the sun or over a fire ". Then the mummy was " wrapped in cloth and hidden away ".[4]

Mr. Elsdon Best states that among the Maori " true

---

[1] Elliot Smith's summary in *The Migrations of Early Culture*, pp. 103-4.

[2] M. Glaumont in *Revue d'Ethnologie*, 1883, p. 73, quoted by Elliot Smith, *op. cit.*, pp. 101-2.

[3] A. Grimble, " From Birth to Death in the Gilbert Islands," in *The Journal of the Royal Anthropological Institute*, Vol. LI (1921), pp. 47 *et seq.*

[4] J. MacMillan Brown, *Maori and Polynesian*, London, 1907, p. 70.

mummification, the embalming of a corpse, was unknown, the process being one of drying. The drying of the head only was a common Maori custom." He goes on to say that Mr. H. Beattie tells that " the custom of drying and preserving bodies was followed to some extent in the South Island, where it was called *whakataumiro*. Oil was used in the process. A dried body seen by Angas in the North Island had apparently been trussed as for burial; the knees were drawn up, and the head rested on them. A few others have been found in caves. Not only was oil rubbed on the drying body, but also gum of the *tarata* tree, a *Pittosporum*, was used to close the pores, as a kind of varnish. Another account speaks of a steam oven being made below the body, which was elevated. This would be the steaming process."[1]

Hare Hongi [2] states that the Maori mummy was prepared in a small temporary building. It was packed with tow and dried over an oven; and it was kept for some time and occasionally exhibited. He has translated important evidence given by Maoris who took part in the process of embalming.[3] One of them, a woman, said:

" There were three which I myself saw at Whanganui mummified for preservation. Two were my aunts, sisters of Parata Te Kiore, one of whom was named Tawhana. The other was my elder sister Kuramoetai.

" They were placed in a sitting position in their own little huts, the walls and roofs of which were lined with Raupo.

" The process of mummifying was carried out with the aid of a hole which was sunk in the earth (beneath the body), into which the contents of the stomach and bowels were drained by the usual passage. The priests frequently carried portions away and buried it (them).

" When properly dried (the bodies) of their chiefs could be gazed upon for long intervals by their people.

[1] Elsdon Best, *The Maori*, Wellington, N.Z., 1924, Vol. II, p. 56. The process was a drying rather than a " steaming " one.

[2] *Journal of the Polynesian Society*, Vol. XXV, 1916, pp. 269–72.

[3] *Ibid.*, pp. 169 *et seq.*

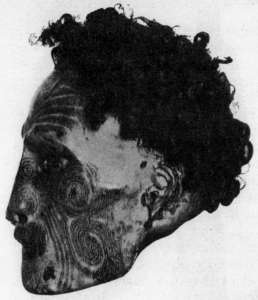

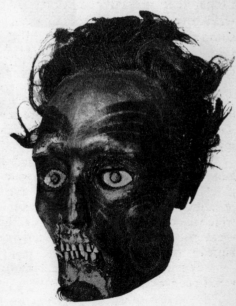

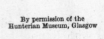

MUMMIFIED MAORI HEADS

The lower head has artificial eyes of pearl-shell

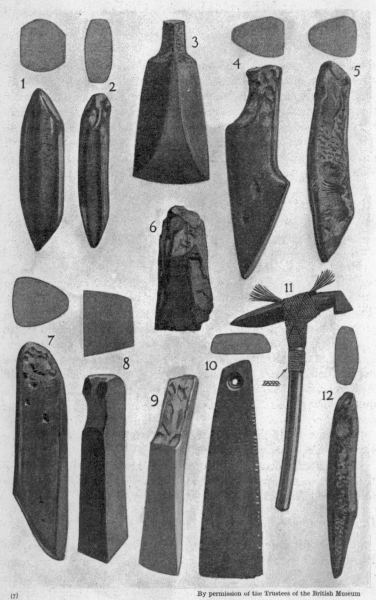

(7)

TYPES OF STONE ADZE-BLADES FROM POLYNESIA

1, Tongan Islands. 2, Marquesas Islands. 3, Hervey Islands. 4, Tahiti. 5, New Zealand (found with Moa remains). 6, Samoa. 7, Easter Island. 8, Chatham Islands. 9, Hawaiian Islands. 10, New Zealand (jade). 11, Tahiti. 12, New Zealand.

" When I gazed upon my elder sister sitting there before me
—I was little at the time, but she was quite a young woman when
she died—it was as if she merely slept, and that ere long she would
awake again and speak to us in the ordinary manner.

" I saw them thus for quite a long period of time. But, when
the people turned in earnest to the practice of the Christian doctrines (the bodies) were carried off to the burial-place and buried.

" I did not witness the manner of preserving heads; but I
did see the heads. The intervals between the lips were filled in
with Pakeha wax. They were most repulsive objects."

A male Maori stated:

" In the case of the death of a chief. If his son or grandson,
or all of his people decide to have him mummified, then a small
enclosure is fenced in, the posts decorated with bird feathers, and
a (small) house is erected therein—a well-built house with carvings,
for it is to be sacred. There is an opening left in its centre. Then
the body (passage) is pierced to allow the contents to get away.
The brain is similarly treated. Then (the body) is placed in the
prepared house. An oven is made beneath it, there are special woods
and leaves used for the process, in order to ensure preservation.
So it is that the skin and bones remain intact. But there is absolutely
no particular change in the appearance of the individual himself.
And so his people are able to gaze upon their chief at intervals for
quite a long period. The house in which he is placed is known as
an Atamira.

" Occasionally the inside of the body is filled with the tow or
scrapings of properly worked flax.

" On special occasions the door of the house is drawn aside, and
the people gaze (upon their chief). They then weep and deliver
suitable and sympathetic addresses."

Hare Hongi continues:

" I myself saw one preserved body at Whangape, that of
Papahia. There were probably two thousand of us present, most
of whom alas! have left this world. Of the living I should name
Re Te Tai and Wi Tana (of Lower Waihou, Hokianga), Anaru
Ngawaka (of Whangape) and Riopo Puhipi (of Puhepoto). I do
not assert that they were present. What I want to convey is that
if they were not present, they should have been. I think that they

were there. . . . This practice of mummification was peculiarly common to the old-time Maori."

E. Tregear [1] says the Maori commoners and slaves were interred in the ground, and chiefs were sometimes laid in the verandas of houses. As a rule, however, the bodies of influential men were flexed and bound tightly and placed in a canoe, a coffin, on a stage or in a tree, either in a deep forest or at some sacred site. After a year had elapsed, the bones were collected, oiled and painted with red ochre. They were then tied up in a bundle and concealed in a cave, among rocks or in a hollow tree.

A jumble of funerary practices, including mummification and some influenced by the rites associated with mummification, may thus be met with in New Zealand. When, however, we go north-eastward to the Marquesas Islands we find abundant evidence of the mummification of persons of importance. In these islands, it would appear, no incision was made to extract the viscera, which was drawn through the anus after putrefaction had set in. The interior of the body cavity was not treated, nor was the brain removed. Both E. S. Craighill Handy and Ralph Linton [2] state, however, that the skin was specially dealt with. Handy says it was " sometimes removed from the body and kept in the house of the family as a sacred relic ", while Linton states that " the epidermis of chiefs and other persons of importance was sometimes rubbed off, apparently with the idea of making the tatoo designs more clearly visible." On some islands mummification was practised in dwelling houses, but in others small temporary structures were erected near the family dwelling. If, however, the corpse was that of a chief or a priest, the temporary structure was erected in the tribal sacred place called the *me'ae* " at which regular religious rites were performed ". The stone platforms on which these mummy houses were built can still be seen on

---

[1] *The Maori Race*, Wanganui, 1904, pp. 386–401.
[2] *Bernice P. Bishop Museum Bulletins*, 9 and 23.   Honolulu, Hawaii.

certain islands, and some of these have pits for drainage, reminding one of the hole, which, according to Ellis, was dug by command of the priest for the collection of the " sins " of the dead. Both portable and stationary biers were in use. The portable bier had a pair of legs at each end and one in the middle. " The legs," Handy says, " were carved with designs and the feet with conventional human figures. Poles for carrying the bier were lashed to the feet on either side. The bottom of the board was either carved or decorated with black or red ornamental sennit lashed over white bark cloth." Stationary biers had a square frame with four legs. C. S. Stewart in his *A Visit to the South Seas* [1], refers to a bier " of spears and other war-like weapons fastened in wicker work together ". The same writer describes a " tomb-house " as follows:

" It stands in the midst of a beautiful clump of trees, and consists of a platform of heavy stonework, twenty feet or more square and four or five high, surmounted in the centre by eight or ten posts arranged in the shape of a grave, and supporting at a height of six or seven feet a long and narrow roof of thatch. Close beneath this the body was enclosed in a coffin." [2]

Vincendon-Dumoulin and C. Desgraz [3] say that the stone platform, on which tomb-houses were erected, were " the base of all Nukahivan edifices ". M. Radiguet [4] mentions the four posts that supported the roof of leaves of the tomb-house, and says:

" Under this roof could be seen the remains of the skeleton, perhaps that of the daughter-in-law of the neighbouring house. . . . At the two ends of the platform two upright stones, about ten feet high, and resembling the Breton *menhirs*, formed an exceptional ornament to this *morai*, which the bushes were in course of invading and the storms of demolishing."

[1] New York, 1831.   [2] C. S. Stewart, *op. cit.*, Vol. I, p. 260.
[3] *Iles Marquises ou Nouka-hiva* (Paris, 1843), p. 253, and J. G. Frazer, *The Belief in Immortality*, Vol. II p. 358.
[4] *Les Derniers Sauvages*, Paris, 1882, p. 92, and Frazer, *op. cit.*, p. 358

F. D. Bennet [1] describes a burial place on the island of Tahuata (Santa Christina) as follows:

" The most picturesque mausoleum we noticed was that which contained the corpse of one of Eutiti's children. It was placed on the summit of an isolated hill, rising from the bosom of a well-wooded savannah, and was covered entirely with the leaves of the fan-palm. The posterior, or tallest wall, was twelve feet high, the anterior was low, closed by a mat, and decorated with six wooden pillars, covered with stained cinnet and white cloth. Strips of tapa (bark cloth), fixed to a wand, fluttered on the roof, to denote that the spot was tabooed; and for the same purpose, a row of globular stones, each the size of a football, and whitened with coral lime, occupied the top of a low but broad stone wall which encircled the building. The interior contained nothing but a bier on which the corpse was laid."

The treatment of the body during the process of mummification varied in different localities. In some cases it was laid out at full length, and in others it was " propped up in a squatting position with the head and arms supported by two sticks lashed together in the form of a cross ".

Mummies were kept for varying periods in dwellings or in embalming houses. On Nukuhiva the coffin containing the mummy was attached to the branches of a tree in the sacred *me'ae* after the mourning period was over.

The use of coffins in the Marquesas Islands and elsewhere is of very special interest. They were generally made of bread-fruit wood, but coffins made of sections of coco-nut logs are referred to.[2] Those for Marquesan adults were from seven to eight feet in length. Some of them were carved. As a rule, they had " a covering of white tapa held in place by elaborate lashings of red and black sennit ". There were designs on the lashings which, as Handy informed Linton, " were derived from string

[1] *Narrative of a Whaling Voyage*, Vol. I p. 331.
[2] C. and S. Lambert, *The Voyage of the " Wanderer '*, London 1883.

figures; . . . their arrangement was the work of special craftsmen ". The mummy was, before being laid in the coffin, "wrapped in a shroud of white tapa and then usually covered with a layer of banana or *ti* leaves ". A heavy mat, instead of a lid, was usually used to close the coffin. Sometimes the coffins of canoe shape had, however, "close-fitting wooden lids ". Linton says that in the Marquesas "coffins were much more used in northern than in southern islands, and it seems probable that in the southern islands they were used only for chiefs and persons of importance ". In some cases the coffins with mummies were laid in caves which were occasionally artificially enlarged. The skulls might be removed from the coffins and kept separate. "It seems probable," says Linton, "that the tapa-covered skulls in some European collections are chiefs' skulls which have been used as cult objects."

Tautain [1] states that in the Marquesas a wooden image of the deceased was utilized in funeral ceremonies. Herman Melville [2] in his description of the tomb of a chief in one of the most secluded portions of the Taipivai Valley, Nukuhiva, which was a high edifice of wood raised on stone, writes as follows:

"On all sides, as you approached this silent spot, you caught sight of the dead chief's effigy, seated in the stern of a canoe, which was raised on a light frame a few inches above the level of the pi-pi (of stones). The canoe was about seven feet in length; of a rich, dark-coloured wood, handsomely carved, and adorned in many places with variegated bindings of stained sinnate, into which were ingeniously wrought a number of sparkling sea-shells, and a belt of the same shells ran all around it. The body of the figure . . . was effectually concealed in a heavy robe of brown tapa, revealing only the hands and head; the latter skilfully carved in wood, and surmounted by a superb arch of plumes. . . . The long leaves of the palmetto dropped over the eaves, and through them you saw the warrior, holding his paddle with both hands in the act

[1] *L'Anthropologie*, Vol. VIII, pp. 538–58 and 667–8, Paris, 1897.
[2] *Typee* (Everyman's Edition), pp. 183–4.

of rowing, leaning forward and inclining his head, as if eager to hurry on his voyage. Glaring at him forever, and face to face, was a polished human skull, which crowned the prow of the canoe. The spectral figure-head, reversed in its position, glancing backwards, seemed to mock the impatient attitude of the warrior."

It is not stated whether or not the mummy lay in the canoe. Probably it did. Linton says that the chiefs of Hakaui valley, Nukuhiva, were buried on the small island of Motuiti. " The coffined corpse was placed on a stage in the centre of a large war canoe. A single steersman sat in the stern while the paddlers were in the bow."[1]

Offerings of food, fruit, flowers, &c., were made to the dead.

Dr. Wyatt Gill in his *Life in the Southern Isles* [2] writes as follows regarding mummification on Mangai Island, the largest of the Cook Group:

" In nothing were the natives of the South Pacific more curious than in their burial ceremonies. The bodies of deceased friends were anointed with scented oil, carefully wrapped up in a number of pieces of cloth, and the same day committed to their last resting-place. A few were buried in the earth within the sacred precincts of the appropriate *marae*; but by far the greater number were hidden in caves regarded as the special property of certain families. . . .

" On the west side of Mangaia is Auraka, the grand depository of the dead of the ruling families who claim to have descended from Rongo,[3] and whose ancestors came from the setting sun. . . .

" The easiest entrance to this cemetery is by a romantic opening called Kauava. . . . Sometimes the cave contracts to the narrowest dimensions; at others its roof can scarcely be seen. Hundreds of well-preserved mummies lie in this natural house of the dead; some in rows on ledges of stalactite, others on wooden platforms. . . .

" If a body were buried in the earth the face was invariably laid downwards, chin and knees meeting, and the limbs well secured with strongest sennit cord. A thin covering of earth was

---

[1] *Bernice P. Bishop Museum Bulletin.* 23, Honolulu, Hawaii, 1925, pp. 54–62.
[2] London, 1876.   [3] God of sky.

laid over the corpse, and large, heavy stones placed over the grave. . . . Numbers were buried in caves easily accessible to enable the relatives to visit the remains of the dearly loved lost ones from time to time. The corpse was occasionally exposed to the sun, reanointed with oil, and then wrapped in fresh cloth. . . . It does not appear that they ever disembowelled the dead for the purpose of embalming. The corpse was simply desiccated (*rara*) and daily anointed."

The editor of the *Journal of the Polynesian Society* (1916) informs us that " he has been into the Kauava cave, and there noted what Dr. Gill has said, numbers of mummies lying on natural shelves, besides many coffins of later date".

In Hawaii, according to David Malo,[1] bodies were preserved by extracting the viscera and packing the cavity with salt. Abraham Fornander states [2] that the embalmers used a preparation from the root of the *ti* plant with which to close the pores of the skin and prevent decomposition. Only the bodies of important individuals were treated in this way. Ellis tells [3] that in Hawaii the bones of the legs and arms and sometimes the skull of " kings and principal chiefs, those who were supposed to have descended from the gods, or were to be deified, were usually preserved ". Apparently these were removed after the modified embalming process had been completed. " The other parts of the body were burnt or buried, while those bones were either bound up with cinet, wrapped in cloth, and deposited in temples for adoration, or distributed among the immediate relatives who, during their lives, always carried them wherever they went."

Ellis adds:

" This was the case with the bones of (King) Tamehameha; and it is probable that some of his bones were brought by his son Rihoriho on his recent visit to England, as they supposed that so long as the bones of the deceased were revered, his spirit would

---

[1] *Hawaiian Antiquities*, B. P. Bishop Museum, Mus. S. P. Vol. VIII, No. 5, p. 132. Malo was an educated native.

[2] *An Account of the Polynesian Race*, London, 1878, Vol. I, p. 106.

[3] *Polynesian Researches* (Second Edition, 1831), Vol. IV, pp. 358 *et seq*.

accompany them, and exercise a supernatural guardianship over them."

Bodies of chiefs of inferior rank and of priests were not treated in this manner, but were " laid out straight, wrapped in many folds of native tapa, and buried in that posture ".   Priests were usually interred "within the precincts of the temple in which they had officiated ". Ellis writes as follows regarding Hawaiian customs:

" A pile of stones, and frequently a circle of high poles, surrounded their grave, and marked the place of interment, corresponding exactly with the rites of sepulture practised by some of the tribes on the opposite coast of North America.   It was only the bodies of priests, or of persons of some importance, that were thus buried.   The common people committed their dead to the earth in a most singular manner.   After death, they raised the upper part of the body, bent the face forward to the knees, the hands were next put under the hams, and passed between the knees, when the head, hands, and knees were bound together with cinet or cord.   The body was afterwards wrapped in a coarse mat, and buried the first or second day after its decease."

The Tangaloa cult interred their influential men's bodies in stone-lined graves.   Others were interred in caves, in clefts of rock, pits, &c., in sequestered places, and in gardens.   Worshippers of Pele, the volcano deity, threw some of the bones of the dead into the crater, and fishermen " sometimes wrapped their dead in red native cloth and threw them into the sea, to be devoured by sharks ", believing that " the spirit of the dead would animate the shark " and " the survivors would be spared by those voracious monsters in the event of their being overtaken by any accident at sea ".

In the Chatham Islands, off New Zealand, the Moriori laid the bodies buried in the earth " with the face towards the west ".   The custom in Samoa, the Cook Islands, the Gilberts and the Carolines, was to lay the corpse with the face towards the east.[1]

[1] Ralph Linton in *Bernice P. Bishop Museum Bulletin*, No. 23. 1925. pp. 64-9.

Cremation was a rare custom in Polynesia. It has been seen, however, that partial cremation was practised at Hawaii. There the skulls and bones of legs and arms of kings and chiefs were preserved while, as Ellis tells, " the other parts of the body were burnt or buried ". Elsdon Best says with regard to New Zealand customs:

" Cremation was never a common or universal custom with the Maori. It was practised in some areas where no suitable places of concealment for bones of the dead were available, and also by raiding forces that had suffered in enemy territory. It was also occasionally practised in order to stay the spread of disease. Cremation was practised to some extent in the Rangi-tikei district, and on the Waimate Plains. When we were erecting Fort Manaia on the Plains in 1879 natives pointed out two pits hard by wherein, they said, bodies used to be burned. In some cases when men of note were slain in hostile territory, the head would be dried and carried home, while the body was burned. Then would be quoted an old saying: ' *He mata kai rangi, kāpā he mata kai aruhe,*' thus intimating that a person of note cannot be treated as a commoner, hence the preservation of the head." [1]

Cremation was practised by the Melanesians. Dr. Codrington refers to the custom in Sa'a where it was imported from Arosi, San Cristoval in the South-east Solomons. Dr. W. G. Ivens says that in the district called Paasi a hill is named " The burning of Pwai Mweimwei ", and he considers it was " the venue of a special ceremony ". A native informed him that " a chief's body was held in too much respect to be burned ". . . . Dr. Ivens adds that " the Tolo peoples of Mala do actually cremate their dead, but cremation cannot be said to be a practice either native to Sa'a, or generally adopted when introduced there from Arosi ". The four commonest methods in this area were exposure in a canoe, throwing into the sea, exposure on a stage or beach altar and interment. [2]

---

[1] Elsdon Best, *The Maori*, Vol. II, pp. 68–9.
[2] *Melanesians of the South-East Solomons*, London, 1927, pp. 208 *et seq.*

Other Polynesian customs were to dispose of the dead by setting them adrift in canoes, or exposing them on heaps of stones in a forest. Although crouched burials were common, we find that " in Tonga earth burial in an extended position seems to have been the rule for all classes ".[1] On all the islands the bodies of kings and chiefs received special treatment.

Ellis states that the sick were sometimes buried alive. " When this was designed," he writes, " they dug a pit, and then, perhaps, proposed to the invalid to bathe, offering to carry him to the water, either in their arms, or placed on a board; but instead of conveying him to the place of bathing, they would carry him to the pit and throw him in. Here, if any cries were made, they threw down large stones in order to stifle his voice, filled up the grave with earth, and then returned to their dwellings."[2]

According to Turner, when writing of a missionary voyage in 1848 to the New Hebrides and New Caledonia, the burial of sick persons was not uncommon on Vaté. " It is considered a disgrace," he tells, " to the family of an aged chief if he is not buried alive. When an old man feels sick and infirm, and thinks he is dying, he deliberately tells his children and friends to get all ready and bury him. They yield to his wishes, dig a round deep pit, wind a number of fine mats round his body, and lower down the poor old heathen into his grave in a sitting posture. . . . His grave is then filled up, and his dying groans are drowned amid the weeping and wailing of the living." As a rule " if a person in sickness shows signs of delirium, his grave is dug and he is buried forthwith ".[3]

[1] B. P. Bishop Museum Bulletin, No. 10, p. 65.
[2] Ellis, Polynesian Researches, Vol I, p. 282 (First Edition).
[3] Nineteen Years in Polynesia, pp. 450-1.

CHAPTER VIII

Egyptian Links with Polynesia

Embalmed Pharaoh as a God—His Connexion with Heavenly Bodies, Stones, and Trees—Scientific Study of Mummification—Egyptian Embalming House—The Directing Priest impersonated a God—Hereditary Embalmers in Egypt and Polynesia—Sacred Bandages—Intestines as Seat of Evil Emotions—Egyptian Mummies in Houses—Drying Egyptian Mummies—Fires in Old Tombs—Egyptian Mummies with Black Heads, Forehead Band, Red Body, and Artificial Eyes—Similar Mourning Customs in Egypt and Polynesia—Importance of Heads and Faces in Egypt and Polynesia—Polynesian Stone Heads—Distribution of Stone Images—Statues and Standing Stones—Egyptian and Polynesian Biers and Tombs—Polynesian God "Eyeball of the Sun" and Egyptian "Eye of Sun"—Coffins of Polynesia and Egypt—Canoes as Coffins—The Canoe of Osiris—Floral Garlands in Egypt and Polynesia.

The most remarkable thing about the embalming customs and associated beliefs in the South Sea Islands, including New Zealand, is that they bear a wonderfully close resemblance to those of Ancient Egypt.

Originally, on the banks of the Nile, the bodies of the pharaohs only were embalmed. The oldest surviving inscriptions in the world, the Pyramid Texts of Ancient Egypt, are really mortuary texts which " were all intended ", as Breasted emphasizes, " for the king's exclusive use ", and these " as a whole contain beliefs which apply only to the King. . . . The nobles of the (Pyramid) Age made practically no use of the Pyramid Texts in their own tombs." After Osiris died his body, according to the Texts, was embalmed so that it might be reanimated. Sometimes in the Pyramid Texts Isis and Nephthys, the sister goddesses, embalm the body of Osiris " to prevent its perishing "; sometimes Anubis " embalms Osiris ".

When the pharaoh had been mummified he " be-

came Osiris " (or " an Osiris ",) and he was then sup-
posed to rise from the dead " as Osiris did ". One of the
Pyramid Texts, identifying the pharaoh Teti (*c.* 2625
B.C.) with Osiris, reads:

" O Osiris Teti! thou art a mighty god, and there is no god
like thee."

The Pharaoh was also identified with the sun-god
Re. As Breasted puts it, "the sun-god became a kind of
celestial reflection of the earthly sovereign ".

The Pyramid Texts also associated the pharaoh-god
with the stars. He is the north star, and he " voyages
the sky with Orion ". The pharaoh was supposed to
inhabit the holy tree because after Osiris had been laid
in his tomb, a sacred tree grew up and enveloped the body
of the dead god. A Pyramid Text reads:

" Hail to thee, Sycamore, which encloses the god, under which
the gods of the Nether sky stand. . . ."

In Plutarch's story the *erica* encloses the god's body,
having " shot up into a large and beautiful tree ". The
King of Byblos had this tree cut down and the trunk
made into a pillar to support the roof of his house.[1]

Here, then, we have the pharaoh of Egypt becoming,
like the Polynesian King, after being embalmed, a god,
a star or group of stars, a pillar, &c. Fundamentally, the
motive for mummification in Egypt and Polynesia was
identical. In both countries the members of the royal
family and other influential individuals were embalmed
like the chief ruler. The King alone, however, became the
god. It was to enable the King to become " an Osiris "
that the practice of mummification originated in Egypt.

But it was not only the religious ideas behind mummification that links Polynesia with Ancient Egypt. The
technical processes and rituals of the two countries were

---

[1] James Henry Breasted, *Development of Religion and Thought in Ancient Egypt*, London,
1912, pp. 17, 27, 59, 101-2, 144 *et seq.*, 160, and Plutarch's, *Isis and Osiris*, xii *et seq.*

remarkably alike. It is only of late, however, that it has become possible to establish this interesting fact. As Mr. Warren R. Dawson, the well-known authority on mummification, writes:

"With the exception of the works of Professor Elliot Smith, to whom we are indebted for almost all our scientific knowledge of mummification and its significance, and of Professor Wood Jones, the majority of the accounts of mummification, even by modern writers, are of little value."

Professor Elliot Smith began his researches when he occupied the Chair of Anatomy in the Government School of Medicine in Cairo. He wrote various monographs on the royal mummies in the Cairo museum, and these have been drawn upon in a recent work written in collaboration with Warren R. Dawson, Fellow of the Royal Society of Medicine, and a scholarly translator of ancient Egyptian writings.[1] Other works by Professor Elliot Smith which have direct bearing on the subject, include *The Ancient Egyptians*,[2] *The Migrations of Early Culture*[3], and *The Evolution of the Dragon*.[4] Mr. Warren R. Dawson's recent papers include "Making a Mummy", in the *Journal of Egyptian Archæology*[5], "Contributions to the History of Mummification", in the *Proceedings of the Royal Society of Medicine*[6], and "A Mummy from the Torres Straits", in the *Annals of Archæology and Anthropology*.[7]

In his contribution to the *Journal of Egyptian Archæology*, Mr. Dawson adds to our knowledge on the subject of Egyptian mummification by providing evidence regarding "the order of procedure, the method of employing the salt bath, the importance of desiccation, and the temporary nature of the embalmer's workshop".

As we have seen, temporary workshops were used in the South Sea Islands, and the platforms on which these

---

[1] *Egyptian Mummies*, London, 1924. [2] London (Second Edition), 1923.
[3] Manchester, 1915. [4] London, 1919. [5] Vol. XIII, 1927, pp. 40 *et seq.*
[6] Vol. XX, Part 6, April, 1927, pp. 831 *et seq.* [7] Vol. XI, No. 2.

were erected still survive in the Marquesas. Ellis, as indicated, tells us that the "corpse-praying priest" directed the operations in the embalming house. Dawson provides illustrations of ancient Egyptian embalming houses in which we see workmen employed in preparing the mummy, and a directing priest " holding a papyrus and making ceremonial gestures ". The Egyptian priest impersonated the god Anubis, and " during the anointing and bandaging processes " he " recited from a service book the appropriate liturgy ". In the Græco-Roman Egyptian period there were two kinds of workers—" the incision - makers and the embalmers and wrappers ". Certain texts refer to other ministrants, named " lectors, sem-priests, imy-khant priests, and the ' Treasurers of the God '". The " god " here mentioned was originally the deified pharaoh. As Elliot Smith and Dawson remind us in this connexion, mummification was " a divine art in the sense that it was essentially for conferring the boon of immortality which transformed a mortal king into a god ".[1] Similarly the Polynesian king became, as we have seen, " a sun-dried god ".

"In the course of time," add Elliot Smith and Dawson, " the practice of mummification (in Egypt) became more and more widely democratized, until at the beginning of the Christian era it had spread to the whole population ". . . . The attainment of immortality was not then regarded as " the privilege of kings and nobles, but was open to all mankind ".[2]

Turner states, as has been indicated, that the embalming process was in Samoa performed by " a particular family of old ladies ". According to Diodorus Siculus, the embalmer's office was hereditary in Egypt. This statement " is confirmed by a group of demotic papyri published by Revillont ".[3]

In Polynesia the bandages were in some, if not in all

---

[1] *Egyptian Mummies*, pp. 48, 60, 163.   [2] *Ibid.*, p. 163.
[3] "Une Famille de Paraschistes ou Taricheutes Thébains," in the *Aegyptische Zeitschrift*, t. XVII (1879), pp. 83–92, and *Egyptian Mummies*, p. 65 and note 3.

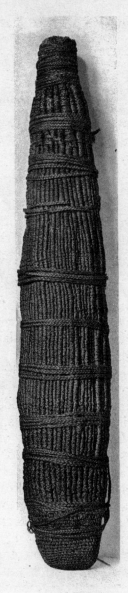

TAHITIAN IDOL

The wrapping of this sacred bundle suggests the influence of the mummification custom

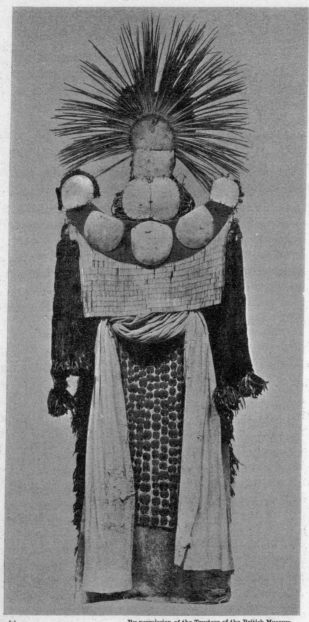

(9)

CEREMONIAL DRESS FROM TAHITI

Worn by the chief mourner at burial rites. See also plate facing p. 112

cases given names, as were the lashings of the sacred
adzes; and the lashings of red and black sennit on the
coffins were covered with symbolic designs. In Egypt
the mummy bandages were similarly named. In a fragmentary papyrus there is

"a long section giving directions for the anointing and bandaging
of the head, with a detailed specification of the bandages to be
used for each part of the head, giving the magical names of each." [1]

The various bandages were, it appears, consecrated
to various deities. Another papyrus brings this out
clearly. A god, addressing a mummified man, says:

"Thou wast rubbed with balsam by Horus. . . . Shesmu
wound with his fingers the divine bandage in order to enwrap
the body with the wrappings of the gods and goddesses. Anubis
as embalmer filled thy skull with resin, corn of the gods . . . cedar
oil, mild ox-fat, cinnamon oil; and myrrh is to all thy members.
Thy body is invested with holy bandages." [2]

The wrapping of amulets, talismans, &c., in various
countries is a significant custom. In Nukuhiva in the
Marquesas Islands " the tapa-wrapped bones were sometimes hung from the roof of the dwelling and kept for
an indefinite period ". Ralph Linton says " it seems
probable that the tapa-covered skulls preserved in some
European collections are chiefs' skulls, which have been
used (in Polynesia) as cult objects, for their decorations
are quite different from those of the war trophy heads
described by early writers ".[3]

Light is thrown on the Polynesian custom, referred
to by Ellis, of digging a hole below the platform on which
lay the corpse during the process of embalming, for the
purpose of receiving the " sins " of the dead, when we
find Plutarch stating that the internal parts of the human
body were regarded " as the seat of evil emotions ".
The exceptions were the heart and kidneys, " the seat of

---

[1] *Egyptian Mummies*, p. 48.   [2] *Ibid.*
[3] *Bernice P. Bishop Museum Bulletin*, No. 23, p. 59.

the mind and the good emotions ", which, Elliot Smith
and Dawson state, were not excised from the body except
by accident or through carelessness on the part of the
embalmers.   Plutarch says that "the intestines were
chargeable with all the sins the man has committed ",
and that when the intestines were removed the body
" became purified ".   Referring to the foreign converts
to Egyptian religion, Plutarch adds:

" In the case of the well-to-do, they imitate the Egyptians,
who open their dead and extract the intestines, which they cast
out before the Sun as chargeable with all the sins the man has
committed." [1]

Warren R. Dawson states that the usual ancient
Egyptian name for an embalmer's workshop was " Pure
Place " or " Pure Place of the Good House ".   Another
name of frequent occurrence is " Tent of the God " or
" God's Booth ".[2] In the " Pure Place " the body of the
" sinner " was made " pure "; his sins were " washed
away ".

Some Polynesians, as we have seen, kept their
mummies in their houses. This custom was not unknown
in Egypt during the late period. According to Diodorus
Siculus, some of the Egyptians placed the embalmed
bodies of their ancestors " in fine chambers " and could
" behold at a glance those who died before they themselves were born ".   In the Syriac version of the Life of
St. Anthony a similar custom is referred to. The saint
says on his death-bed, addressing the faithful brethren:

" And if your minds are set upon me as a father, permit no
man to take my body and carry it into Egypt, lest, according to
the custom which they have, they embalm me and lay me up in
their houses. . . . Dig me a grave and bury me therein." [3]

The technique of Egyptian mummification differed

---

[1] Quoted in *Egyptian Mummies*, pp. 65–7.
[2] *Journal of Egyptian Archæology*, Vol. XIII, 1927, p. 41.
[3] *Egyptian Mummies*, pp. 63, 70; and Budge, *The Paradise of the Fathers*, t. I, p. 382.

at different periods, and even during a single period, as
Herodotus indicates. The particular process of mummification which was adopted in a particular case depended
upon the sum paid by relatives for the work. Rich people
favoured the most elaborate and costly method of mummification for their dead; the poor had to be content
with a comparatively cheap method. In one case the
viscera was removed through an incision, in another *per
anum*, and in a third the body was simply soaked in a salt
bath. We therefore meet with alternative methods of
embalming in Egypt as in Polynesia. The Polynesian
custom of extracting the viscera and brain, packing the
body cavity with cloth soaked in oil, &c., and varnishing
and anointing the skin with oil were all originally Egyptian customs.

Mr. W. R. Dawson has found, by examination of
mummies, that other methods of embalming prevailed
in Egypt than those usually referred to, especially in
modern works. He writes in this connexion:

"Mummies have been found without embalming wounds,
and these were either eviscerated *per anum*, or were not eviscerated
at all. . . . In certain cases some of the viscera were actually
excised *per anum*, and in others no attempt at all had been made
to remove them. I recently examined two well-preserved mummies of the Twenty-sixth Dynasty which had been neither eviscerated nor immersed in a salt-bath, yet both were in an excellent
state of preservation. There was no embalming-wound, nor had
the anal method been resorted to. . . . The bodies had been
merely desiccated, then covered with a liberal supply of resinous
paste. . . . The skin is soft and flexible, and the bodies do not
show the considerable shrinking which inevitably occurs whenever the salt bath has been used."[1]

The drying of the mummy, which had been soaked
in a salt bath and then washed, was of great importance.
Dawson considers that the imperfect method of drying,
or the neglect of it, prior to the Empire period in Egypt,

accounts for the very fragile state of many of the old mummies. He does not think that sun-heat alone was sufficient for the drying process. Fire-heat appears to have been used as well. In 1924-5 an interesting discovery was made in a Theban tomb which, as Mr. Dawson says, " is suggestive in this connexion ". In some of the chambers of the tomb, as the official record states, " a vast number of mummies were piled up almost to the ceiling in a state of disorder. . . . The mummies, to judge from their appearance, seemed to have been dried over a slow fire, which would explain the smoky appearance of all the chambers and passages above." An old empty tomb had evidently been used to dry mummies during the late period. " Many tombs in Egypt," Dawson notes, " bear evidence of having been the scene of fire." [1] The New Zealand custom of using an oven for drying the mummy was apparently not a local innovation. The " portable hearths " found in Cretan tombs may have been intended to dry rather than " warm and comfort the dead ", as has been suggested.

In the Twenty-first Dynasty, the custom was introduced in Egypt of painting the mummy red all over and providing artificial eyes. " In mummies not so painted the innermost wrappings were dyed red." The head was painted black, and a band was traced across the brows.[2] In the course of time " it became usual to dye the outer shroud red ". The cartonnage decorations of the mummy case in Ptolemaic times " were sewn on to this red background ".[3]

The ceremonial mourning for the dead in the South Sea Islands resembled closely that which obtained in Ancient Egypt.

Ellis describes the mournings in the Society Isles,

---

[1] S. Yeivin, *Annals of Archæology and Anthropology*, Vol. XIII, p. 15, and Dawson, *Journal of Egyptian Archæology*, Vol. XIII, pp. 45-6.
[2] Dawson in *Proceedings of the Royal Society of Medicine*, Vol. XX, Part 6, p. 852, and *Annals of Archæology and Anthropology*, Vol. XI, No. 2, p. 93.
[3] *Egyptian Mummies*, p. 120.

and tells that at Hawaii, when a king or chief died, some of the mourners had their heads shaved or very closely cropped, some had front teeth knocked out, and many had black spots or lines tattooed on their tongues. " The Friendly Islanders cut off a joint of one of their fingers." [1] These and the Society Islanders cut their temples, faces, and bosoms with sharks' teeth. Ellis describes the proceedings he witnessed at Maui in the Hawaiian or Sandwich Islands:

" After the death of Keopuolani, we frequently saw the inhabitants of a whole district, that had belonged to her, coming to weep on account of her death. They walked in profound silence, either in single file, or two or three abreast. . . . They were not covered with ashes, but almost literally clothed in sackcloth. No ornaments, or even decent piece of cloth, was seen on one. Dressed only in old fishing nets, dirty and torn pieces of matting or tattered garments, and these sometimes tied on their bodies with pieces of old ropes, they appeared the most abject and wretched companies of human beings I ever saw. When they were within a few hundred yards of the house where the corpse was lying, they began to lament and wail. The crowds of mourners around the house opened a passage for them to approach it, and then one or two of their number came forward, and standing a little before the rest, began a song or recitation, shewing her birth, rank, honours, and virtues, brandishing a staff or piece of sugar-cane, and accompanying their recitation with attitudes and gestures expressive of the most frantic grief. When they had finished, they sat down, and mingled with the thronging multitudes in their loud and ceaseless wailing." [2]

Turner writes of the Samoans lamenting over their dead with " boisterous wailing ", accompanied by " the most frantic expressions of grief, such as rending garments, tearing the hair, thumping the face and eyes, burning the body with small firebrands, beating the head with stones till the blood ran, and this they called an

---

[1] This custom is known in Fiji and New Guinea. " The operation is performed in remembrance of a near relative, such as a brother, &c." Brown's *Melansians and Polynesians*, p. 241.

[2] *Polynesian Researches* (Second Edition), Vol. IV, pp. 179–80 and 359.

' offering of blood ' for the dead ". He adds that " the
death of a chief of high rank was attended with great
excitement and display; all work was suspended in the
settlement ".[1]

Elsewhere in Polynesia, including New Zealand,
similar wailings, lamentations, and mutilations were quite
customary. In Micronesia, " as soon as life was extinct,
the family set up a great wailing and yelling ".[2]

Herodotus [3] writes as follows of the Egyptian manner
of mourning:

" When any person of distinction in a family dies, all the women
of the household besmear their heads and even their faces with
mud, and, leaving the corpse in the house, they wander about the
town beating themselves, with clothes girt up and their breasts
bare, all their relatives accompanying them. The men, too, beat
themselves, their clothes being girt up likewise."

Elliot Smith and Dawson remark that this statement as to mourning in Egypt is " confirmed by numerous
pictures of funeral processions which abound in tombs of
all periods, and in countless papyri. . . . The female
mourners at funeral processions are generally represented with bare breasts and dishevelled hair, and the
usual attitude of their hands suggests that their action
is that of putting mud or dust upon their heads, a practice
which is common in Egypt at the present day. In one
instance at least the female mourners have their clothes
' girt up ' to the pitch of indecency." [4]

It was not until the Eighteenth Dynasty (1580–
1350 B.C.), after about twenty centuries of experience,
that the Egyptians succeeded in making really good
mummies. From the Twenty-first to the Twenty-second
Dynasties (1090–525 B.C.), the art of mummification,
which was " a sacred and religious function ", as Smith
and Dawson constantly remind us, reached its highest

---

[1] *Samoa*, pp. 144–6.   [2] Sir J. G. Frazer, *The Belief in Immortality*, Vol. III, p. 43.
[3] Book II, p. 85.   [4] *Egyptian Mummies*, pp. 57–9.

pitch of excellence. It was in the Twenty-first Dynasty that " the limbs were packed with material to plump them out into a life-like form ". The viscera, having been cleansed, soaked and scented, were wrapped up and re-placed in the body. At an earlier period they were de-posited in Canopic jars. These jars were, however, still included in the " funerary furniture ".

The Egyptians who began to mummify their dead paid special attention to the head and especially the face. It was evidently to them a religious necessity that the dead man should be made recognizable. When, however, they found that the poorly-preserved body no longer retained a facial likeness, the custom was introduced of modelling the head, first by means of linen soaked in resin on which the features were painted, and then by providing mud or plaster heads. Then portrait heads of stone and wood were placed in graves. These were " substitution heads ". In time came the complete statue, a feature of which was the careful attention paid to the face. This is, indeed, an outstanding feature of all the ancient Egyptian statuary. As a rule, the rest of the body was either merely suggested or carved with less attention to detail. In a letter to Professor Elliot Smith, Dr. Alan Gardiner stresses the point that these statues were supposed to be animated by the *ka*-spirit of the deceased. This letter runs:

" That statues in Egypt were meant to be efficient animate substitutes for the person or creature they portrayed has not been sufficiently emphasised hitherto. Over every statue or image were performed the rites of ' opening the mouth '—magical passes made with a kind of metal chisel in front of the mouth. Beside the *up-ro* ' mouth opening ', other words testify to the prevalence of the same idea; the word for ' to fashion ' a statue (*ms*) is to all appearances identical with *ms* ' to give birth ', and the term for the sculptor was *sa'nkh*, ' he who causes to live '."[1]

[1] Quoted in Elliot Smith's *The Migrations of Culture*, p. 42 see also *Egyptian Mummies*, pp. 25-7.

Elliot Smith and Dawson say that "the modelling of a life-like portrait" was "the creation of a living image, a perpetuation of the life of the deceased, in other words, a rebirth or renewal of life". It is, however, worthy of note that this custom of making a substitute body "never deterred the embalmers from their efforts to preserve in the mummy itself the actual lineaments of the dead. Many centuries later they satisfied themselves in their ability to achieve this aim, but during the intervening period the statue contributed much to the consolidation of their ritual and beliefs."[1]

The Polynesian custom of providing a statue of the dead chief who had been embalmed, is, in the light of the Egyptian evidence, a very notable and significant one. It can hardly be characterized as "something quite natural".

Dealing with the Marquesan images in wood and stone Ralph Linton, who makes no reference to Egyptian customs, provides some details of very special interest which still further emphasize that the Polynesian funerary customs have a history rooted in antiquity. He says that there are two classes of Marquesan stone figures: "true images" and "architectural figures". The former "were set up in sacred places" and the latter "incorporated into the walls of terraces of platforms of both secular and ceremonial structures".

Dealing first with wooden images, he tells that in carving the features "the mouth was finished first, then the eyes", and proceeds to say:

"The head was evidently considered the most important part of the figure, and upon it the artist expended his greatest skill. The legs were considered least important; in many figures they are shortened disproportionately or even omitted. . . . The artist followed a definite convention in the representation of all the parts and the grotesqueness of the images is due to this and not to any lack of skill in execution."

Again:

" The bodies of most wooden figures show little or no attempt at modelling. . . . The canons of Marquesan art seem to have permitted only two positions for the arms. Fully eighty per cent of the figures show the upper arms held vertically against the body and the forearms extended forward horizontally with the hands resting upon the stomach."

The arms and hands of many Egyptian mummies are found to be in a similar position.

Mr. Linton goes on to say of the images that " all heads are disproportionately large, some of them forming a third of the total height of the figure ". Stone images reveal similar characters to those of wood and Linton writes of these:

" The great importance attached by the Marquesan sculptor to the heads of figures probably led to the practice of making heads to which no bodies were attached. Most of these heads were used as architectural decorations, but two very large ones in the temple of Oipona, Puamau, Hivaoa, seem to have had a significance similar to that of the true images. The larger of these was removed some years ago by a German trading company and its fate is unknown. It is said to have resembled the remaining head in all important details but to have been much larger. A trustworthy European who helped to remove it estimated its weight at three tons. I saw the smaller head in position. It stands on the corner of the main platform, which also bears the large images. Like these images, it had an individual name, Makii-tauapepe, and seems to have been considered of equal importance with them. . . . The total height of this head at the front is three feet one inch."

According to Linton some of the most important images were " unquestionably figures of the deified dead ". He refers to the statue of Takaii, in Puamau, as an example. In a legend this man is " an important warrior with no divine attributes ", but " at a later period he is considered a god ".

As in Egypt, offerings were made in the Marquesas

to the images of the deified chiefs and kings. " Offerings ", says Linton, " were placed before the image or
hung up near by. Gracia mentions having seen priests
put food offerings to the mouth of the image. According to Handy the offerings were placed on the head of
images on *tokai*. The Puamau images are said to have
been dressed in native costume, and decorated with
ornaments at the time of ceremonies. Stone hats were
used as on Easter Island and elsewhere.

Mr. Linton notes that many small carvings of the
Igorot in the Philippines " show a striking resemblance
to the Polynesian forms in their pose and body treatment, although there is little facial resemblance, and
some carved faces from the island of Engano, south of
Java, are remarkably similar to the Marquesan forms ",
and he suggests that " the ancestral Polynesian conven-
tions for image carving may have been developed somewhere in Indonesia ".

The distribution of stone images is limited in Polynesia. They " seem to be entirely lacking in Samoa.
Tonga, and Micronesia ". In Melanesia " they occur
sporadically ". Linton says that " a few rough attempts
at large sculpture in stone occur in Hawaii ", but large
statues " were numerous only in the Marquesas, in
Raivavai, and in Easter Island ". He adds, however,
that " the Marquesan statues agree so closely with the
wooden images in form and use that it seems that they
are only stone imitations ".[1]

Some peoples who had adopted the custom of providing stone images, but had not amongst them men
sufficiently skilled to carve portraits, provided instead
blocks or pillars of stone on which were carved the eyes
and eyebrows, or simply religious symbols. Others
erected pillars which " tapered downward like the human
body ". Perhaps that was why it was believed in Samoa

[1] Ralph Linton, *Bernice P. Bishop Museum Bulletin*, No. 23, pp. 70 *et seq.*, Honolulu.
Hawaii, 1925.

the spirits of chiefs, who, after embalming, became
" sun-dried gods ", inhabited " blocks of stone ".

In Ancient Egypt the idea of God was closely associated with the beliefs connected with mummification.
An axe-like bundle of linen (*neter*) is the hieroglyph for
" god ". The god was the " embalmed one " or a personification of the completed embalming process. The
god Ptah of Memphis was depicted as a mummy, with
his whole body, except hands and face, completely
wrapped in magical linen bandages. Turner, as we have
seen, tells that in Samoa some of the mummies' heads
and hands were left unwrapped.

In Egypt corpses were laid on biers—that is, on
beds. On the walls of the temple of Dendera there is
a group of scenes, showing Osiris, the first mummy,
being reanimated. He lies on a bier inside a funeral
chest, or tomb-house, supported by symbolic pillars.
Here a life-giving tree is placed at his head, and there
a frog at his feet, while various deities make ceremonial
gestures. In the end, Osiris rises and kneels in a boat
which rests upon a sledge, the supports of which are
lotus flowers.

The funerary bier, as we have seen, was retained in
the South Sea Islands. It was similarly retained, in connexion with mummification, in other countries where the
people did not have beds, as Elliot Smith has pointed
out.[1]

Elliot Smith, referring to the burial customs of East
Africa and of the Asiatic littoral, Indonesia, Melanesia
and Polynesia, writes:

" Another distinctive feature . . . was the idea that the
grave represented the house in which the deceased was sleeping.
How definitely this view was held by the proto-Egyptians is seen
in their coffins, subterranean burial chambers, and the super-
structures of their tombs, all three of which were originally represented as dwelling houses." [2]

---

[1] *The Migrations of Culture*, pp. 45 *et seq.*   [2] *Ibid.*, p. 46.

Reference has been made to Polynesian burials in dwelling houses which were closed and tabooed, and in caves, some of which were artificially enlarged. Ellis tells us that several of the burial caves in Hawaii were " barricaded to prevent any but the proprietors entering them or depositing bodies there ".[1] He also describes a royal tomb-house in Hawaii as " a compact building, twenty-four feet by sixteen, constructed with the most durable timber and thatched with *ti* leaves, standing on a bed of lava. . . . It is surrounded by a strong fence or paling." Outside the enclosure were " several rudely carved male and female images of wood ". These and other images were " perpetual guardians of ' the mighty dead ' reposing in the house adjoining ". Fragments of the offerings of calabashes, coco-nuts (instead of pottery), wreaths of flowers, &c., " the accumulated offerings of former days ", formed " an unsightly mound immediately before each of the images ".[2]

In the previous chapter is a quotation from Herman Melville's description of the tomb-house of the dead chief, and the dead chief's effigy " seated in the stern of a canoe ". The Marquesan " Kory-Kory ", who accompanied Melville to the tomb, told him that " the chief was paddling his way to the realms of bliss and bread-fruit—the Polynesian heaven ", where every moment the bread-fruit trees dropped their ripened spheres to the ground, and where there was no end to the coco-nuts and bananas; there they reposed through the live-long eternity upon mats much finer than those of Typee; and every day bathed their glowing limbs in rivers of coco-nut oil. . . . Best of all, women, far lovelier than the daughters of earth, were there in abundance." Here the Egyptian Paradise of Osiris, with its corn-fields and orchards, is localized, and there are added the Apsaras (fairy women) of the Hindu Paradise.

[1] *Polynesian Researches* (Second Edition), Vol. IV, p. 144.
[2] Ellis, *op. cit.*, Vol. IV, pp. 165–6.

Ellis was told in Hawaii that

" there were two gods who conducted the departed spirits of their
chiefs to some place in the heavens, where it was supposed the
spirits of kings and chiefs sometimes dwelt, and afterwards returned
with them to the earth, where they accompanied the movements
and watched over the destinies of their survivors. The name of
one of these gods was Kaonohiokala, ' the eye-ball of the sun ';
and the other, Kuahairo."

The priest of the latter god promised the king that his
spirit would be taken " to the sky ", and would return
again with the god to the earth " when his body would
be reanimated and youthful ".[1]

The god who was " the eyeball of the sun " recalls the
Egyptian " Eye of Re (the sun-god) ". Horus, as the
solar " eye ", conducted royal souls to Paradise, as did
the gods Agni and Indra in India, and also the god
Yama of another cult.

In Polynesia, as in Egypt, coffins were of as much
importance in funerary practice as the magical wrappings
of the dead. It is remarkable to find that in decorating
these and the biers the colours red, black and white
were of special significance in both areas. In a curious
ceremony in Hawaii these colours again appear. After
a chief had been interred, a man who was supposed to
be possessed by his spirit armed himself and, heading a
procession, went through a village for the purpose of
revenging any injury the chief had suffered during life,
and to punish those who had not shown due respect to
his remains. This man wore a mask with pearl-shell eyes,
and surmounted by feathers of white and red. He and
his followers had smeared their bodies with white and
red clay. " Sometimes," says Ellis, " the body was
painted red, with black and white stripes; at other times
the face was painted red or black, and the rest of the
body red and white." [2]

---

[1] Ellis, *Polynesian Researches* (Second Edition), Vol. IV, pp. 144-5.
[2] *Ibid.*, Vol. I, pp. 532-4.

Canoes were, as has been noted, sometimes used as coffins, or coffins were shaped somewhat like canoes. Corpses, embalmed or not embalmed, were in certain areas set adrift.[1] Rivers considered that the canoe burial " can be regarded as a result of the fact of migration ", the canoe not having been used in the " original home ".[2] Elliot Smith admits that " the special circumstances of the people of Oceania naturally emphasized what may be called the 'boat element' in the funerary ritual ", but he points out that the use of boats with burial prevailed elsewhere, including Egypt; and he considers that the custom could hardly have arisen independently in Oceania and elsewhere in the area of distribution as well.[3] It has been shown that Osiris, as a mummy, appears in a boat in the temple of Dendera scenes.

The offerings of garlands of flowers were not peculiar to Polynesia. Elliot Smith and Dawson note that among the numerous spells in the Egyptian *Book of the Dead*, some refer to " the Crown of Justification, which is a floral wreath or garland to be placed upon the head of the mummy ", and we are reminded that " floral garlands are not uncommon in Egyptian tombs, and that several fine specimens were found in the tomb of Tutankhamen. The mummies of Aahmes I and of Amenophis I were decked with floral garlands. According to Gardener these garlands were placed on mummies in memory of the wreaths given to Osiris on his triumphant exit from the judgment-hall of Heliopolis." [4]

[1] W. H. R. Rivers, *The History of Melanesian Society*, Vol. II, p. 270.
[2] *Ibid.*, p. 169.   [3] *Migrations of Culture*, p. 106.   [4] *Egyptian Mummies*, pp. 148–9.

CHAPTER IX

Ancient Mariners and the Diffusion of Culture

Far Eastern Mummification — Egyptian Technique detected — Long Voyages of King Solomon's Ships—The Phœnician Mariners—Colonies founded by Sea-farers—Caste Burials—Torres Straits Mummies—Treatment of Nails—The Guanche Mummies similar—Diffusion of Mummification in Africa—Scythian and other Mummies—Ancient Hindu Mummies—Modern Indian Mummies cremated—Mummies of Indonesia, Philippines, and Australia—Aino Mummies—Peruvian and Mexican Mummies—Treatment of Nails in Peru—Preservation of Skulls—Indian Ocean Mariners—Dravidian Sea Power—Shore-sighting Birds on Ships—Buddhist's Voyage from India to China—Navigation by Sun, Moon, and Stars—India's Ancient Sea-trade—Culture Drifts into Indonesia and Polynesia—Types of Ancient Ships—Long Voyages—Horus-eye on Boats—Racial and Cultural Drifts.

It is a " far cry " from Egypt to Polynesia, and the question arises as to how the burial customs of the Nile valley reached the distant isles of the Pacific. Withal, it has to be recognized and remembered that mummification was introduced into the South Sea Islands long after it had ceased to be practised at all, or to any extent, in the land of Egypt. The Polynesian people were never, and could not possibly have been, in direct touch with Egyptian civilization, from which they were far separated by space and in time.

In investigating the problem of transmission, we find, in the first place, that those who have made a scientific study of mummification by conducting an examination of mummies from various countries, emphasize in the light of their accumulated knowledge that the technique of mummification in the Far East is that of the late Egyptian dynasties. The sea-farers who migrated

117

towards the Pacific and formed colonies displayed a knowledge of the technique of embalming which had been acquired in Egypt after many centuries of experience. Indeed, it may be said that they really began where the Egyptians, at a particular period, had left off.

During the late Egyptian period there was great maritime activity not only on the part of the Egyptians themselves, but the Phœnicians and other peoples. In the Twenty-Second Dynasty, for instance, King Solomon, the son-in-law of Pharaoh Sheshonk I (the Biblical Shishak) possessed a navy which set out on voyages that lasted for three years, returning with " gold and silver, ivory and apes and peacocks ". His navy was associated with that of the Phœnician King, Hiram of Tyre.[1] " The King's ships went to Tarshish with the servants (sailors) of Huram (Hiram) "; they also visited Ophir (in Arabia) from which they brought " gold . . . algum-trees, and precious stones ". Some of Solomon's vessels were wrecked in the Red Sea.

The sea-farers who reached the land of the peacock in Malay and the Dutch East Indies, and the islands of the Torres Straits, formed colonies from which other colonies " budded ". These colonists appear to have perpetuated religious beliefs and practices long after these had become extinct in the western areas of origin. Mixing with various Eastern peoples at various periods, they acquired other religious beliefs and practices which were fused into an illogical whole. Certain practices were perpetuated by a class. The ruling families had their own religious systems and customs, and their own Paradises. In certain areas the kings and chiefs were mummified, and other classes were interred, exposed, or thrown into the sea. Some ruling classes cremated the dead; other ruling classes practised water burial. As we have seen, the Samoan and Marquesan ruling families practised mummification.

---

[1] *1 Kings*, Chapter x, and *2 Chronicles*, Chapter ix.

One of the interesting and important facts which have emerged from the scientific study of mummification is that the embalming practices of the Twenty-first Egyptian Dynasty certainly reached the Torres Straits islands. We should not be surprised, therefore, to find them repeated in Polynesia. In his paper " A Mummy from the Torres Straits ",[1] Mr. Warren R. Dawson furnishes ample proof of the transmission of a very distinctive technique which cannot be explained by the hazardous theory of " psychic unity ". He deals in his paper not only with a British Museum mummy from the Torres Straits, but with others from the same region which display similar treatment.

We cannot help sharing Dawson's astonishment and interest in finding the late Egyptian embalming customs perpetuated in the Torres Straits area. These include the painting of the head black and the body red, the tracing of a band across the forehead, the insertion of artificial eyes, the making of similar incisions to extract the viscera and of incisions for draining and packing the corpse. The treatment of the skin is of special significance. As we have seen, it was occasionally taken off in Polynesia, the body not having been soaked in a salt bath but simply dried. In Egypt the skin peeled off in the salt bath, and the Torres Straits islanders and the Polynesians, having apparently traditions in this connexion which were derived from some common centre, considered it to be a religious necessity to flay the corpse.

It was in Egypt a religious necessity to preserve the finger-nails and toe-nails. To prevent these coming off in the salt bath, " the embalmers either tied them on to the fingers and toes, or placed a metal thimble over the tip of the finger or toe. Many of the Egyptian mummies which have been examined still have this thread, or well-marked impressions of it, and on some others

---

[1] *Annals of Archæology and Anthropology*, Vol. XI, No. 2, pp. 87 *et seq.*

thimbles have been found."[1]   Tutankhamen's mummy
has a complete set of gold finger- and toe-thimbles.
Another method of preserving the nails was to cut the
skin around finger or toe, and draw it forward and tie
it over the nail as a thimble.

Dr. Hamlyn Harris, as Mr. Dawson notes, states [2]
with regard to Torres Straits mummification " that the
skin was cut round the tip of each finger and the skin,
with the nail attached, was pulled off ".   Here " the
traditional treatment of the nails survives ", says Mr.
Dawson, " but is reversed in practice ".[3]

In his paper on mummification as practised by the
Guanches of the Canary Islands, Mr. Dawson states
that he has detected a similar attention to the nails.   He
found on examining a Guanche mummy at Cambridge
University, which displays the late Egyptian technique,
that the nails had been tied on with leather thongs,
although the corpse had not been immersed in a salt
bath.   Like the Polynesians the Guanches used biers and
deposited mummies in caves, thus following the Egyptian custom of depositing them in rock-cut tombs.

Dealing with the diffusion from Egypt of the practice of mummification, Elliot Smith and Dawson write:

" In the course of their trafficking with neighbouring peoples,
in Nubia and the Sudan, in the Mediterranean islands and coasts,
in East Africa and the Erythræan coasts, Egyptians had introduced many of their customs and practices. . . . Long settlement
in some of these places led to the adoption by the local people of
the Egyptian custom of mummification; and when in later times
the population of these colonies imitated their teachers and ex-
ploited countries still farther afield, a variety of modified forms
of Egyptian embalming were handed on stage by stage to distant
lands, until every continent in the whole world was practising
some of *the many varieties of Egyptian mummification* in a more or
less modified form." [4]

---

[1] *Egyptian Mummies*, p. 88.
[2] *Mem. Queensland Museum*, Vol. I, 1912, pp. 1 *et seq.* and Plate.
[3] *A Mummy from the Torres Straits*, pp. 93–4.   [4] *Egyptian Mummies*, pp. 163–4.

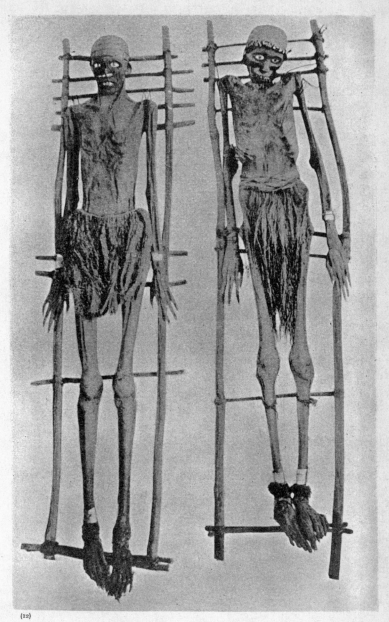

(12)

MUMMIES FROM TORRES STRAITS ISLANDS

Female on left: male on right.   From the Brisbane Museum, Australia

(11)

FUNERARY BIER, TAHITI

From an engraving published in 1836 illustrating the account of a voyage in Oceania by Domeny de Rienzi, the French explorer
See also plate facing p. 97

It is necessary to keep in mind that in Egypt there were "many varieties", because some writers, ignoring Herodotus, who mentions three, assume that there was only one method of Egyptian embalming.

The Egyptian methods of embalming spread into East, Central, and West Africa, "and eventually even as far as Southern Rhodesia and Madagascar". Elliot Smith and Dawson write in this connexion:

"The use of butter as packing material for the mouths of Egyptian mummies 1000 B.C. assumes special importance when we recall Roscoe's account of a similar practice among the modern Baganda of East Africa, and the ritual importance attached to it. Then again, the insertion of mud and onions into the bodies of Egyptian mummies of the same period (XXIst Dynasty) becomes something more than a mere fantastic curiosity, when we discover that the Kilba of Northern Nigeria still adopt this strange method with the definite idea of retarding decomposition." [1]

Instances of the spread into Asia of Egyptian mummification customs are given by Elliot Smith in his *The Migrations of Culture*, and these are supplemented by Mr. W. J. Perry in his *The Children of the Sun*.

Mummification was of sporadic ocurrence in Mesopotamia where honey was used. Instances of the use of bees-wax are known in Egypt. Cicero refers to the use of wax by the Persians. Herodotus tells that the Scythians extracted the viscera and filled the body cavity with pounded stems, perfumes, aniseed, and wild celery seed, and that they coated the mummy with wax. Honey has been used for embalming in modern times in Burmah. In India, even at the present day, according to Mr. Cooke, "several of the ascetic orders bury their dead in salt". Mummies have been found in the sands of Chorassan, or the ancient Bactria. The features of these could be plainly distinguished, so well were the bodies preserved.[2]

---

[1] *Egyptian Mummies*, pp. 165–6.   [2] *The Migrations of Culture*, pp. 66–8.

The Hindu customs are of special interest because the ancestors of the Polynesians were undoubtedly connected for a long period with India. Dr. Crooke points out that in certain Deccan tales there is a belief " in the possibility of securing the body from decay ". In the Vishnu Purana the body of Nimi, the grandson of " Vaivaswata, the Son of the Sun ", is said to have been embalmed with fragrant oils and resins ", with the result that it " remained as entire as if it were immortal ".[1] In the same work it is stated that a Brahman embalmed the body of his mother, making use of the " five pure fluids ", which are milk, curds, ghee, honey, and sugar, for washing and anointing the corpse. The body cavity was packed with camphor, musk, saffron, sandal, and a resin called " kakkola ". Then the mummy was wrapped with muslin, silk, cotton, cloth dyed with madder and Nepal blanketing. Red clay was smeared over the wrapped mummy before it was placed in a coffin of copper.[2] One of the practices of the Aryans was to disembowel their dead and pack the cavity with butter and curds.

In the seventeenth century the Todas opened a corpse at the loins, extracted the entrails and dried it by smoking it. Then they wrapped the body in silk. After keeping it for some time—perhaps for a year—they burned the body.[3] Dr. W. H. R. Rivers [4] refers to a similar custom among the Khasi, who preserve the bodies of chiefs in honey for a period and then cremate them. Here we have the custom of cremation superimposed upon that of mummification. Similar examples of culture mixing, have been recorded in connexion with pre-Columbian America funerary customs.

Captain T. H. Lewins, in his *The Wild Tribes of South-eastern India*,[5] writes as follows regarding the disposal of the dead:

[1] H. H. Wilson, *The Vishnu Purana*, London, 1840, p. 388.
[2] H. H. Wilson, *op. cit.*, p. 387, No. 2.   [3] *The Migrations of Culture*, pp. 68 *et seq.*
[4] *The Todas*, London, 1906, p. 246.   [5] London, 1870, p. 274.

"Among the Dhun and Khorn clans the body is placed in a coffin made of a hollow tree trunk, with holes in the bottom. This is placed on a lofty platform and left to dry in the sun. The dried body is afterwards rammed into an earthen vase and buried; the head is cut off and preserved. Another clan sheathe their dead in pith; the corpse is then placed on a platform, under which a slow fire is kept until the body is dried. The corpse is then kept for six months. . . . It is then buried. The Howlong clan hang the body up to the house-beams for seven days, during which time the dead man's wife has to sit underneath spinning."

The late Mr. W. Crooke gives further evidence regarding the treatment and disposal of the dead in India.[1]

Elliot Smith shows that "a great variety of burial customs, in most respects analogous to the practices of the Naga tribes of India, is found in Indonesia—exposing the dead on trees or platforms, burial in hollow trees, smoking, and other methods of preservation, temporary burial and cremation", and he adds,

"Apart from the definite evidence of preservation of the dead found in scattered islands from one end of the archipelago to the other, there are much more generally diffused practices which are unquestionably derived from the former custom of mummification."

The practice of rescuing the skull, after the disintegration of a poorly mummified body sets in, was practised by the savage tribes of Africa, as well as by Asiatics and Polynesians.[2]

Mr. W. J. Perry, referring to the disposal of the dead in Indonesia, says that he has found evidence of mummification.

"In Timor the Children of the Sun were mummified. They were placed, after death, in open coffins in the branches of trees, and only when the flesh is decayed and the remains are reduced to a mummified condition are they buried facing the Sun, the

---

[1] *Journal of the Anthropological Institute*, Vol. XXIX, 1899, pp. 272 *et seq.*
[2] *The Migrations of Culture*, p. 88.

chief's Father. Heer Kruyt has lately told me that mummification of chiefs is practised by the Toradja of the Sadan district of Central Celebes, a region closely connected with the archaic civilization." [1]

Mr. Perry writes further:

"The Igorot of the Philippines, who ascribe their culture to beings from the sky, practice mummification.[2] The custom is also reported, in the Philippines, among the Bicol, Visaya, Tinguinan and Gaddanes. Farther south the practice occurs in Dutch New Guinea at Mairassi and in Geelvink Bay." [3]

According to W. Roth [4] the bodies of the dead are preserved by the tribes of Queensland, Australia. "Desiccation," says Roth, "is a form of disposal of the dead practised only in the case of very distinguished men. After being disembowelled and dried by fire, the corpse is tied up and carried about for months."

The practice of mummification spread north to Saghalien. According to St. John, who writes of the Ainos, "when a chief of a tribe or village died, his body was laid out on a table close to the door of his hut; his entrails were then removed, and daily, for twelve months, his wife and daughters wash him thoroughly. He is allowed . . . to dry in the sun." [5]

Elliot Smith, referring to the evidence accumulated by R. Hertz [6] says that:

"the disgusting practice of collecting the fluids which drip from the putrefying corpse and mixing them with the food for the living occurs in Indonesia, in New Guinea, and the neighbouring islands, in Melanesia, Polynesia, and in Madagascar." [7]

Mummification was practised in pre - Columbian America. Prescott tells in his *History of the Conquest of*

---

[1] *The Children of the Sun*, pp. 198–9.   [2] Sawyer, *Inhabitants of the Philippines*, p. 259.
[3] Perry, *op. cit.*, (quoting authorities) p. 199.   [4] Quoted by Perry, *op. cit.*, p. 200.
[5] *Journal of the Anthropological Institute*, Vol. II, 1873, p. 253.
[6] "Contribution à une Étude sur la Représentation Collective de la Mort," in *L'Année Sociologique*, 1905–6, p. 83.
[7] *Migrations of Culture*, p. 92.

Peru, that a deceased Inca—one of the ruling class—was disembowelled and embalmed, and that the mummy was placed in the Temple of the Sun. In Mexico, according to Bancroft,[1] a process of embalming was "occasionally resorted to". When the body had been dried and dressed, "water was poured on its head with these words: 'This is the water which thou usedst in this world'". The painting of the mummy red was a common American custom. In his description of a Peruvian mummy, Dr. Daniel Wilson says it is in "the usual sitting position with the knees drawn up to the chin", and that it "possesses a peculiar penetrating odour, somewhat similar to that of an Egyptian mummy".[2]

Mr. Warren R. Dawson recently examined a Peruvian mummy in the British Museum, and comments on the manner in which the knees are so sharply flexed. "The femur and the tibia are parallel, and in close opposition; they are pressed so tightly together and to the body-wall, that they have become alternately convex and concave, so as to nest completely into one another. Considerable pressure, while the body was still plastic, must have been necessary to give effect to this attitude." Apparently the posture can hardly be described as "the usual sitting position". Mr. Dawson found that the lower viscera had been extracted *per anum*. The skin of the body had been varnished with "some resinous or gum-like material". The brain had not been removed. Mr. Dawson also found that the nails had been taken off all the fingers and toes.[3] As will be seen, the Peruvian mummy had been treated similarly to those of the Torres Straits.

The custom of preserving the skull or the mummified head in Oceania and elsewhere is commented upon by Dr. W. H. R. Rivers as follows:

---

[1] *The Native Races of the Pacific States of North America,* Vol. II, p. 604.
[2] *Prehistoric Man,* pp. 440–1.
[3] *Proceedings of the Royal Society of Medicine,* Vol. XX, Part VI, April, 1927, pp. 845 *et seq.*

"Many practices become intelligible as elements of a single culture if we suppose that a people imbued with the necessity for the preservation of the body after death acquired . . . the further idea that the skull is the representative of the body as a whole; if they came to believe that the purpose for which they had hitherto preserved the body could be fulfilled as well if the head only were kept." [1]

It must be borne in mind at the same time that, as has been shown, special attention was paid to the head in Ancient Egypt and in Polynesia, not only in preparing the mummy but in providing an image of the dead.

The evidence of the world-wide diffusion of the technical processes of Egyptian mummification and of the associated beliefs is of great importance in connexion with the study of the origin of Polynesian religious customs and beliefs. Certain Oceanic problems are simplified when it is found that similar curious practices occur elsewhere, and cannot consequently be explained away by the theory of their independent origin on one or other of the South Sea Islands.

As reference has been made in this chapter to the maritime activities of the Egyptians and Phœnicians during the late Dynasties, it would be well, in dealing with the diffusion of religious beliefs and practices by groups of mariners, to draw attention to the evidence regarding ancient shipping in the Indian Ocean and beyond.

In the Hindu epic, the *Mahábhárata*, the ocean is referred to as the habitation of peoples referred to as Nāgas and Asuras. Mr. C. F. Oldham, in his work, *The Sun and the Serpent*,[2] has shown that when the Aryans entered India, the Asuras, whom he identifies with the Dravidians, were in a high state of civilization—"higher", he thinks, "than their Aryan rivals". Brahmanical writers ascribe to them the ability "to restore the dead to life", which may be a reference to

---

[1] Rivers, *op. cit.*, Vol. II, p. 273.　　[2] London, 1905, pp. 53 *et seq.*

their mummification customs. They worshipped the sun, held sacred the Nāga, or hooded serpent, deified kings and ancestors, venerated certain trees, used tribal emblems or totems, and had " much in common with the early inhabitants of Babylonia and, perhaps, even more with those of Elam (Western Persia) and the neighbouring countries ". Of special significance is the fact that the Asuras were " a maritime power ".

Rhys Davids draws attention to the evidence in Buddhist literature regarding the ancient mariners of India. Sakya Buddha himself refers to their voyages as follows:

" Long ago ocean-going merchants were wont to plunge forth upon the sea, taking with them a shore-sighting bird. When the ship was out of sight of land they would set the shore-sighting bird free. And it would go to the east and to the south and to the west and to the north and to the intermediate points and rise aloft. If on the horizon it caught sight of land, thither it would go. But if not then it would come back to the ship again." [1]

In the fifth century of the Christian era Fah Hian, the Chinese Buddhist pilgrim, sailed from the mouth of the Ganges to Ceylon in a merchant vessel. From Ceylon he sailed to Java in a great ship " which carried about two hundred men, and which was navigated by observing the sun, moon, and stars ". At a port in Java the pilgrim embarked for China. " All these ships appear to have been Indian and not Chinese." [2]

Mr. Kennedy has shown that the Dravidian mariners of India were busily engaged in trade in the seventh century B.C.[3]

Oldham [4] writes as follows regarding the drift of civilization and religious systems from India eastward:

" The civilization of Burmah, and other Indo-Chinese countries, is ascribed by legend and by the native historians to

---

[1] *Journal of the Royal Asiatic Society*, April, 1899, p. 432.
[2] Authorities quoted in *The Migrations of Culture*, pp. 84–5.
[3] *Journal of the Royal Asiatic Society*, April, 1898.   [4] *Op. cit.*, p. 166.

invaders from India. And these are connected with the Naga people of Magadha, and of the north and west of India. The ancient navigators, too, who carried the Brahmanical and Buddhist religions, the worship of the Nāga [1], and the Sanskrit and Pali language to Java, Sumatra and even to distant Celebes, were Indian people. And they were, doubtless, descendants of those Asura dwellers in the ocean, which are mentioned in the *Mahábhárata*, and have already been referred to."

A Western Indian proverb keeps alive the memory of ancient trading voyages to Java. It says:

"He who goes to Java never comes back; but if he does return, his descendants, for seven generations, live at ease." [2]

The Indian mariners visited the Persian Gulf. Rhys Davids says in this connexion that " it may now be accepted as hypothesis that:

" 1. Sea-going merchants availing themselves of the monsoons, were in the habit, at the beginning of the seventh (and perhaps at the end of the eighth) century B.C., of trading from ports on the south-west coast of India (Sovīra first, afterwards Suppāraka and Bharukaccha) to Babylon, then a great merchant emporium.

" 2. These merchants were mostly Dravidian, not Aryan. Such names of the goods imported as were adopted in the west (Solomon's ivory, apes, and peacocks, for instance, and the word ' rice ') were adaptations, not of Sanskrit or Pali, but of Tamil words."

Rhys goes on to speak of the importation into India of Babylonian script and charms, and says:

"The priests were, as a body, exceedingly keen to keep the knowledge of *mantras* (the charms or verses), on which the magic of the sacrifice depended, in their own hands. There are some pretty rules about this."

It was considered as an offence for a commoner even to preserve a charm " in his memory ". The priests had it " that God himself had bestowed the exclusive right of

---

[1] Serpent god—the Indian Dragon.   [2] *Bombay Gazetteer*, Vol. I, 402.

teaching upon the hereditary priests, who claimed to be, each of them, great divinities, even to the gods ".[1]

In his review of the evidence regarding the activities of the ancient mariners, Professor Elliot Smith writes:[2]

" It is surely something more than a mere coincidence that the period of the greatest maritime exploits of the Phœnicians, in the course of which, according to many authorities, they reached India or even farther east, should coincide with those of the great pre-Aryan maritime race of India, whose great expeditions . . . were primarily for the purpose of commerce between the Persian Gulf and the west coast of India. There is gradually accumulating a considerable mass of evidence to suggest that, if the Asuras were not themselves Phœnicians, they acquired their maritime skill from these famous sailors and traders. The same hardy mariners who brought the new knowledge and practices from the Persian Gulf to India and Ceylon also carried it farther, to Burmah and Indonesia. . . . These customs spread to Indonesia and the Pacific before cremation was introduced. . . . The advancing wave of western culture swept past India into Indonesia, carrying into the isles of the Pacific and on to the American littoral the products of the older civilizations at first almost, but not altogether, untainted by Indian influence; but for centuries afterwards, as this same ferment gradually leavened the vast bulk of India, the stream of western culture continued to percolate eastward and carried with it in succession the influence of the Brahmanical, Buddhist, and, within a more restricted area, Mahometan cults."

This view regarding the diffusion of certain cultural elements from west to east is supported by the evidence regarding ships which has been accumulated by men competent to deal with the subject.[3]

H. Warrington Smyth and E. Keble Chatterton have, for instance, shown that the Burmese and Chinese junks retain features that characterized the Ancient Egyptian

---

[1] T. W. Rhys Davids, *Buddhist India*, pp. 116 *et seq.*

[2] *The Migrations of Culture*, pp. 86–7.

[3] Outstanding authorities include Cecil Torr (*Ancient Ships*, 1894), Sir George Holmes (*Ancient and Modern Ships*, 1900–6), H. Warrington Smyth (*Mast and Sail in Europe and Asia*, 1906), E. Keble Chatterton (*Sailing Ships and their Story, Ships and Ways of other Days, &c.*), G. Elliot Smith (*Ships as Evidence of the Migration of Culture*), J. H. Breasted in *Journal of Egyptian Archæology*, Vol. IV, &c.

vessels. " I am not contending," writes Chatterton in this connexion, " that the Chinese junk is identical with the Ancient Egyptian ship, but I submit that between the two there is such close similarity as to show a common influence and a remarkable persistence in type."[1]

The Phœnicians adopted the Egyptian type of ship, as did the Cretans, Greeks, and Romans, the Veneti of Brittany and the Scandinavians and Saxons of early times. Even in our own day the racing yachts perpetuate Egyptian shipbuilding fashions. " I suppose," remarks E. Keble Chatterton, " if you could, by sending a current of electricity through one of the Egyptian naval architects now lying as a mummy in one of our museums, bring him to life, so that you might take him to see the yachts racing during Cowes Week, he would not hesitate to say that such ships as *White Heather II* and the newest *Shamrock* were based on designs he had made for his masters under the Twelfth Dynasty."[2]

Those who are sceptical about the vessels of the ancient mariners circumnavigating Africa, crossing the Indian Ocean and the vaster Pacific Ocean, are reminded by Mr. Chatterton that he has seen " a little seven-ton cutter ", not " half the size of the old Phœnician ships ", which had crossed the Atlantic " on her own bottom ". He adds:

" Even still more wonderful and more to the point, as having sailed to the entrance of the Mediterranean, is the passage of the *Columbia II*, a tiny ship only 19 feet long with 6 feet beam. Navigated solely by Captain Eisenbram, she sailed from Boston, U.S.A., to Gibraltar, encountering severe weather on the way, in 100 days." [3]

The " dogged conservatism " of naval architects for many centuries is not the least interesting feature of ship designing. Even more remarkable is the persistence of immemorial superstitions connected with sea-faring. In

---

[1] *Sailing Ships and their Story*, pp. 31–2 and pp. 310 *et seq.*   [2] *Op. cit.*, p. 10.
[3] Chatterton, *op. cit.*, p. 50. and *Times* (London), November 21, 1903

this regard no one has conducted more interesting research than has Mr. James Hornell, late Director of
Fisheries, Madras. He drew attention in the *Memoirs
of the Asiatic Society* (Vol. VII, No 3) to the survival in
the use of the Egyptian Horus eye on the prows of the
older types of boats in Eastern Seas, particularly in India
and China, and to the *Journal of the Royal Anthropological
Institute* (Vol. LIII, 1923) he contributed a fascinating
paper entitled " Survivals of the Use of the Oculi in
Modern Boats ". He gives examples from the Mediterranean area, the Indian Ocean, Malay, and both sides
of the Pacific, as well as Oceania. Referring to the eye
on the boats of the British Columbian Indians, he points
out that it is " nearly related to the types common in
India ", and he considers that there was a time when
" a truly anthropomorphic and realistic form of oculus
was found continuously along the southern and eastern
coasts of Asia from Western India to Northern China,
and thence across the Pacific to what is now British
Columbia. All these forms probably originated from those
of India." In tracing the origin of the boat eyes of India,
he writes:

"The key to this problem is to be found, I believe, in Egypt.
Everyone acquainted with the antiquities of that country is familiar
with the Uzat (or uchat) ornament, commonest of all ancient
Egyptian amulets against the evil-eye. This represents the eye of
the hawk-headed deity Horus, and is also associated with the
sun-god Rā (Rē)."

Having dealt in detail with the Egyptian " sacred
eye " and its Indian forms, he reminds us that no modern
Hindu or other inhabitant of India " can explain its
significance ", and then continues:

" In other papers I have attempted to show that the cata-
marans of the East Coast of India are modelled upon the ancient
Egyptian form of reed raft [1]: with this weightier and more direct

[1] *Man in India*, Vol. I, June, 1921.

corroborative piece of evidence, the inference is strengthened that there are close ethnological affinities between Egypt and the Coromandel coast of India, where customs are still extremely archaic and little affected either by European or Hindu culture. It is my belief that these affinities are due fundamentally to racial relationship, and that a strong strain of the same blood as that which produced the Egyptian type is present in these lowly fisherfolk of the East Coast of India. Both appear, therefore, to be offshoots of that race at present termed ' the Mediterranean '. If so, this strengthens my theory that this race, or their direct progenitors, peopled a tract extending from the Mediterranean eastwards through Egypt, Southern Arabia, and India, and thence through Indo-China into Indonesia and the Pacific, finally impinging on the western coasts of central and equatorial America." [1]

There is no necessary connexion between races and cultures. One race acquired from another in ancient times certain customs, ideas, habits of life, and the knowledge of technical processes, without necessarily acquiring wives to alter or influence the breed. The knowledge of how to build and navigate ships, the perpetuation of superstitions connected with ships, including the use of the Horus eye, may well have passed freely from one people to another after new habits and customs, and new modes of life and ideas regarding the disposal of the dead and the destiny of souls, had been introduced into a particular area. At the same time it has to be recognized that evidence has been forthcoming which suggests that a dominant part was played in ancient times by a particular racial type. Professor Elliot Smith, the distinguished anatomist, has shown, for instance, that the Giza type of skull, which he detected in his studies of the crania of Ancient Egyptian tombs, which date as far back as late pre-dynastic times is repeated in the South Pacific. A skull, preserved in the University of Cambridge, which came from the Chatham Islands, near New Zealand, was, he found one day, an

---

[1] James Hornell, *op. cit.*, pp. 300–2

excellent example of the Giza type.   At first he was
amazed at this unexpected discovery but,

" further examination of the available craniological material and
literature revealed the widespread distribution of what I have
called ' Giza traits ', not only in Polynesia, but also in the Malay
Archipelago and at certain places on the southern Asiatic littoral. . . .
But even more startling was the discovery that crania revealing
the same distinctive traits were by no means rare on the Pacific
coast of Central and South America." [1]

Writing further regarding the distribution of skulls with
" Giza traits ", Elliot Smith tells that, after examining
thousands of crania, he has detected Giza specimens
from Syria across Asia to the Punjab, where they " were
found to be fairly common ", although " rare elsewhere
in India ". The Giza skulls were " widespread in Polynesia and the Pacific coast of America ".[2]

The prototypes of the various classes of Polynesian
vessels are to be found in Indonesia and India. Outriggers, for instance, are still to be met with as far east
as the Red Sea.

In his address to the Ocean in *Childe Harold*, Lord
Byron says:

"Time writes no wrinkle on thine azure brow."

No tracks have been left by the ancient vessels whose
daring navigators ventured to cross uncharted seas.
Nor have, as Elliot Smith remarks, any ancient " bills
of lading " survived. Written records of ancient voyages
are very scanty, but in Polynesia there are, as has been
indicated, many tales and traditions of voyages of exploration and discovery which throw light on the peopling
of the South Sea Islands, and the subsequent maritime
activities of their inhabitants.

The evidence afforded by embalming customs, by
skulls, by types of vessels, and by superstitions and

---

[1] *The Ancient Egyptians* (Second Edition, 1923), pp. vi–viii.   [2] *Ibid.*, p 160.

customs connected with the building and navigation of vessels, which has been accumulated and studied by specialists of late years, has undoubtedly greatly extended our knowledge regarding racial and cultural " drifts " in ancient times. Such evidence is of much more substantial character than that afforded, for instance, by the study of pottery, flints, and even of implements of metal and stone. Its cumulative effect is such that we are enabled to have glimpses of the motives which impelled men to venture into distant lands, and to discover the means by which they accomplished their desires. In short, it throws a flood of light on human behaviour in ancient times such as no piece of pottery can possibly do, interesting and important as pottery evidence may often be.

We appear to be fully justified in concluding that the Polynesians did not embalm their dead, build boats, carve statues in wood or stone, and so on, simply because it was " natural " for them so to do, but because they had acquired the elements of a highly complex culture that had origin in a distant area.

CHAPTER X

Island Megalithic Remains

Skilled Marquesan Stone-workers—Theory of American Origin—Polynesians visited Peru—Melanesia and America—Ellis's View—Did Polynesians influence Peruvians?—Limited Stone-working in New Zealand—Marquesan Wood-working and Stone-working — The Tongan Trilithon Mystery— Japanese and Chinese Symbolic Gateways—Stone and Wood in Micronesian Temples—Why Stone was Used—Gods in Blocks and Pillars of Stone— Hawaiian Sacred Stones—Hindu Gods as Standing Stones—Shiva's Trident in Hawaii—Stone Platforms and Pyramid-like *Maræ*—Sacred Groves—Captain Cook on Polynesian Structures—Ellis on Temples and Ceremonies—The "Horus-eye" in Polynesia—R. L. Stevenson visits "Cannibal High Place"— Migrations and Culture-mixing.

The Polynesians made use of stone not only for making idols but for building, and in some of the communities a high degree of skill in masonry was displayed long before the European explorers discovered the coral islands. In the Marquesas " the construction of many of the ordinary platforms ", says Ralph Linton, " could hardly be bettered by Europeans ", and he thinks " it is not improbable that the ancestors of the Polynesians were familiar with the construction of stone-faced terraces before their departure from their Asiatic and Indonesian home-land ".[1]

E. S. Craighill Handy, on the other hand, considers that stone work was not a trait attributable to the " Indo Polynesians ". He looks to America for a solution of the problem and writes:

" What probably happened is that during the hundreds of years of very active voyaging some Polynesians visited America and

[1] *Bernice P. Bishop Museum Bulletin*, No. 23, p. 5.

returned to Polynesia, having seen the Mexican or Peruvian stonework, and possibly bringing a few stone craftsmen with them. The fact that both in quantity and skill there is a diminution in the art of building with stone, beginning with the Marquesas, running through the Society Islands and ending at Tonga, is strong evidence in favour of the hypothesis that some eastern Polynesians, probably Marquesans, borrowed the art of stone construction from the west coast of South America; and that within Polynesia the art spread from east to west."

Handy states that he has found evidence which points to the Polynesians having visited the American continent. It is a story " taken from the lips of an old man on Hivoa which describes the construction, by a chief of Puamau valley, of a great canoe, and his sailing towards the rising sun till he reached a land, whence he returned again to his Marquesan home ".[1]

The late Dr. W. H. R. Rivers, when writing his *The History of Melanesian Society*, considered the question of American influence. Having dealt with the cultural influences that entered Melanesia and Polynesia from South-eastern Asia, he wrote:

"The possibility must be borne in mind, however, that influences from America may have reached Polynesia and spread thence to Melanesia. It is indeed probable that elements of culture have passed from America to parts of Polynesia, but it is most unlikely that American influence has been of a kind which could have penetrated, directly or indirectly, as far as Melanesia. For the present, by far the most probable working hypothesis is that the direction of the movements has been from west to east, and that with the exception of relatively recent movements from Polynesia, all the peoples who have influenced Melanesian culture have come from the islands south and east of Asia or from the mainland of that continent." [2]

William Ellis, the missionary, recognized that there had been some ancient cultural connexions between America and the South Sea Islands. He deals with " the

[1] *Bernice P. Bishop Museum Bulletin*, No. 34, p. 329, Honolulu, 1927, and Note 33.
[2] *The History of Melanesian Society*, Vol. II, pp. 581-2.

numerous points of resemblance ", including customs, beliefs, myths, and physical character, and says that " many words in the language and several of the traditions, customs, &c., of the Americans, so strongly resemble those of Asia, as to warrant the inference that they originally came from that part of the world ". He wonders if some of the Asiatic mariners who endeavoured to reach America were driven by the trade winds to the Sandwich Islands, " whence they proceeded to the southern groups ", or whether some sailed from America to Easter Island and, sailing westward, met a tide of emigrants from the Malays. He then writes, leaving the problem an open one,

" A variety of facts connected with the past and present circumstances of the inhabitants of these countries, authorize the conclusion that either part of the present inhabitants of the South Sea Islands came originally from America, or that tribes of the Polynesians have, at some remote period, found their way to the continent." [1]

J. Macmillan Brown takes the latter view. Dealing with the evidence afforded by stonework, he says:

" Every feature of Polynesian great-stone work is repeated in the great-stone work of the Andes; and the impetus did not come from America, if we are to judge by the absence of all American products and arts in the Pacific; it must be the other way, as we find purely Polynesian products and methods on the coast of America and evidences that Polynesian warriors swooped down upon the wealthy cities that were approachable by sea. The most probable history is that since even the fatherland, Hawaiki, began to be too narrow for its population, expeditions went off in search of new lands; most went west; but some must have made for the east by getting south into the latitude of the westerlies. And these may have taken the taste for cyclopean stonework and the art of it; and from the coast their influence went up with the people of the coastal empires to the high valleys and plateaus of the Andes.

[1] *Polynesian Researches* (First Edition 1829), Vol. II, pp. 45–9

Handy's view that the "Indo-Polynesians" were not stone builders is strongly influenced by the fact that the Maori did not make much use of stone.[1] Stone-cutting, for instance, appears to have been confined to the Lake Rotorua region, and Ralph Linton suggests that it may have developed spontaneously there, "deposits of easily worked tuffs"[2] being available. But a people are either a stone-working people or they are not.

Linton, dealing with the varieties of stone construction in the South Sea Islands, points out that there was, especially in the Marquesas, a "close correspondence between the methods used in wood-working and stone-dressing". It may well be, therefore, as he suggests, that in some areas stone may have been used to face certain structures previously faced by wood. Perhaps, too, wood was at times utilized as a substitute for stone.

Of special interest in this connexion is a much-discussed big trilithon at Nukualofa, Tonga Islands, which has been compared to a lower, although heavier, trilithon at Tiahuanaco in Bolivia, South America, and also to the comparatively small and low trilithons of the Banks Islands, and the ancient European trilithons. Ralph Linton points out that the Tongan trilithon "differs from the European megalithic structures, however, in having the crosspiece deeply socketed into the uprights", and he says that "it seems probable that the Tongan trilithon represents a purely local development".[3] It may be, on the other hand, that the socketing of the crosspiece was due to the fact that trilithons of wood had previously been erected, and that the Tongan trilithon is an imitation in stone of wooden trilithons which have

---

[1] *Bernice P. Bishop Museum Bulletin*, No. 34, pp. 328–9.

[2] Tuff is a term applied to light porous lava and soft rocks composed of dust, ashes, and stones from a volcano.

[3] *Bernice P. Bishop Museum Bulletin*, No. 23, p. 16. Mr. Linton appears to overlook the fact that at Stonehenge "the cross-pieces of the trilithons are", as Mr. T. D. Kendrick says in his *The Druids* (p. 154), "secured on to the uprights by means of a peg-and-socket lock". Kendrick suggests that "perhaps the pillars, whose sockets still remain, stood in place of tree trunks" (p. 150).

TRILITHON IN TONGATABU, AN ISLAND OF THE TONGA GROUP

The upper stone is morticed into the two uprights

(14)

(158)

PROW OF MAORI CANOE

By permission of the Royal Scottish Museum, Edinburgh

The eyes of the monsters are of glistening pearl-shell (*Haliotis*)

not survived. Wooden crosspieces would have had to be socketed. The "tori-wi" of Japan is a wooden trilithon, and it evidently imitates the elaborate stone trilithons of China. These symbolic "gateways" of China and Japan have an interesting history. In India and Egypt temples were "monstrously overgrown doorways and pylons". Elliot Smith writes in this connexion:

"The significance of gates was no doubt suggested by the idea that they represented the means of communication between the living and the dead, and, symbolically, the portal by which the dead acquired a rebirth into a new form of existence. It was presumably for this reason that the winged disk as a symbol of life-giving, was placed above the lintels of these doors, not merely in Egypt, Phœnicia, the Mediterranean area, and Western Asia, but also in America, and in modified forms in India, Indonesia, Melanesia, Cambodia, China, and Japan." [1]

Both wood and stone were used in the erection of temples. Turner, writing regarding the island of Peru in the Gilbert Group, notes that some "standing stones" there have been taken for prehistoric megaliths. His explanation of them is as follows:

"On giving up heathenism a number of large temples were burned, leaving the stone pillars standing on which the roof rested. These upright stones, four or five feet high, and from ten to twenty in number, according to the size of the house, reminded me first of a burying ground, and then of Druidical times. Beams were laid horizontally along the top of the pillars, and from these beams the rafters ran up towards one, two, or three centre posts, supporting the ridge pole. Whatever may be the solution of the antiquarian problem at Stonehenge, these relics on Peru are simply the lower stone pillars of ancient temples for heathen worship, night dances, and other gatherings." [2]

In considering the problem presented by the stone constructions in the South Sea Islands, it must be re-

---

[1] *The Evolution of the Dragon*, p. 185.   [2] *Samoa*, pp. 298-9.

cognized at the outset that it cannot be solved by dealing
with the technique alone. Some communities may have
cut and dressed stone, and others simply used the undressed stones which were available. In a single area,
as we find, dressed and undressed stones were simultaneously utilized. The vital point is the psychological
motive for the use of stone.

As we have seen, when investigating the symbolism
of jade, that hard stone, which was shaped with immense
difficulty, was searched for and utilized mainly because
of its traditional sanctity. It possessed for those who
used it a religious or magico-religious value. Those
who searched for and found and treasured it believed
that it was a " life giver ", a " god body ", and the Maori,
as we have seen, had twin-deities who were personifications of jade.

But jade was not the only sacred stone in the South
Sea Islands. There is abundant evidence to indicate that
all stones were more or less invested with sanctity.
Turner tells that on the island of Nikunau of the Gilbert
Group sandstone slabs or pillars were regarded as repre-
sentatives of deities:

" Before these (stone) shrines offerings of food were laid during
the day, which the priests took away stealthily by night and made
the credulous believe that gods and not mortals had done it. If
the stone slab represented a goddess it was not placed erect, but
laid down on the ground. Being a lady, they thought it would
be cruel to make her stand so long." [1]

In Samoa the gods Fonge and Toafa were " two
oblong smooth stones which stood on a raised platform
of loose stones ". They were supposed to be the parents
of the god Saato " who controlled rain ". Offerings were
made to the stones.[2] In a village temple two unchiselled
smooth stones represented the god who made yams,
bread, fruit, and coco-nuts, and the god who sent fish
into nets.[3] Turner tells that stone was similarly reverenced

[1] *Samoa*, p. 296.   [2] *Ibid.*, pp. 24-5.   [3] *Ibid.*, pp. 44-5.

elsewhere. On the island of Fakaofo (or Bowditch Island) he was told by natives that men had their origin from a small stone kept there. The chief god was Tui Tokelau, and " he was supposed to be embodied in a stone which was carefully wrapped up with fine mats, and never seen by anyone but the King, and that only once a year ".[1] On Nanumanga, or Hudson's Island, the principal gods were Foelangi and Maumau. The former " had an unchiselled block of stone to represent him ".[2] A stone slab from the beach represented the god Maumau on Nanumea, or St. Augustine Island.[3] Turner tells further that on the island of Aneiteum of the New Hebrides " smooth stones apparently picked up out of the bed of the river were regarded as representatives of certain gods, and wherever the stone was, there the god was supposed to be ".[4] Certain stones near Savaii in Samoa were reverenced and feared because they had originally been octopus gods.[5] Men were supposed to have sprung from stones, as has been indicated. On the Loyalty Islands the god Laulaati was credited with having made a stone " out of which came the first man and woman ".[6]

The Rev. Dr. John Inglis tells of a New Hebridean god named Rangitafu, who was " a block of whinstone, about five feet long, a foot and a half broad, and a foot thick ". He was " a sea-god, and presided over ship-wrecks ". On Aneiteum, according to the same writer, " the idols were all of uncarved, unhewn stones ", except the *natmasses*, which were of rudely-carved wood. When a chief died his name was given to the village *natmas*.[7]

Dr. W. H. R. Rivers provides a number of instances of " stone worship " in Melanesia. Some stones which possessed *mana* (power) due to the presence of a spirit, not a ghost, were kept by individuals; some carved stones

---

[1] *Samoa*, p 268.   [2] *Ibid.*, p. 289.   [3] *Ibid.*, p. 291.   [4] *Ibid.*, p. 327.   [5] *Ibid.*, p. 31.
[6] *Ibid.*, p. 338.   [7] *In the New Hebrides*, London, 1887, pp. 32 *et seq.*

were used to mark boundaries. The latter appear to have had a similar significance to Polynesian images.[1]

Abraham Fornander, formerly a circuit judge in Polynesia, in his great pioneer work,[2] gives much important information regarding " stone worship " in the islands. The Hawaiians, he tells, connected with the god Kane (Tane) "upright stones of from one to six and eight feet in height, the smaller size portable, and the larger fixed in the ground ". These " formerly served as altars or places of offering at what may be called family worship ". Fornander compared these with the phallic stones of the Shiva cult in India, and held that Shiva's name was represented by the Polynesian word *siwa* or *hiwa*, signifying " dark-coloured, black or blue ", but also having the meaning " sacred ", as in *Nuka-Hiwa*, " dark or sacred island ", and *Fatu-Hiwa* or *Patu-Hiwa*, " sacred rock or stone " in the Marquesas. In India a black stone is the emblem of the god Vishnu, and a grey one of Shiva. The Hindus of North-west India worship the sun-god Surya " under the emblem of a black stone ". Describing Polynesian customs connected with stones, Fornander writes:

" In the Hawaiian group these stone pillars were sprinkled with water or anointed with coco-nut oil, and the upper part frequently covered with a black native tapa or cloth, the colour of garment which priests wore on special occasions, and which was also the cloth in which the dead were wrapped."

The emblem of the Hindu god Shiva is a double trident, and Fornander has detected it in Polynesia. He writes as follows regarding it:

" On a hill called *Kaulana-hoa*, back of Kalae, island of Molokai, of the Hawaiian group, are a number of large, irregularly-shaped volcanic stones, standing on the brow of the hill. One is shaped like a high-backed chair, and, judging from analogy to

---

[1] W. H. R. Rivers, *op. cit.*, Vol. II, pp. 406, 416, and 421.
[2] *An Account of the Polynesian Race: Its Origins and Migrations*, London, 1878, Vol. I, pp. 46 *et seq.*

others like it in other parts of the group, may have served as a seat for the chief, or his priest, from which to look out over the ocean, or to watch the stars. On the east side of this, and near to, stands another large stone, marked with a double trident in two places."

William Ellis, the missionary, commented on the great abundance of stone monuments in the Society Islands. These were to be seen " in the bottom of every valley, even to the recesses in the mountains, on the sides of the inferior hills, and on the brows of almost every promontory in each of the islands ", and included " stone pavements of their dwellings and court-yards, foundations of houses and ruins of family temples ". Similar relics were to be seen on deserted islands.[1]

Ellis was informed that the gods were supposed to enter images of wood at certain seasons. " During this indwelling of the gods," the people " imagined even the images were very powerful." There were also stone images, and some were " calcareous or siliceous ", but " the greater part were rude, uncarved, angular columns of basalt, various in size, and destitute of carving or polish ", and " they were clothed or ornamented with native cloth ".[2]

There can be no doubt that throughout the South Sea Islands stone was generally regarded with superstitious reverence. The people had therefore a psychological motive for working stone and erecting pillars, and more or less elaborate stone structures.

In his fine and exhaustive study of the archæological remains of the Marquesan islands,[3] Ralph Linton deals with the various types of stone structures which include walls, terraces and platforms, passages, vaults, chambers, pits, steps and stairways, fortifications, &c. He shows that there were two main classes of ceremonial structures —the *tohua* and the *me'ae*. The former were tribal

---

[1] *Polynesian Researches*, Vol. I (First Edition), pp. 29–30 and p. 50. [2] *Ibid.*, pp. 203–4.
[3] *Bernice P. Bishop Museum Bulletin*, No. 23, Honolulu, Hawaii, 1925.

assembly places, and although " sometimes the scene of public religious rites ", they were " essentially secular and could be visited by all classes of the population ". A level paved dance floor was laid out, and these were long rectangles. Some were parallel to a hillside which was terraced with retaining walls as supports. Special platforms were, as a rule, provided for chiefs or priests. Near a tohua was the warriors' house, and the chief's house was not far off.

The *me'ae* (in Samoa and Tonga *malae*, in New Zealand *marae*, and in some Marquesan islands and on Easter Island *ahu*) was " a tribal sacred place at which regular religious rites were performed ". There were two classes of *me'ae*—the tribal and the mortuary. The tribal *me'ae* were usually small and were often small platforms built at the end of a *tohua*, and surrounded by banyan trees, but some *me'ae* were larger than the *tohua*. Some of the sacred structures had images and were used for special religious ceremonies. " Food offerings were brought to it (the *me'ae*) and human sacrifices were performed at it during the ceremony of dedication."

More numerous than the public or tribal *me'ae* were the mortuary *me'ae*. The corpse was taken to the mortuary *me'ae* and certain rites performed. In his *Life in the Southern Isles*, W. Wyatt Gill, the missionary (quoted by Linton), writes regarding the " spirit burial " of the Mangaians at the mortuary *me'ae* or *marae*:

" Chiefs and priests occasionally received the honour of ' spirit burial ' (*tanu vaerua*); the corpse being borne to the most renowned *marae* on the island and allowed to remain within the sacred enclosure for some hours, but the same day hidden away in the tribal cave. In such cases the depositing of the body in the *marae* was ' the burial ', or the committal of the spirit to the care of the god worshipped by him in life, while the letting down of the corpse into the deep chasm was designated ' the throwing away of the bones ' (*tiringa ivi*), the well-wrapped body being regarded as a mere bundle of bones after the exit of the spirit."

As a *marae* has a resemblance to a pyramid, it will thus be seen that it is absurd to contend that pyramid-like structures found in Oceania and elsewhere should not be regarded as of mortuary character, although no human remains may be found in many of them. The custom of " spirit burial " emphasizes their essential significance in connexion with the destiny of the human soul. Linton writes regarding the *me'ae* or *marae*:

"Though intended primarily for the disposal of the dead, mortuary *me'ae* were also the scene of some of the most important religious rites, and many more human sacrifices were offered there than in the public *me'ae*. This was no doubt due to the fact that the tribal deities were nearly all deified chiefs or priests. No sacred places seem to have been built in honour of the creation gods or of the great deities of Polynesian mythology."

Most of the mortuary *me'ae* were erected on high ground, and some were surrounded by rows of rough stones. Sacred groves were connected with them, and the trees included the sacred banyan—an imported " milk-yielding " tree of the fig family.

Linton shows that the public *me'ae* on the island of Nukuhiva became fused with the *tohua*, and the resulting structure is in a general way comparable to the enclosed sacred places of Hawaii and Tahiti. In some cases the *me'ae* were " a series of platforms " or a " series of super-imposed terraces ". Some had connected with them " skull pits " and " sacrifice pits ". On Uapou and Uahuka the *me'ae* were " small platforms without a sacrifice pit or a pit for skulls ".

In the Marquesas there were also the *tokai*—platforms, cairns, or outcrops of bare rock on which images were placed. These were " sacred to the memory of women who had died in childbirth ". A place of circumcision described by Linton, " consists of two low walls of very large stones ", about fifteen feet apart. The child who was to be circumcised was seated " on a

large stone at the end of one of these walls ". On the
wall sat the spectators. Sacred places of fishermen were
houses built on stone platforms at the edge of the sea.

The *tohua* are peculiar to the Marquesas. Linton,
however, suggests a resemblance to the Hawaiian " dance
platforms ", constructed by terracing hillsides, and building stone wall supports. At the same time he says that
" the resemblances between the Marquesan *tohua* and
the enclosed *marae* of Tahiti are so numerous that I
believe the two forms represent only slightly divergent
developments of the same idea ". When certain ceremonies were performed, women were excluded from the
tohua in the northern Marquesan islands, and " a
sacred character ", Linton says, " was thus constantly
attached to some parts of the *tohua,* and this character
was sometimes extended to include the whole structure ".
He thinks it possible that " through the fusion of the
assembly place and sacred place, *marae* or *me'ae* came in
time to be applied to all sacred structures and finally
passed to the southern islands of the Marquesas with
this significance ". At the same time it is probable that
even the so-called " secular structures " had a fundamental religious significance. Public assemblies, dances,
&c., were connected with the worship of deities or
deified rulers.

Mariner, Cook, and others refer to the sacred mounds
and stone structures of the South Sea Islands. In the
account of Cook's last voyage we obtain vivid glimpses
of those of the Hawaiian people:

" As the ships worked down the coast, we had observed at
every village one or more elevated white objects, like pyramids,
or rather obelisks; and one of these, which I guessed to be at least
fifty feet high, was very conspicuous from the *Resolution's* deck
at anchor, and seemed to be at no great distance up this valley."

Cook landed and had a near inspection of one of the
structures:

"It was an oblong space of considerable extent, surrounded by a wall of stone about four feet high. The space enclosed was loosely paved with smaller stones; and at one end of it stood what I call the pyramid, which appeared to be an exact model of the larger one, observed by us from the ships. It was about four feet square at the base and about twenty feet high; the four sides were composed of small poles, interwoven with twigs and branches. . . . It seemed to be in a rather ruinous state, but there were sufficient remaining marks to show that it had originally been covered with a thin, light grey cloth, which these people appear to consecrate to religious purposes. . . . Before the pyramid were a few pieces of wood, carved into something like human figures, which, with a stone near two feet high, covered with pieces of cloth, called 'hoho' and consecrated to Tongarooa (Tangaloa), who is the god of these people, completed the resemblance to the morais (maraes) of the islands we had lately left."

Adjoining the *marae* Cook saw a house about forty feet long opposite the entrance of which were wooden images "which were said to be representations of goddesses". One had a cap and the other a warrior's helmet, and both had loin cloths. A grave of seven chiefs was enclosed by a low edging of cloth-covered stones in the middle of the house.

Cook also describes a Tongan sacred mound "in a kind of grove open only on the side which fronted the high road. On the summit was "a house of worship". The mound was enclosed by "a wall or parapet of stone".

Ellis tells us that "the national temples" of the Society Islands "consisted of a number of distinct maraes, altars, and sacred dormitories, appropriated to the chief pagan divinities, and included in one large stone enclosure of considerable extent". The gods were kept in distinct temples which had small inner courts:

"The form of the interior or area of their temples was frequently that of a square or a parallelogram, the sides of which extended forty or fifty feet. Two sides of this space were enclosed by a high stone wall; the front was protected by a low fence; and opposite, a solid pyramidal structure was raised, in front of which the images were kept and the altars fixed. These piles were often immense. That which formed one side of the large temple in Atehuru . . . was two hundred and seventy feet long, ninety-four wide at the base, and fifty feet high, being at the summit one hundred and eighty feet long, and six wide. A flight of steps led to its summit; the bottom step was six feet high. The outer stones of the pyramid, composed of coral and basalt, were laid with great care, and hewn or squared with immense labour, especially the *tiavâ*, or corner stones."

Ellis states that "the trees growing within the walls, and around the temple, were sacred". The priests of the national temples "were a distinct class; the office of the priesthood was hereditary in all its departments". Offerings of animals, fruit, &c., were made to the idols; human sacrifices were frequently made. When a man's body was placed before an idol, a curious ceremony took place:

"The priest in dedicating it, took out one of the eyes, placed it on a plantain leaf and handed it to the king, who raised it to his mouth as if desirous to eat it, but passed it to one of the priests or attendants stationed near him for the purpose of receiving it."

Some of the victim's hair was then placed before the idol. The body, which had been wrapped in leaves, was afterwards deposited on the branches of one of the holy trees, and the bones were ultimately burned beneath the pavement of the marae.

Here, it may be noted in passing, we have, as in the case of mummification, a remarkable survival of ancient Egyptian ideas and customs. The offering of the eye of the sacrificed victim was, the Polynesians informed Ellis, made because the eye was "the organ or emblem of power".[1] In Egypt the Horus-eye, especially if offered to the dead, was "the symbol of all sacrifice". When

---

[1] *Polynesian Researches* (Second Edition), Vol. I, p. 357.

Horus, according to the version of the Osirian myth in the Pyramid Texts, performed the ceremony of raising his father from the dead, he offered to him his eye. " Excepting the sacred beetle, or scarab," says Breasted, " it (the Horus eye) became the commonest and most revered symbol known to Egyptian religion, and the myriads of eyes, wrought in blue or green glaze, or even cut from costly stone, which fill our museum collections, and are brought home by thousands by the modern tourist, are survivals of this ancient story of Horus and his devotion to his father."[1]   The eye-offering in Polynesia, as in Ancient Egypt, was intended to stimulate and reanimate the deity.

Robert Louis Stevenson, in his *The South Seas* (Chap. XI) tells of a visit he paid to a deserted Marquesan " cannibal high place ". He and Father Simeon were guided to it by a native boy through a deep, dim forest and he found it to be " a thing on a great scale ". He writes of it:

" As far as my eyes could pierce through the dark undergrowth, the floor of the forest was all paved. Three tiers of terrace ran on the slope of the hill; in front, a crumbling parapet contained the main arena; and the pavement of that was pierced and parcelled out with several wells and small enclosures. . . . In the old days the high place was sedulously tended. No tree except the sacred banyan was suffered to encroach upon its grades, no dead leaf to rot upon the pavement. The stones were smoothly set, and I am told they were kept bright with oil. On all sides the guardians lay encamped in their subsidiary huts to watch and cleanse it. No other foot of man was suffered to draw near. . . ."

On a festival day the clan trooped in a body to the " high place ". Stevenson pictures the gathering of priests and drummers and dancers, warriors and women, and children; he makes us hear the drums throbbing, the singers rendering their long-drawn song, and see the costumed dancers gesticulating in their finery, " their plumed

---

[1] *Development of Religion and Thought in Ancient Egypt*, London, 1912, p. 31.

fingers fluttering in the air like butterflies ". Then he makes us feel the horror of the cannibal feast:

" Men banqueted on the poor clay of a comrade with whom they had played in infancy, or a woman whose favours they had shared."

At first he felt as if he were visiting an antique place like Stonehenge.

" As I began," he says, " to appreciate that the thing was still living and latent about my footsteps, and that it was still within the bounds of possibility that I might hear the cry of the trapped victim, my historic attitude entirely failed, and I was sensible of some repugnance for the natives."

The stone structures in Polynesia show considerable diversity, as do the burial customs, and, perhaps, for the same reason. There were several migrations into the islands, and the cultural elements imported betrayed the impress of religious influences, which had been operating in Indonesia and elsewhere at different periods. In addition, a certain amount of culture-mixing, caused by the fusion of cults, appears to have taken place in the island groups, and there were consequently local variations and local developments in religion which appear to be reflected, for instance, in the peculiar character of the Marquesan stone structures. In some areas, too, stone-working was practised with greater skill than in others.

Linton, in his comparative notes in connexion with his study of Marquesan archæology, says that " the custom of reserving an open space in or near each village as an assembly place was almost universal in Polynesia. It was also of wide occurrence in Micronesia and Melanesia." Except in the Marquesas, where the *tohua* was of elaborate construction, as has been indicated, the assembly places " seem to have been nothing more than cleared level areas ". Linton refers to these as " secular ", but while the term may serve to distinguish them from the *maraes* with their temples, it cannot be overlooked that as Ellis[1] is at pains to remind us, " religious rites were connected with almost every act of their (the Polynesians') lives ".   Even the stone platforms (*paepae*) for houses were invested with a degree of sanctity.   " Although," says Handy, " the house itself was not sacred, yet the work on it, like all labour, was *tapu*, and required consecration of the workers."   When the first stones were laid " a ceremonial priest intoned the *pu'e* chant, ending that day's labour, the actual building of the platform being done the following day. . . . When the house was completed the *pu'e* was again intoned."[2]

In New Zealand, the Maoris, as Linton emphasizes, " had no permanent sacred structures ".   They had, however, " sacred places without structures, and also sacred trees and stones. . . . The *wharekura* (sacred house) in which the young men were taught is the nearest approach to a temple ".

We should not wonder to find the Maoris differing in their religious practices from the Marquesans, Society Islanders, &c.   In New Zealand they mingled with and absorbed in areas the earlier people represented by the Moriori of Chatham Islands, and this fusion appears to have influenced religious beliefs and customs.   Withal, part of the east coast of New Zealand was peopled by " a separate migration into the Pacific from Indonesia ".[3]   These late-comers became very influential; their priesthood appear to have been subjected to different influences in Indonesia from those of the earlier Marquesans or the Samoans.

In the next chapter the problem of the ancient monuments will be studied over a wider area than that embraced by Polynesia.

---

[1] *Polynesian Researches* (First Edition), Vol. I, p. 216.
[2] *Bernice P. Bishop Museum Bulletin*, No. 9, pp. 150–1.
[3] S. Percy Smith, *Hawaiki* (Fourth Edition), p. 102.

CHAPTER XI

The Micronesian Venice

Stone not used because it was plentiful—Marquesan Methods of Quarrying and Transporting Stone—Egyptian Quarrying—New Zealand Stoneworkers—Stone Structures of Caroline Islands—Metal Tools imitated in Stone and Shell—Seafarers and Pottery—Lele Island Ruins—Cyclopean Walls—Canals for Transport—Artificial Islands of Ponape—Great Breakwater—Walled Enclosures and Stone Tombs—Obsidian Find—A Resonant Stone—Caroline Quarries—Native Traditions regarding Builders—Relics on Yap—Megaliths of the Marianas (Ladrones)—Burials on Tops of Monoliths—Megaliths of the Solomons—Sacred Mounds with Dolmens and Shaft Tombs—Sacred Trees connected with Sacred Stones—Stone Circle connected with Sacred Snakes—Polynesians not Savages—Traces of Ancient Culture.

The South Sea Islanders practised the craft of the stone mason, which, it should be recognized, has a history like that of the boat-builder. This interesting fact opens up a problem of great importance in the history of civilization.

There are some who are prone to assume that any isolated people may have begun spontaneously to use stone for building without ever having received a single hint from an outside source, and that we may expect to find they have " quite naturally " developed architectural features similar to those developed elsewhere. The reason usually given for an isolated people making use of stone is that they found stone to be plentiful in their particular area. But a preliminary necessity to using such a material for the construction of buildings of even the simplest character is a certain amount of skill in the quarrying and transporting of blocks of stone. A quarrier has first to select suitable stone *in situ*; then he must undertake the laborious task of cutting, lifting, and

152

removing the blocks. When he has accumulated at a selected site a sufficient quantity of stone, the problems presented by building with this new material must be gradually solved.

Before one can admit that a people who are found to be, or to have been at one time, expert in quarrying and transporting stone and in constructing edifices with it, received no instruction from experienced stone masons, it must be conclusively proved that they developed the stone-mason's craft from its rude beginnings. One expects to be shown, or informed of, their early failures and experiments at the quarry or the building site. It is not sufficient to have examples of their successes alone. Further, in each isolated area one looks for evidence of originality in technique and architectural features. Those who support the theory of independent origin should be able to supply in each case the psychological motive for the erection of pyramid-like structures, walled enclosures of a sacred character, and for the construction of temples of stone instead of wood or earth. Indeed, the act of erecting a temple is one which has surely a history in itself.

Similar stone structures are found in widely-separated areas, and it cannot be urged that there is a human instinct that prompts man to develop spontaneously in different areas the stone-mason's craft for the purpose of ensuring the welfare of his soul. If it was " natural " for the ancient Egyptians to build temples of stone, was it also " natural " for the Babylonians to build them of brick? If it was " natural " for some peoples to make images of their gods, was it also " natural " for other peoples to refuse to have their gods represented in stone or wood in the form of any living creature?

The theory that a particular people may be expected to make use of stone in an area in which stone happens to be plentiful is not supported by the facts of history. An excellent illustration in this connexion is afforded by the Vikings who discovered and settled on Iceland. Stone is plentiful on that island, but the Norsemen did not erect stone houses. In their homeland they had been accustomed to erect timber houses, and they erected timber houses in Iceland. Trees were scarce on the island, but they imported timber from Britain and Norway. As one gathers from their heroic lays, they were great admirers of the stately elm which does not grow in Norway or Iceland, but is a common tree in northern Scotland.

There are references in the sagas to the Icelandic timber trade. In the *Saga of Burnt Njal*, for instance, it is told that when the warrior Flosi had grown old, he " fared abroad . . . to seek for timber to build him a hall; and he was in Norway that winter; but the next summer he was late *boun*; and men told him that his ship was not seaworthy. Flosi said she was quite good enough for an old and death-doomed man, and bore his goods on shipboard and put out to sea. But of that ship no tidings were ever heard." [1]

The Scots similarly built houses of wood. Bede, the " father of English historians ", tells that when missionaries from Scotland were converting the Angles of Northumbria to the Christian faith, they erected a church on the island of Lindisfarne (Holy Island) " after the manner of the Scots, not of stone, but wholly of hewn oak, and covered it with reeds ". There was no lack of stone in western Scotland and northern England, but the Scots had not learned to practise the craft of the stone-mason. Nor did they " borrow " from or imitate the Picts of northern Scotland. The Picts were accustomed to erect stone Brochs—circular towers from 40 to 60 feet high, and from 12 to 15 feet thick.

In the South Sea Islands one does not find evidence of the independent origin of the stone-mason's craft. From the outset the Marquesans, who had no metal tools,

[1] Dasent's translation.

displayed considerable skill in selecting, quarrying, and transporting suitable stone. "Many of the stones in ceremonial structures, and even in the dwelling platforms of chiefs and important persons are," writes Ralph Linton, "of surprising size and weight. The most massive native construction seen is the *tohua* of Uahakekua, which includes boulders weighing from three to ten tons. To transport and place such masses of rock was an engineering feat of no mean order."[1] Some of the stone erections are situated several miles from the places where the stone was obtained.

At the Marquesan quarries the methods adopted in splitting and removing blocks of stone can still be detected. First of all the quality of the stone was tested by making holes in it. Then markings were made on the rock face to guide the workers, who proceeded laboriously to sink grooves. When these were deep enough they undertook the work of undercutting to release the slab. After it was, at length, levered out, the slab was roughly dressed with adzes and rubbed with harder stones until the surface was fairly level. Linton writes regarding the further treatment of the slabs:

"Rarely, the finished slabs were ornamentally adzed or chiselled. The designs were limited to the face, and consisted of simple lines or herring-bone patterns. It is impossible to say whether this work was done at the quarry or after the slabs had been set in place. On the islands of Hivoa and Tahuata (in the Marquesas) many of the slabs in ceremonial structures are decorated with carvings in high relief. To provide for this, projecting blocks were left on the face of the slab at the time it was quarried, but the figures were carved after the slab had been transported and placed."[2]

According to Linton, slabs "as much as 4 feet long and 30 inches wide are still used by the natives for building tombs". He describes how these are transported:

[1] *Bernice P. Bishop Museum Bulletin* 23 (1925), p. 7.   [2] R. Linton, *op. cit.*, p. 9.

" The slabs are slung from a stout pole on their shoulders. The tuff of which the slabs are made is light and more than six bearers are rarely required. Nine of the very large slabs have been transported in recent times, but it is probable that the present method was used in ancient times. . . . In country as rough as the Marquesas, transportation on skids or rollers would have been impossible without the construction of graded ways, and no traces of such ways were seen either at the quarries or in the neighbourhood of ceremonial structures. . . . In some quarries located on very steep hillsides, skids were probably employed for lowering the slabs to level ground. Ropes, held from above, would serve to brake the descent. Once on the level, the main difficulty involved in carrying the slabs would lie in the construction of a frame strong enough to bear the weight and large enough to provide grips for a great number of bearers." [1]

In Ancient Egypt, the home of stone building, obelisks were extracted in a manner similar to that adopted by the Polynesian quarrymen who cut slabs from rock faces. The outline of an obelisk was first marked on the surface of the rock. No chisels were used in cutting. The quarriers had for tools dolerite balls of from 5 to 12 inches in diameter and averaging 12 pounds in weight. Blows were struck with these balls to break the granite, and the pounding caused that hard material to come away " in the form of powder and not as flakes ". A large number of men were employed at this work, and they cut out in the granite round the block to be extracted a trench about 2 feet 6 inches in width. R. Englebach calculates, after practical experience of the work that a " beater " could extract about 3.15 inches of powdered granite in an hour.

After a trench of sufficient depth had been sunk in the hard rock the work of separating the block beneath had to be undertaken. This was accomplished by " undercutting " as in the Marquesan quarries. The great block had then to be removed. Levers and ropes were used for this purpose and the obelisk was placed on a

[1] Linton, *op. cit.*, p. 10.

sled which was drawn over wooden rollers by gangs of labourers.[1] In Assyria similar methods were adopted in transporting great statues, while idols were carried shoulder high as were the blocks of stone in Polynesia.

When we find a people possessed of the knowledge how to select and transport suitable stone and use it for building with considerable skill and success, it is evident that they are drawing upon long-accumulated experience. Beginners cannot be expected to adopt spontaneously the methods of quarrying and transporting stone which had been learned very slowly in the centres of ancient civilization. If they have not received a hint or an instruction from outside, we should be able to follow every stage of the development of their industry from its rude beginnings, and to detect their blunders and failures as well as their successes. We should, further, be able to discover the psychological motive for the use of stone for religious purposes and demonstrate how that motive had origin in ideas rooted in local experiences. The Egyptians, for instance, attached a religious value to stone because they found that corpses, previously preserved in graves dug in the hot, dry sand, decayed in stone-lined graves. It was believed that the stone " ate the flesh "—an idea perpetuated in the Greek name of a stone coffin—the sarcophagus ("flesh-eater"), as Elliot Smith has pointed out. Having assumed that the flesh and therefore the spirit and personality of the dead man entered stone, they regarded stone as holy. It was possessed by the spirit of the great man who was regarded as a god. We cannot trace in Polynesia the history of what is called "stone worship", which, as we have seen, was imported from an outside source with the religious ideas connected with mummification and other methods of dealing with the dead.

Even when we find a people imitating in stone constructions of wood, it does not follow that because they

[1] R. Englebach, *The Problem of the Obelisks*, pp. 41 *et seq.*

have proved themselves capable as wood-workers they could easily become stone-workers. Quarrying work alone requires a great deal of specialized knowledge and skill not obtained in procuring wood. Different methods and different tools were necessary. It is, therefore, hazardous to assume that anywhere in the South Sea Islands, including New Zealand, a people began spontaneously and independently to undertake the laborious and skilled work of quarrying stone without a single suggestion from an outside source, whether or not wood was easy to obtain. The fact that the use of stone was adopted in a part of the South Island of New Zealand does not necessarily afford proof of the independent origin there of stone working. It is probable that certain settlers in the South Island imported the knowledge of how to work stone, and having found a suitable stone, proceeded to excavate it by the methods familiar to them.

In New Zealand the use of stone for facing ramparts no doubt helped to perpetuate the craft of the stone-builder.[1] Stockades and earthworks were more common, however. Throughout the South Sea Islands forts made or faced with stone, stockades, &c., were common in former times.[2]

That the early peoples who migrated into the South Sea Islands from Indonesia were possessed of considerable knowledge of how to quarry and transport stone and use it for building is made evident by the wonderful megalithic buildings of the Caroline Islands. These are not only walls and enclosures of impressive character, but also artificial islets of solid masonry.

In dealing with the early settlers in the Carolines, F. W. Christian[3] brings forward interesting evidence which suggests that they were acquainted with the use of metals for manufacturing axes and knives, but that

---

[1] For stone-faced ramparts see Elsdon Best, *The Maori* (1924), Vol. II, p. 321.
[2] R. Linton, *Bernice P. Bishop Museum Bulletin* 23 (1925), pp. 20–3.
[3] *The Caroline Islands*, London, 1899, pp. 132 *et seq.*

their descendants reverted " through long isolation to the primitive Stone or Shell Age ". The peoples of the western islands of the South Seas refer to iron as *wessa*, *wasai*, *wasi*, *asi*, and *wasei*, and Christian compares these forms with the Finnic *was* or *as*, the Caucasian *asa* and *vasa*, the Magyar *vas*, the Sanskrit *asi* (iron, bronze, copper) and the Latin *æs*. After the South Sea Islanders ceased to use metal they called their weapons of shell and stone by the names applied originally to metal weapons. Christian writes in this connexion:

" It stands to reason that as the basaltic or coral lands of the Pacific produce no iron, steel is unobtainable. It may be presumed that some of the early settlers in the Carolines brought with them a stock of iron or steel weapons, or wrested them from stray pirates of a later day. When these rusted or got broken, and could not be replaced, the traditional name would in all probability remain, and the natives under stress of necessity would fall back upon the handiest materials available to supply their place. Those who live on low coral islets would find the shaft of the Tridacna (Kima or Pachu), a shell very abundant on their reefs, a convenient substitute. Those who inhabited high basaltic lands, as Tahiti or the Marquesas (on the first of which the water is always deep over her coral reefs, and the latter has no reefs at all), would fall back on the black basalt stone to fashion their cutting instruments. Samoa and Fiji have done the same." [1]

Maritime peoples could build and navigate their vessels without metal implements; and, as in Ancient Egypt, stone-workers could extract blocks of stone from quarries by making use of tools of stone and of wooden levers and sleds and ropes.

In these days when so much interest is taken in ancient pottery, and racial and cultural drifts are traced by the evidence afforded by pottery fragments, it should be recognized that sometimes the pottery clue fails us. Migrating peoples did not always carry characteristic pots from the areas whence they migrated, and when,

---

[1] F. W. Christian, *op. cit.*, pp. 132–6.

after settling in a new area, they began to make clay pots, they did not necessarily repeat the forms of those to which they had formerly been accustomed. Cretan pottery, for instance, was not a servile imitation of that of Egypt whence many settlers in Crete appear to have come. After all, pottery was not likely to have been popular on small ships, being too fragile. In the South Sea Islands pottery was made only in restricted areas. It has been found in parts of Eastern New Guinea, in areas in the Solomons, and on the Admiralty Islands, the New Hebrides, New Caledonia, and Fiji. " The former population of Easter Island made pottery." Mr. W. J. Perry, who gives the authorities in this connexion, takes the view that " the craft belonged to the early people ", and that " it has persisted in certain spots that show strong traces of the former civilization ".[1] The islanders had substitutes for clay pots, carrying water in sea-weed bags, &c., and making use of wooden bowls, coco-nut shells, sea-shells, &c., and cooking food in *umu* (ovens).

The suggestion that the early peoples of the Carolines had some knowledge of metals is of extraordinary interest even in connexion with the pottery problem, for it supports the view that certain crafts were lost in the course of the migrations of sea-faring peoples, and especially after settlement in areas where no suitable clay for pots, and no ores for metal tools and weapons could be found.

The builders of the megalithic monuments of the Carolines must, as has been indicated, have come from some centre of civilization where the quarrying and transporting of stone had reached a high state of development, and where impressive buildings were constructed. They were imitators rather than originators. As much is made manifest by the evidence placed on record regarding their activities as stone-builders.

[1] *The Children of the Sun*, p. 32.

(16)

RUINS AT NANMATAL, ISLAND OF PONAPE, CAROLINE ISLANDS

(15)

STONE PYRAMID OF MARAE, TAHITI

From an engraving published in 1836 illustrating the account of a voyage in Oceania by Domeny de Rienzi, the French explorer

On Lele Island, also called Strong's Island, in the eastern Carolines, there are great walled enclosures about 200 feet in length and over 100 in breadth. The walls are constructed of blocks of basalt and are from 9 to 15 feet in thickness.

In his description of an enclosure the " Pot Falat " ruins, Christian says it forms a parallelogram. The wall at the west angle is still 25 feet high, and at the north 26 feet, while at the east angle it is 20 feet; at the south-east the wall is in a dilapidated condition, and varies from 8 to 15 feet in height; it reaches its greatest altitude of about 30 feet at the south angle.

Some of the stones are large. In the south angle, about 20 feet from the ground, is a corner stone of which Christian gives the measurements: " length, 10 feet; depth, 4 feet; breadth across face, 2 feet 6 inches "; while the foundations of the wall are " three roundish masses of basalt piled together, the lowest measuring " 6 feet in length, 4 feet in depth, and 3 feet in thickness ". At the northern angle there is a corner stone which measures " 9 feet in length, 3 feet 6 inches in breadth, and 3 feet in depth ". Another corner stone at the eastern angle " 3 feet 6 inches across, 3 feet 10 inches in depth, and 6 feet 2 inches in length ". At the west angle a massive slab of basalt in the wall is 9 feet 6 inches in length, 2 feet 4 inches in depth, and 3 feet 6 inches in breadth.

The interior is divided by a ruined wall into two courtyards. There are four gateways. A canal runs along the western and northern sides and is about 9 feet in breadth. Christian thinks that this canal, like others on the island, " was constructed for the purpose of rafting up these huge blocks of stone from the beach whither they were brought from South Harbour ". There are other impressive ruins on Lele. Christian says that the south-eastern and south-western portions of the island were " laboriously reclaimed in olden time from the

sea ", and that " a network of canals—very much out of
repair—intersects this portion, many of these partially
filled or banked up by the natives in modern times to
keep the tides from turning their taro-patches and
cleared lands into a salt swamp ".

More remarkable than these ruins are the fifty or
sixty rectangular islets, mainly of artificial formation, in
a lagoon on the eastern coast of Ponape, one of the chief
islands of the Carolines. These islets occupy an area of
about 11 square miles. " Nan Matal " (" The Place of
the Waterways "), as the natives call this strange " city ",
has been compared to Venice. It was protected by a
great breakwater of solid masonry, several miles in
length, and some of the islets are enclosed in thick
basaltic walls. Shallow canals, on which native canoes
were used as gondolas, intersect this Micronesian Venice.

The most remarkable of the islets is Nan-Tauach
(" Place of Loftiness " or " High Walls "). Massive
blocks of basalt form around it a terrace which rises
about six feet above the water, and above the terrace is
a wall of " immensely solid Cyclopean stonework ", says
Christian, " formed of basaltic prisms laid alternately
lengthwise and crosswise after the fashion of a *chock and
log* fence, or, as masons would style it, *Headers and
Stretchers* ". A great gateway opens in the wall, and is
about 25 feet high on the left side and about 30 feet
on the right. Luxuriant vegetation almost concealed the
walls when Christian visited the islet. " Somewhat
similar in character," Christian writes, " would be the
semi-Indian ruins of Java, and the Cyclopean structures
of Ake, and Chichen-Itza in Yucatan."

The islet walls enclose a great structure which is a
double parallelogram. In the outer courtyard, which is
reached by huge steps like those of an Egyptian pyramid,
are fragments of fallen pillars. It measures about 185 by
115 feet, and the outer wall, which averages about 15 feet
in thickness, varies in height from 20 to 40 feet. The

inner enclosure has a wall of from 15 to 18 feet high, its average thickness being about 8 feet. It is reached by steps. The court is roughly paved and measures about 85 feet by 75 feet, and in its centre is a stone-built royal tomb, said to be that of an ancient monarch named Chau-te-reul or Cha-te-leur. Christian notes with regard to this name that "*Chau* was the ancient Ponape word denoting (*a*) the sun, (*b*) a king", and he compares *Chau* with the Rotuma *Sau* (king), and the Polynesian *Hau* and *Au* (king, chief). According to native tradition, therefore, the Nan Tauach tomb is that of a monarch of sun-worshippers.

Besides the royal tomb of the inner court there are three other tombs in the outer court, one being enclosed by two walls between the walls of the inner and outer main walls, and another being shut off at the northeast corner of the outer courtyard by a single wall. "A certain irregularity in the whole building," wrote Kubary, "as in the differing height and breadth of individual terraces, betokens a variety of builders, following one another, and knowing how to give expression to their respective ideas."

The natives regard Nan-Tauach, as they do the other islets, with superstitious reverence, so persistent is tradition, and when Christian was engaged in clearing the undergrowth in the inner court, one of them exclaimed, "The eyes of the spirits are watching everything you do. They will not hurt you because you are a white man, but they will punish us. I cannot sleep at night; I am very much afraid, and I should like to go home."

The central tomb was explored by Christian, who obtained, after digging, some significant relics. It is about 8 feet deep and "roofed in by six enormous blocks or slabs of basalt". Loose coral lay on its floor. Among the rubbish was collected about a quart of rose-pink beads, from the size of a threepenny bit to a shilling, which had been made "by rubbing from the *spondylus*

strombus and *Conus* shells ". Some were " very minute
and delicate in design ". Christian says " they answer
exactly to the *Wampum* or shell-bead money of the North-
American Indians, who use them for ornamenting pouches,
moccasins, and girdles ". Some beads were circular and
others rectangular. " Beads exactly similar in design,"
Christian says, " have recently been discovered in the
ruins of Mitla in Central America." Other relics included about eighty pearl-shell shanks of fish-hooks
similar to those formerly used throughout Polynesia.
Fragments of pearl-shell which were evidently barbs of
bone hooks,[1] five shell axes, five carved shell bracelets
" of elegant design ", about twelve " needles " of shell
which were used for sewing the mat-sails of canoes and
apparently also as necklaces when strung together, and
" thirty or forty large circular shells, bored through the
centres and worn as a pendant ornament on the breast ".
Of very special interest among the finds were " a piece of
iron resembling a spear-head " and a fragment of obsidian, " the *itztli* of the ancient Mexicans ". The tomb
contained " a vast number of fragments of bones ", and
" portions of skulls ". Apparently several " kings " had
been buried in it.

At the back of another tomb, the one shut off by
walls in the southern part of the outer courtyard, Christian happened upon a significant relic. This was " a
long basalt slab carved into a shallow crescent and
balanced on two projecting shafts of masonry. . . . When
tapped it gave a clear ringing sound, and was probably
used for an alarum or for a sort of bell in sacred ceremonies. We found just such another subsequently in
Nanapei's settlement of Ronkiti. I brought it home and
it is now in the British Museum."

In Chapter IV the resonant stones of New Zealand,
China, &c., are dealt with.

Commenting on the ruins at Lele, Christian writes:

---

[1] Like the Tardenoisian pigmy flints.

" In careful and minute adjustment they are inferior to the structures of Java, but doubtless the work of a kindred race of builders labouring under less favourable conditions. Looking at their solid outlines, seamed and furrowed with the rains and sun of untold generations, one cannot help marvelling at the ingenuity and skill of these primitive engineers in moving, lifting, and poising such huge and unwieldy masses of rock into their present position, where these mighty structures, shadowed by great forest trees, stand defying time's changing seasons and the fury of tropic elements." [1]

The quarrying, transporting, and raising the stones, some of which, as we have seen, are of considerable bulk and weight, could never have been accomplished by " beginners ". It was evidently because the builders had been accustomed to handle stone that on arrival in the Carolines they were able in the first place to select their material. Both on Lele and Ponape Nature provided them with ready-made pillars like the " organ pipe " blocks of Staffa and Iona in the Hebrides, the Giant's Causeway in Northern Ireland and, as Christian reminds us, the rocks of the southern promontory of Tasmania.

If the Caroline Islanders began to build simply because suitable stone was available, the Hebrideans, the ancient Irish and the Tasmanians should likewise have utilized the natural pillars provided for them, but, as we know, they did not make any use of them. Nature's generosity is one thing; mankind's ability to take advantage of it is another. It was evidently because the Caroline islands builders were possessed of the necessary skill and knowledge to enable them to remove and transport the basaltic pillars that they utilized them for constructing walls, tombs, and artificial islets. Christian and Kubary, the Polish investigator, both interested themselves in the problems of quarrying and transportation. They show that the Ponapean stones were obtained from two quarries. In one case, Kubary says, " the stones

---

[1] Christian, *op. cit.*

were brought here by means of an inclined plane ".
In the absence of cranes and other machinery Christian
considers this " very feasible ", and writes :

> " In my mind's eye I viewed an even slope of felled tree trunks
> copiously sluiced with coco-nut oil, to avoid friction, up which the
> great blocks would be hauled, one relay of workmen above pulling
> upon long and thick cables of coir fibre or cinnet and supplementary
> ropes of green hibiscus bark, another relay below with solid staves
> and handspikes by turns pushing the huge mass upwards and resting
> with their poles set against and below it to prevent it slipping
> back."

Blocks had to be rafted, landing-stages constructed
to receive them, and, as we have seen, canals made in
some cases so that these blocks might be transferred to
a building site. A great deal of skilled work had to be
performed by men of experience before a wall or tomb
of basaltic pillars could be constructed. The work of
dressing the stones had not to be undertaken. Nature
had provided ready-made pillars which are " polygonal
or multi-angular, some five and some eight-sided ";
many are " six sided, but by no means uniformly so ".[1]
But if it was unnecessary to shape the stones, it was
necessary that they should be raised after arrival at the
building site. As we have seen, the islanders constructed
very thick and high walls. The breakwater and artificial islets of the " Micronesian Venice " were the work
of men possessed of considerable engineering skill;
withal they were experienced builders with a social
organization which made it possible to provide immense
gangs of workmen who had been well trained and
disciplined.

Who were the builders of the impressive stone
structures of Lele and those of much finer design and
finish at Ponape? Admiral Sir Cyprian Bridge, who had
served on the Pacific and Australian stations for a number

---

[1] Christian, *op. cit.*, pp. 81 *et seq.*

of years during the latter half of the nineteenth century, expressed the view that " these great ruins were built by a race entirely passed away . . . long before any white man visited the islands ".[1]   This view, having been criticized unfavourably, he wrote later:

" Whether the ancestors of the present Ponapeans or an earlier people built the great island Venice at Metalanim, it will not, I expect, be denied that the builders must have vastly outnumbered the existing population. The same may be said of every Pacific Island on which prehistoric remains are found. . . . A tradition of a larger population in early times is very common in the South Seas." [2]

Sir Hercules Read and Horatio Hale rejected the view that the ancient builders were not the ancestors of the present Caroline Islanders, the former pointing out that the builders of the great pyramids, &c., in the Nile valley were the ancestors of the modern fellaheen of Egypt.[3] Christian suggests that the builders were " an intelligent minority swaying an ignorant majority ". Kubary's view was that the stone buildings of Nan Matal " were erected by a race preceding the present inhabitants of Ponape ", and that this was a " black race " from whom the present Ponapeans, a mixed race, are in part descended. One of the disinterred skulls from the ruins was very long, the index being 70·2 while the average aphalic index of modern Ponapeans is 79·7.

Native tradition, according to Christian,[4] tells that the breakwater and island " Venice " of Ponape were built by two brothers named Olo-chipa and Olo-chopa. By the magic spells of these men " one by one the great masses of stone flew through the air like birds, settling down into their appointed place ". Hahl, the German

[1] *The Geographical Journal*, XIII (1899), p. 132.
[2] His Introduction to F. W. Christian's *The Caroline Islands*, 1899, pp. 13–4.
[3] *The Geographical Journal*, XIII, p. 135, and *Ethnography and Philology of the United States Exploring Expedition*, pp. 86 et seq.   [4] *Op. cit.*, p. 81.

investigator, quoted and summarized by Perry,[1] refers to a tradition which tells that the founders of Ponape came from the island of Yap "on stones that swam on the water", which recalls the Arthurian tradition of swimming stones. Perry, drawing upon Hahl, says further:

"It is said in Ponape that certain spirits came from the sky and changed into stones; and the gods cannot be approached except through these stones, which are only found in certain places; if they are lacking in any place, so is the cult of gods. These stones are not only used in connexion with offerings made to gods, but also possess magical power and healing properties. When, for example, men wish to go fishing, they drop a holy stone into the sea."

Hahl shows further that the priests belong to the commoners, and that they are matrilineal in hereditary succession. The ruling class is evidently descended from the conquerors of the ancient civilization which is represented by the great stone structures. When that civilization was broken up an end came to the work of building walls, tombs, and islets with blocks of stone.

Christian says of the people of the island of Yap, the most westerly of the Carolines, whence the Ponapean stone-builders are said to have come, that their language "appears to be a crabbed form of some ancient Asiatic tongue allied to the Dravidian (of India), coloured with a tint of Malay and Japanese, and crossed or chequered, in a very remarkable way, with unmistakable Polynesian words".[2] There are two classes on Yap, the *Pilung*, or chieftains, and the *Pimlingai*, or slaves. The latter are darker in colour and "their hair is more curly, and in speaking they have a slightly different pronunciation. It looks," says Christian, "as if they belonged to an earlier race."[3] The same writer refers to a wharf "neatly built of coral blocks", and to structures, called *kades* or *kachers*, similar to those of the Pelews, and writes:

[1] *The Children of the Sun*, pp. 398–9.   [2] *Op. cit.*, pp. 51–2.   [3] *Op. cit.*, p. 288.

" The island is full of the relics of a vanished civilization—
embankments and terraces, sites of ancient cultivation and solid
roads neatly paved with regular stone blocks, ancient stone platforms and graves, and enormous council lodges of quaint design,
with high gables and lofty carved pillars. The ruins of ancient
stone fish-weirs fill the lagoon between the reef and the shore." [1]

In the Marianne group to the north of the Carolines

" there exist certain pyramids and truncated cones, on the top of
which are placed *semi-esferas*, i.e. half-spherical bodies. These
cones or pyramids on the island of Guahan do not exceed three
feet in height, the diameter of the curious pieces on the tops being
about two feet. Those seen on the island of Saipan near the village
of Garapui on the west coast are somewhat larger and generally
composed of stone. Amongst the natives these go by the name of
Houses of the Ancients. They face each other in two parallel lines
like a regular street. According to tradition the old inhabitants
used to inter their dead in these houses or cairns. Many even of
the present generation have a superstitious fear of touching the
stones or cultivating the ground in their neighbourhood." [2]

The megalithic monuments in the Marianas (or
Ladrones) are described by Lieut.-Commander P. J.
Searles in the *Scientific Monthly* for November, 1927. He
deals especially with the upright monoliths known as
the *lat'te*. These are surmounted by hemispherical
capitals and are arranged in rows of four to six stones
which run parallel to the sea-shore or a river bed.
These megaliths are comparable to the famous Stonehenge
group. In Tinian, where they are most impressive, the
blocks of stone are about 12 feet high and about 18 feet
in circumference while the capitals are 5 feet 6 inches in
diameter. The estimated weight of each monolith is
about thirty tons.

Lieut.-Commander Searles states that in an un-
published manuscript of a nineteenth-century Spanish
Governor, it is recorded that human bones were discovered in a hollow at the top of one of the big stones of

[1] F. W. Christian, *op. cit.*, p. 19.   [2] F. W. Christian, *op. cit.*, p. 53.

the "House of Taga". According to local tradition Taga had the bones of his daughter deposited on the summit of a monolith. It used to be thought that the *lat'te* were dwelling houses. Recent research has, however, demonstrated that these megalithic groups were really of religious significance. That the ceremonies performed had a connexion with cannibalism is suggested by the mutilated condition of skeletons found in and near the megalithic enclosures, but on this point there is no certainty.

The *lat'te* in Guam are of very special interest. They are connected with three areas. One area is apparently an ancient burial place in which the dead were laid with feet towards the water and the head inland. A second area suggests by its broken human bones that cannibal feasts were held. As, however, broken weapons are found associated with these, it may be that the breaking of bones and weapons was a final religious ceremony in connexion with the disposal of the dead. Remains of ornaments, weapons, stone implements and pottery have been found in the third area.

Important evidence regarding the use and sanctity of stone in San Cristoval (an island near the end of the Solomons to the east of New Guinea, and between New Britain and the New Hebrides) is given by Dr. C. E. Fox.[1] He describes several kinds of burial mounds called *heo* or *hera*. The *heo* is really the burial mound with a shaft and a dolmen on the top; the *hera* is the square or courtyard used for dancing which lies in front of the mound (*heo*). The dolmen (*hau suru* = " exalted stone ") forms " a kind of box of stone or little stone temple ". The skulls of the dead were placed inside it. Sacrifices were burned on the dolmen, and on it were placed round stones, carved stone heads, or small stone statues into which the " double " (*adaro*) of the dead man passed and resided. The shaft led to a burial chamber

---

[1] *The Threshold of the Pacific*, pp. 218 *et seq.* and 281 *et seq.*

or cave. As elsewhere, sacred trees were associated with the sacred stones. Dr. Fox tells that on the mound there was " at least one sacred tree and some sacred shrubs ", and either on the mound or at the base of it grew " a sacred coco - nut ". Occasionally " stone pillars and other mysterious stones whose use is unknown " were placed on the *heo*. On the coast the *heo* " are made of rubble of earth and stones bordered by large slabs of rock "; the inland *heo* are of " red clay ". The size of the *heo* vary considerably, the largest being 60 feet by 40 feet and 20 feet high. Small ones, 6 feet by 4 feet and 1 foot high are commonest. These burial places are connected with chiefs and with certain clans.

Stone platforms (*ariari*) " very regularly constructed " on sea-fronts, or in front of " sacred houses ", were used for offering sacrifices, and sacred trees were associated with them. Stone walls (*du'a*) marked boundaries and clan battles were fought at them. Some walls ran out into the sea, and were consecrated to sacred sharks. Dr. Fox tells of

" a famous *du'a* running out into the sea, connected with the *figona* (spirit) Wamarea who is said to be the *koa*, or fellow, of Hatuibwari, the Winged Serpent. On this dogs were sacrificed, and it was very sacred, no one daring to approach it."

Among the sacred stones (*Hau mæa*) is Wabina or Waibina, " named after the hawk *Bina*. It is " a large bright red stone about 2 feet square " and formerly stood on a *heo* (sacred mound) encircled by carved stones, one with an incised figure of a shark, another with the incised figure of a bonito, and others of white coral and diorite shaped to represent sacred birds—the frigate hawk of the Araha clan and the sea-gull which was sacrificed to in war. Near the Wabina stone was a sacred coco-nut tree, the nuts of which were not eaten. An evil ghost inhabited this tree. A priest conducted the ceremonies at the sacred red stone to which burnt offerings of pig and puddings were made, and he had a wagtail as his oracular bird.

Another sacred stone was supposed, like Chinese jade, to shine in water by night. A " whistling stone " whistled when one of the clan was about to die. Carvings on rock of the pig, turtle, crocodile, birds and fish were sacred.

" Stones are sometimes placed on graves, and many graves have an edging of small upright stones round them. The graves of Araha are sometimes lined with stones."

Dr. W. G. Ivens has collected important evidence regarding sacred stones on the islands of Mala (or Malaita) and Ulawa in the South-east Solomons. On Ulawa there is a snake grove with its hereditary priests. Young men who died were supposed to change into a dreaded winged snake; " its sides were yellow, its back grey, its under part like the belly of a turtle, and just below its head were two wings like the wings of a flying fish ". It was a " composite wonder beast " like the dragon of China and the winged serpent of pre-Columbian America.

Sacred snakes were fed with lizards. " At Ripoo," says Dr. Ivens, " there was a ring of stones associated with snakes." [1]

On Mala and Ulawa are stone walls which were sacred. Offerings of bonito and coco-nuts were placed upon them.[2] There were stone platforms also. On Ulawa coco-nuts used in the opening ceremonies when the bonito were first caught were placed as offerings on the stone platform, *räi seu*, outside the canoe house, and lay bleaching there. On the landing place called " The Descent of the Bonito " the following salutation was recited:

[1] *Melanesians of the South-East Solomons*, London, 1927, pp. 284-5.   [2] *Ibid.*, p. 477.

NATIVE GIRLS DANCING THE SITTING "SIVA-SIVA", SAMOA

(195)

(17)

STONE MONUMENTS ON TINIAN ISLAND, MARIANNE ISLANDS

From an engraving published in 1836 illustrating the account of a voyage in Oceania by Domeny de Rienzi, the French explorer

"Where the nuts are bleaching,
Where the big bonito descends,
Where they descend in pairs,
Where the young men descend." [1]

It would appear that among the settlers in the South Sea Islands were worshippers of the sun and the serpent, who erected megalithic monuments, including walled enclosures, stone-built tombs, platforms, &c., having connected stone as a " life giver " and " spirit body " or " god body " with the sky world, who constructed canals for irrigation and transport, practised agriculture and were accomplished navigators and builders of vessels. They had evidently before reaching the Pacific come under the influence of an ancient civilization. The traditions of that civilization survived in some areas until those were reached by Europeans. " Several South Sea Island races are not now savage in any sense," wrote Sir Cyprian Bridge, " and never deserved that epithet in its sense of ferocious. There is no finer people on earth than the Tongans, and the closely related and but slightly less vigorous Samoans. . . . The grace of manner and general dignity of bearing habitual with members of chiefly families could not be surpassed in the most polished European courts." [2]

Tregear, an authority on Maori life, religion and history, writes of the South Sea Islanders:

" who shall say that, being barbarians, they have always been barbarians? It would, indeed, be impossible to prove, and my own belief is opposed to such a notion. . . . They may be, and probably are, the degenerate descendants and broken remnants of mighty peoples, and their simplicity is not the result of innocence, but of ignorance and decay." [3]

The megalithic structures of the South Sea Islands, which are eloquent of ancient cultural influences, may

[1] *Melanesians of the South-East Solomons*, London, 1927, p. 159.
[2] Introduction to F. W. Christian's *The Caroline Islands*, p. 11.
[3] Quoted by Perry, *op. cit.*, p. 108.

differ greatly in detail on various islands and even in single groups of islands, but behind them all remains the psychological motive for the use of stone for religious purposes, and the arbitrary connexion of stone with the gods and the sky world. If we concentrate too much on local variations of type, design, and workmanship, we may, in dealing with the problem presented by the megalith remains as a whole, be unable to see the wood for the trees. Allowance must be made for local developments, for the clash of cultures in areas, and for other historical events, including a change in the ruling class owing to local conquests by intruders. In time it may be possible to discover the historical causes which led to the outstanding differences in the use of stone in various areas. But no doubt can remain that the peoples who " scorned delights and lived laborious days " that they might express their religious ideas in stone were impelled by motives rooted in a traditional reverence for stone, and that that reverence was an inheritance from the ancient cultural areas whence came the ancestors of the South Sea Islanders at various periods and by different routes.

CHAPTER XII

Creation Myths

Imported Religious Ideas and Customs—Culture Mixing on South Sea Islands—Hereditary Priestly Caste—Aristocratic Type of Maori Religion—Cult of Io the Supreme Being—Lower Grade Priests as Shamans—Doctrine of the World's Ages in Asia, Europe, Polynesia, and America—Cataclysms before Creation of Present World—Tangaroa (Tangaloa) as Polynesian Creator—Lofty Religious Poem—Stretching out of Sky in Polynesia, India, and Egypt—The Creation Egg Myth in Polynesia, India, and Egypt—The Sun-egg and the Moon-egg—Io not a Maori Concept—An Io Chant—Metaphysical Views of Creative Process—Hindu Parallels—Schools of Thought—Brahma and the Ages—The World Tree.

The religious ideas of the South Sea Islanders reveal, as do their social organization and physical achievements, the inspiring influences of complex cultures with long histories of development in the areas whence their ancestors had migrated to the various groups of basaltic or coral islands. It is evident that the sea-farers who discovered new homes in the Pacific did not forget all they had previously known and begin afresh to formulate religious beliefs and customs of a " primitive " character. They were accompanied by priests who formed a hereditary caste and perpetuated the lore and mental habits of that caste. At sea they acted as pilots, and were supposed to be able to propitiate the gods in times of peril: on land they were the spiritual guides of the people. The chiefs ruled by divine right, and were supposed to be descended from and to be earthly representatives of the gods.

It has been found that various groups of islands were peopled at different periods by bands of migrating sea-farers. In the areas whence they came there had been from time to time ethnic and cultural changes. One group of settlers introduced the royal custom of mummification and the associated religious ideas; another introduced the custom of cremation, and another introduced extended burial in stone-lined graves. Invasions and conquests by groups of peoples within Polynesia alone brought about changes in religious ideas and customs in this area and that. There were thus, in varying degrees of intensity, a good deal of culture mixing after the islands had been well populated. The original complexity of imported cultures was, as a result of local fusions, thus greatly increased. In some cases the conquerors imposed their religious ideas upon the conquered; in others the conquered achieved, as in New Zealand, a partial intellectual conquest of their rulers.

It has to be recognized further, in studying the religious ideas of the islanders, that the priests did not reveal all they knew or believed in to the common people. The caste they formed was a most exclusive one. In New Zealand, for instance, there were grades in the priesthood and those of the higher ranks " were ", as Eldon Best reminds us, " the exponents and upholders of what may justly be termed the aristocratic type of Maori religion, the cult of the Supreme Being, Io of the Hidden Face ". Best writes of the caste of intellectual aristocrats:

" This higher-class cultus was confined to that grade of priests and to men of superior rank; its secrets, practices, and teachings formed the most highly venerated and most intensely *tapu* portion of the esoteric lore of the Maori. The common people were not allowed to gain any knowledge of its ritual or practices. The aforesaid priests appear to have also practised the cult of the secondary or departmental gods, but had no dealing with low-class shamanistic performances indulged in by third-rate *tohunga* (priests); nor did they teach or practise the arts of black magic."

The lower-grade priests were concerned with the departmental and tribal gods and some were no better than shamans, and it was their customs and ideas that the early observers and recorders became acquainted with. It was consequently assumed that Polynesian religion as a whole was of quite primitive character, and writers like E. B. Tylor, Andrew Lang, and others drew upon the statements of early missionaries and travellers for data regarding " savage religion " in its rudimentary phases. But, as Best says:

"The lower grades of a religious system are by far the easiest for any alien observer to become acquainted with; in many cases this is the only aspect they ever gain any knowledge of. Among such a people as the Maori the higher type of religion is by no means conspicuous: it is in the hands of a small class, and is most jealously guarded." [1]

In dealing with Polynesian cosmogony one meets at the outset with undoubted traces of the ancient doctrine of the World's Ages which appears to have had origin in Babylonia and passed westward into the mythologies of the Greeks, the Celts, and the Teutons, and eastward into those of the Persians, the Hindus, and the Chinese, ultimately reaching the Aztecs of Mexico in pre-Columbian times. [2]

There are references, as in India and Mexico, to cataclysms by fire and flood before the creation of the present world. " Creation begins," as Dixon says of the Hawaiian account, " in the origin of a new world from the shadowy reflex of one that is past. . . .

"Unsteadily, as in dim moon-shimmer,
    From out Makalii's night-dark veil of cloud
    Thrills, shadow-like, the prefiguration of the world to be." [3]

In a lofty religious poem from the Society Islands, collected by Moerenheut and translated by Fornander, [4]

---

[1] *Some Aspects of Maori Myth and Religion* (Dominion Museum Monograph No. 1) Wellington, N.Z., 1922, pp. 6, 7.

[2] See my *Myths of Pre-Columbian America*, pp. 64 *et seq.*

[3] *Oceanic Mythology*, p. 15, and Bastian, *Die heilige Sage der Polynesier*, p. 70.

[4] *Voyage aux Îles du Grand Océan* and *The Polynesian Race*, Vol. I, pp. 220 *et seq.*

(D 917)

the Supreme Being is the creator of the universe and the gods. He is identified with the god known in the various Polynesian dialects as Tanaoa, Taaroa, Tangaroa, Tangaloa and Kanaloa. The poem runs:

> " He abides (exists). Taaroa by name
> In the immensity (space).
> There was no earth, there was no sky,
> There was no sea, there was no mankind,
> Taaroa calls on high.
> Existing alone he became the universe.
> Taaroa is the root (origin),
> The rocks (foundation),
> Taaroa is the sands,
> Taaroa stretches out the branches (is wide-spreading).
> Taaroa is the light;
> Taaroa is within;
> Taaroa is (? the germ);
> Taaroa is below (beneath);
> Taaroa is enduring (form);
> Taaroa is wise;
> He created the land of Hawaii,
> Hawaii great and sacred
> As a crust (or shell) for Taaroa."

The poem goes on to refer to the stretching out of the sky:

> " Stretch out the seven heavens; let ignorance cease.
> Create the heavens, let darkness cease.
> Let anxiety cease within . . .
> Let repose (immobility) cease.
> Let the period of messengers cease.
> It is the time of the speaker (as creator).
> Fill up (or complete) the foundations,
> Fill up the rocks,
> Fill up the sands.
> The heavens are enclosing (surrounding),
> And hung up are the heavens
> In the depths:
> Finished be the world of Hawaii."

The Ancient Egyptians celebrated in their Spring festivals the " hanging out of the heavens " as an act of creation. In Sanskrit literature the Hindu god Agni is said to have stretched out the heavens, and the same act is credited in Rig-vedic hymn (I, 103, 2) to Indra.[1]

E. S. Craighill Handy [2] quotes a more explicit account of the creation from the Society Islands which is as follows:

" Taaroa was the ancestor of all the gods; he made everything. From time immemorial was the great Taaroa, Tahitumu (The-origin). Taaroa developed himself in solitude; he was his own parent, having no father or mother. . . . Taaroa sat in his shell in darkness from eternity. The shell was like an egg revolving in endless space, with no sky, no land, no sea, no moon, no sun, no stars. All was darkness, it was continuous thick darkness. . . ."

Taaroa broke his shell which became the sky. Then he entered a new shell and used it " for the great foundation of the world, for stratum rock and for soil for the world. And the shell Rumia that he opened first became his house, dome of the god's sky, which was a confined sky, enclosing the world then forming."

The egg myth is found in one of the Hindu stories of creation. In the *Laws of Manu* it is related that the Self-Existent Being desired to create living creatures. He first created the waters which he called " narah ", and then a seed; he flung the seed into the waters, and it became a golden egg which had the splendour of the sun. From the egg came forth Brahma, Father of all, and having come originally from the waters the god was called Narayana.[3]

In Manu's account of the creation it is said that " after dwelling for a year in the egg the glorious being, by his own contemplation, split it in twain ". [4]   The

---

[1] Budge, *The Gods of the Egyptians*, II, 63; Muir, *Original Sanskrit Texts*, IV, p. 100, and V, p. 214, and my *The Migration of Symbols*, pp. 110-1.

[2] *Polynesian Religion (B.P.B. Museum Bulletin* 34), Honolulu, Hawaii, 1927, pp. 11, 12.

[3] My *Indian Myth and Legend*, p. 101.   [4] Muir's *Sanskrit Texts*, Vol. I, p. 35.

Vayu Purāna says that " at the beginning of the day ",
the Supreme Lord " entering the egg " became the
" stimulating cause " of creation. In the *Bhāgavata
Purāna* " the living soul which resides in time, action
and natural quality, gave life to that lifeless egg floating
on the water. Purusha then having burst the egg, issued
from it." In another version the egg is broken in twain,
" from these two halves of the shell he (the creator)
fashioned the heaven and the earth, and in the middle
(he formed) the sky, and the eight quarters, and the
eternal abode of the waters ".[1] The Harivamsa version
says that the god having dwelt in the egg for a year
" divided it into two parts, heaven and earth ". In the
Vishnu Purāna the mundane egg is compared to the
coco-nut " surrounded by the outward husks ".[2]

The egg myth was known in Egypt at an earlier
period than in India. Re (Ra), the sun-god, rose from
the primordial waters as the sun-egg. Ptah of Memphis
likewise emerges from an egg, and he was also " father
of the mighty fathers (the other gods), and father of the
beginnings, he who created the sun-egg and the moon-
egg ". Shu, the god who raised the sky, had for his
sacred animal the goose, " and sometimes he is supposed
to be connected or even identical with the goose which
laid the egg whence issued the world ".[3] In the *Book of
the Dead* there are allusions to " the egg of the Great
Cackler ", which is sometimes identified with Geb, the
earth-god, and the sky goddess Nut.

In New Zealand the Supreme Being, " Io of the
Hidden Face ", was also referred to as " Io the Parent ",
" Io the Parentless ", " Io the Great ", &c. " It is
evident," says Eldon Best, " that he is not a local (Maori)
production, that the concept must hail from other lands,"
and he goes on to say:

" It is just possible that the ancestors of the Maori brought the

[1] Muir, *Sanskrit Texts*, pp. 35, 74, 156, 503.   [2] Muir, *op cit.*, Vol. IV, pp. 32 and 41.
[3] A. Weidemann, *Religion of the Ancient Egyptians*, pp. 131-2 and 231.

name of Io from an Asiatic homeland. In Renan's *History of the People of Israel* the author states that the name of Iahveh, or Iahoue, became contracted into Iahou, or Io. Of a verity it would be a startling discovery to find that Io is but a form of the name Jehovah." [1]

Hare Hongi [2] has translated a remarkable Maori chant which he gives with comments, and the following quotations illustrate its remarkable beauty and impressiveness.

" Io dwelt within the breathing-space of immensity.
The Universe was in darkness, with water everywhere.
There was no glimmer of dawn, no clearness, no light.
And he began by saying these words,
That he might cease remaining inactive:
' Darkness, become a light-possessing darkness.'
And at once light appeared.
(He) then repeated those self-same words in this manner,
That he might cease remaining inactive:
' Light, become a darkness-possessing light.'
And again an intense darkness supervened.
Then a third time he spake saying:
' Let there be one darkness above,
Let there be one darkness below (alternate) . . .
Let there be one light above
Let there be one light below (alternate) . . .
A dominion of light, a bright light.'
And now a great light prevailed.
(Io) then looked to the waters which compassed him about,
And spake a fourth time saying:
' Ye waters of Tai-Kama, be ye separate:
Heaven be formed.'
                Then the sky became suspended.
' Bring forth thou Tupua-horo-nuku.'
And at once the moving earth lay stretched abroad.

"Those words (of Io) (the supreme god) became impressed on the minds of our ancestors, and by them were transmitted down through generations; our priest joyously referred to them as being:

[1] *Some Aspects of Maori Myth and Religion*, pp. 20-1.
[2] *Journal of the Polynesian Society*, Vol. XVI, pp. 109-19.

"The ancient and original sayings,
The ancient and original words,
The ancient and original cosmological wisdom (wananga)
Which caused growth from the void,
The limitless void,
As witness the tidal-waters,
The evolved heaven,
The birth-given evolved earth."

"And now, my friends, there are three very important applications of those original sayings, as used in our sacred rituals. The first occurs in the ritual for planting a child in the barren womb. (*kopu pakoka*), or barren womb. The interest in this term centres in the idea which gives it materialization. We are clearly to understand that as Io, by using certain words, caused the solid substance of matter to issue from the void of space, so man, by using these words, can cause the barren womb to conceive and bring forth.

"The next occurs in the ritual for enlightening both the mind and body.

"The third and last occurs in the ritual on the solemn subject of death, and of war, of baptism, of genealogical recitals and such like important subjects, as the priests most particularly concerned themselves in.

"The words by which Io fashioned the Universe—that is to say, by which it was implanted and caused to produce a world of light—the same words are used in the ritual for implanting a child in a barren womb. The words by which Io caused light to shine in the darkness are used in the rituals for cheering a gloomy and despondent heart, the feeble aged, the decrepit; for shedding light into secret places and matters, for inspiration in song-composing, and in many other affairs, affecting man to despair in times of adverse war. For all such ritual to enlighten and cheer includes the words (used by Io) to overcome and dispel darkness. Thirdly, there is the preparatory ritual which treats of successive formations within the universe, and the genealogical history of man himself."

In an ancient Maori lament translated by John White [1] occur the lines:

---

[1] *The Ancient History of the Maori*, Vol. I, pp. 7-8.

" From germ of life sprang thought,
  And god's own medium came:
  Then bud and bloom; and life in space
  Produced the worlds of night . . .
  'T was Nothing that begat
  The Nothing unpossessed,
  And Nothing without charm . . .
  'T was Rangi who, with Atu-tahi,
  Brought forth the moon.
  And Rangi Wero-wero took,
  And, yet unseen, the sun produced.
  He silent, skimmed the space above,
  And then burst forth the glowing eye of heaven
  To give thee light, O man!"

A New Zealand, South Island, myth opens:

" The Atua (god) began his chant of creation at Te Po (darkness), and sang: Po begat Te-ao (light), who begat Ao-marama (daylight), who begat Ao-tu-roa (long-standing light), &c." [1]

The metaphysical concepts of the Maori, which appear to have a history rooted in India, are of striking character. White gives a creation chant connected with the " discovery of man " by the god Tane which he translates as follows:

" Night had conceived
  The seed of night.
  The heart, the foundation of night,
  Had stood forth self-existing
  Even in the gloom.
  It grows in gloom—
  The sap and succulent parts,
  The life pulsating,
  And the cup of life.
  The shadows screen
  The faintest gleam of light.
  The procreating power,
  The ecstacy of life first known,

[1] White, *op. cit.*, pp. 17–8.

> And joy of issuing forth
> From silence into sound.
> Thus the progeny
> Of the Great-extending
> Filled the heavens' expanse;
> The chorus of life
> Rose and swelled
> Into ecstacy,
> Then rested in
> Bliss of calm and quiet."

Taylor[1] gives another Maori metaphysical view of the creative process which refers to six periods beginning with the first movement of life and ending with the appearance of the gods and human beings. The first period traces life from its beginnings:

> "From the conception, the increase,
> From the increase, the swelling,
> From the swelling, the thought,
> From the thought, the remembrance,
> From the remembrance, the consciousness, the desire."

In the second period:

> "The word became fruitful;
> It dwelt with the feeble glimmering;
> It brought forth night:
> The great night, the long night . . .
> The night ending in death."

The third period follows:

> "From the nothing, the begetting,
> From the nothing, the increase,
> From the nothing, the abundance,
> The power of increasing, the living breath;
> It dwelt with the empty space,
> It produced the atmosphere which is above."

In the fourth period the sun and moon appear; in the

---

[1] Richard Taylor, *Te ika a Maui*, London, 1870, pp. 109-11.

fifth the sky is part of the earth, or dwells with the earth, not having been separated from the earth, and the islands are born. As stated, the gods and human beings have origin in the sixth period.

These extracts from the memorized ancient literature of the higher priestly cults resemble the speculations of the early Hindu thinkers regarding the origin of all things. E. B. Havell has compiled the following " Hymn of Creation " from surviving fragments:

> " There was neither existence, nor non-existence,
>   The Kingdom of air, nor the sky beyond.

> " What was there to contain, to cover in—
>   Was it but vast, unfathomed depth of water?

> " There was no Death there, nor Immortality.
>   No sun was there, dividing day from night.

> " Then was there only THAT, resting within itself.
>   Apart from IT, there was not anything.

> " At first within the darkness veiled in darkness,
>   Chaos unknowable, the All lay hid.

> " Till straightway from the formless void made manifest
>   By the great power of heat was born that germ." [1]

In the Hindu *Upanishads* the fundamental idea is the identity of Brahmă and the supreme and eternal Atman (self) which is the creative power. One account of creation begins:

> " At first the Universe was not anything. There was neither sky, nor earth, nor air. Being non-existent it resolved, ' Let me be '. It became fervent. From that fervour smoke was produced. It again became fervent. From that fervour fire was produced."

The fire became rays, the rays condensed like a cloud and the cloud produced the water which formed the sea.

[1] E. B. Havell, *Benares, The Sacred City*, pp. 4–5.

" Mind (or soul, *manas*) was created from the non-existent," explains a priestly commentator. " Mind created Prajapati (the god). Prajapati created offspring. All this, whatever exists, rests absolutely on mind." [1]

As in Hindu so in Polynesian religious literature the various narratives of creation are not easy to reconcile. The speculations of various " schools of thought " of various periods and from different areas of origin are to be detected. It would appear, however, that the metaphysical views of creation from the various island groups in which they have been collected were imported by the exclusive higher priesthoods who had been in contact with the Brahmanic " schools " in Indonesia or in India itself. It is now being generally recognized that in Brahmanic religious literature are to be traced the ideas of the pre-Aryan Dravidian teachers of India who were in touch with Mesopotamia.

In no other country was the doctrine of the World's Ages more highly developed than in Brahmanic India, and, as has been indicated, there are traces of that doctrine in Polynesia. After a succession of Ages the Universe, according to Brahmanic ideas, was destroyed. All life and all matter then returned to the supreme Atman (self), the Germ. " The whole universe," says the *Katha Upanishad*, " trembles within the life (Brahmă); emanating from it (Brahmă) the Universe moves on." When the Universe was at the end of a succession of Ages, a Kalpa (Day) of Brahmă, returned to the Atman, Brahmă slept and when consciousness was revived, the process of " creating anew " began again.

The " World Tree " is to be met with in Polynesian as in Hindu mythology and in the mythologies of other peoples.

[1] Muir's *Original Sanskrit Texts*, Vol. I, pp. 29–30. Deussen's *Philosophy of the Upanishads*, p. 39. My *Indian Myth and Legend*, pp. 99 *et seq.*

CHAPTER XIII

Traditions of the Deluge

The Deluge and the World's Ages—Hindu, Aztec, and Greek Doctrines—
Buddha and the Maori Puta—Puta causes Flood—Maori Three Destructions
of World—South Island Maori Myth—Traces of Christian Influence—Hindu
and Babylonian Features — Hawaiian Version — Marquesan Chant of the
Deluge—Taaro (Tangaloa) causes Flood in Society and Windward Islands—
Refugees on Mountains—Shower of Stones from the Sky—Sea-god causes
Deluge—Island of Refuge—Babylonian Origin of this Island—The Deluge
Storms—Peruvian and Aztec Myths—Fijian Deluge — Human Rebellion
against God—Links with Egyptian Myth—Flood Myths and Creation
Myths—Flood caused by Rival Gods—Micronesian Flood Stories—Mouse-
woman causes Yap Flood—The Mouse as a Life-giver.

Throughout the South Sea Islands there existed in
pre-Christian times a number of versions of the ancient
Deluge story. In some cases, as has been indicated, the
story is connected, as in India, with the doctrine of the
World's Ages. As is indicated in the previous chapter,
it was believed by the ancient Hindus that a group of
Ages (Yugas) formed a Kalpa, or Day of Brahma. " At
the close of this Day of Brahma," according to ancient
texts, " a collapse of the universe takes place, which lasts
through a Night of Brahma, equal in duration to his
Day, during which period the three worlds are converted
into one great ocean. . . . At the end of that Night he
(Brahma) awakes and creates anew." [1]

There is no trace in the Rig-veda of this doctrine of
Ages. In the *Satapatha Brahmana* and certain other
Hindu sacred works no mention is made of any great
mundane periods in connexion with the Deluge. Manu,

[1] Muir's *Original Sanskrit Texts*, Vol. V, pp. 43-4.

the Hindu Noah, survives the flood in his ship which ultimately grounds on a high mountain. It is possible that the doctrine of the World's Ages was a Dravidian one, which was originally derived from Mesopotamia.

The Aztecs of Mexico acquired the doctrine of the World's Ages, but they believed there was a cataclysm at the end of each of the four Ages. At the end of the first Age came a deluge; the second Age was brought to an end by violent winds, and the third Age by fire. Famine destroyed a " considerable portion " of the people at the end of the fourth Age.

Hesiod gives the Greek system of Ages. At the end of the Bronze Age Zeus said: " I will send a great rain such as hath not been seen since the making of the world, and the whole race of men shall perish. I am weary of their iniquity." [1]

In one of the Maori stories of the Deluge the disaster is brought about by Puta. S. Percy Smith compares this name with that of Buddha of India. " The word Buddha," he writes, " is an impossible form in any Polynesian dialect as at present constituted, and it is quite clear that the form the name would take in Polynesia would be Puta." [2]

According to Maori tradition Puta was " the man who was commissioned to call on all the people of the world to believe in God. He built a temple in which to teach men how to become noble." But the people would not heed him and said: " Your words are lies." In the end Puta placed sacred offerings in a calabash.

" Having arrived on the bank of a stream, he opened the calabash, and then closed it again; and saw a cloud standing in the heaven, bright as the brightness of a fire burning on the earth. He called to Raki to overturn the earth, and he struck the earth with his knife (*maipi*), and the earth turned upside down, and all the

---

[1] My *Myths of Pre-Columbian America*, pp. 64 *et seq.*
[2] *Hawaiki*, (Fourth Edition), p. 70.

people of the world perished. Puta and his people alone were saved." [1]

White gives a Maori summary of three separate destructions of the earth:

" Puta was the cause of the land being turned upside down in the days of Mata-iho (face bowed down), or Mata-aho (shining face), when trees and vegetation, and also the greater part of men were destroyed.

" The second upsetting of the land was in the days of Wi (dread), or I (was) and A (am). This was of the same destructive character as the first. Then Hapopo (decay) folded up the sun, and caused the death of a vast multitude.

" To Ui (ask) belonged the fire of destruction, and Puta caused the commotion which overthrew the earth, so that the animals of this world, and the birds, and the *moa*, and others of the same kind, were destroyed." [2]

Another Maori myth makes Tupu-tupu-nui-a-uta " the cause of the flood ".

" He asked for rain, and such torrents descended as produced a flood, which continued to rise until the plains, the hills, and the highest peaks of the mountains were covered by it; and all mankind, except those who had prepared a raft, and had taken refuge on it, perished in the water." [3]

The longest Maori version is full of interesting details. It opens as follows:

" Men had become very numerous on the earth. There were many great tribes. Evil prevailed everywhere. The tribes quarrelled and wars were frequent. The worship of Tane (the god) was neglected and his doctrines openly denied. The teachings of Para-whenua-mea (*débris* of the flood) and Tupu-nui-a-uta (the King of the interior) respecting the separation of Rangi (heaven) and Papa (earth) were disputed, and men obstinately opposed their doctrines, and declared them to be false teachers, and asserted that

---

[1] John White, *The Ancient History of the Maori*, Vol. I, pp. 168–9 (Wellington, N.Z., 1887).

[2] J. White, *op. cit.*, p. 181.   [3] J. White, *op. cit.*, p. 180.

Rangi and Papa were now as they were when the world was made, and that Tane had not done any of the things he was said to have done."

The Teachers referred to above endeavoured to establish the sacred doctrines of their faith, but the people flouted and cursed them. Then Tupu-nui-a-uta and Para-whenua-mea cut down trees with their stone adzes and made a " very wide raft " which was bound together by ropes and vines. On this raft they erected a house in which they put " much food—fern-root, Kumara (sweet potatoes) and dogs ". In a *paua*-shell (*haliotes*) they put holy water, which they used in their ceremonies, when repeating incantations. The myth proceeds:

" Para-whenua-mea and Tupu-nui-a-uta then repeated incantations, and prayed that rain might descend in such abundance as would convince men of the power of Tane, and prove the truth of his existence and the necessity of the ceremonies of worship for life and for peace, and to avert evil and death."

The teachers and some females go on the raft; Tiu prays for rain which falls in torrents. " When it had so rained for four or five days and nights, he (Tiu) repeated incantations that it might cease, and it ceased." The flood comes next day, the raft floats down the river Tohinga and unbelievers are drowned.

The myth goes on to tell that the raft drifted to various places. At one a sacrifice is offered to the gods. At another " sacred fire " is produced by friction:

" Para-whenua-mea took grass, and held it over the sacred fire and took it away again; again he held it over the sacred fire. This he did so that they might cook food for themselves on that fire."

Offerings of fire-sanctified grass are made to the gods, and bundles of grass are consecrated to the males and females on the raft.

"When these presentations and thank - offerings had been made to the gods, they took fern-root, and with it touched the lips of all—first of the men, then of the women, and then of the children. Then, for the first time, they partook of cooked food."

Goddesses were afterwards seen "wandering on the face of the ocean". The raft drifts about for seven months. Then Tiu expresses the belief that they will all reach land and not perish. On the eighth month he observes that the sea "has begun to subside". He is asked how he knows and answers, "By the sign of my staff". The myth goes on to say:

"He had kept his *wananga*, or altar, on one side of the deck, where he performed his ceremonies and repeated his incantations, and observed his staff, which he also kept there; and by his knowledge and constant devotion to his ceremonies he understood the signs of his staff. Hence he again said to his companions, ' The blustering winds of the past moons have become less strong. The great winds of the past moons have become weaker now, and the winds of this month have died away, and the sea has become calm.' "

In the end the raft reaches dry land at Hawaiki. They found that all human beings except themselves had been destroyed, " and the land had materially changed: it had cracked in parts, had been turned upside down, and had been confused by the power of the flood . . . the earth had completely changed in appearance ".

On landing they perform ceremonies to Tane, Rangi and Rehua and other deities, and repeat incantations. Offerings of sea-weed were made:

"As they addressed each god consecutively, a portion of the sea-weed of the length of the two thumbs of the priest was broken off the main piece. Each god was addressed at a different spot. The altar to each god, on which each offering was left, and before which the incantations were repeated, was a root of grass, a shrub, or tree, or flax-bush."

The ceremonies were afterwards observed, but only the chief priest could approach the altars. Ordinary people who did so would die because the food would swell in their stomachs. The myth explains in detail the entire ceremony.

Next day food was offered, and it was partaken of, first by the high priest and then by the others. Then they beheld the rainbow and a star to which sacrifices were made.[1]

Elsdon Best regards with suspicion this myth from the South Island of New Zealand and inclines to reject it. " It seems," he says, " to be based upon missionary teachings. A number of expressions used, such as *whakapono*, are employed in such a way as to show that the relator was conversant with the Maori edition of the Bible. Evidently some enthusiastic Christianized native introduced a number of names of mythical beings of Maori lore into a garbled description of the old Babylonian myth beloved of our own teachers. The statement that a great flood was sent to punish men because they refused to heed the admirable teachings of Tane is certainly Biblical, but is utterly opposed to the trend of Maori lore." [2]

This seems to be too sweeping a judgment. If the Maori teller of the myth had been drawing upon the Maori bible alone, he would scarcely have omitted mention of the animals taken on board Noah's ark, and the sending forth of the birds to ascertain if the flood was subsiding. In some of the Hindu myths the rain is mentioned as the cause of the flood. The storms of wind are a feature of the Babylonian myths and are not mentioned in the Biblical account.[3] In this Maori myth we are told that as the flood subsides, " the great winds of the past moons have become weaker ". It may be that the reason for the flood being sent as given in this

[1] J. White, *op. cit.*. Vol. I, Chap. XII.   [2] *The Maori*, Vol. I. pp. 150–1.
[3] The only wind is the one which God made " to pass over the earth, and the waters assuaged ", *Genesis*, viii, 1.

Maori myth is really of Biblical origin. The rest appears to be mainly of pre-Christian character. Best's " enthusiastic Christianized native " had apparently a genuine Maori flood-myth to repeat, and prefaced it with a paraphrase of the Biblical narrative.

Fornander refers to several Hawaiian versions of the flood myth. " Some," he says, " indicate the decay and corruption of the original legend." In one version the Noah is Nuu or Nana-Nuu or Lana (*l* and *n* being interchangeable). Nana or Lana means " floating ". The " Floating Nuu " may well be the Biblical Noah. He is commanded by his god to build a large vessel for himself and his wife and his three sons and their wives. When the flood subsides their vessel strands on the top of Mauna-Kea, the highest mountain on the island of Hawaii, where there is a cave which is called after the wife of Nuu. Before leaving the ship the three gods Kane, Ku and Lono enter it and tell Nuu to go out.

A Marquesan myth, " Chant of the Deluge ", is " a remarkable specimen of native poetry ". It relates that the Lord of the Ocean is to overwhelm the land. A respite of seven days is granted. The myth names the animals which are to be saved, and tells that a house is built " high above the waters ". This house has several stories " with chambers, with openings for light, stored with provisions for the preservation of the various animals ". The animals are tied in couples and marched into " this big, deep house of wood. Then the family enter; it consists of four men and four women. . . . Then the storm bursts over them; the rain is pouring fearfully, and gloom prevails; all on earth is displaced and mixed up with the waters ". After a time a dark bird is sent out. It returns, but when it is sent out a second time it alights on sand; it is, however, recalled. Another bird is liberated and it returns with young shoots or branches. " The land is now dry," and the men and animals leave the " house ".

Fornander translates the poetical chant which his friend Lawson had collected. It opens as follows:

" The Lord Ocean is going to pass over the whole dry land.
  A respite is granted for seven days.
  Who would have thought to bury the great earth in a roaring
      flood?"

The singer rejoices that he and the others are to be " reserved on the flood ":

> " The flood, the roaring.
>   And it will fall over the valleys,
>   Pass over the plains,
>   It will bury the mountains,
>   And envelope the hill-sides,
>   O the flood, the roaring."

In the " house " the human beings and the animals are carried " away to sea ". The singer complains of the discomforts experienced:

> " Crush, crackle, a stinking crowd.
>   Bring together, pell-mell,
>   All the heaven-fed animals.
>   Sleeps the sacred supporter in this noise.
>   Noise, God, noise, with God arise!
>   God wills it."

The wind roars, the rain falls, " shaken up and mixed up is the earth ". In time the flood subsides and the singer says:

> " I will offer seven sacred offerings
>   And seven sucklings that shall cry
>   To the Lord Ocean.
>   The Lord has assented that the earth
>   Shall now be dry."

Fornander notes that this chant, " like all the ancient Polynesian chants, is replete with tropes and allusions of which the original meaning is in many instances now forgotten ".[1]   Here again an old myth seems to have been influenced by the flood narrative as related by missionaries.

Ellis[2] was not surprised to find that "traditions of the Deluge, the most important event in reference to the external structure and appearance of our globe that has occurred since its creation, have been found to exist among the natives of the South Sea Islands, from the earliest period of their history ". He considered that " the striking analogy between those (traditions) religiously preserved by the inhabitants of the islands of the Pacific, and the Mosaic account, would seem to indicate a degree of high antiquity belonging to this isolated (Polynesian) people ".

Ellis found that different versions existed in the island groups—different " in several minor particulars ". One group which recognized Taaroa (Tangaloa) as the principal god and creator, told that this deity became angry with men on account of their disobedience to his will and " overturned the world into the sea ". The earth sank in the deep, " excepting a few *aurus*, or projecting points, which, remaining above its surface, constituted the present cluster of islands ". The people of Eimeo believed that after the flood subsided " a man landed from a canoe near Tiataepua, in their island, and erected an altar, or *marae*, in honour of his god ". This was the Polynesian Noah.

Mr. Orsmond gave Ellis the following translation of the Deluge tradition preserved among the Windward Islands:

" Destroyed was Tahiti by the sea; no man, nor hog, nor fowl, nor dog, remained. The groves of trees and the stones were carried away by the wind. They were destroyed, and the Deep was over the land. But these two persons, the husband and the

[1] A. Fornander, *An Account of the Polynesian Race*, London, 1878, Vol. I, pp. 88 *et seq.* and 225 *et seq.*

[2] *Polynesian Researches* (First Edition), Vol. II, pp. 57 *et seq.*, and (Second Edition), Vol. I, pp. 382 *et seq.*

wife, (when it came in), the wife took up her young chicken; the husband took up his young pig; the wife took up her young dog and the kitten; the husband took up that.[1] They were going forth and looking at Orofena:[2] the husband said, ' Up, both of us, to yonder mountain high.' The wife replied, ' No, let us not go thither.' The husband said, ' It is a high or long rock, and will not be reached by the sea'; but the wife replied, ' Reached will be it by the sea yonder, we two on the mountain round as a breast, O Pito-hito; it will not be reached by the sea.'[3] They two arrived there. Orofena was overwhelmed by the sea; that mountain, Pito-hiti (alone) remained; that was their abode.

" There they watched nights ten,[4] the sea ebbed, and they two saw the little heads of the mountains in their elevation. When the sea dried or retired, the land remained without produce, without man, and the fish were putrid in the caves and holes of the rocks. They said, ' Dig a hole for the fish in the sea.' The wind also was becoming feeble, and when it was dead or calm, the stones and the trees began to fall from the heavens; thither they had been carried by the wind. All trees of the land had been torn up, and carried high by the wind. They two looked about, and the woman said, ' Safe are we two from the sea, but death, or hurt, comes now in these stones that are falling. Where shall we abide? Torn by the roots up had been all the trees, and carried above the pathway of the rain in the heavens.

" ' Dig a hole for us two, a dwelling place.' The hole was dug, covered with grass the bottom of the hole or cave; stones were spread on the top of the hole, and these covered over with earth. While these two were sitting within, they heard with terror the loud voice of the falling stones. Now they fell more thinly, then one little stone at a time fell, and afterwards ceased entirely.

" The woman said, ' Arise you, and advance without, and see if the stones fall.' The man replied, ' I go not out, I shall die.' He waited till night and till day, and then said, ' The wind is truly dead, and the stones and the trunks of trees cease to fall, neither is there the sound of the stones.' They went out, and like

---

[1] The translator notes that " these were all the animals known to the people, and the term *fanaua* (young) is both singular and plural, so that it may apply to one, or to more than one chicken, &c."

[2] High mountain in Tahiti.

[3] She meant " Let us to the other mountain which will not be reached by the sea."

[4] The natives reckoned time by nights instead of days.

a small mountain was the heap or collection of the stones and the wood. The earth and the rocks remained of the land; the shrubs were destroyed by the sea. They descended, and gazed with astonishment. There were no houses, nor coco-nuts, nor palm trees, nor bread-fruit, nor hibiscus, nor grass; all was destroyed by the sea. They two dwelt together. The woman brought forth two children; one was a son, the other a daughter. They grieved that there was no food for their children. Again the mother brought forth, but still there was no food. The children grew up without food; then the bread-fruit bore fruit, and the coco-nut and every other kind of food. In three days encircled or covered was the land with food. The land became covered with men. From two persons, the father and the mother, filled was the land."

Ellis gives the Deluge tradition of the island of Raiatea. It tells that after the peopling of the world, the sea-god Ruahatu, was reposing in slumber in his sacred place " among the coralline groves in the depths of the ocean ". This place was taboo (*tapu*), but a fisherman paddled his canoe upon the forbidden waters and cast out his hooks. These hooks " became entangled in the hair of the sleeping god ". The fisherman tugged for a long time. They became disentangled but the god had been rudely awakened and he arose to the surface. He upbraided the fisherman for his impiety and declared " that the land was criminal, or convicted of guilt, and should be destroyed ". The fisherman confessed his sorrow and implored the god to forgive him, asking that the threatened destruction should be averted, or that he himself might escape.

" Ruhatu, moved by his penitence and importunity, directed him to return home for his wife and child, and then proceed to a small island called Toamarama which is situated within the reefs on the eastern side of Raiatea. Here he was promised security, amid the destruction of the surrounding islands.

" The man hastened to his residence, and proceeded with his wife and child to the place appointed. Some say he took with him a friend who was residing under his roof, with a dog, a pig, and a pair of fowls, so that the party consisted of four individuals, besides the only domesticated animals known in the islands.

"They reached the refuge appointed, before the close of the day; and as the sun approached the horizon, the waters of the ocean began to rise, the inhabitants of the adjacent shore left their dwellings on the beach and fled to the mountains. The waters continued to rise during the night, and the next morning the tops of the mountains only appeared above the wide-spread sea. These were afterwards covered, and all the inhabitants of the land perished. The waters subsequently retired, the fisherman and his companions left their retreat, took up their abode on the mainland, and became the progenitors of the present inhabitants."

Ellis goes on to say that the people of the northern and southern groups of islands with whom he conversed on the subject of the Deluge knew nothing of " the windows of heaven having been opened, or the rain having descended ". He adds:

" In the legend of Ruahatu, the Toamarama of Tahiti, and the Kai of Kahinarii in Hawaii, the inundation is ascribed to the rising of the waters of the sea. In each account the anger of the god is considered as the cause of the inundation of the world, and the destruction of its inhabitants. The element employed in effecting it is the same as that mentioned in the Bible; and in the Tahitian tradition the boat or canoe being used as the means of safety to the favoured family, and the preservation of the only domestic animals found on the islands, appear corrupted fragments of the memorial of Noah, the ark, and its inmates."

It is more probable that the Polynesian myths of the Deluge were derived from Indian and Babylonian sources. The Babylonian Noah Ut-napistim (Sumerian Ziusudu) and his wife who escaped in their boat during the Deluge, afterwards resided on an island. The memory of this island may have given the Deluge tradition of Raiatea its distinctive character, the island being confused with the ark or boat. In the earlier Sumerian version Ziusudu, after escaping the Deluge, is sent by the gods to the " land, the land of Dilmun "[1] or to dwell " on a mountain,

---

[1] Identified with the island of Bahrein in the Persian Gulf.

the mountain of Dilmun ".[1] The Babylonian deluge was preceded by a great storm:

"The whirlwind of Ramman mounted up into the heavens."

In the Sumerian version the flood " overwhelmed the land " for seven days and seven nights, and in the Babylonian for six days and six nights. " The wind storm," says the former, " had driven the great boat over the mighty waters."[2]

In the Peruvian myth the Noah is warned by a Uama of the approaching deluge, and told to seek refuge on the summit of a mountain for five days. On reaching that retreat the Noah finds that numerous animals have already arrived there. The sea rose and covered the land, and all living beings were destroyed, except those on the mountain summit. Ellis draws attention to the resemblance of this myth to the Deluge myth of Hawaii. The Aztec myth of Mexico, he considers, corresponds, on the other hand, to the Tahitian story. It, however, bears a closer resemblance to the Babylonian myth. The Noah is named Coxcox and he and his wife survive in a boat. The people of Michuacan called their Noah Tezpi and tell that his boat was filled with various kinds of animals. Two birds were sent out to ascertain if the flood had subsided, one being the vulture and the other the humming bird. A Codex of the Nahuath tells that a god warned Nata and his wife Nena of the coming flood, instructing that a boat should be constructed from a tree. In this boat the couple, during the deluge, lit a fire and cooked fish. The smoke rose to the heavens and a god became angry.[3] In the Sumerian version of the myth Ziusudu offers up a sacrifice in his boat to acquaint the gods with his survival.[4]

---

[1] Leonard W. King, *Legends of Babylon and Egypt in relation to Hebrew Tradition* (The Schweich Lectures, 1916), London, 1918, p. 90, and Note 1.

[2] L. W. King, *op. cit.*, p. 78.

[3] Prescott, *History of Mexico*, Appendix 1 quoting authorities.

[4] L. W. King, *op. cit.*, p. 84.

The Rev. Thomas Williams and the Rev. James Calvert collected in the Fiji group of islands several versions of a Deluge myth and write regarding them:[1]

"They speak of a deluge which, according to some of their accounts, was partial, but in others is stated to have been universal. The cause of this great flood was the killing of Turukawa—a favourite bird belonging to Ndengei—by two mischievous lads, the grandsons of the god. These, instead of apologizing for their offence, added insolent language to the outrage, and fortifying, with the assistance of their friends, the town in which they lived, defied Ndengei to do his worst. It is said that although the angry god took three months to collect his forces, he was unable to subdue the rebels, and, disbanding his army, resolved on more efficient revenge. At his command the dark clouds gathered and burst, pouring streams on the devoted earth. Towns, hills, mountains were successively submerged; but the rebels, secure in the superior height of their own dwelling-place, looked on without concern. But when, at last, the terrible surges invaded their fortress, they cried for direction to a god who, according to one account, instructed them to form a float of the fruit of the shaddock; according to another, sent two canoes for their use; or, says a third, taught them how to build a canoe, and thus secure their own safety. All agree that the highest places were covered, and the remnant of the human race saved in some kind of vessel, which was at last left by the subsiding waters on Mbenga; hence the Mbengans draw their claim to stand first in Fijian rank. The number saved—eight—exactly accords with the 'few' of the Scripture record. By this flood it is said that two tribes of the human family became extinct. One consisted entirely of women, and the other were distinguished by the appendage of a tail like that of a dog. The highest point of the island of Koro is associated with the history of the Flood. Its name is *Ngginggi-tangithi-Koro*, which conveys the idea of a little bird sitting there and lamenting the drowned island. In this bird the Christians recognize Noah's dove on its second flight from the ark. I have heard a native, after listening to the incident as given by Moses, chant ' *Na qiqi sa tagici Koro ni yali*—The Qiqi laments over Koro, because it is lost.' "

This Fijian version of the flood is reminiscent at

[1] *Fiji and the Fijians* London, 1858, p. 196.

the outset of the Ancient Egyptian myth of the " Destruction of Mankind ".   An offence is committed against the god who takes some time to collect his forces. The rebels flee to the mountains and in their high fortress think they are secure.   A flood is sent but at first they regard it without concern.   As the waters rise, however, they become alarmed, and a god instructs them to make a float, or he sends two canoes for their use, or teaches them how to build a canoe.

The Egyptian myth tells that when the sun-god Re (Ra) grew old " mankind took counsel against his majesty ".   The god grew alarmed and consults, among others, his father Nu, the god of the primeval waters, to whom he says, " Mankind, who had their being from mine eye, hold counsel against me.   Tell me what ye would do in face of this."

Nu advises him, " Turn thine eye gainst those who conspire against thee."

Re says, " Behold men flee unto the hills; their heart is full of fear because of that which they said."

The " eye " is the goddess Sekhet-Hathor who goes against the rebels armed with a knife.   She slaughters the human rebels until she " waded in the blood of men ".

Re becomes alarmed at the slaughter and causes a great quantity of beer to be prepared.   It is made the colour of blood with a red substance.   Seven thousand jars of this mixture are emptied and the goddess finds the fields inundated.   She drank of the soporific liquid, became intoxicated, and " took no more cognizance of men ".   It was Re who said, " I shall protect mankind against her (the destroying goddess) ".

There is no trace in the Hindu Deluge myths of a story of this kind.   The Fijian account of a human rebellion, or of a wrong done by human beings against a god, and of a god taking pity on the men on the mountains and arranging to rescue them, appears to be remotely connected with the Ancient Egyptian myth which may have been carried to Oceania by the ancient mariners who introduced the Egyptian custom of mummification and Egyptian ideas regarding the sun's connexion with stone.

The South Sea deluge myths have an essential connexion with the myth of the origin of the world from the primordial deep. The mysterious sacred bird in the Fijian myth is to be found in the Samoan story of creation as given by the Rev. George Turner[1] of the London Missionary Society, which is as follows:

" The earliest traditions of the Samoans describe a time when the heavens alone were inhabited, and the earth covered over with water. Tangaloa, the great Polynesian Jupiter, then sent down his daughter in the form of a bird called the turi (snipe), to search for a resting-place. After flying about for a long time, she found a rock partially above the surface of the water. . . . Turi went up and told her father that she had found but one spot on which she could rest. Tangaloa sent her down again to visit the place. She went to and fro repeatedly, and, every time she went up, reported that the dry surface was extending on all sides. He then sent her down with some earth and a creeping plant, as all was barren rock."

The plant grew, spread, withered and decomposed and worms which appeared on it became human beings. Turner, in a footnote, refers to another account which represents Tangaloa " rolling down from the heavens two great stones, one of which became the island of Savaii, the other Upolu ".

The Egyptian god Re, against whom men rebelled, ascended to the sky world. In a Maori myth the god Ta-whaki " at one period lived on earth. . . . Ta-whaki caused the deluge by stamping on the floor of heaven until it cracked, and a flood of water flowed down and covered the earth ". Like Osiris (who was fused with Re) " Ta-whaki was killed by his brother-in-law ", but " came to life again ".[2]

[1] *Nineteen Years in Polynesia*, 1861. pp. 244–5.
[2] John White, *The Ancient History of the Maori*, Vol. I, p. 55.

The Rev. W. W. Gill gives a myth from Mangaia in the Cook group of islands which tells of the rivalry between the sea-deity Ake and the sky-deity Aokeu. The former makes the sea rise and flood the land, and the latter sends rain which increases the flood. A small portion of land is left and the king who takes refuge on it prays to Rongo who forces Ake and Aokeu to cease, and the flood then retreats.[1]

The Pelew Islanders have, according to Kubary, a myth which tells that a god was killed by the wicked natives in days of old. A woman informs the other gods who resolve to send a flood. The woman is advised to make a raft. She does so and ties it to a tree. As the rope was too short she was drowned. The gods restore her to life and decide to make her an immortal by giving her to drink of the Water of Immortality. One of the gods, however, pricks the leaf in which this water was carried and the water all escaped. This woman was the sole survivor after the flood and became the ancestress of mankind.[2]

On the island of Yap the flood is caused by a mouse-woman or mouse-goddess. The daughter of this woman was a beautiful girl who dwelt under a stone in a grassy field. As she sat on this stone watching kites that were being flown, a man threw a net over her and thus captured her. The girl became his wife. After her baby was born the grandmother appeared in her mouse form. The man killed the mouse with the result that after seven days a typhoon came and caused a flood. His wife caused the waters to retreat by muttering a spell over boiled coco-nut milk which she sprinkled on the waters. This woman was the ancestress of the Mouse Clan.[3] Here we have the flood caused by the slaying of a sacred

---

[1] Rev. W. W. Gill, *Life in the Southern Isles*, London, 1888, p. 80.

[2] J. Kubary, *Die Religion der Pelauer*, in Berlin work, and Sir J. G. Frazer's *The Belief in Immortality*, Vol. III, p. 259 *et seq.*

[3] W. Müller, *Yap*, pp. 622 *et seq.*, and Sir J. G. Frazer, *The Belief in Immortality*, Vol. III, pp. 199–200.

mouse instead of a sacred bird. The sun-god Apollo had a mouse form. In India the god Ganesha was connected with the mouse. There were " mouse-lords " in ancient Ireland, and mouse-feasts in ancient Scotland. Mr. Warren R. Dawson has dealt with the mouse in religion in an article in *Folk-lore*.[1] There can be little doubt, in view of the evidence brought together by Mr. Dawson that the widely-scattered beliefs connected with the mouse as a " life-giver " had their origin in Ancient Egypt.

[1] Vol. XXXVI, pp. 227 *et seq*. A Perthshire standing stone is connected with the mouse.

CHAPTER XIV

Marriage of Heaven and Earth

Classic and Hindu Myths—Sky-god and Earth-goddess—Sky-goddess of
Egypt and India—Separation of Heaven and Earth—Egyptian and Hindu
Versions—Maori Versions—Rangi as Sky-god and Papa as Earth-mother—
Tane, the Polynesian Shu—Tane sets Stars in their Places—The Sky Covering
—Magical Separation Chant—A Sky-god who formerly was a Man—The
Maori Osiris-Re—Mountain Road to Sky World—Slain God comes to Life
Again—The Wars of the Gods—Rebels expelled from Sky—Separation Myths
from Various Island Groups—Ruu and Maui as Gods of Cardinal Points—
How they raised the Sky—Octopus holds down the Sky—Micronesian Myths
—The Serpent Props of Sky—Indonesian Myths—Asiatic and European
Myths—Polynesian Concepts not "Primitive".

"The marriage of Heaven and Earth," writes a
French author,[1] "forms the foundation of a hundred
mythologies." In the Greek Theogony of Hesiod
"broad-bosomed Earth" rises out of Chaos and becomes
"the firm abode of all things", and she "produces the
starry Heaven, co-extensive with herself, to envelop her
on every part". In Hesiod's *Work and Days*, Earth is
"mother of all things", and in the Homeric hymns she
is "the universal mother . . . the mother of the gods,
and the spouse of starry Uranus (the sky)". "Mother
Earth" is addressed and invoked by several Greek poets.

In India Dyaus (Heaven) and Prithivī (Earth) are
the "prolific parents" of all creatures. The ancient
Vedic hymns have many references to the sky-father and
the earth-mother. "Heaven and Earth," writes Dr.
J. Muir, "are regarded as the parents not only of men,
but of the gods also." [2]

"Contrary to the usual mythical conception," says Sir

---

[1] A. Réville, *Essais de Critique Religieuse*, p. 383.
[2] *Original Sanskrit Texts*, Vol. V, pp. 21 *et seq.*

J. G. Frazer, " the Egyptians regarded the earth as male
and the sky as female ".[1] But Sir James overlooks the
evidence regarding the Hindu goddess Aditi who was
the mother of Varuna and Mitra, and other gods called
" Adityas ". She appears to be sometimes identified with
the sky. In a Vedic hymn she is " the sky, Aditi, towering
to the empyrean ". As a rule, " her sons the Adityas are
. . . mentioned separately from the other gods ". Muir
notes that Aditi was " distinguished from the Earth ",[2]
but he does not seem to recognize sufficiently that even
in Vedic times the process of blending two different
groups of deities was already well advanced.

In Egypt, according to one of the cosmogonical
myths the god Shu separates Heaven and Earth. A text
in a Theban tomb says of him: " He has divided the
heaven from the earth; he has uplifted the heaven in
eternity above the earth." As Wiedemann notes " other
texts ascribe to him the uplifting of the primeval waters
(Nû), the pillars of heaven and the like. . . . The radical
meaning of his name can scarcely be other than ' the
Uplifter', corresponding to the root *shu*, ' to uplift, to
uplift oneself', and expresses the belief that he was the
supporter of the heavens, or the divinity who had once
uplifted them and thus separated them from the earth.
In later texts he becomes the representative of the glowing heat of the sun, or the hot wind. This is a misplaced
identification, doubtless brought about by the accidental
assonance of the above-mentioned root *shu*, with the roots
signifying ' to be hot, to be parched up' and ' wind ' ".[3]

The myth of the separation of Heaven and Earth has
been traced in India. In the *Aitareya Brāhmana* (iv. 27),
as translated by Professor Haug [4] we read:

" These two worlds (heaven and earth) were once joined.
(Subsequently) they separated. (After their separation) there fell

---

[1] *The Golden Bough* (*Adonis, Attis, Osiris* vol.), 1907 Edition, p. 237, Note 3.
[2] *Original Sanskrit Texts*, Vol. V, pp. 35 *et seq.*
[3] A. Wiedemann, *Religion of the Ancient Egyptians*, pp. 32–3.   [4] Vol. II, p. 308.

neither rain, nor was there sunshine. The five classes of beings (gods, men, &c.) then did not keep peace with one another. (There-upon) the gods brought about a reconciliation of both these worlds. Both contracted with one another a marriage according to the rites observed by the gods. . . . That world approached this world: thence were produced heaven and earth: neither the heaven nor the earth was produced from the air."

In the Taittirīya Āranyaka it is definitely stated that " the Earth is the wife, the Sky is the husband, they are a pair ".[1]

In Indonesia and Polynesia there are a number of versions of the myth of the separation of Heaven and Earth, and Maori mythology tells not only of this separation but of the war of the gods.

Sir George Grey, in one of the classics of Polynesian mythology, gives a Maori version of the ancient myth:

" Men had but one pair of primitive ancestors; they sprang from the vast heaven that exists above us, and from the earth which lies beneath us. According to the traditions of our race Ranga and Papa, or Heaven and Earth, were the source from which, in the beginning, all things originated. Darkness then rested upon the heaven and upon the earth, and they still clave together, for they had not yet been rent apart. . . .

" At last the beings who had been begotten by Heaven and Earth, worn out by the continued darkness, consulted among themselves, saying: ' Let us now determine what we should do with Rangi and Papa, whether it would be better to slay them or to rend them apart.'

" Then spoke Tu-matauenga, the fiercest of the children of Heaven and Earth: ' It is well, let us slay them.'

" Then spake Tane-mahuta, the father of forests and of all things that inhabit them, or that are constructed from trees, ' Nay, not so. It is better to rend them apart, and to let the heaven stand far above us, and the earth lie under our feet. Let the sky become as a stranger to us, but the earth remain close to us as our nursing mother."

Five of the brother gods consented to this proposal,

but one of them, Tawhiri-ma-tea, the father of winds and storms, objected, fearing that his power was to be overthrown.

The first god who attempted to separate the sky and the earth was Rongo-ma-tane, god of agriculture. When he failed, Tangaroa, god of fish and reptiles, Haumia, god of food which is not cultivated, and Tu-matauenga, god of fierce human beings, each tried in vain to accomplish the task. Then slowly arose Tane-mahuta, the god of forests, birds, insects, &c. He failed at first, but after a pause he stood on his head and thrust the sky upward with his feet.

Rangi, the sky god, and Papa, the earth mother, groaned and shrieked in their sorrow because they were separated. " Wherefore," they cried, " slay you thus your parents?" Grey's narrative proceeds:

" But Tane-mahuta pauses not, he regards not their shrieks and cries; far, far beneath him he presses down the earth; far, far above him he thrusts up the sky.

" Hence these sayings of olden time. ' It was the fierce thrusting of Tane which tore the heaven from the earth, so that they were rent apart, and darkness was made manifest, and so was the light."

Tane was the Polynesian Shu, but had acquired the attributes of Re-Osiris, Indra, Marduk and other deities. Elsdon Best writes of him:

" He is the Fertilizer, the power that fertilized the Earth Mother and caused her to produce vegetation of all kinds. He represents light, and brought light into the world. He is the parent of the Dawn Maid, and the renewer of the life and light of Hina, the moon. He has many names to accord with his many functions. For instance, as Tane-mahuta he represents trees; as Tane-i-tewananga he represents occult knowledge; as Tane te Waiora he represents sunlight. . . . Tane it is who warms the body of the Earth mother, and is the cause and conserver of all life. Tane is the personified form of the sun." [1]

---

[1] Elsdon Best, *Some Aspects o Maori Myth and Religion*, Dominion Museum, Monograph No. 1 Wellington, N.Z., pp. 13–4.

In another Maori version of the myth [1] the sky-god is called Raki, and Tane takes him on his own back while his younger brother, Paia assists him and utters prayers. One prayer runs:

> " Cary Raki on the back.
> Carry Papa.
> Strengthen, O big back of Paia,
> Sprained with the leap at Hua-rau."

The myth proceeds:

" Now Raki was raised with the aid of this prayer, and spoke words of *poroporoaki* (farewell) to Papa, and said, ' O Papa! O! You remain here. This will be the (token) of my love to you: in the eighth month I will weep for you.' Hence the origin of the dew, this being the tears of Raki weeping for Papa.

" Raki again said to Papa, ' O old woman! live where you are. In winter I will sigh for you.' This is the origin of ice.

" Then Papa spoke words of farewell to Raki and said, ' O old man! go, O Raki! and in summer I also will lament for you.' Hence the origin of mist, or the love of Papa for Raki.

" When the two had ended their words of farewell, Paia uplifted Raki, and Tane placed his *toko* (pole), called Toko-maungi (prop of the mountain), between Papa and Raki. Paia did likewise with his *toko*. . . .

" Then Raki floated upwards, and a shout of approval was uttered by those above, who said:

> " O Tu of the long face,
> Lift up the mountain."

The applause came because Tane " having disconnected the heaven . . . propped up its sides and made them stable ".

There had been long and dense darkness, another version of the myth tells, before sky and earth were separated. Then Rangi took Te-ata-tuhi (the first streak of dawn) to wife, and begat the moon; he begat the sun by Wero-wero. These two were " placed for eyes in the sky ".

[1] John White, *The Ancient History of the Maori*, Vol. I pp. 47-9.

Tane, like the Babylonian Marduk, is said to have set the stars in their places. But, in the first place he stretched out the sky as did the Hindu gods Indra and Agni. Rangi " had no covering by which he could appear seemly ", and Tane obtained sacred red cloth and fastened it over him. As, however, it did not suit the sky god by night he swept it off. Then Tane obtained a suitable covering for Rangi. In one of the versions Tane stretches mats over the sky, the fastenings being stars. In the day-time the stars " were not beautiful " but at night Rangi " looked grand ".

Among the stars which Tane placed in the sky were Manako-tea (white Magellan Cloud), Manako-uri (black Magellan Cloud), and Mango-roa (big Magellan Cloud). The myth proceeds:

" He (Tane) also brought (to Rangi) Ao-tahi (' first light '), the sacred star, and Ariki (queen of all stars of the year). Puaka (in a heap) was her father and Taku-rua (double rim) was her mother. She will not associate with the others. When she appears in the east the people repeat incantations, weep, and welcome her.

" When Puaka twinkles and flashes its rays towards the north, it is an omen of a fine year; when it twinkles and flashes its rays towards the south, it is an omen of a bad year of rain and wind. These seasons are called after the stars which influence those periods of the year for good or evil." [1]

There was, according to one Maori school of thought, hostility between Rangi and Papa after they were separated. This was because, at the time they were separated, an ancient goddess " of the first generation of the Po ", who was named Whai-tiri, composed and chanted the following incantation:

" Rough be their skin—so altered by dread
As bramble and nettle, repugnant to feel.
So change, for each other, their love into hate.
With dire enchantments, oh! sever them, gods.

[1] J. White, *op. cit.*, Vol. I, pp. 52-3.

And fill with disgust to each other their days.
Engulf them in floods, in ocean and sea.
With dire enchantments, oh! sever them, gods.
Let love and regret for each other be hate.
Nor affection nor love of the past live again." [1]

As we have seen, one Maori school of thought believed that sky and earth were separated by physical
force by their athletic Atlas-like god Tane, and another
that it was due mainly to enchantments that the sky
" floated " up from the earth.

Like the Ancient Egyptian priests those of the Maori,
however, blended many myths. In the story of Ta-whaki,
for instance, which was incorporated in their complex
mythology, one finds echoes of the stories of the Egyptian gods Re and Osiris, which were originally quite independent of one another, but had been fused in Egypt
as a result of the fusion of the solar and Osirian cults.

The ancient goddess Whai-tiri, who chanted the
incantation to separate the earth and the sky, is said to
have taken as her husband Kai-tangata and their daughter
was Hema (procreating power). A son of Hema was
Ta-whaki (rush about). He loved Hine-nui-a-te-kawa
(the great daughter of baptism) who had been betrothed
to another, and because she returned his love her relatives
conspired to slay Ta-whaki.

It is told in one version of the Ta-whaki story that
at one period he lived on earth and had the appearance
of a man.

" His garments were like those of a poor man. He went up
to the top of a mountain and sat down, where he put off his earthly
garments and clothed himself in lightning. Now, there was a
man on that mountain, who, when he saw Ta-whaki coming,
secreted himself, and from his hiding-place he saw Ta-whaki thus
transform himself. He informed the people of the fact, and thence
the people looked on Ta-whaki as a god, and all the tribes chanted
and offered sacrifices to him."

[1] J. White, *op. cit.*, p 51.

As has already been noted, Ta-whaki caused the deluge by stamping on the floor of heaven until it cracked, thus causing the waters to flow down and cover the earth.

It is told that Ta-whaki twice attempted to reach the sky by climbing up a *ti*-tree on the mountain top and then up a spider's web which was stretched between the tree and the sky. Twice the web broke. On the third attempt, however, he gained the sky.

Another reading tells that "when Ta-whaki arose from the water he saw a peak (or road) and he climbed on it to heaven". On the mountain top he found his grandmother who was blind and he restored her sight by means of wet clay and enchantments. As Ta-whaki climbed he repeated the incantation:

> "Ta-whaki climbed to the first heaven;
> Climbs up Ta-whaki to the second heaven.
> Ta-whaki goes on to the tenth heaven,
> And arrives at the pleasant heaven
> Where man is nourished."

In the end he "made openings in the fourteen heavens", his object being "to acquire a knowledge of the incantations known to Tami-i-waho, and also to obtain a sight of him who was hanging in space in the heaven". After obtaining what he sought, "Ta-whaki retired to the heaven of Rehua, where he took up his abode". He took as his wife a "mountain lifter" and their grandson was Rata.

While on the earth Ta-whaki is said to have been slain by his elder brothers. According to an incantation his blood glows in the sun, the moon, and the red sky. The birds *Kaka* (*Nestor productus*) and *Kaka-riki* (small green parrot) "took some of his blood and stained their feathers with it". It is said that "Ta-whaki by his own inherent power came to life again". Then he set out for the sky. The version of the myth which tells that he rose from the sea suggests that he had been drowned. While in the sea he took as his wife Hine-tu-a-tai (daughter of the sea-coast) and their family were fishes of various kinds.[1]

Another myth which enters into the Maori complex was that of the war of the gods.

One version tells that when Rangi and Papa were separated, Tawhiri-ma-tea, god of winds and storms, attacked his brothers. He is the " Wild Huntsman in the Raging Host ".

" He . . . sends forth fierce squalls, whirlwinds, dense clouds, massy clouds, dark clouds, gloomy thick clouds, fiery clouds, clouds which precede hurricanes, clouds of fiery black, clouds reflecting glowing red light, clouds wildly drifting from all quarters and wildly bursting, clouds of thunderstorms and clouds hurriedly flying. In the midst of these Tawhiri-ma-tea himself sweeps wildly on. Alas! alas! then rages the fierce hurricane."

He smites the forests and trees fall; he swoops down upon the seas, raising billows and causing whirlpools.

When this god of storms and wind attacked his brothers, Tangaroa " fled for safety to the ocean "; others fled inland. Ever since that time Tangaroa has waged war against Tane and Tane against Tangaroa. Tane supplies canoes and Tangaroa overwhelms them. Other deities were separated and made enemies by the god of winds and storms.

Another myth tells that when Tane had arranged the stars and introduced " the laws of *tapu* (taboo) " he visited the earth and then returned to the sky.

Certain spirits which had been driven from the sky for disobedience to Rangi caused evil among the fish so that multitudes perished. They did likewise among the birds and they slew mankind.

" Thus was evil introduced into this world, and man, birds, and fish became antagonistic. Man killed man, birds destroyed birds, and fish devoured fish; and thus death was first known in this world."

[1] J. White, *op. cit.*, Vol. I, pp. 53 *et seq.*

There had been wars in heaven even before Rangi and Papa were separated. Two gods, or demons, named Tu and Roko killed some of Tane's creatures. "Then Tu and Roko determined to go up into heaven and there make war, and kill the occupants of that region." A battle was fought on a hill and the tribe there was slaughtered; another battle was fought at Awa-rua (the two rivers) and there Tu was mortally wounded and died.

"Roko rose to revenge the death of Tu; and this was the war that was waged even up to the high peaks of the hills of heaven. . . . A great many beings fell."

Tu and Roko (or Rongo) were "the originators of evil in ancient times. They caused disobedience and war in the heavens." Tane sorrowed because of the evil caused by these beings and he said, "I will not allow you to live here. Go ye below." The myth proceeds:

"He (Tane) then threw all that company—that tribe and their chief, Roko—tumbling down to the worlds below; and this party, which had gone up in confidence, returned in confusion, and came to the place Kai-hewa (eat in doubt) where they lived in dismay and dread."

Another reading tells of three rebellions. The first was caused by the spirits whom Tane had "thrown down from the heavens"; they took revenge on the creatures made by Tane. The second rebellion was caused by Ru and Ro "who gave battle in heaven". There were beings whom Tane had fostered, and they fled to this world and "from them sprang the *aruhe* (fern root) and other foods. This is why the fern root was used by man as a sacred offering to be given to the gods." In the third rebellion Tu (god of war) was killed by the beings of Tane, "and his spirit was allowed to go to the Po". Thousands of the rebels were slain.

The myth of the separation of heaven and earth is found to be widely spread in the South Sea Islands. In

the Chatham Islands the god who raises the sky is called
" Heaven Propper ". He made use of ten pillars in all,
placing one above the other.[1] Ellis the missionary tells
that according to the Tahitian version of the myth " at
first the heavens joined the earth, and were only separated
by the *teva*, an insignificant plant, *Draconitum polyphillum*
till their god, Ruu, lifted up the heavens from the earth ".
In one of the religious chants this event is referred to in
the line

> " *Na Ruu*[2] *i to te rai*."
>
> " Ruu did elevate or raise the heavens." [3]

In the Hervey group the sky is said to be of " solid blue
stone ". Formerly it was so low that it rested on the
leaves of the *teve* (which grows about 6 feet high) and of
the arrow-root (about 3 feet high). The god Ru came
up from the Underworld and was sorry for the inhabitants
of the earth who had such a confined residence and endeavoured to raise the sky a little.

" For this purpose he cut a number of strong stakes of different
kinds of trees, and planted them in the ground at Rangimotia, the
centre of the island (of Mangaia) and of the world. This was a
considerable improvement, as mortals were thereby enabled to
stand erect and to walk about without inconvenience. Hence
Ru was named ' the sky-supporter '. Wherefore Teka sings:

> ' Force up the sky, O Ru,
> And let the space be clear.' "

One day Maui, son of Ru, in revenge for an insult,
assumed gigantic proportions, and running towards his
father, muttered the incantation:

> " Ru, who supports the many heavens—
> The third, even to the highest, ascend."

Then placing his head between the legs of the Polynesian Atlas, he gave a heave with his shoulders, hurling

---

[1] A. Shand, *Journal of the Polynesian Society*, Vol. III, p. 121.   [2] Ru.
[3] *Polynesian Researches* (Second Edition). Vol. I, p. 116.

Ru and the sky to a tremendous height from which there was no return. Ru's head and shoulders " got entangled among the stars ".

Another myth makes Ru a god of the South and Maui, his son, a god of the North. Gill gives it as follows:

" Originally the heavens almost touched the earth. Maui resolved to elevate the sky, and fortunately succeeded in obtaining the assistance of Ru. Maui stationed himself at the north, whilst Ru took up his position in the south.

" Prostrate on the ground, at a given signal they succeeded in raising a little with their backs the solid blue mass. Now pausing awhile on their knees, they gave it a second lift. Maui and Ru were now able to stand upright; with their shoulders they raised the sky higher still. The palms of their hands, and then the tips of their fingers, enabled these brave fellows to elevate it higher and higher. Finally, drawing themselves out to gigantic proportions, they pushed the entire heavens up to the very lofty position which they have ever since occupied.

" But the work was not complete, for the surface of the sky was very irregular. Maui and Ru got a large stone adze apiece, and therewith chipped off the roughest parts of the sky, thus giving it a perfectly oval appearance. They now procured superior adzes, in order to finish off the work so auspiciously commenced. Maui and Ru did not cease to chip, chip, chip at the blue vault until it became faultlessly smooth and beautiful, as we see it now."[1]

In Samoa Turner was unable to find any consecutive tales of the early period when the universe was being constructed or set in order.[2] He writes in this connexion:

" They say that of old the heavens *fell down*, and that people had to crawl about like the lower animals. After a time, the arrow-root and another similar plant pushed up the heavens. The place where these plants grew is still pointed out, and called the Te'enga-langi, or heaven-pushing place. But the heads of the people continued to knock on the skies. One day, a woman was passing along, who had been drawing water. A man came up to

[1] W. W. Gill, *Myths and Songs from the South Pacific*, pp. 59 and 71.
[2] The myths in question, as collected by another missionary, are given below (Chapter XVII).

her and said that he would push up the heavens if she would give him some water to drink.

" ' Push them up first,' she replied.

" He pushed them up.

" ' Will that do?' said he.

" ' No; a little farther.'

" He sent them up higher still, and then she handed him her coco-nut shell water bottle.

" Another account says that a person named Tiitii pushed up the heavens; and the hollow places in a rock, nearly six feet long, are pointed out as his footprints." [1]

In the Society Islands the hero Maui finds the sky held down close to the earth by the tentacles of a gigantic cuttle fish. He dives into the sea and dismembers the monster. Then the sky rises and expanding forms the blue arch of heaven with the sun at noonday as the keystone.[2]

Various versions of the myth are found in Micronesia. One which recalls the Hindu-Buddhist concept of four nāgas (serpent deities) supporting the sky, is from Nukufetau. It tells that " the fish had a meeting to devise some plan of raising the heavens, but failed, when the sea-eel, or serpent offered his services and did the business.[3] On Tamana the sky is separated by " a man called Liki ". According to the myth of Nikunau in the Gilbert group the sky was " resting on the earth until raised by two brothers, Naleau and Laki. They had a third brother whose right eye was plucked out and thrown up into the heavens and became the sun." On Peru, another of the Gilberts, Naleu raised the sky by means of poles.[4]

The serpent-prop is met with again on the island of Onoato. There it is told that the god Naleau made an opening in the sky, went down and prevailed upon the sea-serpent to assume an erect position and elevate

[1] George Turner, *Nineteen Years in Polynesia*, pp. 245–6.

[2] D. Tyreman and G. Bennet, *Journal of Voyages and Travels,* Vol. I, p. 526.

[3] Turner, *Samoa*, p. 285.   [4] Turner, *op. cit.*, pp. 293, 297.

the sky. Afterwards stones were transformed into men.[1]

In the New Hebrides the story tells that a woman was engaged pounding food and owing to the lowness of the sky, struck it with her pestle. She told the sky to go up higher, and it rose in response to her angry words.[2]

W. J. Perry gives various versions of the sky-tale.[3] A Dutch collector tells that on the island of Roti, near Timor, and to the east of Java, it was believed the sky was formerly so close to the earth that men could reach it easily. " If there was no fire on the earth, they went up to the sky to get it." A man named Laihamak grew very tall and was then unable to walk upright. He asked the sky to " push up a little higher " so that he might walk without stooping. The sky was angry and receded. Laihamak then left Roti and went eastward, utilizing various islands as " stepping stones ". Perry points out that he moved in the direction " the stone-using immigrants are supposed to have taken ".

The story of the woman hitting the sky with a rice pestle when she was preparing food is found among the Manobo of Mindanao. In northern Luzon a similar story is told. A sitting Ifugao deity (Luzon) is credited with the feat of pushing up the sky. " The Tagolog say that the sky was once very near to the earth: men threw stones at it, and thus made the deity very angry, so that he drew the sky up to its present position." According to the Minahassa people the sky was formerly reached by way of Mount Lokon, but a man named Warere " cut it in two and thus severed the connexion ".

In Borneo the Olo Ngadju tell that the sky retreated because its god was offended, his son having taught the people how to grow rice. Perry continues:

[1] Charles Wilkes, *Narrative of the U.S. Exploring Expedition*, Vol. V, p, 86.
[2] R. B. Dixon, *Oceanic Mythology*, p. 36.
[3] *The Megalithic Culture of Indonesia*, pp. 167 *et seq.*

" The sky was formerly near the earth in Nias, so that the priests could get there up a ladder. People used to scrape off the fat from the underside of the sky and eat it. One day a man sent his wife to get some of the fat. She was angry and hit the sky, which thereupon was drawn up."

This old woman, and others who, in the myths, behave like her, was probably an ancient goddess. Perry writes regarding the Indonesian evidence:

" The sky-beings figure in the tales of origin of several peoples, and the supreme beings are sometimes supposed to have lived on earth. The whole of the associations of the sky-world, from the point of view of the indigenous peoples, therefore date from a time subsequent to the arrival of the strangers in Indonesia. No signs exist of any beliefs in a world in the sky, or in beings connected with it, previous to the arrival of the stone-using immigrants."

In India where, as we have seen, the sky and earth were supposed to have been joined and to have been separated, there are references to Krishna, the avatar of Vishnu, supporting the sky with a single finger. Hercules in like manner relieved Atlas of his burden for a time.

Traces of the myth of the raising and propping of the sky are to be met with from China to Western Europe. When Alexander the Great received a visit from Celtic envoys he asked them what they feared most, and he was surprised and annoyed when they answered that their only fear was that the sky should fall down upon them.[1] Apparently he expected them to say that they greatly dreaded himself.

The South Sea Islands myths of the raising of the sky are not accurately described as " child-like inventions and imaginings ". They are rather the fragments surviving in folk-lore of ancient mythology. The Maori versions which were collected from the priests, not from " the folk ", are of more dignified character than those

---

[1] Ptolemy, son of Lagus, quoted by Arrian, *Anabasis*, I, 4, § 6.

collected on the small islands, and resemble more closely the Hindu material. Dixon regards the Maori myth as " a special or locally developed form " of the widespread sky-raising theme " which reaches back almost without a break from Central Polynesia to Indonesia ".[1]

[1] *Oceanic Mythology*, p. 36.

CHAPTER XV

Tane the Divine King

Polynesian Gods and Hindu Gods—Rival Supreme Deities—Tane and Indra—Links with Marduk of Babylonia and Ptah of Egypt—Sky-makers and Sky-props—Tane's Connexion with Trees and the Adze—Tane sets the World in Order—The War in Heaven—Tane creates a Goddess—Tane Myth and Japanese Myth—Tane in the Underworld—Tane and the "Well of Life" —The "Waters of Kane (Tane)"—Searches for the "Well of Life"—"Milky Way" as a Sky River—The "Sky Pool"—Sun Gods and the "Water of Life"—Creation of the First Man—Tane as Tiki—Image Making and Creation Myths—Fusions of Myths in Polynesia—Tane as "Life-giver" and Ruler of the Universe.

Among the gods of Polynesia Tane was one of the most important, but in some areas he was less prominent than in others. In the South Sea Islands, as in India, it is found, however, that the leading god of a particular cult might be overshadowed or supplanted by the leading god of another cult, perhaps for political reasons, or perhaps because of the introduction of new doctrines. The process of change sometimes brought about the fusion of the attributes and myths of rival deities, and sometimes the exaltation of a new deity above the older group of deities. As the Hindu gods Varuna and Mitra, for instance, were displaced and obscured by Indra and Agni, who usurped their functions during the Vedic Age, so did a Polynesian deity like Tangaloa displace Tane and even the supreme god Io, especially in Samoa, Tonga and the Society Islands. It may be that the rise of Tangaloa was in no small measure due, in the first place, to the intrusion of new and influential settlers from a distance. At the same time it has to be recognized that the glorification, in religious literature, of a particular deity at the expense of other deities can sometimes be otherwise explained. Max Müller [1] has drawn attention to the fact that in the Vedic Age of India all the principal deities were addressed as supreme:

" When these individual gods are invoked, they are not conceived of as limited by the powers of others as superior or inferior in rank. Each god is to the mind of the supplicants as good as all the gods. He is felt, at the time, as a real divinity, as supreme and absolute, in spite of the necessary limitations which, to our mind, a plurality of gods must entail on every single god. All the rest disappear for a moment from the vision of the poet, and he only who is to fulfil their desires stands in full light before the eyes of the worshippers. ' Among you, O gods, there is none that is small, none that is young: You are all great indeed ',[2] is a sentiment which, though, perhaps, not so distinctly expressed by Manu Vaivasvata, nevertheless, underlies all the poetry of the Veda. . . . It would be easy to find, in the numerous hymns of the Veda, passages in which almost every single god is represented as supreme and absolute. In the first hymn of the Second Mandala, Agni is called the ruler of the universe, the lord of men, the wise king, the father, the brother, the son, the friend of man; nay, all the powers and names of the others are distinctly ascribed to Agni . . . Indra is celebrated as the strongest god in the hymns as well as in the Brahmanas, and the burden of one of the songs of the Tenth Book is: ' Indra is greater than all ' . . . He conquers everyone. He is called the King of the world, he has the power to prolong the life of men, and in one verse he is called the maker of heaven and earth, of Agni (fire god), of Surya (the sun god), and of Vishnu (the preserver)."

Indra was, to begin with, pre-eminently the god who slew the water-confining serpent-dragon, Vrittra, to provide the world with life-giving and sustaining water. He wielded the thunderbolt and caused the thunder and lightning which brought rain. As a warrior-god, he not only slew the drought-causing, water-confining serpent-dragon, but waged war against the

---

[1] *Ancient Sanskrit Literature*, pp. 532 et seq.   [2] *Rig Veda*, VIII, 30, 1.

demons who were enemies of the gods, and he was therefore recognized as the patron of warriors. His wars were waged to establish law and set the world in order. He was credited with having placed " yonder sun a brilliant light in the sky ", and with having " fixed " other lights of the sky, including the " moon and stars ". He " directed downwards the action of the waters "; he " spread out the sky " or the sky cover, and " established the earth and stretched it out ". Agni, the fire-god, is similarly credited with having stretched out heaven and earth " like two skins ". Indra " by his skill ", we read in a Vedic hymn, " has propped up the sky from falling ". He " ordained the course of the months in heaven ", and it was also said of Indra that " the father (the sky) has a circumference divided by thee ". As Muir puts it, " the attributes which are ascribed to him (Indra) are chiefly those of physical superiority and of dominion over the external world ". But, at the same time, Indra was lauded as " the lord of the whole moving and breathing world ", as one who " generated at once the sun, the heavens, and the dawn ", as the creator of the vegetation which the waters he released had nourished and as the god of life and death who had a Paradise of his own. " A variety of vague and general epithets are lavished upon Indra," comments Muir.[1]

The god Tane of Polynesia has much in common with Indra, and especially the post-Vedic Indra who became identified with the dragon as a rain-giver and season-controller. Both have links with the sky-shaping, hammer-wielding Ptah of Egypt, and the composite sky and earth-god Ptah-Tanen, with the Hittite rain-bringing and season-controlling Tarku, and with the thunderbolt - wielding Marduk (Merodach) of Babylonia who absorbed the attributes of other deities, including those of the sun-god and of Ea, god of fertilizing

---

[1] Muir's *Original Sanskrit Texts*, London, 1884, Vol. V, pp. 77 *et seq.* and pp. 214 *et seq.*

water. In like manner the Hindu fire-god Agni became identified with the sun and absorbed the acquired solar attributes of other deities previously exalted. A significant text reads:

"Agni becomes Varuna in the evening; rising in the morning he is Mitra; becoming Savitri he moves through the air; becoming Indra he glows in the middle of the sky."[1]

Tane was connected with life-giving water as well as with the sun and sunlight, and so was Agni, who was said sometimes to be "concealed in the receptacle of the waters", or "in the waters and the plants"; the waters are "the mothers of the god of fire, who being generated from fire-sticks is connected with trees, and being a fire-god is in the lightning and in the sun".[2] The Hindu reasoned somewhat in this manner: "The thunder weapon (bolt or axe) causes lightning and thunder which brings rain; the rain causes floods, and fertilizes the earth in which trees and crops spring up and in these trees there is fire which is generated by the friction of fire-sticks. Agni therefore hides in the water; he also hides in the trees and in the thunder weapon, and he is in the sun. Water, trees, sunlight, fire, and the thunder weapon are all manifestations of Agni."

The Polynesian god Tane is similarly a deity with many manifestations. Like Indra and Agni, as we have seen, he played a prominent part when sky and earth were separated and stretched out; he provided the sky-cover for Rangi and, as will be shown, acted in like manner to Indra in setting the universe in order. He is found wielding an axe or adze as Indra wields a thunderbolt, and other deities wield an axe or hammer; he is, indeed, the dragon-god of the sacred adze which, as has been shown, causes thunder and lightning. As a tree-feller he was the patron of artisans. But he was not only in the tree-felling adze, but in the tree which owed

[1] Muir, *op. cit.*, Vol. V p. 219, note 341   [2] Muir, *op. cit.*, pp. 202, 207, 208, 210.

its origin to the sunlight and water he had provided. When a tree was felled, it was said, " Tane has fallen."

As the warrior-god who set the world in order and was a " life bringer " (a provider of sunlight and water), Indra, as stated, waged war against the forces of disorder. " Even all the gods," says a Vedic hymn, " assailed thee, Indra, when thou didst prolong (?) day and night. When thou didst fight alone against all the furious gods, thou didst slay the destructive." [1]

Tane, in Maori mythology, acts as does Indra in his rôle of a warrior god. He wages war against the rebels in heaven. These include " the deformed offspring of Rangi ", and he consigns them to outer darkness.

" These (rebels) were not willing to obey the commands of Rangi; they persisted in disobedience and wrongdoing, and were swept by his orders down to the lower worlds."

The rebels plotted to be " revenged on Rangi " because he had expelled them from the Celestial regions:

" They first caused evil amongst the fish of the sea, and multitudes of them were destroyed. Then they caused evil amongst the birds of the air, and flocks of them perished. And when men were multiplied, they also caused evil among them. Tu-mata-u-enga and Rongo-ma-rae-roa were the leaders of the hosts of the war spirits which slew mankind. Thus was evil introduced into this world, and man, birds and fish became antagonistic. Man killed man, birds destroyed birds, and fish devoured fish; and thus death was first known in the world." [2]

Like Marduk and Indra, Tane " arranged the stars ", placing them in their proper positions as guides to mariners, as heralds and controllers of the seasons, &c.

" These seasons are called after the stars which influence those periods of the year for good or evil."

[1] Muir, op. cit., Vol. V, p. 18.
[2] John White, The Ancient History of the Maori, Vol. I, pp. 44-5.

The " queen of all the stars of the year " is Ariki, and " when she appears in the east the people repeat incantations, weep, and welcome her ".[1] Sirius (Taku-rua) and Rigel (Puanga) were selected " to preside over planting and harvest time ", and others were selected " to preside over winter ".[2]

As we have seen, the stars were used as a covering for the sky-god Rangi, who was " standing naked ". A myth tells that Tane admired them greatly when, having ascended to the upper regions, he first saw the glittering host on " the shore of heaven ". To his younger brother, Wehi-nui-a-mamao, who dwelt in these upper regions, he said he wished to get the stars " to beautify our father ", and the brother consented to their suggested distribution in the sky.

It was during this visit to the upper regions that Tane obtained trees, which were named " the travellers of Tane of the south-east breeze ", and were, as indicated, identified with the god. His brother had offered him as food a *tui* (parson bird), taking off its head, " but Tane would not partake of it, because of the sanctity of the place whence it was taken ". He wished, however, to take some of the birds down to the earth, but his brother said, " Do not take any (of the birds) below—there is no food (for them there): rather take trees down and plant them." Tane agreed, and " he took some of each sort of tree ". Another myth tells that as soon as Rangi and Papa were separated, trees were discovered, but they were growing upside down. Tane reversed them, and they are now called " the defiant offspring of Tane ".[3] Still another myth refers to vines and creepers, and tender plants growing in red water between Rangi and Papa before they were separated. The sky-props were cut from trees which were in existence when the couple were yet in close touch. Tane's intimate con-

---

[1] J. White, *op. cit.*, pp. 52–3.   [2] J. White, *op. cit.*, pp. 148–9.
[3] J. White, *op. cit.*, Vol. I, p. 143.

nexion with trees is emphasized in the myth which tells
that one of his wives was a tree, and that their offspring
" were trees and not men ".[1]

Night and day first began to be when Tane, according to Maori doctrine, took as his wife Hine-ti-tama.
The story of her origin is related in the myth which
tells that the hosts of Heaven cried out, " O Tane!
fashion the outer part of the earth: it is bubbling up."
The god repeated incantations, and fashioned from the
mud the body of a woman. She was made to live by
Tane, and she gave birth to a daughter whom Tane
called Hine-ata-uira, and she, too, became Tane's bride.

The myth regarding Tane and this goddess resembles that of the Japanese couple Izanagi and Izanami.
When the latter dies, she departs to Yomi, the dark
underworld. Izanagi follows her to entice her to return,
but he fails, and is pursued by demons to the Borderland
of life and death.[2]

The Maori myth tells that Tane's wife hid herself
and her children by going into " the lower world ", and
was there when Tane returned from the sky to his
earthly home.

" Tane was so grieved at the absence of Hine-ata-uira that he
forgot to plant the trees, and resolved to follow her. She arrived
at Te Po, the place of Hine-a-te-ao (daughter of the light). Hine-
a-te-ao said to her, " Go back. I, Hine-a-te-ao am here. This is
the division between night and day '. Hine-atu-uira took no heed:
she persisted in her endeavours to go and prevailed over Hine-
a-te-ao and passed on. Then Tane arrived. Hine-a-te-ao asked
him, " where are you going?' Tane answered ' I am in pursuit of
my wife '. Hine-a-te-ao replied, ' She will not be overtaken by
you. She has rushed recklessly on. . . . ' Tane said, ' Nevertheless, let me pass,'. That *tipua*, the goblin, Hine-a-te-ao, said to
Tane, ' Come on, follow your wife.'

Tane went till he came to the Po of Hine-a-te-po. She asked
him, ' where are you going?' Tane replied, ' I am in pursuit of
my wife.' She said, ' I have spoken thus to her, " Return from this

[1] J. White, *op. cit.*, p. 158.   [2] See my *Myths of China and Japan*, pp. 357 *et seq.*

place, as I, Hine-a-te-po, am here. I am the barrier between night and day "; but she did not hearken to me.' Tane said to Hine-a-te-po, ' Let me pass,' and the goblin gave him permission."

Tane at length reached the Underworld house in which his wife was concealed. The door was shut, and he could not gain admittance. Calling out, he pleaded with her to return with him, but she replied:

" Return you to the world (day) and nourish some of our progeny, and leave me down below, so that I can drag some of them down here."

Then the couple sang songs to one another, but the goddess bade Tane, whom she addressed as " Great provider of food ", a final farewell. Tane returned to the world, but he was not pursued by demons, as was the Japanese hero god Izanagi. Both the Japanese and Polynesian myths link with that of Orpheus, who went to the Underworld to recover his lost bride Eurydice.

In New Zealand, where we find a mosaic of myths imported at various periods, the story of Tane's bride appears to have been given a secondary meaning, for she was identified with the dawn and the twilight. But her resemblance to a dawn goddess like the Hindu Ushas is superficial. That deity is followed by the sun-god as by a lover, but Indra is represented as being hostile to her, and he crushes her chariot with his thunderbolt. The Polynesian goddess does not return like Ushas from the Underworld as " the giver of joy ", " the bringer of food ", " the preserver of order ", &c., nor can it be said of her, as of Ushas, that " she is the life and breath of all things, causing the birds to fly from their nests ... awakening the five races of men, yea all creatures, as if from death ".[1] Tane's lost wife remains instead in the dark underworld as queen of the dead. The original myth appears to have been influenced by the myth of the sky-god Rangi and the

Muir's *Original Sanskrit Texts*, Vol. V, pp. 181 *et seq.*

earth goddess Papa. In China, Yang, the male principle, is connected with the sky and with warmth, life-giving and activity, while Yin, the female principle, is connected with the earth, inactivity, cold, and death. Tane may be said to represent Yang, in one of his phases, and his lost bride Yin.

As the " Great provider of food ", and therefore a life-giver and life-sustainer, Tane is connected with water and especially the " Well of Life ". According to a Maori myth:

" When the moon dies she goes to the living water of Tane— to the great lake of A-ewa, to the water which can restore all, even the moon to its path in the sky."

Another reading is:

" When man dies, his body does not come to life again: it is sucked into the mouth of Hine-nui-te-po (great daughter of night. Not so is it with the moon: the moon when it dies, goes to bathe in the great lake of Aiwa (or Aewa), the living water of Tane which renews life." [1]

In Hawaiian mythology Tane figures as Kane, and is associated with the gods Ku and Lono, forming a trinity, and also with Kanaloa (Tangaloa). " Kane and Kanaloa," writes W. D. Westervelt,[2] " were the water-finders, opening fountains and pools over all the islands, each pool known now as Ka-Wai-a-ke-Akua (the water provided by a god)." When the query was put in one of the very old Hawaiian newspapers, "What are the waters of Kane?" the answers were, Westervelt informs us:

" The heavy showers of life-giving rain, the mountain stream swelling into a torrent lifting and carrying away canoes, the rain-bow-coloured rain loved by Kane, the continually flowing brooks of the valleys and the fresh waters found anywhere—these were the waters of Kane."

---

[1] J. White, *op. cit.*, Vol. I, p. 142.
[2] *Legends of Old Honolulu*, Boston, U.S.A., 1915, pp. 32 *et seq.*

Westervelt goes on to say " it may reasonably be surmised that from the realization of the blessing of fresh waters the ancient Polynesians as well as the Hawaiians looked up to some waters to be found somewhere in the land of the gods, which were called ' the waters of life of Kane ' ". According to Hawaiian myths:

" If anyone is dead and this water is thrown upon him, he becomes alive again. Old people bathing in this water go back to their youth."

Stories tell that Kane found water with the aid of a long and strong staff, or a spear, which he carried as does a " water diviner " his hazel stick. A missionary, writing about 1868, recorded a myth of Kane and Kanaloa appearing " more like man than gods ", and wandering all through the islands gathering the *awa* root, which when crushed and mixed with water makes an intoxicating drink. On one particular island Kane thrust his staff through a rock, " breaking open a hole, out of which water leaped for them to mix with their prepared *awa* ". . . . " This pool of fresh water," says Westervelt, " has been known since the days of old as Ka-puka-Wai-o-Kalihi (the water door of Kalihi)." [1]

David Malo [2] gives Hawaiian metrical prayers referring to the " water of life " of the god which fertilizes the world, and emphasizing the character of the god as a " food-giver " and " life-giver ":

> " Green are the leaves of God's harvest fields.
> The net fills the heavens—shake it!
> Shake down the god's food!
> Scatter it, O heaven! . . .
> Life to the land!
> Life from Kane,
> Kane the god of life . . .
> Life to the people!
> Hail, Kane of the water of life!   Hail!

[1] Westervelt, *op. cit.*, p. 35.
[2] " Hawaiian Antiquities ", *B. P. Bishop Museum Special Publication* No. 2, pp. 205 *et seq.*

One is reminded by this of Norman Gale's poem

> " God comes down in the rain,
>   And the crops grow tall:
> This is the country faith
>   And the best of all."

Hawaiian legends tell of a distant Paradise, in which dwelt the first human pair, and amongst its names are " Blue Mountain ", " The Land of the Heart of Kane ", and " The Land of the Divine Water of Kane ". This is a sacred land which may be reached by the righteous. It is said " that he must prepare himself exceedingly holy who wishes to attain it; if faulty or sinful, he will not get there: if he looks behind, he will not get there:[1] if he prefers his family, he will not enter Paliuli ". Fornander quotes an ancient chant which describes this " hidden land of Kane " as the

> " Land with springs of water, fat and moist,
> Land greatly enjoyed by the god." [2]

Fornander says that " the living water of Kane " is frequently referred to in the Hawaiian folk-lore.

" According to traditions this spring of life, or living water, was a running stream or overflowing spring, attached to or enclosed in a pond. It was beautifully transparent and clear. Its banks were splendid. It had three outlets; one for Ku, one for Kane, and one for Lono, and through these outlets the fish entered in the pond. If the fish of the pond were thrown on the ground or on the fire, they did not die; and if a man had been killed and was afterwards sprinkled over with this water, he did soon come to life again." [3]

Fornander also makes reference to the Hawaiian legend of the young man who visited the land in which Kane's " Water of Life " is to be found, and a popular rendering of the narrative is provided by W. D. Wester-

[1] This prohibition is in the Orpheus myth, in the story of Lot's wife, &c.
[2] A. Fornander, *The Polynesian Race*, London, 1878, pp. 77-8.
[3] A. Fornander, *op. cit.*, p. 78

velt,[1] who reminds us that mention of the life-giving
water " is found in many of the Pacific island groups,
such as New Zealand, the Tongas, Samoa, Tahiti, and
the Hawaiian Islands ". He might have also added the
Chatham Islands.

The Polynesian story resembles closely the Celto-
Irish and Celto-Scottish stories of searches made for the
" Well of Life " at the " World's End ", in the Underworld, or on some distant island of Paradise. It relates
that an old king was very ill and was informed by a
mysterious stranger, who subsequently disappeared, that
he must drink of the " Water of Life of Kane ".

Three sons set forth to search for it in turn. The
first son, after a long journey, reached a forest in which
he met a dwarf. The dwarf asked him where he was
going, but the searcher pushed him aside roughly and
tried to force his way through dense vegetation. But
the tendrils of the vines and creepers in this land of
the supernatural beings twined round him until he was
overcome and lay down like one who was dead. The
second son set out after a time, and he acted towards
the dwarf like the first, and was similarly overcome.

Then the youngest son undertook to find the " Water
of Life ", and rescue his brothers. When he met the
dwarf, he answered his questions, and appealed for his
help. The dwarf was well pleased with the young man's
civility, and gave him a staff which would open a way
for him to the " Well of Life ". The dwarf told that
this well was in the house of a royal sorcerer, and that
the house entrance was guarded by two dragons which
were ready to devour an intruder, but that they could be
pacified with food which the dwarf gave to the young man.

The younger brother reached the house, gained
admittance, and fell in love with a beautiful maiden
who assisted him to obtain the water. He filled his
calabash, and hastened away with it.

[1] *Legends of Old Honolulu*, Boston and London, 1915.

The narrative continues:

" With great joy he hastened from land to land and from sea to sea watching for the little man, the *a-a*, who had aided him so much. Almost as if his wish were known, the little man appeared, and asked him how he fared in his journey. The prince told him about the long way and the success and then offered to pay as best he could for all the aid so kindly given."

The dwarf refused to take any reward. Then the prince asked another favour. He wished to know where he could find his lost brothers. The dwarf gave the desired information, and then the young man found his brothers, whom he restored to life and strength by sprinkling over them a few drops of the " Water of Life ".

On their way homeward the elder brothers stole the " Water of Life " and filled the calabash of the younger brother with salt water. When they reached home their father was made sicker than he had been before by drinking from the calabash of the younger son, but he was restored to health and strength when the elder sons gave him the real " Water of Life ".

The younger son was in disgrace for a long time, but ultimately three great kings,[1] came from distant lands and revealed who had found the " Water of Life ", and the younger son was honoured and restored to favour. He afterwards married the beautiful maiden who had helped him to obtain the life-giving water. His wicked and ungrateful brothers fled to distant parts and never returned.

William Ellis, the missionary, refers to the account of the Hawaiian hero who made a voyage to " the land where the inhabitants enjoyed perpetual health and youthful beauty, where the *wai ora* (life-giving fountain) removed every internal malady, and every external deformity, or paralysed decrepitude, from all those who were plunged beneath its salutary waters ".[2]

---

[1] Like the earlier mysterious visitor each of these was probably a god.
[2] *Polynesian Researches* (First Edition, 1829), Vol. I, p. 48.

Westervelt [1] gives a Hawaiian tale of a drowned man having been restored to life by the goddess Hiiaka, who forced the ghost to re-enter the corpse. She sprinkled water in the eyes and over the face of the dead man, repeating a spell addressed to the god Kane (Tane) which concluded with the significant lines:

> " Here is the water of life.
> Awake! Arise!
> Let life return.
> The taboo (of death) is over.
> It is lifted.
> It has flown away."

The man was revived, and he rose up and walked to his home.

The Hindus believed that the dead were purified by bathing in the Celestial Ganges as the living were purified by bathing in the Earthly Ganges. In the " Swargarohanika Parva " of the Mahábhárata, the hero Yudhishthira reaches the heavenly regions in the flesh. " Having bathed in this stream (the Celestial Ganges)," says a god to him, " thou wilt be divested of thy human nature. Indeed, thy grief dispelled, thy ailments conquered, thou wilt be freed from all enmities." When Yudhishthira bathed in the river, " he cast off his human body " and " assumed a celestial form ".

Ellis, discussing the Polynesian belief in the " Well of Life ", reminds us that Sir John Mandeville states he saw a " fountain of youth " in India, and goes on to say:

" The expedition which led to the discovery of Florida was undertaken not so much for a desire to explore unknown countries, as to find an equally celebrated fountain, described in a tradition prevailing among the inhabitants of Puerto Rico, as existing in Binini, one of the Lucayo Islands. It was said to possess such restorative powers as to renew the youth and vigour of every person who bathed in its waters. It was in search of this fountain,

---

[1] *Hawaiian Legends of Volcanoes*, Boston and London, 1916, pp. 112–5.

which was the chief object of their expedition, that Ponce de Leon ranged through the Lucayo Islands, and ultimately reached the shores of Florida." [1]

E. S. Craighill Handy, in his fine and elaborate study of Polynesian religious ideas and practices,[2] would have it that " the ' water of life of Kane ' in Hawaiian mythology, as in Maori lore, was a figurative expression signifying sunlight ". He notes in this connexion that in the mythology of the Society Islands the " Milky Way " is sometimes spoken of as " Water-of-Life-of Tane " and " Water-of-Life-of-Taaroa ".[3] But in other mythologies the " Milky Way " is regarded as a heavenly river. The Ganges, for instance, according to ancient Hindu belief, has its source in the sky, and in China we have stories of sages sailing up the Yellow River and reaching the " Milky Way ".[4] It is told of one Chinese sage who reached the " Milky Way " from the Yellow River that his oar fell from the sky and was treasured afterwards in the Royal Palace. The ancient Egyptians believed that the Nile had its source in the " Milky Way ". In the Pyramid Texts Osiris is the " new water " (the inundation), and it is said that

" The waters of life that are in the sky come,
    The waters of life that are in the earth come." [5]

Assyrian symbols of the sun show streams of water flowing down to plants. Mexico had its " water sun ". In Australia, according to Strehlow, " the ' Milky Way ' is a Great River with inexhaustible reservoirs of sweet water ".[6] The Ainu of Japan regard the " Milky Way " as the river of the Gods.[7] In Japanese mythology the

[1] W. Ellis, op. cit., Vol I. p. 47.
[2] "Polynesian Religion" (Bernice P. Bishop Museum Bulletin 34, Honolulu Hawaii, 1927), p. 103.
[3] E. S. Craighill Handy, op. cit., p. 101.
[4] My Myths of China and Japan, pp. 110–11 and pp. 144 et seq.
[5] Breasted, Religion and Thought in Ancient Egypt, p. 145.
[6] Quoted by Dr. Goldenweiser, Early Civilization, London, 1922, p. 211.
[7] Batchelor, The Ainu and their Folklore, p. 70.

" Milky Way " is the " Tranquil River of Heaven ",
and there is a " True-Pool-Well-of-Heaven ".[1] Pliny
refers to the " Milky Way " as " a circular track ", and
says that from it comes the milky nutriment of the
vegetable world.[2]

Handy, in support of the theory that the " water of
life of Kane " must be a " figurative expression signifying sunlight ", refers to a Hawaiian legend given by
Fornander in which a hero, who searches for the water,
flies " in a straight line to the rising sun "; after flying
for " six moons ", he arrives at the " edge of a hole, in
the bottom of which was kept the water of everlasting
life of Kane ". Handy comments:

" The association in this story of the ' water of life ' with the
sun and its light is so obvious that it seems unnecessary to dwell
upon it further." [3]

Handy follows, in this connexion, Mr. Elsdon Best,
who writes:

" The *waiora* of Tane is light, sunlight which is the welfare
of all things. Tane-te-waiora is Tane as dispenser of life-giving
sunlight. The dying moon bathes, not in water, but in this life-
bringing light, and *in this esoteric version we see that the Maori of
yore hit upon a scientific truth.* With this knowledge *waiora* must
be written as one word, and not as *wai* (water) *ora* (life, living)." [4]

The fact that the Polynesians had stories about life-
giving wells of water does not strengthen Mr. Best's
view. These stories are too like others found in Asia
and elsewhere to be dismissed lightly. Life-giving wells
in the sky are not uncommon in many mythologies. The
Arunta of Australia, for instance, regard the Pleiades
as women who went up to the sky to live " at a place
called Intitakula, near to what is now called the Deep

---

[1] *Transactions of the Asiatic Society of Japan*, Vol. X, and Aston's *Shinto*, pp. 96 *et seq.*
[2] *Natural History*, Book XVIII, Chap. 69. In Hindu mythology the milk of the cow
goddess is mixed with river water.
[3] E. S. Craighill Handy, *op. cit.*, p. 103.
[4] *The Maori*, Vol. I, pp. 138-9. The italics are mine.

Well ".[1] In ancient Egypt, as has been noted, the belief obtained that there were waters in the sky.[2] Maspero, writing of these, says:

"The Nile was said to have its source in Paradise, to traverse burning regions inaccessible to man, and afterwards to fall into the sea whence it made its way to Egypt. Sometimes it carried down from its celestial sources branches and fruits unlike any to be found on earth." [3]

As we have seen, the Polynesian god, Tane, obtained trees from the sky, and saw great birds there.

The ancient Egyptians transferred Egypt and the Nile to the sky. In the Pyramid Texts (1209–16) Horus leads Pharaoh Pepi to the heavenly " great isle in the midst of the Field of Offerings over which the gods make the swallows fly ", and it is explicitly stated that " the swallows are the Imperishable Stars (the Northern Stars) ".[4] The well of life, or the " lake of life " in the sky was connected with the sun-gods Re or Horus and other deities. In a funerary papyrus the soul of the Pharaoh cries out to the nine deities:

"May I proceed upon the course of your lake, may I be the companion of your servants. May I stand up to walk like those who are (alive) on earth. May I breathe the wind that issues from you, the north wind that issues (from) Nut. May I imbibe the water whence ye issued, upon the brink of the lake of Horus, that my soul (bai) may be divine, my spirit (ikh) beatified." [5]

The sun-god Re was supposed to bathe each morning in the horizon pool of the Celestial Dewat. When the dead Pharaoh reached this pool, he bathed in it, too, and then passed to the sun-boat which sailed across the sky daily in the river called the " waters of turquoises ".[6]

---

[1] Spencer and Gillen, *The Arunta*, London, 1927, Vol. II, p. 500.
[2] See also *Genesis* i, 7, "And God made the firmament and divided the waters which were under the firmament, from the waters which were above the firmament."
[3] *The Dawn of Civilization* (McClure's translation), London, 1894, p. 20.
[4] Breasted, *op. cit.*, p. 134.   [5] *Journal of Egyptian Archæology*, Vol. IV, p. 126.
[6] Breasted, *op. cit.*, p. 144, note 2.

The earthly well of the sun-god Re at Heliopolis is reputed to be the well in which the Virgin Mary washed the infant Christ after taking flight from Herod to Egypt.

It is more probable that the Polynesians were, in their myths regarding the " Water of Life " in the sky, perpetuating the ancient concepts of the Old World than that they " hit upon a scientific truth " by stating in figurative language that the moon received its light from the sun. The ancient Egyptians, the ancient Hindus and others, as we have seen, believed that the sun, at the beginning, rose out of the dark primordial waters, or was hatched from a cosmic egg. Hare Hongi, in his paper on " A Maori Cosmogony ",[1] quotes the Maori chant which tells that, in the beginning:

" The Universe was in darkness, with water everywhere,
    There was no glimmer of dawn, no clearness, no light."

Then light was created, and the waters were separated—the waters above the sky from the waters beneath. As we have seen, the cosmic egg myth was known in Polynesia. As the Asiatic ideas regarding the sun, moon, the " Milky Way ", were likewise familiarly known throughout Polynesia, it would appear that the " water of life of Tane " was really " life-giving water ", and not sunshine. The sky pool, well or lake of Polynesia was a concept similar to that which obtained in ancient Egypt, India, and elsewhere.

Like Marduk of Babylonia, Tane was credited with being the creator of the first man, Tiki, and as Tane-Tiki he was identified with the first man.

A Maori myth tells that " Tiki was the first man, and his wife, Ma-riko-riko (glimmer), was the first woman in his world. Arohi-rohi (mirage) formed Ma-riko-riko from the warmth of the sun and Pa-oro (echo); therefore she was of this world—not of Divine origin." Another myth of the origin of man sets forth:

[1] *Journal of the Polynesian Society*, Vol. XVI, 113 et seq.

"An aquatic plant growing in swamps was the male pro-creating power which engendered the red clay seen in landslips, whence came the first man. This man was discovered by one of the gods before light had dawned on this world. It was the grand-son of this man who separated earth and heaven, and caused light to be, and divided the world of light from the world of darkness."

Here the "first man" is the grandfather of Tane, or Tane-Tiki.

Other versions say:

"Tiki (Tane) made man by mixing his own blood with clay, and forming it into a figure like himself; and by breathing into it he gave it life."

"Tiki was made of red clay and the centre shoot of *raupo* (*Typho* angustifolia). He was made in the resemblance of the god who made him."

"Tiki-ahua made the first man—of red clay. He also lifted and propped up the heaven from the earth; and light came on to the world we live in. The heaven lay on the earth and caused night until it was thus lifted up."

The myth of the making of the first man from red clay is found in Egypt, where the god Ptah fashioned man on the potter's wheel. In one of the Babylonian creation myths Marduk makes man of mud mixed with his blood. He also forms the earth by laying a reed on the water to collect mud. The custom of presenting blood to clay images of deities with purpose to animate them was very widespread.

Fornander, in his summary of Hawaiian legends regarding the creation of the first man, says that it was accomplished by the three gods Kane, Ku, and Lono.

"They created man on the model or in the likeness of Kane. The body of the first man was made of red earth—*lepo ula* or *ala-ea*—and the spittle of the gods—*wai-nao*—and his head was made of whitish clay—*palolo*—which was brought from the four ends of the world by Lono. When the earth image of Kane was ready, the three gods breathed into its nose and called on it to rise, and it became a living being." [1]

It will be recalled that from the saliva of certain Egyptian gods, which drops upon the earth, spring various forms of life, including serpents, trees, and herbs.

In the Maori myths which tell of Tane forming the first woman, whom he took as his wife, and from whom the races of man are descended, are a manifest fusion of earlier myths regarding the descent of chiefs and kings from the gods, with later myths which came into being after images were made and ceremonies were performed to animate them. We should not be misled by the gross details in the latter class of myths into assuming that these are necessarily of primitive character. The gross details rather suggest the influence of a decadent period, or a rationalizing process when secondary meanings were sought for and morbid sensualists were active. Withal, it was the custom on the part of the priests to relate myths in the language understood by the common people.

Some of the Polynesian myths which have been collected reveal the influence of Christian missionary teaching. The priests having heard fragments of Biblical stories, worked these into their own inherited myths. This process of fusion had always been active in Polynesia. In pre-Christian times fragments of myths were imported from India and other areas in Asia and treated in like manner. Those Polynesians who had acquired a knowledge of mummification acquired also the beliefs and myths connected with mummification, just as those who had been influenced by jade symbolism and searched for jade, perpetuated the myths connected with jade, as we have seen. When we find in Polynesia myths about a god forming the first man and woman from clay or

---

[1] A. Fornander *The Polynesian Race*, London, 1878, Vol. I, p. 62.

river mud mixed with blood or saliva, it is manifest that we are in contact with that stage of civilization when images were provided for the souls of chiefs or kings and for gods, and the custom prevailed of animating the images with body moisture, including blood, or by using red substances which were surrogates of " the blood which is the life ". We do not in Polynesia discover what can rightly be described as " primitive religious ideas ", but rather mosaics composed of fragments of the religious systems of ancient civilizations with which the ancestors of the South Sea Islanders had been brought into touch during their wanderings at various periods and in different areas.

The imported myths were certainly localized in Polynesia. The attributes of deities to which prominence were given were those which had an intimate connexion with Polynesian habits of life. Tane's connexion with trees, for instance, was emphasized on the islands where trees provide food as do coco-nut and bread-fruit trees, and where it was so necessary to have timber for boat-building, for the construction of houses, and for weapons, implements, &c. Maori proverbial sayings are of interest and significance in this connexion. These include " the narrow path used in crossing belongs to Tane ", applied to a canoe, and " the bold and daring children of Tane, defying the storm ", applied to trees used for constructing houses.[1]   Carpenters, boat-builders, and wood-workers in general regarded Tane as their patron because he provided timber and the adze. As " lord of the forest ", Tane was associated with the birds which congregate because trees bear fruit. The Maori liked to see birds numerous in a wood, for it meant that food was abundant there.

Being a " life-giver ", Tane was the divine physician who cured sickness, and he was connected with the Underworld and the sky world as the god who gave life

[1] J. White, *op. cit.*, Vol. I, p. 143.

to the dead. Withal, Tane, like the Hindu Indra and the Babylonian Marduk, was a warrior king god who ruled the world, controlled the seasons and cared for human beings in this world and the next. He was essentially a " life-giver " as is emphasized by his connexion with sunshine, the " water of life ", and vegetation. His supplies of light and water were made possible by his control of the heavenly bodies. He had brought order out of chaos, and he had disciplined the forces of Nature for the benefit of mankind. The stability of the world and the protection and perpetuation of human life had been ensured by Tane as the divine law-giver and ruler of the Universe whom mankind worshipped and obeyed.

CHAPTER XVI

Symbolism of the " Tiki "

Tane and Tiki, the First Man—Maori " Tikis "—Easter Island Images as " Tikis "—Stone Images of Marquesas called " Tikis "—Gods as " Tikis "— " Tikis " of Dead Friends—Ceremony of singing and weeping over " Tikis "— " Tikis " deposited with Dead—Coffins carved as " Tikis "—Lizard Symbol on Coffin—Hare Hongi on " Tiki " Symbolism—The Phallic Theory—Male and Female " Tikis "—Three Types of " Tikis "—" Tikis " and Ancestor Worship —" Life Substance " in " Tikis "—" Tiki " Symbolism and Jade Symbolism— Chinese Mortuary Jades—Maya Frog Symbol and Maori " Tiki "—Chinese Jade Frogs—Frog Symbolism of India and Egypt—Frogs and Rain—Frogs and Mice—Frog Deities of pre-Columbian America—The " Tiki " and the Frog Symbol of Rain-giving, Life-giving, and Resurrection.

As we have seen in the previous chapter, the first man was called Tiki and Tane was identified with him. It now remains for us to deal with the Maori neck pendants known as " tikis ", and with other Polynesian " tikis " in their relation to the god Tane and to Tiki " the first man ".

Specimens of Maori " tikis " are to be seen in many of our museums. These are small and grotesque jade anthropomorphic images, with heads tilted sideways, large grinning mouths, round staring eyes, bent arms and hands, usually with three fingers in each, or spirals instead of hands, and with bent and attenuated legs, the feet having each three toes and meeting below. Some images suggest the squatting posture of Buddha figures.[1]

The early Christian missionaries and others collected many specimens of Maori " tikis ", but " tikis "

---

[1] I have met natives of Siam who carried in their pockets, carefully wrapped up, small images of Buddha. These are reputed to protect individuals, bring luck, and so on.

have now become very scarce. When a good specimen is put up to auction it usually fetches a high price.

Some writers have referred to " tikis " as " idols " or " gods ", and others as " portraits of ancestors ", or " fœtus images ". It has been asserted, too, that the correct Maori term to apply is " hei-tiki ", and Mr. John White, author of *The Ancient History of the Maori*, has translated " hei " as " for ", or " to be used as ", believing that " hei-tiki " meant " to be used as ", or " to be like Tiki ". He says that " the value or sacredness of these (" tikis ") was derived from the fact of their having been worn or handled by the dead of past ages ".[1]

F. R. Chapman has taken exception to White's derivation. " Hei," he writes, " is a neck ornament. This name is given to me by competent Maori scholars to represent several forms of bone ornaments hung from a string round the neck. *Tiki* is the name given to the large carved figures on the gables of houses or set up near houses. This, then, is a small copy—a neck-*tiki*. The *tiki* represents, and the word is derived from, the name of the god Tiki. He is sometimes spoken of as the progenitor of mankind, and enters into numerous mythical tales. According to some authorities, there were several gods Tiki." [2]

Hare Hongi, the Maori scholar, writing with intimate knowledge of the language, customs and beliefs of his race, says of the pendant:

" The ' tiki ' is sometimes, and quite improperly, termed a *hei-tiki*. This *hei* is merely the cord or necklet worn around the neck, from which the ' tiki ' itself depends. For instance, to speak of a chain and locket (*hei-tiki*) is all very well; but it is obviously improper to apply that term to the locket (*tiki*) itself." [3]

E. S. Craighill Handy translates " tiki " as " idol, image, representation, design ", and shows that the

[1] *Transactions of the New Zealand Institute*, Vol. XXIV, p. 511.
[2] *Ibid.*, Vol. XXIV, p. 520.
[3] *Journal of the Polynesian Society*, Vol. XXIV, Part I, pp. 162–3.

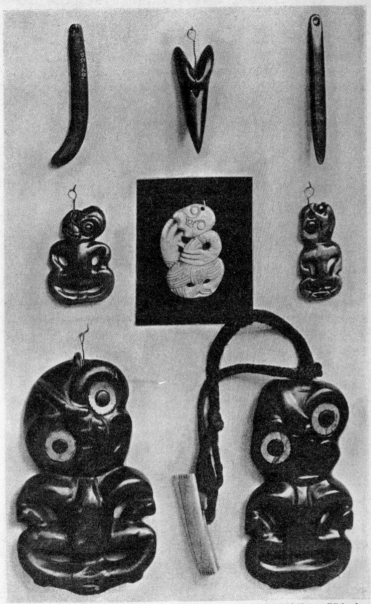

(20)

GREENSTONE TIKIS AND EAR-RINGS

The small tiki in centre is of bone; the eyes of the two lower tikis are inlaid with pearl-shell

Photo. A. J. Iles

MAORI METHOD OF GREETING BY PRESSING NOSES

One girl wears a flax cloak and a huia feather, the badge of rank, in her hair; the other a cloak
of feathers on a flax fabric

images carved in the Marquesas on blocks or boulders
(*Ke'a*) were called "tiki Ke'a". These images, he
would have it, represent "tribal gods", and usually
have, like the Maori jade "tikis", large, staring eyes
and long grinning mouths.[1]

"Tikis" might be carved in the round like the
Easter Island images, or the grotesque eyes and mouths
might simply be incised on the square stones of a temple
platform. As we have seen, in the case of Samoa, the
spirits of the mummified and deified dead were supposed
to enter stones, which therefore became, like the Japanese
shintai, "god bodies". Fishermen in the Marquesas
had their sacred precincts and their special gods.
Ceremonies were performed and operations directed by
the chief fisherman. In a special house was kept a shrine
which was used in the fishing rites, and " secreted by
being buried in the ground were the stone fish gods
(*tiki*) ". Handy says that " at Ta'a Oa there was a stone
platform on which the rites were performed, and the
tiki were buried in it when not in use ". At Atu Ona
the fishing rites were performed in a large house which
was so *tapu* (sacred) " that only the chief fisherman, who
performed the rites, could enter.

" Inside were a small staging (*fata'a*) that served as an altar,
and two parallel rows of peeled fau stakes (*koufau*) wrapped with
cloth and ornamented with coco-nut leaves which were woven
around them. During the rites the stone image of the fishing god
was placed midway between these two rows. . . . I was told that
the sleeping houses, the ceremonial house, and the house for
storing the nets were all elevated on short posts with roofs coming
to the floor on either side, ends closed, and a rectangular door in
one end. The precincts as a whole were *tapu* to women."

Stone platforms at villages, on which images (" *tiki* ")
of gods were carved on blocks of stones, were called

---

[1] " The Native Culture in the Marquesas " (*B. P. Bishop Museum Bulletin* 9). In *Bulletin*
34, however, Mr. Handy says that "the word *tiki* never means image, an idea that was
expressed in the old dialect by quite another word, *ata*. In modern usage *tiki* signifies figure,
design ". (p. 121.)

paepae, and had a sacred character, as we have seen, as feast- and dancing-places, tombs, &c.[1]

Elsewhere throughout Polynesia the " tiki " might be made either of stone or wood. The " tiki " was also carved on clubs, &c., and the eyes and ears were sometimes represented by spirals. Ruth H. Greiner writes regarding the " tiki ":

" In most of the carvings the head of the ' tiki ' is disproportionally large and has as its most prominent feature round or pointed oval spectacle eyes, with a high ridge through the centre terminating in the ears and the nose. Superorbital ridges are generally indicated, and these likewise terminate in the ears which on small figures are usually represented by two connected spirals turned towards each other. On a few specimens only single spirals are seen, and on larger figures a projecting longitudinal flange replaces the spiral. . . . The mouth is very large, and is always open, showing the tongue. . . . Some ' tikis ' have five fingers on each hand; others have only three or four." [2]

The symbolism of the Maori " tiki " was of somewhat complex character. F. R. Chapman has insisted that a " tiki " was not regarded as a god or an idol, and that it was not " in any way worshipped ".[3] But there can be no doubt as to its haunting sanctity. The Rev. William Tate, who lived in New Zealand from 1828 till 1835 and laboured among the natives, considered that the superstitions connected with the greenstone " tiki " arose from certain customs. He has told, for instance, that

" the *hei-tiki* was taken off the neck, laid down on a tuft of grass or a clean leaf in the presence of a few friends meeting together, and then wept and sung over, in order to bring more vividly to the recollection of those present the person recently slain, whose body they will never see again, to whom the *hei-tiki* belonged. In this way it is used as a remembrance of all those who have worn

---

[1] E. S. Craighill Handy, "The Native Culture in the Marquesas" (*Bernice P. Bishop Museum Bulletin* 9), Honolulu, Hawaii, 1923, pp. 148 *et seq.*, 165 and 355.

[2] "Polynesian Decorative Designs " (*Bernice P. Bishop Museum Bulletin* 7), p. 5.

[3] *Transactions of the New Zealand Institute*, Vol. XXIV, p. 520.

it, *and is called by the name of the individual whom it for the moment represents.* It is wept over and caressed with much affection, and those present cut themselves severely in token of their regard for the deceased. These (' tikis ') amongst other *manatungas* (keepsakes or heirlooms) are much valued."[1]

Chapman quotes Thomson, who found that a " tiki " varied in size from a shilling to a plate, as saying:

" When a long-absent relative arrives at a village the *hei-tiki* is taken from his neck and wept over for the sake of those who formerly wore it. There is no doubt they (the ' tikis ') are handed down from father to son for generations, indeed, for centuries. They were deposited with the bones of the dead until they were removed to their final resting place."

Chapman adds, writing in 1891, that the practice of burying " tikis ", when the last of a family dies, " continues to this day, and is doubtless the reason why so many of them and other valuable objects are found buried ".[2]

Dr. Shortland, formerly Native Secretary, New Zealand, considers that the " tikis " are " merely grotesque representations of the human form ", and continues:

" Their value greatly depends on their antiquity. It is the practice to bury such, and other valued articles with the dead. After a time they are removed, and then are specially valued. I remember a chief excusing himself from giving me an eardrop because it was a pirau-tupapaku—i.e. a thing with a dead taint."[3]

The Rev. J. W. Stack, formerly missionary to the South Island Maoris, has expressed the opinion that the " tikis " were " highly prized as heirlooms for having been actually in contact with the sacred bodies of their revered and noted ancestors ". He tells of a particular " tiki " which had passed backwards and forwards from one branch of a family to another for successive genera-

---

[1] Quoted by Chapman, *op. cit.*, pp. 520–1.   [2] Chapman, *op. cit.*, p. 521.
[3] *Transactions of the New Zealand Institute*, Vol. XXIV. p. 516.

tions, the relatives who performed the ceremony of removing it from a body before the final burial of the bones took place, " taking possession of it each time ". He tells that a chief showed him this particular " tiki ", stating that it belonged originally to Marutuahu, son of Hotunui, one of the original immigrants from Hawaiki.

The Rev. Mr. Stack was of opinion that the custom of wearing the " tiki " was imported into New Zealand from Hawaiki. Most of the authorities quoted by Chapman were agreed that the " tikis " were made on the North Island, but he notes in this connexion that Major Heaphy, when at Arahura, South Island, in 1846, saw the " tikis " receiving " their last polish ".[1]

The association of the " tiki " with the dead is of very special interest. As has been stated, it was buried with the body, which was afterwards disinterred. The ceremony of preparing for secondary interment, when the bones were deposited in the tribal burial cave, was known as the *hahunga*. Mr. Colenso, in his *Essay on the Maori Races of New Zealand*, writes of this ceremony:

" After being exhibited, seen, wept and wailed over, they (the bones) were carried by a single man and near relative to their last resting place, the exact spot of deposit, for wise political reasons, being only known to a select few. Sometimes the bones were thrown into some old volcanic rent or chasm; sometimes thrown into very deep water-holes; and sometimes neatly and regularly placed in a deep, dark cave; always, if possible, wherever those of his ancestors happened to be." [2]

Carved wooden coffins were occasionally used for the bones, and specimens of these are preserved in New Zealand museums. In 1902 two Europeans, who were engaged in pig-hunting, discovered quite by chance in *Waimamaku* Valley, two small burial caves which are situated on the face of a precipitous cliff. These were

[1] Chapman, *op. cit.*, p. 522 and Rev. J. W. Stack, pp. 512-3

[2] Quoted by T. F. Cheeseman in *Transactions of New Zealand Institute*, Vol. XXXIX, p. 451.

"literally packed with human skeletons", and there were no fewer than "eight carved burial-chests, most of them full of bones". Mr. Louis Morrell, one of the discoverers, informed Mr. T. F. Cheeseman [1] that "all the chests, except one carved on the back to resemble a lizard, were found in the largest cave. . . . The chests were standing up with their backs against the wall". One small carved and painted box was, however, "resting on its lid". Six of the chests resemble greenstone "tikis", but have, in proportion, much longer bodies. The heads survive on all save one, and the mouths are large and the eyes round and staring. The legs of two are mere stumps: those of the others are bent, and represent the toes in touch. Two have large three-fingered hands pressing flat on the breast; another shows similar hands over the stomach. All are more or less adorned with symbolic designs. The chest with the lizard is a fine specimen of Maori carving, and is worthy, indeed, of a Chinese art-craftsman. Two of the chests—the lizard one and another—had been painted red, but there is no trace of colour on the others.

Mr. Bloomfield, the resident magistrate, heard and recorded evidence from Maoris in the vicinity immediately after the coffins had been discovered. One of these, Heremaia Kauere, referred to five of the burial chests as "tikis", and gave the name of the priest who made them for certain individuals whom he named. The lizard coffin had been provided for the remains of Tangataiki, which were first placed in a hollow tree. "Some years after, when they went to get his bones they found the skin dried over the head, which was preserved, showing the elaborate tattooing. The skin was also preserved over the other parts of the body; the legs were the only parts that had gone. The body was taken down and placed in the cave at the time of the fight of Motokauri. . . . A 'tiki' was placed at each side of

---

[1] *Transactions of New Zealand Institute*, Vol. XXXIX, p. 452.

the entrance to the cave. The *waka*, with the lizard on it, stretched across the mouth inside."

This Maori informant went on to tell that his grandfather, some time later, entered the cave to deposit the bones of a relative. He " walked over the top of the lizard and placed the bones at the end of the cave ":

" He must have been confused; he did not go round the *waka* (lizard coffin) as was the custom. He stepped back again over the lizard, and was bitten by the spirit of the lizard. He felt sick when he got out; went home, and died. . . . The lizard was endowed by the incantations of our forefathers with powers of evil. It was placed as a guard over the bones of the dead to prevent interference."

The chests called " tikis " were, when found, about 200 years old, but the lizard-chest called " waka " (canoe shaped) was no more than about 75 years old.[1]

Hare Hongi, the Maori scholar, who urges the view that a " tiki " is a phallic symbol, says that Heremaia Kauere referred to five of the carved coffins as " tikis " because the figures display the organs of reproduction, and he contends that Heremaia should have said, or did say, " six " and not " five " " tikis ". The other coffins or caskets " do not show the organs ", and (adds Hare Hongi) " Heremaia applied the term " tiki ' to what was proper to the term. They are ' tiki ' because they represent the reproduction and the decay of man."

Hare Hongi's view is that the ideograph of " tiki " is " that of the original production and the reproduction of man. As woman is the bearer of man, it is proper that woman only should wear the ' tiki '; this, with few eccentric exceptions, she does." He then goes on to describe what he calls the perfect forms of the " tiki " which he has seen in greenstone and ivory:

" The most perfect form of the ' tiki ' is that which shows both the male and female figures in loving or amatory embrace (organs conspicuous). The next most perfect form is that which shows the female figure only, with the male and female organs in juxtaposition. . . . Tiki (Tane-Tiki) is the emblematical form of that which pierces (solar ray; male organ) and brings forth (from the female). So far then Tiki, speaking of life. In its last phase, Tiki speaks of death. The carved or plain pillar, post, canoe, mausoleum, or other memorial which is set up to the memory of a deceased chief is probably referred to as a ' tiki ' or ' pou-tiki '." [1]

Hare Hongi is not only assured that the " tiki " is " emblematical of the principle of (human) reproduction and decay ", but that the greenstone or ivory symbol should be connected with Tiki, " the first man ", to whom three prominent names were applied. These are:

Tiki Tawhito Rangi—" Tiki of ancient days ".
Tiki Tawhito Ariki—" Tiki, ancient *ariki* (*ariki* senior in line of descent)."
Tiki Hawaiki—" Tiki of Hawaiki—mythical home of race." [2]

Hongi's theory of the phallic significance of the " tiki " appears to be but a " half truth ". It certainly does not account for the custom of friends assembling to weep over and caress the " tiki " of a dead man, as they weep over and caress his bones. The ceremony is suggestive of ancestor worship rather than of the adoration of the Linga. Although Hongi insists that women only should have worn the " tiki ", it was certainly worn by men as well and, as Thomson has said, a specially venerated " tiki " was " handed down from father to son for generations ". As a family or tribal relic, a " tiki " was apparently supposed to be impregnated with the " life substance " of ancestors. The fact that some " tikis " are female, is one that cannot be regarded as at all favourable to Hare Hongi's somewhat narrow interpretation of the symbol. Withal, the Marquesan " tikis " —the carved platform blocks of stone—are heads or faces alone, and have no apparent connexion with Linga

worship. The idea that the shape of these stones emphasize their phallic significance is rather far fetched. But
once the phallic-worship theory is adopted, its adherents
discover phallic symbols everywhere. Even the belfries
of churches have been proclaimed by some as phallic
symbols.

It cannot be overlooked that the vast majority of the
Maori "tikis" are of jade. They must consequently
have had, like the sacred jade axes, the jade ear-rings,
&c., an intimate connexion with the symbolism of jade
as a "life-giver". Jade objects were not necessarily
phallic symbols. The Chinese regarded jade, as we have
already seen, as a symbol of Heaven and a depository of
Heavenly influence, which endowed all those who wore
it during life with vitality, health, and prosperity, and,
after death, prolonged life by strengthening the vital
energy, thus protecting the body against decay.
"When," says a Chinese writer of the fifth century, "a
grave of ancient date is dug up and the corpse is found
to look as if it were alive, then there is everywhere both
upon it and inside it a great quantity of gold and jade.
It was an established rule with the house of Han to bury
every prince or feudal lord with clothes adorned with
pearls and with boxes of jade, in order to prevent putrefaction." In the *Khai Yuen* codex it is stated that "gran-
dees and officials of the first, second, and third rank
shall receive in their mouths circular pieces of jade,
those of the fourth and fifth rank blue jade, those of the
sixth and lower rank cowries". Wang Chao Yū, a
scholar of the Sung Dynasty of China, says regarding jade:

"When the energy of the soul has reached its highest stage,
then it is able to have intercourse with the spirits composed of Yang
matter (shen); and jade being the purest part of the essence of the
Yang, it may, when swallowed, assist the soul to gain that end." [1]

The jade "tikis" and other jade objects which the

[1] J. J. M. De Groot, *The Religious System of China*, Vol. I, p. 271 *et seq.*

Maoris deposited with their dead may, simply as jades, have been supposed to vitalize the dead, protect them against evil influences, and bring them into communion with the spirits and gods.

It may well be, too, that the Maori "tiki" was an ancient symbol which was imported into New Zealand long after its primary precise significance was obscured. Originally it may have been a frog. It certainly bears a striking resemblance to the Maya frog or toad symbol.

Hare Hongi suggests that the sideways tilted head of the "tiki" is a female characteristic in connexion with "child getting". But this does not explain why the heads of male "tikis" are similarly treated. A more probable explanation is that the head was tilted sideways to indicate the great antiquity of the individual (the first man) which the "tiki" symbolized. Before the sky was raised and propped up, the beings who had come into existence between Rangi and Papa were bent and crouched in the confined space. The sky was so low that they could not stand erect, or even raise their heads. As a frog, or "first man", the "tiki" crouched, as shown in the symbols, until Tane set the world in order. The crouching frog retained the characteristics of the earliest beings.

"Dealing in his "Jade" [1] with jade objects used by the ancient Chinese in dressing the corpse, Dr. Laufer refers to "the small jade carving of a frog found in a Chinese grave of the Han Period". It is

"a four-footed frog with three toes, in a squatting position; the head is rather massive in proportion, the mouth being indicated by an incised half-circular line, the two eyes by two concentric circles."

Laufer also quotes a Chinese record which says:

"The King of Kuang-ch'uan opened the grave-mound of

---

[1] Field, *Museum of Natural History Publication* 154 (Anthropological Series, Vol. X, pp. 306 *et seq.*), Chicago, 1912.

Duke Lung of Tsin and found there a striped toad of jade of the size of a fist and hollow inside. . . ."

The frog figures prominently in the folk-lore of India. "Mother frog", for instance, is invoked in rain-making ceremonies to "pour rain by potsful".[1] As a "rain-giver" the frog was, of course, a "life-giver".

A Vedic hymn [2] was devoted to the frogs. It is said that "these vow-fulfilling Brahmans, the frogs" which, after lying silent for a year, utter cries, "stimulated by Parjanya (the rain god)". The frogs are compared to the soma-drinking Brahmans because they perform similar functions:

"They (the Brahmans) have observed the divine ordinances of the year; these creatures (the frogs) do not disregard the season; when autumn has arrived these heated kettles obtain their release. The frog who lows, and the one who bleats, the speckled and the brown, have bestowed on us riches: giving us hundreds of cows, the frogs prolong our lives in the season of a thousand shoots." [3]

In ancient Egypt the frog-headed goddess Hekt was regarded as a form of the goddess Hathor. The four primeval gods had frog's heads, the frog, as a "life-giver" having been concerned with the creation of the world and fertility. Wiedemann says that the great men of the Old Kingdom prided themselves "on being ' prophets' of truth and of Hekt". The ancient Egyptian frog-lore survived into Coptic times, and Coptic lamps bear the image of a frog with the inscription, "I am the resurrection". That the frog was supposed by the ancient Egyptians to give life to the dead, is made evident by the fact that it figures prominently in connexion with the resurrection of Osiris. In one particular scene on the walls of the temple of Dendera, Osiris lies on his bier in mummified form, while at his head kneels the goddess Hathor with outstretched hands,

[1] E. Thurston, *Omens and Superstitions of Southern India*, pp. 252–3, 305–6.
[2] *Rig-veda*, VII, 103.   [3] J. Muir, *Original Sanskrit Texts*, Vol. V, pp. 436–7.

and at his feet, on a pedestal, squats an enormous frog.

Greek writers have preserved for us significant Egyptian lore regarding the frog. According to Horapollo (I, 25) it symbolized an imperfectly formed man. When the "new water" of the Nile, at the beginning of the Egyptian year, as it did at the beginning of time, fertilized the mud, it was believed that the frogs were spontaneously generated as were the mice. The Greeks accepted the view that the slime-coated frogs were half-formed—part of their bodies being still mud as they crawled about or squatted awkwardly. It was believed that if the river fell, the frog would be left incomplete— half mud, half frog. Ælian (II, 56) refers to a shower of incomplete frogs. Apparently, according to Wiedemann, the ancient Egyptian idea was that frogs were "the first living beings" that "originated in the valley of the Nile".[1] But the mouse, which was also supposed to be generated from Nile mud when the river began to rise, may be regarded as the frog's early contemporary. This fact may account for the close association of the frog and the mouse in so many Eastern stories.

The frog deities were connected with the sun, and so were the mouse deities. Mouse-Apollo became a prominent solar deity in Anatolia. The frog-goddess, which was given a solar significance in the Old World, was imported into pre-Columbian America. The Tunica Red Indians of the Lower Mississippi Valley had among their gods "a frog and a figure of a woman which they worship, thinking that they represent the sun". Mr. John R. Swanton comments that "it is hard to understand what connexion there could have been between the sun and the frog. This, in fact," he adds, "presupposes an explanatory myth which is unfortunately now lost."[2]

[1] A. Wiedemann, *Religion of the Ancient Egyptians*, London, 1897, pp. 129, 130. E. A. Wallis Budge, *The Gods of the Egyptians*, Vol. II, pp. 136-7, pp. 378-9.
[2] John R. Swanton, "Indian Tribes of the Lower Mississippi Valley" (*Bureau of American Ethnology Bulletin* 43), Washington, U.S.A., 1911, pp. 318-9.

Frogs figure in the Maya Codices and stone carvings of Central America. Tozzer and Allen, in their notes on Maya amphibia, refer to frog deities " with water coming from their mouths ", and in their illustrations these are seen to have hands with three fingers and feet with three toes. " God B in Tro-Cortesianus 12B should," they write, " be associated with the frog. His legs are those of a frog and he appears as if swimming in the water. ' Frog ', in Maya, is ' *Uo* ', which is also the name of the second month of the Maya year . . . the height of the rainy season in the Maya region . . . There seems to be no distinction in the treatment of frogs and toads in the codices." Toad gods, with three or four fingers on each hand, and human faces, bodies, and three-toed feet, are identified by Tozzer and Allen with the " tree toad " (*Hyla eximia*) which is common in the valley of Mexico. It is conspicuous at the beginning of the rainy season, croaking loudly. Tree-toad gods were " associated with agriculture and the sowing of grain at the beginning of the rainy season ".[1]

The identification of the Maori " tiki " with the ancient frog symbol of rain-giving, life-giving and resurrection, would appear to account for its various uses and connexions much more satisfactorily than does the phallic theory of Hare Hongi. Tiki, the god, has, as Tane-Tiki, a solar connexion and a connexion with life-giving water. As the technique of Egyptian mummification, and the complex ideas connected with mummification, " drifted " across the world into India, Indonesia, and into America on the one hand and Polynesia on the other, so may have the frog-lore and the frog symbol which, as has been shown, had a very early and intimate connexion with mummification. Combined in the Maori " tiki " with the symbolism of the frog as a life-giver was, apparently, the symbolism of life-giving jade,

[1] A. M. Tozzer and G. M. Allen, " Animal Figures in the Maya Codices " (*Papers of the Peabody Museum*, Vol. IV, No. 3, pp. 308–10 and plates 7 and 8), Cambridge, Mass., 1910.

which was also connected with the sun, the sky, and life-giving water—"the water of Kane (Tane)". The frog being anciently the first form of life, and a symbol of "imperfectly formed man", Tiki was in Polynesia thought of as the first man as well as a god, and the Maori jade "tiki" was, it would appear, supposed to contain the "mana" of generations, to stimulate fertility and to ensure the resurrection of the dead. It was evidently something more than a mere phallic symbol. Indeed, the phallic theory does not afford a full explanation of the various uses to which the "tiki" was put. There is not a single text which can be quoted in support of such a theory.

The making of "tikis", ear-rings, &c., from jade entailed considerable labour and no small degree of skill. Mr. John White, author of *The Ancient History of the Maori*, says that the greenstone "was broken as best they could break it into pieces when in boulders or large blocks, but it was not chipped—it was bruised to take any angle or point off". It was then rubbed on or with sand-stone and a drill was used to cut holes. Two stones were tied to the upper end of the drill to steady it, and a string was wrapped round the spindle above the stones. With a string-end in each hand the worker then made the drill rotate. Pounded stone or gritty sand and water "were put to the point of the drill at various times of the work".

The Rev. J. F. H. Wohlers tells that when in 1844 he began to labour among the Maoris of Southland he found among the *tohungas* (wise men) "some learned in old tales" and "some skilful in works of art". He describes one of the "old artists" at work:

"He is advanced in years, and hard labour no longer agrees with him. Sitting and doing nothing, his nerves will not be quiet; so he takes in hand a piece of raw greenstone, looks at it, and thinks what can be made of it. By and by he begins to rub it on a suitable stone. It takes a long time before a bright smoothness appears; but even a very slow progress cheers his mind, and the monotonous rubbing quietens his nerves. When he feels tired he ceases rubbing and enjoys rest. So it goes on through, perhaps, many years."

Mr. Wohlers describes the drill:

" To bore a hole or to make fine depressions he has a wooden staff about 18 in. or 2 ft. long; at the lower end is fastened a sharp splinter of hard stone; in the middle of the staff is fastened a small fly-wheel; round the upper end he winds a cord, and holds the two ends of the same one in each hand. Now, while comfortably sitting, and the greenstone being fastened below him with the sharp end of the bore upon it, he skilfully balances the latter in an upright position, and as he draws alternately with his hands the tool revolves in fast motions forwards and backwards. Formerly time was not considered among the Maoris."

Dr. Shortland, formerly Native Secretary, tells that the house of a South Island Maori chief which he visited was " like a stone cutter's shop ". The chief and another man sat beside a large slab of sandstone on which they ground by turns a piece of greenstone, rubbing it backwards and forwards. " They made so little progress during my stay," writes Dr. Shortland, " that it seemed probable that it would be left for some one of the next generation to finish the work."

Mr. Chapman, dealing with the Maori drill, tells of a friend seeing an old Maori at Rotorua in the North Island, " sitting on the ground, holding down a *hei-tiki* (" tiki ") by means of his two great toes, and drilling a hole through it, using such a drill . . . supporting it by merely balancing it ".

Captain Cook was puzzled to know how the Maoris bored holes in greenstone. He appears not to have seen the wooden drill with stone point which was kept twirling backwards and forwards, and constantly " fed " with hard sand and water, " in order ", as Chapman says, " to eat its way through the Pounamu or other

stone, on which steel would make no impression ".[1]
The Maori drill bears a remarkable resemblance to the
ancient Egyptian crank drill of the Early Dynastic
period. It had similarly two stone weights on the shaft
which served the same purpose as does the modern
fly-wheel and the forked point of the shaft held a hard
splinter of stone, the "cutter". The Egyptian drill
had, however, a handle which was used to make it re-
volve. One hand grasped the handle and another
steadied the shaft.[2] The Maori drill was made to re-
volve by cord like the fire-drill of other peoples.

[1] *Transactions and Proceedings of the New Zealand Institute*, 1891, Vol. XXIV, pp. 511
et seq.
[2] My *Footprints of Early Man*, pp. 143–5.

Neck Ornament (Tiki), from New Zealand, made from a
Human Skull

CHAPTER XVII

Tangaloa the Creator

Forms of Tangaloa in Polynesia and Melanesia—Hawaiian Farmer's Gods
—The Samoan Tangaloa—Tangaloa and Io—Antiquity of Samoan Concept—
Paradise and the Land of Origin—Divinity of Samoan Kings—Tangaloa and
Brahma—Tangaloa as an *Atua*—Sanctity of Manu'a—Samoan Creation Myth
—Tangaloa and the Rock—Cardinal Points in Polynesia and elsewhere—
Origin of Earth and Water—First Human Pair—Creation of Spirit, Heart, Will,
and Thought—Samoan Atlas as Sky-prop—Origin of Heavenly Bodies—
Peopling of the Isles—"Peopling Vine" myth—New Zealand not mentioned
in Samoan Creation Myth—The Bird-god Turi—Family Tutelary Animals—
Australian Creation Myth—Samoan Creation Poem—Sacred Vine and Hindu
Soma—Trees as Sky-props—Marae of the Sky-world—Earthly Maraes and
Chiefs—Tangaloa's Race—Indonesian Parallels—Sacred Rocks and Stones in
Fiji and Hawaii—Hindu God Shiva and Sacred Stones.

The god Tangaloa was in central and western
Polynesia of much greater importance than Tane. In
Samoa he was the Creator and Supreme Ruler of
the Universe as he was also in Tahiti where he was
known as Taaroa. The Maoris knew him as Tangaroa,
a lesser deity than his brother Tane, but, as will be
shown, there are indications in Maori mythology that
he once occupied a higher position. In the Hervey
Islands, where he was also known as Tangaroa, he was
regarded as a son of Vātea who ruled over sky and sea
and personified the sun at noon-day. An interesting
fact is that he himself, although regarded as a sky-god,
was expelled by his twin-brother Rongo, an underworld
deity and god of war. In Hawaii, Tangaloa was known
as Kanaloa (*t* and *k* being interchangeable), and was
associated there with the trinity Kane, Ku and Lono.
He was also, as we have seen, coupled with Kane as a

great traveller who searched for water, and the pair were especially mentioned in the prayers of agriculturists:

> " Here is food,
> O Gods Ka-ne and Kanaloa!
> Here is food for us.
> Give life to us and our family.
> Life for the parents feeble with age.
> Life for all in the household,
> When digging and planting our land
> Life for us—
> This is our prayer." [1]

As Tagaro he was known in the New Hebrides, where he was a *Wui* (supernatural being) who came down from the sky, lived for a time among men in human form, gave origin to the coco-nut tree and, because he had been wronged, departed either by setting out on a voyage towards the horizon of the sky-world, or returning direct to the sky.

It is in Samoa that we find Tangaloa in his most sublime form. He is there, indeed, a deity of such lofty character that the question arises whether he was of early, or comparatively late importation. As the Supreme Being, the only other Polynesian god who is comparable to him is the Maori Io, who, as we have seen, was known only to the higher ranks of the priesthood in New Zealand —*Io-i-te-wahi-ngaro* ("Io of the hidden place"), *Io, te atua nui ki te rangi tuatini* (" Io, the great god of the vast heavens "). As Elsdon Best says of *Io-matua* (" Io the Parent "):

> " He is truly the life, the welfare, the acme, the head of all things in all realms. There is nothing to be controlled by any other being, save as a subordinate of Io." [2]

It may well be that the Samoan Tangaloa was not of late importation. S. Percy Smith,[3] after careful in-

---

[1] W. D. Westervelt, *Legends of Old Honolulu*, Boston and London, 1915, p. 33.
[2] Elsdon Best, *The Maori*, Wellington, N.Z., 1924, Vol. I, pp. 90-1.
[3] *Hawaiki* (Fourth Edition), 1921, pp. 91-2.

vestigation of the available evidence, came to the conclusion that "the Samoans and part of the Tongans
formed part of the first migration into the Pacific, and
they have been there so long that they have forgotten
their early history". He emphasizes in this connexion
that " all the numerous legends as to their origin seem
to express their own belief in their being autochthones,
created in the Samoan Islands ". Both the Samoans
and the Tongans believed in a spirit land called Pulotu
"which", S. Percy Smith reminds us, "is not known
to other branches of the race—except indeed in Fiji,
where it is found under the variant Mbulotu ". Obviously
this is " also the name for the ancestral home in the far
west . . . The Samoan belief is identical with that of
the other branches (of Polynesians) as to the flight of
the spirits of the dead to the west." Dr. Carroll[1] has
suggested that Pulotu is identical with Burattu or Burutu
in Mesopotamia. On the other hand it may have a
connexion with Bharata, the name of a king and his
race in ancient India. There are indeed Hindu references to India as the land of the Bharata people.

It does not follow that because Tangaloa is found
to have been in Samoa a god of lofty conception he
was necessarily a late importation. As we have seen,
the Samoans perpetuated very ancient beliefs and customs.
Like the ancient Egyptians, for instance, they believed
that after being embalmed, their chiefs became. " sun-
dried gods " and that one spirit (Polynesians thought
that each individual had two spirits)[2] went to the sky
and another entered a stone or some other " spirit body ".

It may well be that the Samoan Tangaloa was, as
a creator, in large measure a memory of the Hindu god
Brahma. Dr. John Fraser, in his notes on a Samoan
Creation poem, draws attention to Tangaloa's love of

---

[1] *Journal of the Polynesian Society*, Vol. IV, p. 153.

[2] Dr. John Fraser writes in this connexion: "The Melanesians and Polynesians believe
that man has two spirits—the one may leave him for a time when he is dreaming or in a faint;
the other finally leaves his body at death." *Journal and Proceedings of the Royal Society of
New South Wales*, Vol. XXV, p. 280.

rest and peace and the fact that he is represented as a
" quiescent god ", and says that " in these respects he
resembles the Indian Brahma ", and that " although
he rests in the heavens, he intervenes in the affairs of
men " and " in his active manifestations he has many
forms ".[1]

There is nothing improbable in the view that the
chief god imported by the earliest settlers in Polynesia
may have more closely resembled the high god of the
area whence their ancestors came, than did the high
god or gods of the later settlers. The myth of the expulsion and partial degradation of Tangaloa, as preserved
by the Hervey Islanders, may well reflect a historical
happening. Tangaloa, the Brahma, may have been
supplanted by the Polynesian " late-comers " who worshipped a god of war, offered up human sacrifices and
practised cannibalism. Among these late-comers, as,
for instance, the Maori, the practice of mummification
was, as we have seen, somewhat rare. The expression
" le atua Tangaloa " used in Samoan myth is especially
suggestive, for, as Dr. Fraser notes, the word atua
(" god ") was " almost obsolete when the first missionaries
went to Samoa ".

The most complete form of the Samoan "story of
Creation ", in which Tangaloa figures as a Brahma,
was collected by the Rev. T. Powell and translated by
the Rev. G. Pratt, both of whom had been Samoan
missionaries for about forty years. The former settled
on the island of Tutuila and had under his charge the
island Taū, " the largest of a cluster of three islands—
Manu'a—which forms an eastern portion of the Samoan
group ". Dr. John Fraser notes that " all Samoan
traditions centre around Manu'a as the first resting
place of the race, and there alone dwelt the *Sacri Vates*
whose duty it was to preserve in their memories and

[1] *Journal and Proceedings of the Royal Society of New South Wales*, Vol. XXIV, p. 213,
note 3.

to recite the old legends and myths. . . ." Mr. Powell was thus on classic ground; and, having gained the confidence of the bards, he wrote down from their lips many of "the traditions which they had received from their ancestors ".[1]

The original manuscript left by the Rev. Mr. Powell gives the title of the Creation Story as ' *O le tala i le tupuaga o Samoa* ' ("the story of the growing up of Samoa"). It was taken down in June 1867,[2] and opens as follows:

"The god Tangaloa dwelt in the Expanse; he made all things; he alone was (there); not any sky, not any country; he only went to and fro in the Expanse [3]; there was also no sea, and no earth; but, at the place where he stood, there grew up a Rock. Tangaloa-fa'a-tutupu-nu'u was his name; all things were about to be made by him, for all things were not yet made; the sky was not made, nor anything else; but there grew up a Rock [4] on which he stood."

The god then spoke to the Rock saying, "Be thou split up "—that is to give birth to children. The Rock then brought forth seven "children" which have names meaning flat-land, land rambling like creeping plants, land like a flat reef, land like a honeycomb, land like soft volcanic rock that can be cut up, land which juts up like a rock on a path, and land which is branching coral. Dr. Fraser says that the mountains being mostly volcanic were not supposed to belong to the earliest stages of creation.

As the god utters the words which cause things to be, he faces the west, having the north on his right hand and the south on his left. The Aztecs of Mexico, in like manner, faced the west. Their god of the south,

---

[1] *Journal and Proceedings of the Royal Society of New South Wales*, Vol. XXIV, pp. 195–6.

[2] *Ibid.*, Vol. XXV, pp. 261 *et seq.*

[3] *Va-nimo-nimo.* " Va " means " space "; " nimo-nimo " means " unlimited ".

[4] The word used is " Papa ". Dr. Fraser says "Papa" is not a rock "in our sense of the word, but " merely something flat and solid " he prefers the translation " foundation " as used in *Isaiah*, xxxi, 17.

Huitzilopochtli, was consequently, as his name is translated, "Humming-bird *to the left*".[1] The Egyptians
and Chinese looked to the south and had the east on
the left and the west on the right, the Babylonians,
Semites, and Celts looked to the east and had the north
on the left and the south on the right. The Greek augurs
looked north as do the Shiva worshippers in India,
although the Vedic Indians looked east.[2] It may be that
the Polynesians looked west because their original
"Mecca", Hawaiki, lay in that direction.

The Samoan creation myth proceeds:

"Tangaloa stood facing the west, and spoke to the Rock.
Then Tangaloa struck the Rock with his right hand, and it split
open towards the right side.[3] Then the Earth was brought forth
(that is the parent of all the people in the world), and the sea was
brought forth. Then the sea covered the Papa-sosolo [4]; and Papa-
nofo (that is Papa-taoto [5]) said to Papa-sosolo, 'Blessed are you in
(the possession of) your sea.' Then said Papa-sosolo, 'Don't bless
me; the sea will soon reach you too.' All the rocks in like manner
called him blessed.

"Then Tangaloa turned to the right side [6], and the Fresh
Water sprang up. Then Tangaloa spake again to the Rock, and
the Sky was produced. He spake again to the Rock and Tui-te'e-
langi [7] was brought forth; then came forth Ilu,[8] 'Immensity',
and Mamao, 'Space' came (that was a woman); then came
Niuao." [9]

The Rock, in response to Tangaloa, next produced
a boy called Lua-'o and a girl called Lua-vai. The former
name appears to mean "two clouds" and the latter
"two fresh waters". The god appointed them to the
Sā-tua-langi, "the race at the back of the sky (i.e.

---

[1] My *Myths of Pre-Columbian Mexico*, p. 287.
[2] My *The Migration of Symbols*, pp. 29–30.
[3] That is "north side".
[4] The land rambling like creeping plants.   [5] Flat land.
[6] The north.   [7] A king to prop the sky.
[8] Dr. Fraser says that *ilu* means "innumerable", i.e. "100,000 or any vast number": it
appears to refer to the distance between the south and the north.
[9] Ilu, Mamao, and Niuao appears to mean "Length, Breadth, and Height", each, however
"limited to the sky" (Fraser).

the north) ". Another boy and girl issued forth, the latter being named " Desolate Sea ". Next came Man (" tangata ", Hawaiian " Kanaka " i.e., " the human race "). After Man came forth " the Spirit, then the Heart, then the Will, then Thought ", but all these " were only floating about on the sea; there was no fixedness there ". As Dr. Fraser points out, Man was at first " a dull, inert mass of matter ", when, however, Tangaloa, having created Spirit, Heart, Will, and Thought, put them into Man, he became a " living soul ", or an " intelligent being ".

The myth proceeds to tell how Tangaloa set the world in order; allotting to his children their places and duties:

" Then Tangaloa made an ordinance to the Rock and said:—

" ' Let the Spirit, and the Heart and Will and Thought go on and join together inside Man,' and they joined together there and man became intelligent. And this was joined to the earth ('ele-'ele), and it was called Fatu-ma-le-'Ele-'ele, as a couple, Fatu [1] the man, and 'Ele-'ele,[2] the woman.

" Then he said to Immensity and Space, ' Come now; you two be united up above the sky with your boy Niuao,' [3] then they went up; there was only a void, nothing for the sight to rest upon.

" Then he said to Lua-o and Lua-vai,[4] ' Come now, you two, that the region of fresh water may be peopled.'

" But he ordains Aoa-lālā and Ngao-ngao-le-tai to the sea, that they two may people the sea.

" And he ordains Le Fatu and Le-'Ele-'ele,[6] that they people this side; he points them to the left-hand side,[7] opposite to Tua-langi.

" Then Tangaloa said to Tui-te'e-langi, ' Come here now, that you may prop the sky.' Then it was propped up; it reached up on high. But it fell down because he was not able for it. Then Tui-te'e-langi went to Masoa and Teve; he brought them and used them as props; then he was able. (The *masoa* and the *teve* [8]

---

[1] The seed giver.   [2] The receptacle of the seed.   [3] Symbol of altitude.
[4] Clouds and fresh water.   [5] Sea beings.   [6] First man and woman.
[7] The south.
[8] Both are arrow-root trees. The leaves are on the top alone and spread out like a table.

were the first plants that grew, and other plants came afterwards).
Then the sky remained up above, but there was nothing for the
sight to rest upon. There was only the far-receding sky reaching
to Immensity and Space.

" Then Immensity and Space brought forth offspring; they
brought forth Po and Ao (Night and Day), and this couple was
ordained by Tangaloa to produce the ' Eye of Sky ' (the Sun)."

Nine heavens in all are provided, and then comes
the production of other gods who are really emana-
tions from Tangaloa.

" Then Tangaloa sat (still); he is well-known as Tangaloa-
fa'a-tutupu-nu'u [1]; then he created Tangaloa-lē-fuli [2] and Tan-
galoa-asiasi-nu'u [3] and Tangaloa-tolo-nu'u [4] and Tangaloa-
sāváli,[5] and Tuli [6] also and Longonoa.[7] "

The stars were the progency of Night (Po) and
Day (Ao). As we have seen Tangaloa had ordained
this couple to produce the sun ("Eye of the Sky ").
When Tangaloa the Messenger asks them if they have
any children Night and Day make answer:
" There remain four boys that are not yet appointed
—Manu'a, Samoa, the Sun and the Moon."
An assembly is held in the " House Beautiful "
in the Ninth Heaven where dwelt Tangaloa the Creator
and Tangaloa the Immovable and various decrees were
formulated.

" Then said Tangaloa, the Creator, to Night and Day:—
' Let those two boys (Manu'a and Samoa) go down below to be
chiefs over the offspring of Fatu and 'Ele-'ele (the first man and
woman). But to the end of the names of the two boys was attached
the name of Tangaloa-lē-fuli who is King (tupu) of the Ninth
Heavens; hence the (Samoan) Kings (tupu) were named 'Tui o
Manu'a-tele ma Samoa atoa '.[8]
" Then Tangaloa, the Creator, said to Night and Day:—

---

[1] Creator of lands.   [2] Immovable.
[3] Omnipresent, the visitor of lands and peoples.
[4] Extender, increaser of lands and peoples.
[5] Envoy or messenger.   [6] Bird form of God.   [7] Reporter of happenings.
[8] King of Great Manu'a and all Samoa.

' Let those two boys, the Sun and Moon, go and follow you two; when Day comes, let the Sun follow; also when Night comes, the Moon too comes on.' These two are the shades of Tangaloa; they are well known in all the world; the Moon is the shade of Tangaloa; but thus runs the decree of Tangaloa the Creator:— ' Let there be one portion of the heavens, in which to pass along; in like manner also shall the Stars pass along.' " [1]

Samoa and Manu'a having been created, Tangaloa, the Messenger, causes other island groups to spring up. The Eastern group comes into being:

" Then he went off to cause the group of Fiji to grow up; but the space between them seemed so far off that he could not walk it; then he stood there, and turned his face to the Sky, (praying) to Tangaloa, the Creator, and Tangaloa, the Immovable; Tangaloa looked down to Tangaloa, the Messenger; and he made the Tongan group spring up; then that land sprang up.

" Then he turns his face to this Manu'a; and looks up to the heavens, for he is unable to move about; then Tangaloa, the Creator, and Tangaloa, the Immovable looked down and caused Savai'i to spring up; then that land grew up.

" Then Tangaloa, the Messenger, went back to the heavens, and said:—' We have now got countries, the Eastern group [2] and the Fiji group, and the Tongan group, and Savai'i. Then, as all these lands were grown up, Tangaloa, the Creator, went down in a black cloud to look at the countries, and he delighted in them; and he said, ' It is good'; then he stood on the top of the mountains to tread them down, that the land might be prepared for people to dwell in. Then he returned (on high). And Tangaloa, the Creator, said (to Tangaloa, the Messenger):—' Come now; go back by the road you came; take people to possess the Eastern groups; take Atu and Sasa'e; that is a pair; they are called conjointly Atu-Sasa'e; these two people came from the heavens from among the children of Tangaloa."

Tangaloa, the Messenger, places on Fiji the pair named Atu and Fiji and on Tonga the couple named

---

[1] Here Tangaloa is identified with the sun and moon, both being forms, emblems, or " shades " of the god. Light appears (as dawn) before the sun rises and the sun is regarded not so much as the light given as the ruler of day as the moon is of night.

[2] Tahiti and the adjacent islands.

Atu and Tonga. The Samoan first parents, Fatu and
'Ele-'ele, had children and from these were selected
Valu'a and Ti'ăpă to people Savai'i.

The land of Upolu was then made to spring up
and after it came the land of Tutuila.

Tangaloa, the Creator, next said to Tangaloa, the
Messenger,

" ' Come now; go you with the Peopling-vine; take it and
place it outside in the Sun; leave it there to bring forth." [1]

This Fue or " Peopling-Vine " brought forth " something like worms ", and Tangaloa, the Creator descending from the sky, shredded the worms " into strips, and
fashioned them into members, so that the head and the
face and the hands and the legs were distinguishable".

Four worms being completed like human bodies
(male and female) Tangaloa, the Creator, " gave them
heart and spirit" and "four persons grew up". These
were the vine children named Tele and Upólu and
Tutu and Ila. The former pair were placed on Upólu
to people it and the latter pair on Tutuila.

The sacred vine had its representative spirit in the
sky world and we are told that he was Tangalao's son.

" Fue, the son of Tangaloa, that came down from heaven had
two names, Fue-tangata and Fue-sā; he peopled the two flat lands."

The Creation story concludes with,

" Then Tangaloa gave his parting command thus:—' Always
show respect to Manu'a; if any one does not, he will be overtaken
by calamity; but let each one do as he likes with his own lands."

The antiquity of this myth is emphasized by its
limited knowledge of Polynesia. The Eastern or Tahiti
group, the Tongan group and the Fiji group are referred
to. There is no reference to New Zealand, which had
apparently not been discovered. Had the Samoan

---

[1] This vine has, probably on account of its growth in spiral form, a connexion with the
sun. Some vines grow " sun-wise ", and others " against the sun ".

priests known of that land, they would have had surely
something to say about it. Hawaii was likewise unknown,
It will be noted that Tangaloa requires the Polynesians
to " show respect to Manu'a " the group of islands
of which Tau was the chief and where the priesthood
had their headquarters.

In addition to this elaborate Creation myth, the
Rev. T. Powell collected in 1871 a poem called " O
le solo o le Va ", in which Tangalao is associated with
his bird form Tuli or Turi. Dr. Fraser says that the
bird is the " Golden Plover " and adds,

"Every family in Samoa has its own 'tutelary animal'—
aitu[1]—a pigeon or some other bird, a fish, &c. This aitu is specially
reverenced by the members of the family from generation to
generation, and none of them will ever mention its name. A
convert renounces heathendom by publicly destroying his aitu,
the spectators standing by expecting that he will immediately fall
down dead."

An interesting fact mentioned by Dr. Fraser in
connexion with the plover is that some of the " Australian blacks " connect it with the acts of Creation.
" The tribe of Lake Tyers, Victoria," he says, " call
the 'grey plover' bunjil borandang. Now Bunjil is the
Victorian name for the Creator of all things, and the verb
punjiliko means 'to make, fashion, create'."[2] It may be
that this is no mere coincidence. The ancient mariners
who introduced the custom of mummification and the
associated beliefs and myths, may well have influenced
those Australian tribes who practised mummification.

The Samoan Creation poem refers to Tuli (the
Golden Plover) as " the emblem of Tangaloa the Messenger ", who carries out the instructions of Tangaloa,
the Creator. Its opening stanzas describe the primeval
sea before any land appeared.

[1] Totem.
[2] *Journal and Proceedings of the Royal Society of New South Wales*, Vol. XXIV, p. 213, note 2.

" Rollers flooding, rollers dashing,
　Rollers fighting, rollers clashing,
　The sweep of waters and the extension of waves,
　Surging high but breaking not.—
　Waves reclining; waves dispersing;
　Waves agreeable; waves that cross not;
　Waves frightsome; waves leaping over;
　Waves breaking; waves warring;
　Waves roaring; waves upheaving;
　The peopled waves; waves from east to west;
　Whose companion is the wandering current." [1]

Tuli the bird speaks, addressing Tangaloa who sits
" at the helm of affairs ", saying it desires to find rest
from the ocean in the sky. There is but a single rock in
the primeval deep and it is Manu'a. The moon looks
down on this rock, and so does the unchanging sun;
the fresh waters are in their place (above the sky) and
so are the salt waters (the sea); " heaven ascends, the
sky is clear ". Here the bird-messenger appears to
report to Tangaloa on the progress of creation.

Tangaloa descends, and desiring to have a place
whereon to stand, bids land arise. Then up sprang
Savai'i with its high mountain and up sprang Fiti (Fiji)
and all the Tongan group. The " two Samatas " (now
villages on the south side of Savai'i) also appeared—
Samata-inland and Samata-by-the-sea. These were
" the seats of Tangaloa and his footstool ". But Manu'a
" grew up first "; it is " the resting-place of Tangaloa ".
The god passed over the face of the waters and was
affrighted by the waves.

" ' Oh for a little coral strand!' thus to heaven he cries:
　Upolu, a very small bit of rock,
　And Tutuila, a little stony land,
　Are isles that thereupon immediately arise:
　Where chiefs in after times may find a place of rest;
　And gods though pinched for room, have many a feast."

[1] Apparently the Equatorial current crossing the Pacific from east to west.

The first human beings come from the sacred " vine ", which is a native climbing-plant called *fue*, Dr. Fraser suggests a connexion between the " vine " and the Hindu " soma ". One variety in Samoa is a Hoya. " Another variety of the *fue*," he says, " is full of refreshing juice which the natives drink; so also the Soma juice was used as a drink in the Vedic sacrifices. The Soma had reference to the generative power of the sun; so also the *fue* in the Samoan legend."

The poem continues:

" And hither came from heaven the peopling vine,
Which gave to Tutuila its inhabitants,
And to Atua, and A'ana, with Le-tuamasaga in Upolu.[1]
(Forth from the vine they come)
The bodies only move, they have no breath,
Nor heart's pulsation.
The god-like Tangaloa learns (in heaven) above,
The sacred vine to gender life has now begun,
But that its offspring only wriggle in the sun;
No legs, no arms they have;
No head, no face,
Nor heart's pulsation.
Tangaloa then, descending from the west,[2]
Speaks but the word and it is done:
' These fruits, the product of the vine, are worms,
But them I fashion [3] into membered forms;
To each of you from above I now impart a will.' " . . .

Fiji, Tonga, and other islands are then referred to and it is emphasized that they are of lesser importance than Manu'a. Nor can the sky-supporting arrow-root tree (the *Masoa*), " supplant the firm seed-stone of Manu'a, the Stone (father) and the Earth (mother) ". The " seed-stone " is the source of life: it came before the tree as Manu'a came before other island groups. But the " seed-stone " was sacred also because it was a

---

[1] These are three portions of Upolu Island.   [2] On the rays of the sinking sun.
[3] Cut up so as to form legs, arms, &c.

(22)

TANGALOA, THE POLYNESIAN GOD

Wooden figure from Rurutu Island, Austral group. Represented in the act of creating the
other gods and men. When found, the hollow back contained a number of small images

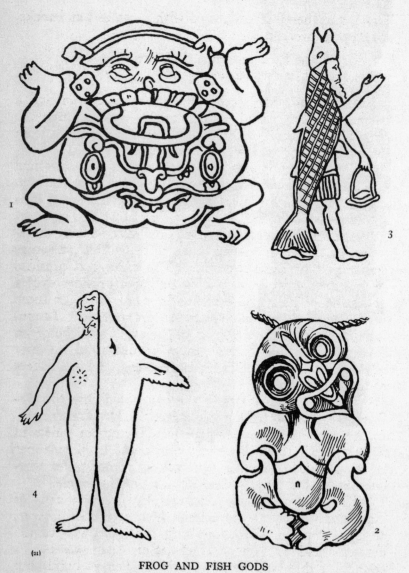

(21)

FROG AND FISH GODS

1, Maya frog deity. 2, Maori tiki (see p. 256). 3, Babylonian fish-god (Ea-Oannes). 4, Vătea,
the fish-god of Hervey Islands (see pp. 290–1)

stone, and therefore connected with megaliths and rocks. The poem proceeds:

> " The Rock produced and soon could show
> At least ten hundred sons."

After death, the spirits of chiefs or kings entered a sacred megalith. The Samoan priests reasoned that the first manifestation must, therefore, have issued from sacred stone (or rock)—the " seed-stone ".

The poem proceeds to tell that Tangaloa convened a council in the *fono* of Tranquillity—that is in the sky. A *fono* was a place of assembly, and in the poem it is referred to as the *malae* (that is, *marae*). The circle of chiefs in the heavenly *marae* sit in silence. Here, therefore, we have an assembly at a megalithic structure transferred to the sky-world. The chief god presides over the lesser gods, as a king on earth presides over a gathering of chiefs at a stone circle, a *marae*, or some other sacred place, and edicts are pronounced. Tangaloa decrees that the first cup of " Kava " shall be given to him. To him likewise must be dedicated the first offerings. The special offering, however, by the fishers must be the bonito.

Tangaloa then refers to the assembled chiefs as *Sa-Tangaloa*, that is, " Tangaloa's race ". Dr. Fraser notes in this connexion that " there were numerous chiefs in Samoa who bore the name of Tangaloa ". In like manner there were kings called Quetzalcoatl among the worshippers of the Aztec (Mexican) king of that name.

The Samoan poem concludes by giving details of Tangaloa's edicts at the council held at the sky *marae*, as if to impress the people with the sacredness of the councils held by Samoan chiefs at an island *marae*. A council of this kind must be held " when ye build ship or house ", because at the beginning Tangaloa, the Great Architect of the Universe, held such a council. Manu'a's king was the first man " to own a ship ", and he was the earthly Tangaloa. A chief architect must superintend the building of a ship as Tangaloa superintended the building of the world of islands. The last lines of the poem refer to an independent building of a house—one built without due ceremony:

> " The rafter-breaking god came down "

and the heretical builder had cause to exclaim:

> " Alas! my building all complete
> Is scattered in confusion great."

Similar to the Samoan myths regarding the origin of mankind from creeping-plants, stones, or rocks, are those found among the Indonesian tribes. Mr. Perry, in his admirable summaries from the writings of Dutch collectors, gives several examples.[1]

" The first ancestress of the race in the Luang-Sermata group is supposed to have descended from the sky down a creeper, the petrified roots of which are still to be seen on the island of Nowalna."

The woman thus comes from the sky-world, using the creeper as a ladder, but a myth of the Kayan of Sarawak states:

" ' In the beginning there was a rock. On this the rain fell and gave rise to moss, and the worms, aided by the dung beetles, made soil by their castings. Then a sword handle (*haup malat*) came down from the sun and became a large tree. From the moon came a creeper which hanging from the tree became mated with it through the action of the wind.' From this union the first men were produced."

Human beings also came from rocks and stones. The Taiyal of the mountain region of north Formosa account for their origin as follows:

" A rock once stood on the top of Mount Papakuwake . . . One day this rock split, and out of it came a man and a woman, the ancestors of the Taiyal." [2]

[1] W. J. Perry, *The Megalithic Culture of Indonesia*, Manchester and London, 1918, pp. 69, 77, 92.   [2] W. J. Perry, *op cit.*, p. 77.

A Minahassan myth tells of a stone giving birth to an ancestress because the sun heated it and caused it to sweat.

" Another account states that there was once a stone as large as a house in the middle of the sea. The waves played over it, and after a time a crow emerged. The stone then sweated, and out came Lumimu'ut (the tribal ancestress)."

" The ancestors of the Khasi chiefs of Nongkrem and Myllem are said to have come out of a rock situated not far from the Shillong peak in the Nongkrem direction." [1]

" The ancestors of the Tashon branch of the Chin came out of a large rock at Shunkla and the ancestors of the Whenho came out of the rocks at Sepi." [2]

These are but a few of many examples of stone or rock origin myths given by Mr. Perry, who proceeds to give a selection of those which tell of the first man and woman being shaped by the beings of the sky-world as stone images.

" The creation myths are recorded among the Posso-Todjo group of the Toradja and, in central Borneo, among peoples allied to the Kayan and Kenyah. In both cases it is said that beings of the sky-world made the first man and woman in the form of stone images.

" An analogous form of creation myth is recorded among the Iban of Sarawak. They say that one of the sky-people, Petara, commanded Salampandi, another sky-being to make men. She tried first to carve them out of stone, but the images could not speak. She then tried iron without success. Finally she tried earth and the two images spoke." [3]

Sacred stones under a fine rubber tree, stones rudely carved to represent human beings, a mass of stone " in the form of a human face, menhirs, heaps of stones and rocks are regarded in Indonesia as sacred and the abode of spirits—gods or ghosts of ancestors. The *marae* is known. The Chawte clan of the Old Kuki have " an open space surrounded by a low wall. At the east end of

---

[1] W. J. Perry, *op cit.*, pp. 78, 79.   [2] *Ibid.*, p. 80.   [3] W. J. Perry, *op cit.*, p. 80.

the space is a small house in which are two stones. This is the abode of Pakbangha . . . their supreme being ".[1] "During assemblies the principal chiefs sit on stone seats while "other chiefs sit upon wooden seats ". Stone-lined graves were provided for chiefs.[2]

It would appear that Samoan myths, beliefs, and customs connected with stones were imported from Indonesia at a time when the megalithic peoples were in course of their eastward migrations. Stone " god bodies " and stone-lined graves were conspicuous features of the Samoan cult.

In Fiji sacred stones were similarly " gods " and there were " no true idols ". Rocks were likewise connected with deities. Even a stone no bigger than a swan's egg might be a god as well as a great boulder.[3]

Fornander refers to the sacred stones of Hawaii, and connects the word *Hiwa* or *Siwa* of different Polynesian dialects which meant primarily " dark coloured, black, or blue " and secondarily " sacred " with " god stones ". He says that the Marquesan *Fatu-Hiwa* or *Patu-Hiwa* meant " sacred rock or stone ", while *Nuka-Hiwa*, one of the Marquesas, originally meant " dark or sacred island ". He connects *Siwa* or *Hiwa* with *Siwa* or *Siva* (" Shiva "), the Hindu god who with Brahma and Vishnu formed the trinity, " The Creator, (Brahma), Preserver (Vishnu), and Destroyer (Shiva) ". He notes that in India " a black stone is the emblem of Vishnu " and a grey stone the emblem of Shiva.[4]

---

[1] W. J. Perry, *op. cit.*, p. 57.   [2] W. J. Perry, *op. cit.*, p. 33 *et seq.*
[3] Rev. W. Deane, *Fijian Society*, London, 1921, pp. 65 *et seq.*
[4] A. Fornander, *The Polynesian Race*, London, 1878, Vol. I, pp. 46 *et seq.*

CHAPTER XVIII

Tangaloa and other Gods

Political Aspect of Pantheons—Religious Changes in Polynesia—The Great Revival—Tangaloa and the Floating Stone—Bird-god and Primeval Ocean—Sky Stones—Bird-god and Egyptian Bird Soul—Taaroa of Tahiti—Goddess Hina—Origin of First Human Pair—Windward Islands and Leeward Islands Origin Myths—Sea Gods—Blue Shark as "Makara"—Sky God as Sea God—Boats of the Sky-world—Sky Mariners become Megaliths or Rocks—Sacred Octopus in Old and New Worlds—Octopus and Megaliths—Octopus and Pig—Octopus and Mandrake and Taro—Kanaloa an Octopus in Hawaii—Gods of Sky and Underworld—Kanaloa as Alien God in Hawaii—Tangaroa in Marquesas—Hervey Islands Myths—Vatea the Polynesian Ea, Father of Tangaroa—Tangaro and Rongo—Origin of the Coco-nut Tree—Expulsion of Tangaroa—Mexican Expulsion Myth—Captain Cook and People as "Children of Tangaroa".

Tangaloa received different treatment in different island groups, and one reason for this may be that, as in ancient Egypt and ancient Babylonia, local pantheons were occasionally reflections of local political conditions. The chief god of a conquering tribe was elevated above the chief god of the conquered, and in forming a new pantheon the priests and kings or chiefs effected other changes in the values and attributes of deities. As will be shown. Tangaloa was in one area regarded as a twin-brother of another deity, who was either slightly more powerful than him, or he became, in another area, one of a group of great deities whose attributes were inter-changeable. Elsewhere he was displaced as a sky-god and creator or divine artificer, and had his sphere of influence strictly circumscribed.

But while changes of this kind may have been

277

effected, as a result of intrusions by conquering tribes or families, it cannot be overlooked that new ideas regarding the gods and new religious practices and myths may occasionally have been introduced by the priesthood in consequence of contact from time to time with fresh groups of sea-farers from Indonesia whose religious ideas had been influenced by the settlement in that area of the teachers of the rival faiths of India. As we have seen, the serpent-dragon cult, and the cults which had imparted to jade and obsidian a religious value, had influenced areas in the South Sea islands. We have to take account, too, of the searchers for pearl shell and pearls, who as importers of religious ideas undoubtedly exercised some degree of influence. Withal, although sun-worship never assumed in the South Sea islands the prominence it had in India, there are traces of the ideas connected with solar cults. Tangaroa, as is indicated in the previous chapter, had evidently in Samoa certain solar associations.

The Polynesians appear, when confronted by a crisis, to have ever been prone to adopt either wholly or partly new religious ideas and practices, especially when given a lead by their chiefs and priests. The early Christian missionaries were sometimes embarrassed by the sudden and wholesale conversions effected on some islands. In 1836, for instance, Europe was thrilled by reports of the " Great Revival in the Sandwich Islands ". It took place at a time when the great masses of the people were " upon the verge of starvation ". Hermann Melville says of this " Revival ":

" Several thousands were, in the course of a few weeks, admitted into the bosom of the Church. But this result was brought
about by no sober moral convictions; as an almost instantaneous
relapse into every kind of licentiousness soon after testified. It
was the legitimate effect of a morbid feeling, engendered by the
sense of severe physical wants, preying upon minds excessively
prone to superstition; and by fanatical preaching, inflamed into

the belief that the gods of the missionaries were taking vengeance upon the wickedness of the land."

Melville detected, while living among the Polynesians, an inherent characteristic which was "akin to hypocrisy" and wrote in this connexion:

"It leads them to assume the most passionate interest in matters for which they really feel little or none whatever; but in which, those whose power they dread, or whose favour they court, they believe to be at all affected."

The Polynesians were, at times, as ready to change their religion as to change the little clothing they wore. But they retained some of their old beliefs after acquiring new beliefs. Sunday, for instance, was their "Taboo Day" . . . "the very words", says Melville, "formerly expressing the sacredness of their pagan observances now proclaiming the sanctity of the Christian Sabbath ".[1]

The Maori of New Zealand did not differ much from the Sandwich Islanders after Christianity came into fashion, and especially in those communities in which there was a lack of genuine conviction. Mr. Alfred A. Graves, writing with intimate knowledge in his *Tales of a Dying Race*, pictures for us a particular community which was nominally Christian. A school is kept by a Church of England lady missionary, and is periodically visited by the Bishop. A Mormon missionary appears on the scene, and after a time he is successful in wooing the schoolmistress. The Bishop is furious, but the natives accept the situation with interest and enthusiasm. One Maori voices the sentiments of the others when he says to the Mormon:

"You and te schoolmissis make a *marenatanga*—allasame you say ' marry '. By-and-py the Mormona Church and t'e Church of Englan' make a *marenatanga*, too, here in Omakau, an' we have another werry good time wit' a noo religion."

[1] *Omoo*, Chapter XLV.

The " noo religions " in the old days effected more than one *marenatanga* (marriage) between the Tangaloa and other cults.

In Samoa Tangaloa was, as the chief god, usually referred to as Tangaloa-langi (" Tangaloa of the skies "). As we have seen, he was the divine architect and creator who brought into existence, or set in order, the world of men called Lalolangi (" Under the skies ").

One of the several versions of the origin myth tells that at the beginning when a vast sea covered the world below the skies, Tangaloa looked down and saw a stone floating on the waters.[1] He raised this stone to his sky-world, and carved it into human shape, and breathed into it the breath of life. A maiden thus came into being and he took her as his wife. In time a child was born. According to one collector this child was a boy, but another says a girl.

Tangaloa sent his child to the world below the sky in the shape of Tuli or Turi, a bird (Chapter XIII). Dr. Fraser, as we have seen, identified the bird as the " Golden Plover ". Stair follows him in this regard, but Turner says the bird was a species of snipe.[2]

Another version of the Samoan myth makes Tangaloa himself the bird which descends from the sky-world to search for dry land.

A similar myth comes from Tonga.[3] It tells that there dwelt in the heavens Tama-pouli-alamafoa (" King of Heaven "), Tangaloa - tufuga (" Celestial Artizan "), Tangaloa-atu-logo-logo (" Celestial Messenger "), and Tangaloa-eiki (" Celestial Chief "). Tangaloa the Messenger was sent down to the world to search for land. He assumed the form of a bird, and flew about for a long time, but found only a sandbank on which waves were breaking.

---

[1] Like the floating stone in Arthurian romance. *Morte Darthur*, Book XIII, Chap. II.

[2] J. B. Stair, *Old Samoa*, pp. 212 *et seq.* G. Turner, *Samoa*, pp. 7 *et seq.*

[3] " Traditions tonquiennes," in *Anthropos*, Vol. II, pp. 444 *et seq.*, and summarized by Dr. R. B. Dixon in *The Mythology of All Races* (*Oceanic*, p. 19).

" Returning to the skies he reported that he could find no dry land, but the lords of heaven said to him, ' Wait for seven days, and then go back and look again.' He did so and found the land already risen above the waters. Bringing back tidings of his discovery, he was again instructed to wait and to look once more, for this dry land which he had seen was indeed the earth. Tangaloa, the divine Messenger, then complained that there was no place below where he could rest, and was told to ask Tangaloa, the divine Artificer, to cast down chips and shavings from his work. This he did and the island of Eua arose."

Tangaloa the Messenger, on his return to the world, found the land which had dropped down from the skies. He was ordered to dwell on it, but he flew back to the sky-world and complained that there was no plant or tree.

" Then the divine chief gave him a seed, ordering him to plant it, and when he had done so, the seed germinated and grew, and a great vine arose, spreading until it covered all the land."

There is nothing primitive about a myth of this kind which reflects a civilization in which there were rulers, artificers, horticulturists, &c. The bird form of the god suggests the *bai*-soul of the ancient Egyptians which descended from the sky-world to visit the tomb, while the stone image into which was breathed the breath of life is reminiscent of the Egyptian tomb image which was ceremonially animated so that it might become a habitation of the *Ka*.

Ellis, who mentions a tradition of the Society Islands " that the first inhabitants of the South Sea Islands originally came from a country in the direction of the setting sun ", says that " the origin of the islands, as well as their inhabitants, was generally attributed to Taaroa, or the joint agency of Taaroa and Hina (the goddess) ". He tells that some who ascribed the formation of the islands to Taaroa said he laboured so hard " that the profuse perspiration induced thereby filled up the hollows and formed the sea, accounting this circumstance for its transparency and saltness ".[1] Another myth credits the work of forming the islands to a descendant of Taaroa, a son of the sun and moon. This god embraced the sand on the sea-shore and begat a son called Tii (Tiki) and a daughter named Opiira, who were " the father and mother of mankind ".

Mr. Barff gave Ellis from his collections a myth which tells that man was of the fifth order of intelligent beings created by Taaroa and Hina. Transforming themselves into human shape this couple became the parents of Tii " the first-born of mankind ", and of a daughter, the first woman.

According to another version " Taaroa made the earth, the sun, moon, and stars, heaven, and hell ", and " Tii made man of the earth ".[2]

In the Windward Islands, according to Ellis, the origin of the world and all it contains was ascribed to the procreative power of Taaroa " who is said to have embraced a rock, the imagined foundation of all things, which afterwards brought forth the earth and sea ". The myth proceeds:

" Soon after this the heralds of day, the dark and the light blue sky, appeared before Taaroa, and solicited a soul for his offspring: the then inanimate universe. The foundation of all replied, ' It is done,' and directed his son, the Sky-producer, to accomplish his will. In obedience to the mandate of Taaroa, his son looked up into the heavens, and the heavens received the power of bringing forth new skies, and clouds, sun, moon, and stars, thunder and lightning, rain and wind. He then looked downwards, and the unformed mass received the power to bring forth earth, mountains, rocks, trees, herbs, and flowers, beasts, birds, and insects, fountains, rivers, and fish. Raitubu, or Sky-producer, then looked to the abyss, and imparted to it power to bring forth the purple water, rocks, and corals and all the inhabitants of the ocean. Some of the

---

[1] In ancient Egypt it was said of Osiris, ' The Nile comes forth from the sweat of thy hands." Breasted, *Religion and Thought in Ancient Egypt*, p. 21.

[2] W. Ellis, *Polynesian Researches* (Second Edition) London, 1831, Vol. I, pp. 112 *et seq.*

gods are said to have been produced in the same way, namely by the god Taaroa looking at the goddess his wife, who afterwards became the mother of his children." [1]

In the Leeward Islands Taaroa was said to be Toivi, or "without parents", and to have "existed from eternity". Mr. Barff informed Ellis regarding him:

"He (Taaroa) was supposed to have a body, but it was invisible to mortals. After innumerable seasons had passed away, he cast his *paa*, shell or body, as birds do their feathers or serpents their skins; and by this means, after intervals of innumerable seasons, his body was renewed. In the *reva*, or highest heavens, he dwelt alone. His first act was the creation of Hina, who is also called his daughter. Countless ages passed away, when Taaroa and his daughter made the heavens, the earth, and the sea. The foundation of the world was a solid rock, which, with every part of the creation, Taaroa was supposed to sustain by his invisible power."

Taaroa, with the assistance of Hina, created the gods of the sky, earth, and sea. These included "Rootane, god of peace", the dog god, "Toahitu", gods of war, "Tuaraatai, ", whom Mr. Barff thought was "the Polynesian Neptune". In addition to this Neptune there was Hiro, the sea-god, and the shark-gods. The blue shark was sacred and was supposed "to recognize a priest on board any canoe". Ellis writes of it as a "makara":

"I have been repeatedly told by an intelligent man, formerly a priest of an *atua mao*, that the shark through which his god was manifested, swimming in the sea, carried either him or his father on its back from Raiatea to Huahine, a distance of twenty miles." [2]

Although Tangaloa is in the myths of Central and Western Polynesia a god who has his dwelling in the sky, it must not be assumed that he had on that account no connexion with the sea. In the sky-world, as we have

---

[1] *Polynesian Researches* (Second Edition), Vol. I, p. 324.
[2] *Polynesian Researches* (Second Edition), Vol. I, Chap. XIII.

seen, there were streams, pools, and lakes. Indeed, the lower world in which human beings were to live appears, according to the cumulative evidence of the myths, to have been shaped in imitation of the world of the gods. That was evidently because the ancestors of the Polynesians had before leaving Indonesia acquired the ancient conception of a sky-world which was an imitation of the world of men. They, therefore, began to frame their myths from what may be called " ready made " material. It appears to have been because of the prevalence of the idea that there were waters in the sky that we find in Samoa a myth which tells that Tangaloa and his son Lu " built a canoe or vessel up in the heavens. When finished it was taken down and set on the Laueleele, or surface of the earth. There was no sea at that time." [1]

Another memory of the waters of the " sky-world " is discovered in the myth from Upólu which tells that Tangaloa, who sends thunder, storm, and heavy rain, had fallen in love with the daughter of a chief who lived in a cave. He let down a net from the sky, " caught her and pulled her up to the heavens ". Their son Pili wished to reside in the world of men and Tangaloa said:

" If you go down, come up again. But if you wish to go and not return, take my wooden pillow and fishing net with you." [2]

The god's canoe is mentioned in another myth. " Tangaloa," it says, " was said to have come along the ocean in a canoe, with seven of a crew, and to have taken up his abode in the bush inland of the settlement." The god and his crew were transformed into stones in a sacred grove, and when war broke out two of the chiefs went inland " to consult Tangaloa ". One of the chiefs sat in front of the grove; the other, covered with leaves, went round behind.

" If the stones appeared separated and unusually far apart, that was a sign that the district was about to be broken up and

---

[1] Turner, *Samoa*, pp. 11-2.   [2] Turner, *Samoa*, pp. 232-2.

killed or banished. But if the stones were huddled together, that was a good omen, and indicated union, victory, and strength." [1]

Tangaloa's canoe is reminiscent of the sky-boat of the sun god, the seven members of the crew being the seven stars of the " Great Bear " (Ursa Major) constellation. After the fusion of the stellar and solar faiths in ancient Egypt, a process which can be traced in the Pyramid Texts [2], the star gods " became the rowers of the boat of the sun god ".

The essential connexion of Tangaloa with the sea (the sky sea and the earthly sea), even in Samoa, is emphasized by his connexion with the octopus (cuttlefish). In the Mediterranean area the octopus was a form of Aphrodite and it figures prominently on the pottery of the sea-faring Minoans of Crete. The sea-farers who migrated gradually towards the Far East carried octopus lore with them, and in pre-Columbian America the octopus was a form of the mother goddess. On a number of Central American stone slabs " the head of the goddess is a conventionalized octopus ".[3] M. Siret found the octopus motif among the relics of ancient sea-farers in Spain, "and", says Elliot Smith, "makes the remarkable claim that the conventionalized form of the Egyptian Bes, which, according to Quibell, is the god whose function it is to preside over sexual intercourse in its purely physical aspect, is derived from the octopus ".[4]

Whether Bes was or was not an octopus, it is certain that Tangaloa was, as stated, associated with the octopus (cuttle-fish).

Among the Samoan origin myths given by Turner is one which tells that Tangaloa first shaped the heavens, then the earth and then the fee or cuttle-fish. He told the cuttle-fish " to go down under the earth and hence

[1] Turner, Samoa, pp. 53–4.
[2] Breasted, Development of Religion and Thought in Ancient Egypt, p. 102.
[3] Saville, Antiquities of Manabi, Ecuador, 1907, and Elliot Smith, Evolution of the Dragon, p. 17.
[4] Evolution of the Dragon, p. 171, and Quibell, Excavations at Saqqara, 1905–6, p. 14

the lower regions of sea or land are called Sa le fée, or sacred to the cuttle-fish. The cuttle-fish brought forth all kinds of rocks, and hence the great one on which we live."

Another version says that from the loose rocks and fire sprang a man (? god) called Ariari, and " from him and a woman sprang the cuttle-fish and the race of men ".

A version of the Samoan origin myth " begins ", says Dixon, " with a genealogical series of rocks and cliffs, from which at length arises the octopus, whose children are fire and water. Between their descendants arises a mighty conflict, in which water wins and the world is destroyed by a flood only to be recreated by Tangaloa."[1]

In Samoa the cuttle-fish was a war-god, and its spirit was supposed to be present in the white shell of the *Cypræa ovula*. This is an arbitrary association of very special interest, because Aphrodite was similarly connected with univalvular and other shells.[2]

Turner gives a myth about the octopus gods of Savaii being caught in a net and killed by an Upólu hero. The gods were " changed into stones, and now stand up in a rocky part of the lagoon on the north side of Upólu. For a long time travelling parties from Savaii felt *eerie* when they came to the place—did not like to go through between the stones, but took the outside passage."[3]

An octopus god of Savaii married a chief's daughter, and he built a " stone house " inland. Turner says of this " house " that its " Stonehenge relics " are " still pointed out and named to this day ' the house of the Fe'e '."

Here then we have another arbitrary association—that of the octopus with rocks and megaliths.

[1] Roland B. Dixon, *The Mythology of All Races: Oceanic*, p. 17.
[2] Elliot Smith, *op. cit.*, pp. 166 *et seq.*   [3] Turner, *Samoa*, p. 31.

We find the octopus associated also with the pig. Turner tells of a family which had two gods embodied in the heart of a pig and an octopus. " Men, women, and children were most scrupulous never to eat either the one or the other, believing that such a meal would be the swallowing of a germ of a living heart or octopus growth, by which the insulted gods would bring about death." [1]

The octopus was likewise connected with Moso, " one of the great land gods in opposition to Tangaloa ", whose other forms included the pigeon, a tree, a stone, a large wooden bowl " decorated with white shells " the mullet, the turtle, and the stinging ray fish.[2] The bowl was a symbol of Tangaloa as well as of Moso.

The octopus was prominent in the mythology of the Society Islands. A Creation myth tells that

" when land became land and it was firm, the great octopus, Tumu-ra'i-fenua, held on; one arm was south, one arm was north, one arm was east, and another arm was west; they held the sky down against the earth." [3]

Handy says that " the number eight and the octopus which it symbolized were prominent features in the symbology of the Society Islands, being made the basis of the political divisions of all the islands. For example, the eight districts of Raiatea were spoken of figuratively as the tentacles of the octopus, while the residence of the chief at Opoa was the head." As Ellis says of the Society Islanders, " Raiatea . . . has been celebrated as the cradle of their mythology, the seat of their oracle, and the abode of those priests whose predictions for many generations regulated the expectations of the nation. It is also intimately connected with the most important matters in the traditionary history and ancient religion of the people." [4]

[1] Turner, *Samoa*, p. 72.   [2] Turner, *Samoa*, pp. 36-8.
[3] T. Henry, quoted by E. S. Craighill Handy, *Bernice P. Bishop Museum Bulletin* 34 (1927), p. 129.   [4] *Polynesian Researches*, Vol. I, p. 13.

Elliot Smith shows that the octopus and the mandrake were personifications of the goddess Aphrodite in the Eastern Mediterranean.[1] In the Marquesas the place of the mandrake was taken by the taro, and Handy says that " an octopus, or if one could not be obtained, a taro root with eight rootlets was used ceremonially in certain rites ".[2] It may be that the octopus was originally associated with the goddess Hina who in some of the myths assists Tangaloa at the Creation.

The octopus was fished for and eaten in various parts of Polynesia, but it was taboo to the gods and the priests.[3]

Tangaloa was identified with the octopus in Hawaii. In " The Creation Song of Hawaii ", Kanaloa (Tangaloa) is mentioned, in this form, with the goddess Lailai " of the distant night ", of whom little is known, with Kii (Tiki), the first man, and Kane (Tane):

" Lailai was born a woman,
Kii was born a man,
Kane was a god born,
Kanaloa was born a god, the great Octopus." [4]

Although in some areas Tangaloa is referred to mainly as a sky-god, and in other areas mainly as a sea-god, it would appear that originally he was at once a god of sky and sea—of the waters above the firmament as well as the waters beneath. This view is confirmed by a modern Polynesian lay which the King of Niue (Savage Island) chanted when he welcomed the Right Hon. Mr. Seddon, Prime Minister of New Zealand, who visited him in May, 1900. Apparently the bard drew upon ancient tradition. The following extracts which refer to Tangaroa, the ancient god, are from the translation of the lay by the Rev. Mr. Hutchin, Raratonga:[5]

---

[1] *The Evolution of the Dragon*, pp. 165 et seq.   [3] *Polynesian Religion*, p. 129.
[2] Handy, *op. cit.*, p. 46.   [4] *Journal of the Polynesian Society*, Vol. IX, p. 42.
[5] Communicated by Edward Tregear to *Journal of the Polynesian Society*, Vol. IX pp. 234–5.

" O Tangaroa, thine is the land of wisdom! Niuē is always at peace when you come.

" The Turtle and the Shark are sacred fish that dwell in the ocean. O Tangaroa from the far-off sky (land). . . .

" O Tangaroa, thine is the land of sacred wisdom. O Tangaroa from the ocean, from the far-off sky. . . ."

As we have seen (Chapter XV) Kanaloa (Tangaloa) was in Hawaii associated with the god Kane (Tane) as a searcher for water. These deities, in several of the myths, constitute a pair to the exclusion of Lono and Ku. In Tahiti we similarly meet with the pair Taaroa and Tii (Tiki). According to Ellis " Tii and Taaroa the people imagined to be one and the same being, but that Taaroa dwelt in the region of chaos and Tii in the world of light ".[1]

In Hawaii Kanaloa and Kane were " very closely allied ", says Westervelt, " to the farming interests of the people long ago, and he adds:

" It may be that the close connexion of waters with plant growth made these two gods the especial gods of farmers."

Other gods were sometimes mentioned in the prayers of farmers, and each of these " bore the name Ka'ne (sometimes Ku or Lono would be substituted), followed by an adjective showing some method of work ". Westervelt gives as an example Kane-apuaa (Kane the Pig). He suggests that the word *puaa* " carried the idea of digging or uprooting the soil ".[2] As we shall see, however, in Chapter XXII the pig deity was important in itself.

Fornander was of opinion that the introduction of Kanaloa (Tangaloa) into the Hawaiian group of gods took place about eight centuries ago during the period of immigration from the southern groups of islands. He writes of Kanaloa as a god who embodied the conception of evil, and, as such, was punished by Kane.[3]

---

[1] *Polynesian Researches*, Vol. I, p. 114.   [2] *Legends of Old Honolulu*, p. 34.
[3] *The Polynesian Race*, Vol. I, pp. 84–5.

His dismissal of Kanaloa as "a fallen angel" does not accord with what Westervelt says of him. It may be, however, that as Handy suggests, Kanaloa may have acquired the attributes of Whiro, the New Zealand god of tempests and evil. "This," he says, "may represent some priestly teaching in Hawaii." Handy adds that "neither myths in general nor the worship reveal the theory of this deity's being a 'fallen angel', as Fornander puts it. In prayers Kanaloa is repeatedly appealed to as a beneficent deity, along with Ku, Kane, and Lono; and his name with these three is mentioned by Malo as one of the four major deities venerated by chiefs and people, it being said that he had two days in each moon set aside to be especially devoted to his worship." [1]

In the Marquesas, according to E. S. Craighill Handy,[2] Tana-oa (Tangaloa) "is at one and the same time a mythical figure, a legendary hero, a god of the elements, and the patron of occupations. . . . Tane was of little importance in the Marquesas. His name appears in legends and chants, but not in the genealogies. The sacred adze is associated with his name. . . . Tana-oa, who was god of the sea and winds, was the general patron of fishing." [3]

In the Hervey Islands (Cook Islands) Tangaroa is the twin brother of Rongo, god of war, and their parents are Vātea "father of gods and men" and Papa, a goddess from the Underworld.

Vātea bears a striking resemblance to the Babylonian god Ea, who, as Oannes, was, according to Berosus, "a creature endowed with reason, with a body like that of a fish, and under the fish's head another head, with feet below, like those of a man, with a fish's tail". As Pinches [4] says, "this description applies fairly well to

---

[1] E. S. Craighill Handy, *Bernice P. Bishop Museum Bulletin* 34, Honolulu, Hawaii, 1927, pp. 115 *et seq.*

[2] "The Native Culture in the Marquesas," *Bernice P. Bishop Museum Bulletin* 9, Honolulu, Hawaii, 1923, pp. 244 *et seq.* [3] *Ibid.*, p. 246.

[4] T. G. Pinches, *The Religion of Babylonia and Assyria*, London, 1906, p. 51.

certain bas reliefs from Nimroud in the British Museum. This creature described by Berosus lived in the Persian Gulf, landing during the day to teach the inhabitants the building of houses and temples, the cultivation of useful plants, the gathering of fruits, and also geometry, law, and letters."

Gill's [1] description of the Polynesian Vātea is as follows:

" Vātea . . . was half man and half fish, the division being like the two halves of the human body, the species of fish to which this great divinity was allied being the Taairangi (*Cetacea*), or great sea monsters, i.e. porpoises, whose sides are covered with pure fat, and whose home is the boundless ocean. Thus one eye of Vātea was human, the other a fish-eye. His right side was furnished with an arm; the left with a fin. He had one proper foot, and half a fish-tail."

Gill goes on to say that Vātea (or Avatea) signifies " noon " in all the dialects of Eastern Polynesia. In another of his forms he is a great sky-god, one of his eyes being the sun and the other the moon. His home is given as " The-thin-land " and " The-bright-land-of-Vātea ", implying " the perfect contrast between the brightness of noon-day or Avatea, and the utter gloom of Po, or night, which is the equivalent of Avaiki (the Underworld) ". Vātea was thought of as at once a god of the sky and a god of the sea.

Tangaroa was born from his mother's head, and was referred to as a fair-haired deity. His human descendants were the " fair-haired progeny of Tangaroa ":

" The fair-haired children of Tangaroa
Doubtless sprung from dazzling light." [2]

Tangaroa is represented, like the Babylonian Ea, as the god who introduced agriculture, which he taught to his brother Rongo. On Mangaia he had one *marae*,

[1] Rev. W. W. Gill, *Myths and Songs from the South Pacific*, London, 1876, pp. 3 *et seq.*
[2] W. W. Gill, *op. cit.*, p. 13.

and the only offerings ever presented there were " the first-fruits of all newly-planted coco-nut groves—the tiny buds, which eventually become nuts ".[1] It was supposed that all that was red " on the earth or in the ocean " belonged to Tangaroa, while all of other colours belonged to Rongo. Thus the red and upright plantain was Tangaroa's, while bananas of all sort were Rongo's:

" Of three kinds of chestnuts, but one, the red-leafed, is sacred to Tangaroa. Of the two sorts of the indigenous yam, the red is Tangaroa's. Of the double variety of coco-nuts, one belongs to Tangaroa. All bread fruit was sacred to Rongo.

" In regard to the wealth of the ocean, Rongo was decidedly the gainer. But four sorts of fish—all scarlet, besides lobsters, fell to Tangaroa. The silvery, striped, spotted, and black were all Rongo's." [2]

A myth dealing with the origin of coco-nuts, which were especially connected with Tangaroa, tells of Tuna, the eel, falling in love with the beautiful maiden Ina. He transforms himself into human shape and visited her, resuming his eel shape when he returned to the sea. A time came when they had to part. Tuna told Ina that on the next day heavy rain would cause a flood, and this flood would enable him to reach her door in his eel form. " I will lay my head upon the wooden threshold," said he. " At once cut it off and bury it: be sure daily to visit the spot to see what will come of it."

The flood came as foretold and with it the eel. Ina took an axe and chopped off the eel's head, which she buried at the back of her house. In time there grew up from the head twin coco-nut trees, one being red in stem, branches, and fruit, and the other a deep green. " And thus," says the myth, " came into existence the two principal varieties of coco-nut, the red being sacred to Tangaroa and the green to Rongo." [3]

On Rarotonga, where human beings were sacrificed

---

[1] W. W. Gill, op. cit, p. 19.   [2] W. W. Gill, op. cit., p. 12.
[3] W. W. Gill, op. cit., pp. 77–9.

to Rongo, "the reeking head of the victim was offered to Tangaroa". But Tangaroa had originally no essential connexion with bloody sacrifices.

On Mangaia the sea was sometimes called "the Sea of Vātea" or "the Sea of Tane". The blue vault of the sky was supposed to be of solid stone which was sustained originally by "the frail props of Rū on the central hill of Mangaia". The sky was subsequently elevated by Māui. There were then ten separate heavens, one above the other, and these "constituted the Elysium of the brave". In the sky was "the home of Tangaroa, the scarcely worshipped god of day".[1]

Here we have traces of a fusion of contradictory myths. Māui belongs to a different cycle of myths than that in which Tangaroa is prominent.

A myth tells of the separation of Tangaroa and Rongo. The former was displeased because of the preference shown to his brother, who had all things and creatures of other colours than red. "Rongo became very rich, Tangaroa comparatively poor. . . . The parents declared that Tangaroa carried the palm for beauty, whilst Rongo excelled in abundance."

It is told that Tangaroa set out on a voyage "in search of some other land where he could reign alone. He made a long journey and touched at many islands, scattering everywhere the blessings of food piled up for the purpose in his canoe. Finally he settled down on his beloved islands Rarotongo and Aitutaki, leaving Auau, or, as it was afterwards called, Mangaia, in the quiet possession of Rongo = *The Resounder*." Rongo was worshipped as a war god and human sacrifices were offered to him, and he was connected with the Underworld.

The form of the myth on Mangaia tells that Tangaroa was "expatriated without hope of return". The island was supposed to have been raised from Avaiki, the

W. W. Gill, *op. cit.*, p. 18.

Underworld, by Rongo, and it was regarded as the " outward expression " of Avaiki.[1]

Here we have a myth which closely resembles that of the Aztec expulsion myth of pre-Columbian Mexico. The peace-loving god, white god, Quetzalcoatl, to whom bloodless offerings were made, was expelled by his twin-brother, the blood-thirsty Tezcatlipoca who was dark like the Polynesian Rongo, and was, like Rongo, connected with the Underworld as a dark god. Quetzalcoatl set out on a voyage towards the east, leaving Tezcatlipoca supreme and associated with the terrible war-god Huitzilopochtli to whom human beings were sacrificed, as Rongo was with Rangi. It was prophecied that either Quetzalcoatl, or his white people would return to Mexico. When Cortez was leading his troops towards the Aztec capital, King Montezuma and his subjects believed that the Spaniards were the " white gods ", or " white men from the East "—the people of the white Quetzalcoatl.[2]

When Captain Cook discovered Mangaia from which the fair Tangaroa had been expelled, the natives " were greatly surprised at the fair hair and skin of their visitors, and at once concluded that these were some of the long-lost fair children of Tangaroa ".[3]

[1] W. W. Gill, op. cit., pp. 12 et seq.
[2] My Myths of Pre-Columbian America, pp. 254 et seq.
[3] W. W. Gill, op. cit., p. 13.

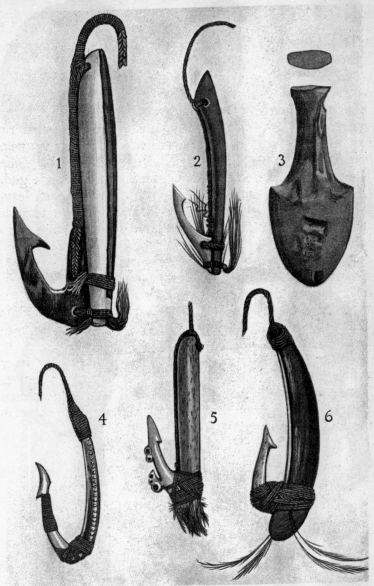

(24)

POLYNESIAN FISH-HOOKS, ETC.

1, Fish-hook of whale's bone, turtle shell, and pearl shell; Tonga. 2, Fish-hook of bone and pearl-shell; Tahiti. 3, Stone bread-fruit splitter; Hawaiian Islands. 4, Fish-hook of bone and haliotis shell. 5, Fish-hook of Moa-bone. 6, Fish-hook of bone, haliotis shell and wood; last three from New Zealand.

Reproduced by permission from the Hunterian Museum, Glasgow

IDOLS

1, 2, 3, and 4, collected on Captain Cook's voyage.   3 is from the Solomon Islands, the others
are from New Zealand.   5 is an idol with *Haliotis* or pearl-shell eyes from New Zealand

CHAPTER XIX

A Sea-god and Culture Hero

Maori Tangaroa as a Sea-god—As a "Lord of Light"—Sky and Sea
Connexions—Tangaroa and Tane—"Great River of Heaven" Myth—"Great
River" God and Thunder-goddess—The Earthly Wife—Punga the Lizard
God—Samoan Myth of Forbidden Sky-fish—Maori Myth of Tangaroa and
Papa—Rangi's Theft of Papa—Tangaroa as Lunar Controller of Tides—New
Hebrides Tangaroa Myths—Tagaro as Giver of Coco-nuts—Sky God who gave
Origin to Sea—Tagaro and Qat—Obsidian Myth—Gods of Sky and Under-
world—Visits to Sky-world—Derivation of Name Tangaloa—Deified Ruler
Theory—Tribal Name—Theory of Chinese Origin—"Egg People" of Burmah
and China—Dragon Kings—Samoan and Indonesian Dualism—Chinese and
Polynesian Jade Symbolism—No Chinese Archæological Relics in Samoa.

The Maori knew Tangaloa as Tangaroa and regarded
him mainly as a deity of the sea. His descendants included the god of whales, the god of sharks, the god of
eels, the god of shell-fish, the goddess of all sorts of
small fish, the goddess of sea-birds, the reptile gods,
and even the god of rats. Hare Hongi [1] has urged the
view, on the other hand, that Tangaroa was not really
an ocean god but a god of light, and points out that he
was "Lord of the Milky Way". But, as we have seen,
the "Milky Way" appears to have been regarded in
Polynesia, as elsewhere, as a Celestial River running
from a Celestial Lake, the source of all the waters in the
world.

In his notes on Samoan folk-songs, &c., translated
by the Rev. T. Powell and the Rev. G. Pratt, Dr. John
Fraser [2] insists on the essential connexion between sea

---

[1] "The Gods of the Maori, Sons of Light," in *The Journal of The Polynesian Society*,
Vol. XXIX, pp. 24–8.
[2] "Some Folk-songs and Myths from Samoa" in the *Journal and Proceedings of the Royal
Society of New South Wales*, 1890, Vol. XXIV, pp. 195 *et seq.*

and sky. The Samoan poet refers to the waters (*vai* and *tai*) being assigned to their places during the creation period, and Dr. Fraser writes: [1]

" The ' waters' here are *vai*, ' fresh water', and in the next line *tai*, ' salt water', is the sea. The poem makes a distinction between *vai*, the waters 'above the firmament' (*Genesis*, i) and *tai*, the waters below."

It may be that before Tangaroa was imported into New Zealand, he had been fused with his father Vātea, the half-fish, half-man god, who was at once a deity of sky and sea.

In the Maori Creation myth Tangaroa, as we have seen, attempts unsuccessfully to rend apart Rangi and Papa before that feat is accomplished by Tane. He is afraid of his brother Tawhiri-ma-tea, " the god and father of winds and storms". When that god wages war to avenge the wrong of separating Rangi and Papa, he takes flight to the ocean. The myth proceeds:

" Tawhiri-ma-tea next swoops down upon the seas and lashes in his wrath the ocean. Ah! ah! the waves steep as cliffs arise, whose summits are so lofty that to look from them would make the beholder giddy; these soon eddy in whirlpools, and Tangaroa, the god of ocean, and father of all that dwell therein, flies affrighted through his seas; but before he fled, his children consulted together how they might secure their safety, for Tangaroa had begotten Punga, and he had begotten two children, Ika-tere, the father of fish, and Tu-te-wehiwehi, or Tu-te-wanawana, the father of reptiles."

The Maori myth goes on to relate that when the war broke out the father of fish and the father of reptiles disputed where they should find safety. The former preferred the sea, but the latter shouted, " Nay, nay, let us rather fly inland. . . ."

" Then without delay these two races of beings separated.

[1] " Some Folk-songs and Myths from Samoa," in the *Journal and Proceedings of the Royal Society of New South Wales* 1890, Vol. XXIV, p. 213, note 8.

The fish fled in confusion to the sea, the reptiles sought safety in the forests and scrubs."

Tangaroa was enraged against Tane because his children who had deserted him were sheltered by that god in his forests on dry land. He has since waged continuous war against Tane, and Tane, in return, has waged war against him.

" Hence Tane supplies the offspring of his brother Tu-matauenga (the god and father of fierce human beings) with spears and with fish-hooks made from his trees, and with nets woven from his fibrous plants, that they may destroy the offspring of Tangaroa; whilst Tangaroa, in return, swallows up the offspring of Tane, overwhelming canoes with the surges of his sea, swallowing up the lands, trees, and houses that are swept off by floods, and ever wastes away, with his lapping waves, the shores that confine him, that the giants of the forests may be washed down and swept out into his boundless ocean, that he may then swallow up the insects, the young birds, and the various animals which inhabit them—all which things are recorded in the prayers which were offered to these gods." [1]

Another Maori deity may have been an older god of the sea and ancestor of fish than Tangaroa. This is Awa-nui-a-rangi (Great River of Heaven), perhaps an ancient personification of the " Milky Way ", the ordinary name for which, according to Elsdon Best, is Te Mangoroa, " mango " denoting a shark.[2]

Awa-nui-a-rangi climbs up to heaven and finds that the thunder-goddess, Whai-tiri, has gone on a man-killing expedition, being in the habit of offering up human victims in her Lightning House. He heard her loud voice which deafened his ears, and had to take shelter from her dropping hail.

When the thunder-goddess appeared she had two prisoners. One was slain, but the other, Fire Attendant, was taken by Awa-nui-a-rangi as his wife. He also married the thunder-goddess, and she taught to her

[1] Sir George Grey, *Polynesian Mythology*, Chap. I.   [2] *The Maori*, Vol. II, p. 214.

fellow-wife " the ceremony and incantations, the performance of which would prevent blight and cause food
to become abundant ". The thunder-goddess refers to
the husband's connexion with the sea when she says to
the other wife:

" When our husband comes back from the sea, tell him to
bring two pieces of seaweed. One must be dried by the heat of the
sun and then thrown on our house; the other you must take and
pass it through the fire, and repeat incantations over it, and breathe
on it, and then throw it away. If you remember to do this, food
will be plentiful for you and our child."

The thunder-goddess, who had been dwelling with
her husband and fellow-wife on the earth, then departs
to the sky in a cloud. When the seaweed ceremony was
performed food was supplied in abundance.

" That night Ika-whenua (fish of the land) fell from heaven
as food for her child. It lay in heaps, and partly covered the trees;
and when Kai-tangata [1] went to sea for fish, he was able for the
first time to procure a quantity."

Another version of the myth says that the first born
of Whai-tiri (thunder-goddess) and Kai-tangata (Awa-
nui-a-rangi) was called Punga and he was the father of
the lizard tribe. The second child was Karihi (sinker of
the bottom of the fishing-net), and the third was a girl
named Hema who married Ara-whita-i-te-rangi (crooked
road to heaven), and was the mother of Ta-whaki.

Punga, who is also mentioned as a son of Tangaroa,
and father of all small fish, is in this myth the father of
lizards and sharks. The off-spring of Punga and Karihi
slay Ta-whaki, as we have seen, while he was " washing
and combing his hair in the pool of Rangi-tuhi ".[2]

In this myth there may well be, as suggested, the
remnants of material which were incorporated in the
Tangaroa myths. The connexion it shows between the

---

[1] The other name of Awa-nui-a-rangi.   [2] J. White, *op. cit.*, pp. 87 *et seq.*

deities of sea and sky—between the river of the sky and the ocean, may explain the origin of the shark name of the " Milky Way ". Punga, the father of lizards and sharks, was a son of the sky-river god and the thunder-goddess.

In a Samoan myth it is told that Sa and Manu dwelt in a place named Afusi-ngalu ("the place where the waves dash over the reef in spray ").

" Tangaloa-le-Mana (Tangaloa the all powerful) went down to them from heaven with a fish for them, the celestial *ana'ana* (a fresh-water fish); he left it with them; they two were to keep it from him; so they placed it in the fresh water. He said to them, ' Do you two feed this my fish and guard it carefully; beware lest you use it ill. Then Tangaloa returned to the sky. They remained and ate the fish, they and their children. Tangaloa knew it. Then he came down again and spake (not as a friend) to them—' The punishment is this; since you have not obeyed my word, bring here your children; henceforth they shall face the coral bottom of the sea; neither shall you look up; now then go and seek for a land (to dwell in).' Then they went and reached Upólu and dwelt under (*lalo*) Mānu. That is the reason why it is called Lalo-Manu. And their children (were various kinds of sea-eggs), the *vatu'e*, the *vana*, the *'ina*, the *tapumiti*, the *ofa-ofa*, and all things in the sea whose eyes turn downwards."

The village of Lalo-Manu is situated at the base of an extinct volcano which about ninety years ago had ashes on its slopes although it is now overgrown with vegetation. Dr. John Fraser explains that the children who were condemned to look downward in the sea because they and their parents had eaten the forbidden fish are varieties of the sea-urchin. He suggests that Tangaloa's fish had a connexion with the " heavenly fishes " of the Zodiac, and adds, " some people, of old, regarded the Zodiac as a celestial river ".[1]

There are traces in Maori mythology of Tangaroa as a god superior to Tane and the brothers and even to

[1] *Journal and Proceedings of the Royal Society of New South Wales*, Vol. XXV, pp. 74–6.

Rangi. The latter god is referred to as Raki. A myth tells:

"Now Raki (Rangi) had no right to Papa-tu-a-nuku. She was the wife of Taka (Tanga)-roa. She went to live with Raki when Taka-roa had gone away with the placenta of his child. On his return, he found she had been living with Raki for some time, and had given birth to Rehua and Tane, and the other children. . . . Raki and Taka-roa proceeded to the sea-beach where they fought with spears. Raki was pierced by Taka-roa with a *huata* (a barbed spear) through both thighs, but he was not killed. The offspring he had by Papa-tu-a-nuku after this were a weak or sickly family."

Among the "weaklings" it is significant to find forms of Tane—Tane-kupapa-eo (Tane who lies on the flat rocks), Tane-tuturi (Tane who kneels), Tane-pepeke (Tane who draws his legs up), and Tane-i-te-wai-ora (" Tane at the living water, or water of life ").

A second version makes Rangi the nephew of Tangaroa, and a third says that " Taka-roa had come from a distance, even from Kara ('flint stone')", was the progenitor of Tama-nui-a-raki ("great son of heaven"), and connected with tribes referred to as " chub nose ", " nipped in nose ", " substantial nose ", " exact nose ", " perfect nose ", and " non-snoring nose ". From Taka-roa-o-te-ihu-pu (" Taka-roa of the perfect nose ") came the Maori people and from Taka-roa-hau-papa (" Taka-roa the cold ") came the European people.

A third version explains that Raki (Rangi) lay flat because he had been speared by Taka-roa (Tangaroa), but Tane came and lifted him up " as high as the mountains ", or as a fourth version puts it Tane and his brothers first rested Raki (Rangi) " thoughtlessly " on " the pinnacles of the mountains " but afterwards lifted him " still higher ".[1]

As controller of the tides Tangaroa was in New Zealand connected with the moon. He personified all

---

[1] J. White, *The Ancient History of the Maori*, Vol. I, pp. 22 *et seq.*

fish and was the patron of fishermen as in the Marquesas. Of special interest is his connexion with jade which, as we have seen, was regarded as a fish—a dragon, or shark-dragon and a "makara". The god took as his wife Anu-matao, a personification of cold, and their twin sons were Pounamu and Poutini. "Pounamu" (greenstone), as we have seen, was simply the animated stone, and Poutini was its guardian. The Jade people or Greenstone people had fled from a distant land where they had been at war with the Sandstone people. In New Zealand they came into conflict in the North Island with the Obsidian people and took refuge in the South Island.

In the southern New Hebrides Tangaloa is an eel or snake god who assumes human form as do the Nāgas of India. He is credited with the origin of the coconut palm which grew up from his buried head.[1] In this area the Polynesians mixed with the Melanesians and some of the islands have Polynesian names. Aniwa, for instance, as Mr. Sidney H. Ray points out, means "a place abounding in coco-nuts".

On the island of Tanna where, according to the Rev. W. Gray, he was called Tangalua it was told that he married an Aniwan woman named Seimata and they had a son. The Aniwans hated Tangalua, because, as they said, he was not a man but only a ghost. So they killed him with a big dose of *kava*. The myth proceeds:

"Before he died he told Seimata to watch the place where he was buried, for something would grow there that would be food for her and her child. As Tangalua lay drunk with *kava* he wagged his tail again and again, and died and was buried. Out of his two eyes grew a coco-nut tree."

The Rev. Dr. Gunn tells that Tangaloa was known in Aniwa as Tangaroa, and was said to have married a woman named Keke. Now and again he "left Aniwa

---

[1] The authorities are not agreed whether the coco-nut tree had its original habitat in America or the East Indian Archipelago. Apparently the coco-nut was carried across the Pacific by man. It was introduced by mariners into Melanesia and Polynesia.

and went over to Rupapu (Port Resolution) and to Nahabusima (Weasisi, Tanna), and to Namera (Kwamera, Tanna), and to other parts of Tanna ". Of special interest is the statement that " when he went away, he left part of him (his reptile or fish tail) behind as he was big and long like a house ", being, as the Rev. Dr. Gunn records, regarded as " a gigantic eel or sea-snake ". The myth goes on to tell that he died after drinking *kava*. His head was cut off and buried and from it grew a sago palm which ultimately became a coco-nut palm. From this tree, after it was cut down, sprang the coco-nut trees of Samoa, Rarotonga and Niue (Savage Island) [1]

In Rarotonga, as we have seen, the coco-nuts are said to have sprung from the head of Tuna who assumed the shapes of an eel and human being at will.

In the northernmost of the New Hebrides Tangaloa was known as Tagaro. He was a *wui* (supernatural) but lived as a man who " created and raised his food ".

" His life was full of wonders; his coco-nuts increased as he ate them; dry nuts out of which he scooped the meat filled up again. Finally Tagaroa became angry because someone stole his pig, and went off to Mamalu no one knows where; he turned the island upside down, and went off eastward in his canoe from the east coast of the island, taking with him the best of everything, and never to return. He put out the fire, but threw back a fire-stick; his shell trumpet lies on the beach in the form of a rock; Lepers' Island is his canoe. His place at Hombio is very sacred; his yams still remain there." [2]

An Aurora Island story tells that Tagaro made the sea, which in old times " was quite small, like a common pool upon the beach . . . this pool was at the back of his house," and " there were fish in the pool ". Tagaro built a stone wall round the pool. He forbade his two children to go to the back of the house, but one day when he was out the boys went to the pool. One shot

---

[1] " Stories from the Southern New Hebrides " in the *Journal of the Royal Anthropological Institute*, Vol. XXXI (New Series, Vol. IV), pp. 147 *et seq*.
[2] R. H. Codrington, *The Melanesians*, Oxford, 1891, p. 168.

a fish and when he tried to seize it, a stone was thrown down and the water poured forth in great volume.

"Tagaro heard the roaring of the water and ran to stop it; and the old woman laid herself down in the way of it, but nothing could be done; those two boys who had thrown down the stone took clubs like knives and prepared a passage for the sea, one on one side and the other on the other side of the place, and the sea followed as it flowed. And they think that the old woman turned into a stone, and lies now on the part of Maewo near Raga." [1]

A Leper Island story makes an old woman the creator of water which was stored in a leaf of the *via* (gigantic caladium). Two boys pierced the leaf which was protected by a fence at the back of the house, and a flood issued forth. When the old woman heard the water surging she cried out in a loud voice, "Pour round about and meet! Round about the world!"

"And thus the sea for the first time stood full around the whole world, for before that they say there was no sea. So the old woman you may say made the sea herself." [2]

It may be that this version of the story is a memory of the water-confining serpent-dragon who was slain by the water-providing deity, or the twin deities. In Melanesia the serpent-god is very common.

Tangaloa is in the Banks Islands recorded evidence referred to as Tangaro. There are several brothers of that name, and their elder brother is Qat who had no father, and whose mother was "a stone that burst asunder and brought him forth". Here again we have a memory of the dragon which, as we have seen, was supposed in the Far East to have been born from the stones called "dragon's eggs".

[1] R. H. Codrington, *op. cit.*, p. 370. Scottish Highland folk-tales tell of an old woman who was a guardian of a well which had to be covered every evening with a stone slab. One evening she failed to cover the well and the water streamed forth and formed a loch. Loch Awe in Argyllshire and Loch Ness in Inverness-shire are reputed to have had origin in this way. The old woman (a goddess) was subsequently transformed into a stone.

[2] R. H. Codrington, *op. cit.*, pp 372-3.

Qat's brothers are called Tangaro the Wise, Tangaro the Fool (who was " ignorant of everything ") &c.— and numbered eleven in all, making with Qat a group of twelve. The names of nine of the Tangaroa brothers " are made up," says Codrington, " of the names of the leaves of trees and plants, Nettle-leaf, Bread-fruit-leaf, Bamboo-leaf, Coco-nut-leaf, Umbrella-palm-leaf, &c.

" These all grew up as soon as they were born, and they took up their abode in the village Alo Sepere, where their mother, turned into a stone, may yet be seen. There Qat began to make things, men, pigs, trees, rocks, as the fancy took him."

Eternal day prevailed, and Qat imported night from " the foot of the sky " which he reached by canoe. An interesting reference to obsidian may be noted.

" When night had lasted long enough. . . . Qat took a piece of red obsidian and cut the night with it."

" Hence," says Codrington, " the expressions *O maran me teve*, the morning has cut, and *O mera ti lamasag*, the dawn strikes upon the sky, *mera* being a common word for red." [1] The dawn (or deity of dawn) was apparently anciently identified with obsidian—the magical fire-making and divination stone associated with tribal gods, and also a totem stone.

Codrington gives a myth from Araga, Whitsuntide Island, New Hebrides, in which the memory of Tangaloa, the sky-god, is preserved:

" Tagaro has ten brothers, besides Suqe, who accompanies and thwarts him.[2] Tagaro came down from heaven, made men and other things, and went back again to heaven. Suqe belonged to the earth; his head was forked, therefore he had two thoughts in it. Whatever Tagaro did or made was right, Suqe was always wrong. . . . Tagaro sent him to a place where is a bottomless chasm, somewhere inland in Araga, where he rules over the ghosts of the dead. Tagaro when on earth, though a *wui*, had a human

---

[1] R. H. Codrington, *op. cit.*, pp. 156–7.
[2] Tagaro wanted everything to be good, and Suqe-mata " would have all things bad ".

form, with superhuman power. He made the plain country by treading the ground with his feet; where he did not tread are the hills."

Tagaro married a woman when on the earth and a boy was born. After Tagaro disappeared " the boy kept asking his mother who his father was, and was told he was in heaven ". The pair climbed to the sky on a plant resembling that in the *Jack-and-the-Beanstalk* nursery story. In the sky-world the boy " found Tagaro sitting in a *salite*-tree and fashioning images of himself out of the fruit." Tagaro descended to earth with the pair, but he cut the plant-ladder and " went back to heaven ".[1]

Here we have again the twin-gods, one in the sky and another in the Underworld of the dead—the dualism so characteristic of Samoan mythology.

According to Codrington it was thought on Leper Island that twins might be a gift of Tagaro. " In some places, as at Saa, twins are liked; at Mottav the people of a village are proud of twins." A survivor of twin sons of Aurese would, it was believed, " turn out a great man " because " Tagaro gave the twins ".[2]

It is of interest to find that while Tangaloa was known as Tagaro in Melanesia, there was no mention of Tane, Rono, or Tu (Kane, Lono, or Ku).

The problem presented by Tangaloa is one of great interest. Some would have it that he was of independent origin in Polynesia; others consider him an imported god. Fornander, as we have seen, regarded him as an alien in Hawaii, where he was known as Kanaloa, and wrote of him as " a fallen angel antagonistic to the great gods, and the spirit of evil and death in the world ".[3] Dr. John Fraser divided the name Tangaloa into two parts—" tanga " and " loa ". He suggested that " tanga " meant " envelopes ", or " encloses ", and that " loa "

[1] R. H. Codrington, *The Melanesians*, p. 169.   [2] Codrington, *op. cit.*, p. 230.
[3] *The Polynesian Race*, p. 83.

(D 917)

signified as in Samoa, "long", "far off". Tangaloa may therefore be translated as "the (far off) god that encompasses all things"; or "the (far off) encircling Aether". In Samoan "tanga" is a "bag" that "envelopes" or "encloses", and in the Maori dialect 'tangai" is the "bark" or "rind" which "envelops", while "takai" is a "wrapper".[1]

The Rev. Dr. George Turner, dealing with the problem, says:

"The derivation of Tangaloa is uncertain. 'Loa' means 'long', and 'tanga', a bag; or as an adjective, 'freedom from restriction'. The unrestricted, or unconditioned, may therefore fairly be regarded as the name of the Samoan Jupiter."[2]

But the question arises whether Tangaloa was the original name of the god, or that of a deified ruler, or the name of a tribe. In Tahiti, Ellis, the missionary, said that "several of their *taata-paari*, or wise men, pretended that, according to other traditions, Taaroa (Tangaloa) was only a man who was deified after death".[3] This statement suggests that some ruler who had established the Tangaloa cult in Polynesia was after death, having been mummified and transformed into a "sundried god", identified with the Creator.

E. S. Craighill Handy suggests that Tangaloa may have been "a name belonging to a later group of seafaring Polynesian immigrants". His researches have inclined him to identify the Tangaloans of Polynesia with a Chinese people, and he writes in this connexion:

"Investigation of the name Tangaloa revealed the fact that this word is applied to the river population of southern China, spelt in redaction Tan-kah-lo, meaning people (*lo*) of the egg (*tan*) family (kah). The discovery of this correspondence in names and in culture traits has led to the conclusion that a group of these seafaring Chinese, whose religion combined the strictly

---

[1] Dr. John Fraser, *Journal and Proceedings of the Royal Society of New South Wales*, Vol. XXV, p. 264.
[2] *Samoa*, p. 52. [3] *Polynesian Researches* (Second London Edition), Vol. I, p. 323.

Chinese worship and philosophy with Buddhism, came into Polynesia, intermarried with Caucasoid Polynesian women, and through organizing ability and genius for trade, succeeded ultimately in dominating Samoa, Tonga, and the Society Islands and later Hawaii and other groups." [1]

Mr. Craighill Handy goes on to say that "the Creation story in the Society Islands, according to which Taaroa (Tangaloa) was born of an egg, is seen perhaps to have relationship to the meaning of the Chinese Tan-ka-lo (Egg-family-people)". But the Yahao branch of the Chin people of Burmah are an "egg people". At any rate, they say that their ancestors "were hatched out of an egg laid by the sun on Webula hill ".[2] Withal, it has been shown that the cosmic egg figures in the Creation myths of India and Egypt.

Mr. Craighill Handy suggests another Chinese connexion when dealing with the Samoan and Tongan paradise of chiefs, called Pulotu which was supposed to be situated on an island towards the north-west. It is ruled over by a being, named Hikuleo, or Si'uleo, who has a human head and the lower part of his body "in the form of the tail of a great eel or serpent ". He points out that Fu-hi, the traditional first Emperor of China is "depicted as a human figure with a fish tail something like a mermaid ".[3]

Hindu Nāgas (serpent deities) had, however, half-human and half-reptile forms, as has been indicated, and the Buddhists carried into China many of the ideas found in the dragon lore of that country.

The Tangaloa octopus was not of Chinese origin. Nor could the Tangaloa coco-nut lore have come from China.

It is unlikely that it was a Chinese people who imported into Samoa the practice of circumcision or the

---

[1] *Polynesian Religion, op. cit.*, pp. 325–6.

[2] J. G. Scott, *Upper Burma Gazetteer*, Rangoon, 1900, p. 458, and W. J. Perry, *Megalithic Culture in Indonesia*, p. 94.

[3] E. S. Craighill Handy, *op. cit.*, p. 326.

practice of mummification, or the beliefs connected with
mummification, including the elevation of the dead
ruler to the sky-world where he became a god. Tangaloa
may have well been, as Ellis was informed, " only a
man who was deified after death ", his name having
been conferred upon the Creator—the Brahma of the
Samoan Creation myth. Handy recognizes a possibility
of this kind when he says that " under the influence of
the Polynesian custom of recording history in genealogies
the name Tan-kah-lo came to be regarded as that of the
divine ancestor Tangaloa ". The Rev. G. Pratt has
shown that " the first kings of Samoa were sacred and
looked upon as gods ".[1] Dr. John Fraser, referring to
the " Sa-Tangaloa " (" Tangaloa's race ") says " there
were numerous chiefs in Samoa who bore the name of
Tangaloa ".[2]

A significant fact is that a Samoan chief was addressed
as " you two ". Dr. Fraser draws attention to this " sort
of dual majesty ", but suggests that " you two " was
used because the chief " is supposed never to be without
an attendant ".[3] But, as we have seen in the Samoan
Creation myth, Tangaloa was a dual personality—Tangaloa
of the sky and Tangaloa the bird or " Messenger ",
Tangaloa the Creator, and Tangaloa the Immovable—
the active Tangaloa, and the passive Tangaloa, like the
active Hindu Brahma, and the passive Brahma. There
was also Tangaloa the Sun, and Tangaloa the Moon—
the two " shades " (emblems, or manifestations) of
Tangaloa. The islands he created were dual. Southern
Savai'i, for instance, was divided between " Samata-
inland " and " Sama-by-the-sea ". When the land of
Tutuila was created, Tangaloa, the Messenger, " faced
the heavens towards Tangaloa the Creator ", and the

---

[1] W. J. Perry, *The Children of the Sun*, p. 299, and the Rev. G. Pratt, " Genealogy of the Sun: a Samoan Legend ", in the *Report of the Australian Association for the Advancement of Science* (1888), Vol. I, p. 657.

[2] *Journal and Proceedings of the Royal Society of New South Wales*, Vol. XXIV 216, note 37.

[3] *Ibid.*, Vol. XXV, p 118.

Messenger exclaimed, "Two lands are now gotten for
me to rest in". Fue, son of Tangaloa, descended from
the sky to rule over the land and he had "two names,
Fue-tangata and Fue-sā"; and "he peopled the two
flat lands".[1]

The dual organization of society which is reflected
in these myths is not a feature of Chinese life, but it
is found to be conspicuous in Indonesia, as Perry has
shown.[2]

There are really more traces in New Zealand of what
may be called "Chinese influence" than there is in
Samoa. At any rate, the Maori greenstone symbolism
resembles closely, as has been shown, the jade symbolism
of China, but the Maoris and the Chinese may have
derived their beliefs connected with jade from a common
source. The same may be said of the Maori and Chinese
dragon lore. That the Chinese did not give origin to
jade symbolism is evident by the finds of jade objects
in ancient Egypt and ancient Babylonia.

Had a Chinese people settled in Samoa, Tonga and
the Society Islands at a later period than the "Indo-
Polynesians", as Mr. Craighill Handy suggests,[3] one
would expect to find their archæological relics of bronze
or iron. But the Samoans were stone-using people until
discovered by the Europeans.

---

[1] *Journal and Proceedings of the Royal Society of New South Wales*, Vol. XXV, p. 274.
[2] *The Megalithic Culture of Indonesia* and *The Children of the Sun*.
[3] *Polynesian Religion*, pp. 323 *et seq.*

CHAPTER XX

Tu and Rongo

Tu as God "Stand"—Samoan Bird Form—As a God of War—Tu in
Maori Myths — As Enemy of Tane and Tangaloa — Tu the Devourer
of Gods—As World-tree, or Sky-prop—Maori Symbols of Gods—Tu and
the Storm-god—Tu as the Progenitor of Mankind—Indonesian Links—Tu
and Tiki—Tu as Controller of Disease—Tu as War-god in New Zealand and
Marquesas—Human Sacrifices to Tu—Tu and Oro—"Water of Tu"—
Human Sacrifices in Tahiti and Hawaii—Tu as Patron of Arts—Fusion of
Rongo and Tane—Set and Horus similarly fused—Maori Rongo and Agri-
culture—Connexion with Moon, Rainbow, and Meteors—Rongo and the
Goddess Pani—Pani and Rice—The Hindu Pani—Pani as Water-confiner—
Rongo and Pani controlled Disease—Rongo and Star Vega—Kumara Con-
nexion—Rongo in Hewn Stone—Hawaiian Lono (Rongo) as Thunder and
Rain God—Rongo as Dark God—Tangaloa and Rongo—Rongo of Under-
world—The Tiki Cave Entrance to Underworld—Priests as Forms of Gods—
Lono of Hawaii—Lono as Controller of Disease—Hindu Trinity and Hawaiian
Trinity—Expulsion of Lono from Hawaii—Boxing and Games in Honour of
Lono.

Other prominent gods of Polynesia, who like Tane
and Tangaloa were " head and shoulders " above the
tribal and family groups of deities, were Tu and Rongo.
As we have seen, Tane as Kane formed a trinity in
Hawaii with Tu as Ku and Rongo as Lono.

In Samoa Tu, whose name signified " stand " and
had the secondary meaning " strike ", was specialized
mainly as a god of war. Turner says of him:

" Stand (Tu) was the name of this war god, as he was said
never to sit down. He was incarnate in the rail. If the bird appeared reddish and glossy, it was a sign the people were to go to
war. If dark and dingy, the omen was bad, and they were ordered
to sit still." [1]

Another god named Tufi had for his symbol a coco-
nut tree spear ten feet long. Turner says that " when the
people met for worship the spear was stood up, and
offerings were laid before it ". The spear was also a
symbol of Tu. " It was taken ", says Turner, " in the
war fleet as a sign that Tu was with them." In Samoa
Tu was in time of peace " a doctor "; he was " supposed
to be powerful in removing sickness in return for prayers
and offerings ".[1]

In Maori mythology Tu is sometimes the elder and
sometimes the younger of the six children of Rangi and
Papa. Certain of his attributes are revealed in his names
Tu (" stand up "), Tu-matauenga (" Tu of the inciting
face "), Tu-rama-rama-a-nuku (" Tu the light of the
world "), Tu-rama-rama-a-rangi (" Tu the light of
heaven "), Tu-taka-hinahina (Tu of the grey hairs ").[2]
When it was proposed to separate the heavens (Rangi)
and the earth (Papa), Tu, " the fiercest of the children ",
suggested that Rangi should be slain. Tane declined
to agree to this, preferring separation from the sky and
continued association with Mother Earth. Rongo first
tried to raise the sky but failed, then Tangaroa tried and
failed, and was followed by Haumia-tikitiki[3] who also
failed. " Then Tu-matauenga, the god and father of
fierce human beings, rises up and struggles, but he,
too, fails in his efforts." Tane was the successful god,
as we have seen.[4] Subsequently Tu (" fierce man ") was
the only one of the brothers who could resist the attacks
of the avenging storm-god Tawhiri-ma-tea. He " still
stood erect and unshaken upon the breast of his mother
earth ". Tane failed to assist him and he became the
enemy of Tane's progeny. He also attacked Tangaroa's
" children " for a similar reason as well as those of
Rongo and Haumia-tikitiki.

[1] Turner, op. cit., pp. 61–2.
[2] J. White, The Ancient History of the Maori, Vol. I, p. 161.
[3] A personification of the bracken, and connected with Tiki.
[4] Grey's Polynesian Mythology, Chapter I.

"Thus Tu-matauenga devoured all his brothers, and consumed the whole of them, in revenge for their having deserted him and left him to fight alone with Tawhiri-ma-tea and Rangi.

"When his brothers had all thus been overcome by Tu, he assumed several names, namely, Tu-ka-riri, Tu-ka-nguha, Tu-ka-tana, Tu-whaka-heke-tan-gata, Tu-mata-wha-iti, and Tu-matauenga; he assumed one name for each of his attributes displayed in the victories over his brothers. Four of his brothers were entirely deposed by him and became his food; but one of them, Tawhiri-ma-tea, he could not vanquish or make common by eating him for food, so he, the last born child of Heaven and Earth was left as an enemy for man, and still, with a rage equal to that of Man, this elder brother attacks him in storms and hurricanes, endeavouring to destroy him alike by sea and land."[1]

Here the steadfast Tu may personify the world-supporting tree, or, as the Samoan coco-nut tree spear symbol suggests, the post that propped the sky. His Maori symbol was a nail-shaped straight stick with a knob at the top and pointed at the other end, while Tawhiri-matea's symbol resembled a corkscrew, apparently symbolizing the whirlwind, Tane's had a semi-circular bend in the middle, Tangaroa's was of zigzag form to symbolize waves, Hauima's had three semi-circular bends and Rongo's was "wavy" to represent the growth of the sweet potato (*kumara*) "as", says White, "it raised the earth in little mounds".[2]

Tu seems also to have symbolized the rock-supporting land, the foundation of the earth. Perhaps his prototype, as a supporter, was a mountain god—an Asiatic Atlas. There is, however, another aspect of Tu's character. He and the god of storms apparently represented, in an ancient mythological system drawn upon by the Maori priests, those twin deities met with everywhere in Polynesia—the fair sky-god and the dark underworld god.

Fornander refers to the Maori Tu as "the progenitor

[1] Grey, *op. cit.*, Chapter I.   [2] J. White, *The Ancient History of the Maori*, Vol. I, p. 2.

of man " and the elder brother of the gods, and he quotes Bopp who connected him with the Hindu Vedic *Tu*, " to be powerful ". " That the name of this god ", says Fornander, " and his character as the forefather of the human family, are older than the arrival of the Polynesians in the Pacific, is plainly shown in the fact that among some of the pre-Malay dialects of the Indian Archipelago, as in Saparua, Ceram, Salibabo and Celebes, we find the words *Tu-mata, To-mata, Tau-mata* and *Tau* as expressing the sense of ' man ' especially, and in a general way ' mankind '." [1]

Best, referring to Colonel Gudgeon's researches, [2] gives the popular Maori myth that Tu, deciding that " supernatural beings were not fitted to populate this world " created Tiki, the first man, " the progenitor of the human race ". Tu formed an image of earth, and endowed it with life. Best notes that Colonel Gudgeon was not satisfied with this myth, having formed the opinion that Tiki was " a personified form of the life principle ", [3] but as has been seen this is not necessarily a final explanation of Tiki. Even Tiki was a complex deity. The Maori priests, like the modern anthropologists, appear to have had more than one theory as to his origin and significance.

Best [4] refers to Tu and Maki-roa " and others " as " controllers of all forms of disease ". [5] His estimate of the character of Tu is as follows:

" In Tu we have the tutelary deity of the war department of Maoriland. Tu represents war, bloodshed, and the present writer is inclined to hold the view that Tu personifies the setting sun, which is ever associated with death. . . . As Tu was the chief war god of the Maori, it was his *tapu* that lay heavy on fighting men when on active service. His *mana* was over the warrior, and any who infringed the many restrictions imposed by his tapu

[1] *The Polynesian Race*, Vol. I, p. 66 and note 2.
[2] *Journal of the Polynesian Society*, Vol. XIV.
[3] *The Maori*, Vol. I, p. 121.   [4] *Op. cit.*, p. 105.
[5] Tane was also appealed to by curers of sickness. Best, *op. cit.*, Vol. II, p. 47.

were indeed in parlous plight. Offerings of the hearts of slain enemies were made to him. He was the presiding genius of war, but, at the same time, any fighting force was also under the sway, *mana*, and guidance of one at least of the many beings who may be termed tribal war gods. These latter belonged to the third and fourth classes of *atua maori*, or native gods." [1]

We learn from Craighill Handy that in the Marquesas Tu had an essential connexion with war.

" While the local tribal god was the deity to whom sacrifices were actually offered, Tu was the patron of war on both Nuku Hiva, and Hiva Oa. On Nuku Hiva, all those taking part in the ceremonial associated with war—that is, the inspirational priest, the ceremonial priest, and the temple assistants (and possibly the warriors)—were known as *ati Tu* (*ati*, ' relations ', or ' people of '; Tu, 'god of war ')." [2]

In Tahiti, where Oro was the war-god, the first wounded warrior seized in battle was offered in a sacrifice as " the-slain-warrior-of-the-water-of-Tu ".[3] Ellis writes in this connexion:

" Sometimes the first victim was called *Te ivi o te vai o Tu*: the head was completely covered as low as the neck with successive bandages of cinet, carried to the temple, and burned before Taaroa (Tangaloa); and was generally regarded as an earnest of the defeat of his party, and the destruction of his family." [4]

According to David Malo the Hawaiian Tu, known in the local dialect as Ku, received human sacrifices in war time. Craighill Handy in his summary of Malo's evidence says that Ku was " first of all, the national war god of the ruling and priestly dynasty ". Under other epithets, however, he was " patron of several peaceful arts ". Canoe-builders, bird-catchers, and fishermen

---

[1] *The Maori*, Vol. I, pp. 236-7.
[2] " The Native Culture in the Marquesas," *Bernice P. Bishop Museum Bulletin* 9, p. 131.
[3] Here Tu is merged in Tane, whose life-giving water (" Water of Kane ") renewed the moon, cured disease, prolonged human life, and strengthened warriors, &c.
[4] W. Ellis, *Polynesian Researches* (Second Edition), Vol. I, p 289.

invoked him. Sorcerers appealed to Ku and kings often
assumed his name.[1]

Craighill Handy notes that as Ku was in Hawaii
a patron of wood-workers, he was in the Society Islands
a great artizan who assisted in shaping the earth. Elsewhere Tane was patron of canoe-makers. Tangoloa, as
we have seen, was referred to in Samoa as an artizan or
architect.[2] Tu thus acquired certain of the attributes of
Tane and Tangaloa.

Fornander says that, in the Hawaiian triad of Kane,
Ku and Lono, Kane was regarded as the superior. Ku
was, however, known as Ku-kau-akahi ("Ku stands
alone" or "the one established"). The three gods were
"worshipped jointly under the grand and mysterious
name of 'Hika po loa', while another ancient name was
'Oi-e', signifying 'most excellent, supreme', sometimes used adjectively as 'Kane-oi-e'." In a hymn
already quoted from, the priest before naming "Lono,
dwelling on the water" couples the names of the other
two gods of the trinity as follows:

"O Kane and Ku, the builder."

In another chant Kane is first mentioned and then
Ku and Lono together.[3] The Maoris sometimes coupled
Rongo (Lono) and Tane (Kane), and worshipped the
pair as a single god named Rongo-ma-Tane.[4] In like
manner Horus and Set were sometimes fused in ancient
Egypt.

The god Rongo, also known in various Polynesian
dialects as Ro'o, Lono, Longo and Ono, was in New
Zealand "the patron deity of art and agriculture", says
Mr. Elsdon Best, who regards him as "the male personification of the moon", adding that the moon was

---

[1] David Malo, "Hawaiian Antiquities", *B. P. Bishop Museum Special Publication*, No 2, pp. 114, 210; and Craighill Handy in *B. P. Bishop Museum Bulletin* 34, pp. 113-4.
[2] Craighill Handy, *op. cit.*, pp. 114, 115.
[3] A. Fornander, *The Polynesian Race*, Vol. I, pp. 61, 62, and pp. 74, 75.
[4] Elsdon Best, *The Maori*, Vol. I, pp. 130 *et seq.*, 236, 281.

connected with agriculture " in many old-world lands ". Mr. Best, dealing with the name Rongo-marae-roa (" Rongo of the far-spread expanse "—that is, of the sea) explains that " moon worship was often connected with water worship in olden times, as in Babylonia. It was the moon that caused crops to grow in Babylonian belief, and this also was the Maori belief." Certain moon markings were called by the Maori " the ovens of Rongomai ". The god was connected with the cultivation of the " sweet potato " (kumara). In one of the myths he is seen with the rainbow " standing in the heavens ". It is evident that Rongomai is a form of Rongonui (" Great Rongo "), and it is of interest to find him under this name referred to by Mr. Best as " the personified form of meteors ". and that as such he was " appealed to in war time " as well as on other occasions.[1]

As a god of agriculture the Maori Rongo was associated with the goddess Pani, whose name, Tregear suggests, is a variant form of *pari*, a well-known rice name of South-eastern Asia. In Hindu Vedic literature Pani is a person who does not worship the gods of the singers and is a term " wide enough to cover either the aborigines or hostile Aryan tribes, as well as demons ". There are Vedic passages which suggest that the Panis were regarded sometimes as mythological beings, " demons who withhold the cows or waters of heaven, and to whom Saramā [2] goes on a mission from Indra".[3] This apparent identification of a non-Aryan deity or group of deities with the water-confining serpent-dragon may explain the Maori goddess Pani's connexion with water which puzzles Best, who writes:

" A curious myth concerning Pani is to the effect that she was taken to wife by Rongo-maui, who is spoken of as the younger brother of Whanui, the star Vega. That star was connected with agriculture, for its cosmic rising about March was the sign that

---

[1] Elsdon Best, *The Maori*, Vol. I, pp. 131 *et seq.*   [2] A goddess.
[3] Macdonald and Keith, *Vedic Index*, Vol. I, pp. 471-2.

sent the Maori to prepare his store pits and lift his crops. This Rongo-maui obtained from Whanui the seed of the sweet potato, not in a proper manner, because he stole it; hence the pests that attack the crops are said to have been sent as punishment for that pernicious act. Rongo then caused his wife Pani to give birth to the *Kumara*, which she did in water; always she entered the water when she was about to produce the tubers. These waters are termed the ' waters of Mona-ariki '." [1]

Best wonders why Pani always enters water in order to produce what is essentially a dry-land product, and mentions Tregear's suggestion that she may have been in Indonesia a rice goddess. He refers to her as the Maori Ceres.[2] Pani was, like Rongo, Tane and others appealed to in sickness.[3]

Pani was invoked when the kumara was planted. Roughly-hewn stones were set up in fields and were called by the natives *taumata*, which Best translates as " resting places or abiding places of the gods ". They were " visible representations of the gods of agriculture, such as Rongo ". A portion of the first tuber planted was offered to the stone which may be referred to as a " god body ". Rongo was sometimes represented by " a double form of stone image " which was probably the dual Rongo-ma-Tane (Rongo and Tane). When the crop was lifted portions were offered to Rongo and Pani.[4]

In Hawaii where, as will be seen, Rongo, as Lono, was a thunderer, he was prayed to for rain and was a controller of the seasons.[5]

As has been indicated, in the Hervey group Rongo and Tangaroa were regarded as twin sons of the sky deity Vātea and the earth goddess Papa. The home of Rongo was Auau (Mangaia). Tangaroa had fair hair, but, as Gill reminds us, " Rongo's hair was raven black ". Tangaroa's home was " in the sky ", but Rongo was

---

[1] " Ariki " means a first-born male or female of high rank.
[2] *The Maori*, Vol. II, pp. 370-1 and p. 380.   [3] *The Maori*, Vol. II, p. 430.
[4] Best, *The Maori*, Vol. II, pp. 386-9.   [5] A. Marcuse, *Die Hawaiischen Inseln*, p. 98.

known as " God-whose-home-is-the-shades "— that is, the Underworld. When Tangaroa left Auau, and settled on " his beloved islands Rarotonga and Aitutaki ", Rongo had complete possession of Auau (Mangaia). Gill gives the meaning of Rongo's name as " The Re-sounder ".

" Ro(ng)o or O Rō," writes Gill, " was the chief object of worship at Tahiti and most of the Leeward Islands. His seat was the *marae*, or sacred grove, at Opoa, on the island of Raiatea; whence this worship extended to all the neighbouring islands, and throughout the Paumotu group. Human sacrifices were continually offered to the great Polynesian god of war, to obtain success in their cruel enterprises."

At Aitu the god Rongo was regarded not as a brother of Tangaroa, but as his son. As Longo, the Samoans also referred to him as the son of that deity.

Rono (Rongo) was the principal god of Rimatara and human sacrifices were offered to him.

There can be no doubt about the association of the Rongo of Mangaia with the underworld (Avaiki). Gill gives a myth which tells that he was the grandfather of three illegitimate children, Rangi, Mokoiro and Aka-tauira, the three chiefs from whom the people of Mangaia were supposed to be descended. " Rongo wished his three grandsons to live with him in Auau in the shades. But Rangi was resolved to pull up this land Auau, after-wards called Mangaia, from Avaiki." This he accom-plished with the aid of his brothers. " Three small rocks, united at the base, close to the *marae* of Rongo and the altar for human sacrifice, are pointed out as symbolizing the threefold lords of the soil." Gill continues:

" Rongo continued to live in Avaiki, in the invisible or nether Auau, of which this island was asserted to be but the outward expression. He directed Rangi to offer bleeding sacrifices on his *marae* in the upper world, from time to time—the decayed corpse to be invariably thrown in the bush to his mother Papa.

" Mangaia now for the first time emerged to the light of day, and became the centre of the universe. Its central hill was accordingly designated Rangimotia = ' the centre of the heavens '. The inhabitants of Mangaia were veritable *men* and *women*, as contrasted with the natives of other outlying islands, who were only *tuarangi*, or evil spirits, in the guise of humanity."

On the brow of the hill, facing the west, and near the *marae* of Rongo, the war god, there is said to have been formerly " a deep gloomy chasm " known as " Tiki's hole ". This was " the regular road to Avaiki, like (as the natives said) the single aperture at the top of a coco-nut. Through it the three brothers descended to Avaiki, or ascended to the light of day, at pleasure ". The three brothers, the grandsons of Rongo, were " joint kings ". According to Gill:

" To Rangi Rono gave ' the drum of peace '; to Mokoiro the direction over food of all kinds; to the pet—the youngest—Akatauira was given the *Karakia* (prayers) and the sway over his brethren."

The cult of Rongo brooked no rivals. Tangaroa was expelled. Tane-papa-kai (Tane-piler-up-of-food), a younger son of Vātea and Papa, was degraded. Rangi, the grandson of Rongo, " was not pleased with Tane ", and after Tane died his son Papaaunuku was considered to be unsatisfactory as the priest through whom Tane spoke. As Rongo " lived only in the shades ", Rangi " wished for a god who would live with him in this upper world ". He sent to Rarotonga and obtained Motoro, son of Tangiia, the brother of Tangaroa, Rangi and Tane, and he became the living god or priest. He had " grown up under the sacred shade of the tamanu leaves ".

The Lono (Rongo) of the Hawaiian group appears to have acquired certain of the attributes of Tangaroa. At Mangaia, as we have seen, Captain Cook and his men were regarded as the descendants of the long-lost and expelled Tangaroa. The Hawaiian idea was that they were the descendants of the fair Lono. Rongo was, as we have seen, regarded at Mangaia as a dark god.

In Hawaii, as has been already indicated, a trinity was formed by Kane, Ku and Lono (Tane, Tu and Ron(g)o), and Kanaloa (Tangaloa) was associated with them. The trinity at Mangaia was formed, as we have seen, by Rongo's grandchildren. The Hawaiian Kane, Ku and Lono were " equal in nature ", says Fornander, " but distinct in attributes ". In one of the hymns the third deity is invoked as " Great Lono dwelling on the water. . . . Lono of the flashing eyes, a god, the god of lightning." [1]

Another hymn runs:

> " An altar for you, O Lono.
> O Lono of the night,
> O Lono of the thunder,
> O Lono of the lightning,
> O Lono of the heavy rain,
> O Lono of the terrible, divine face,
> O Lono, O Lono with the restless eyes,
> Ah, fly to the northern sea,
> Ah, fly to the southern sea,
> To the eastern sea,
> To the dark shore, to the white shore,
> To the dark moon, to the bright moon." [2]

One of the hymns [3] addressed to Captain Cook as Lono has been translated as follows:

"O Lono in heaven! you of the many shapes (or beings). The long cloud, the short cloud, the cloud just peeping (over the horizon), the wide-spreading cloud, the contracted cloud in the heaven, (coming) from Uliuli, from Melemele, from Kahiki (Tahiti), from Ulunui, from Hakalauai, from the country of Lono situated in the upper regions, in the high heavens, in proper order, in the famous order of Leka. O Lalohana, O Olepuu-ka-

---

[1] A. Fornander, *The Polynesian Race*, Vol. I, p. 61 and note 2.
[2] A. Fornander, *op. cit.*, Vol. I, pp. 94-5.
[3] A. Fornander, *op. cit.*, Vol. II, p. 178 note 1

honua; Eh Ku, Eh Lono, Eh Kane, Eh Kanaloa, Eh the god from Apapalani of Apapanuu, from Kahiki east, from Kahiki west,[1] here is the sacrifice, here is the offering. Preserve the chief, preserve the worshippers, and establish the day of light on the floating earth! Amen." [2]

Another hymn or chant is given by Fornander: [3]

" Kane of the great Night,
  Ku and Lono of the great Night,
  Hika-po-loa the King.
        The tabooed Night that is set apart,
        The poisonous Night,
        The barren, desolate Night,
        The continual darkness of Midnight,
        The Night, the reviler.
O Kane, O Ku-ka-Pao,
And great Lono dwelling on the water.
Brought forth are Heaven (and) Earth,
Quickened, increased, moving,
Raised up into Continents.
        Kane, Lord of Night, Lord the Father,
        Ku-ka-Pao, in the hot heavens,
        Great Lono with the flashing eyes,
        Lightning-like lights has the Lord,
        Established in truth, O Kane, master-worker;
The Lord Creator of mankind:
Start, work, bring forth the chief Ku-Honua.
And Ola-Ku-Honua the woman; [4]
Dwelling together are they two,
Dwelling in marriage (is she) with the husband, the brother."

David Malo gives evidence of Lono's connexion with agriculture:

    " O Lono of the blue firmament!
      Here are vegetables, here is meat,
      An offering of prayer, a sacrifice,
      An offering of fat things to you, O Lono!

---

[1] Kahiki (Tahiti) in Hawaiian lore refers to any distant land.
[2] Fornander says the phrase " *Amama, ua noa* " corresponds to the Christian " Amen "
[3] A. Fornander, *op. cit.*, Vol. I, pp. 74–5.
[4] The chief and the woman are the first pair of human beings.

Let the crops flourish in this *ahu-puaa* (district).

. . . .

Send gracious showers of rain, oh Lono.
Life-giving rain, a grateful gift,
Symbols of Lono's blessing . . .
Oh Lono of the broad leaf,
Let the low-hanging cloud pour out its rain
To make the crops flourish,
Rain to make the tapa-plants flourish,
Wring out the dark rain-clouds
Of Lono in the heavens." [1]

In still another hymn by Fornander, quoted by Mr.
E. S. Craighill Handy,[2] Lono is seated in his holy assembly "in the distant sacred place" which is "in
heaven", and the "sacred signs" of Lono's assembly
are given as "thunder, earthquake, wind, clouds, rain
and the rushing stream". Here Lono resembles the
Samoan Tangaloa. Tregear notes that he was sometimes regarded as an uncreated, self-existent deity.[3]
In New Zealand, as we have seen, Rongo was a healer
of disease: in Hawaii Lono had a similar reputation; he
was, Westervelt notes,[4] the ancestor and instructor of
priests who gave healing, while David Malo tells that
Lono-puha was prayed to when diseases were treated.[5]

It would appear that the attributes of Kane, Ku and
Lono were "borrowed" by one another. This was
apparently due to their arbitrary association in a trinity,
in imitation of the Hindu grouping in Brahmanic times,
of Brahma, Vishnu and Shiva. The association of Indra
and Agni as "twins" in India led to a like result. Indra
acquired part of the character of Agni, and Agni exercised Indra's function of slaying the water-confining
serpent-dragon Vrittra.[6]

---

[1] Translation by N. B. Emerson in *B. P. Bishop Museum Special Publication*, No. 2 (1903), pp. 233–5.
[2] *B. P. Bishop Museum Bulletin*, No. 34, p. 111.
[3] Maori-Polynesian Comparative Dictionary under "Rongo".
[4] *Legends of Gods and Ghosts*, pp. 94 *et seq.* Here Lono dwells among men.
[5] Quoted by Handy, *op. cit.*, p. 111. Here the god is "Luna—pig".
[6] Muir's *Original Sanskrit Texts*, London, 1884, Vol. V, p. 220.

Lono may appear to Mr. Craighill Handy in his Hawaiian capacity " the patron of agriculture " as a " god of peace ", but as Rongo he was in Western Polynesia a god of war who required sacrifices of human beings. He was also as Rongo the " dark-haired " god of the Underworld, in opposition to Tangaloa the " fair-haired " god of the sky, but in Hawaii he was fair. Withal he was expelled from Hawaii as Tangaloa had been from Mangaia. Lord Byron[1] gives a folk version of the myth of his expulsion, referring to him as " Rono ". His wife was wooed by another, as was, according to Maori myth, the wife of Tangaloa (Tangaroa) by Raki (Rangi). In a fit of jealousy he slew her, and then maddened by sorrow went about wildly and engaged in boxing with each man he encountered.

" The people astonished, said: ' Is Rono entirely mad?' He replied: ' I am frantic on her account, I am frantic with my great love.' Having instituted games to commemorate her death, he embarked in a triangular boat and sailed to a foreign land. Ere he departed he prophesied, ' I will return, in after times, on an island[2] bearing coco-nut trees and swine and dogs."

This was evidently one of the several folk versions of a persistent tradition regarding a god who had been wronged and expelled.

Ellis in his version of the myth says that Rono (Lono) was said to have been an ancient king of Hawaii who " became offended with his wife and murdered her ". He " lamented the act so much, as to induce a state of mental derangement. In this state he travelled through all the islands boxing and wrestling with everyone he met." Ellis continues:

" He subsequently set sail in a singularly-shaped canoe for Tahiti, or a foreign country. After his departure he was deified by his countrymen and annual games of boxing and wrestling were instituted in his honour."[3]

[1] *Voyage of the " Blonde "*, London, 1826, p. 11.
[2] *Moku* may mean " ship " as well as " island " notes Handy, *op. cit.*, p. 112.
[3] *Polynesian Researches* (Second Edition), Vol. IV, pp. 134-5.

CHAPTER XXI

Worship of Captain Cook as White God

Captain Cook's Discovery of Hawaiian Islands—Ship regarded as Island or Sea-monster—Native Tradition of returning White God—Memories of White Foreigners—Priest greets Cook as a God—Ceremony at Sacred *Marae*—Cook presented to Images of Gods—Offering of Pig to Cook—The Sacrificial Feast —Return Visit of Captain Cook—How Cook was murdered—Bones of Cook as Sacred Relics—Mexican and Polynesian Myths of returning White Gods— Indonesian and Indian Myths—Hindu Rudra as White God and Dark God— Rudra as Controller of Disease—Rudra and Mouse-Apollo—God who removed Diseases was Cause of them—Rudra ceremonially expelled—Rudra's Arrows of Disease, Rain, and Lightning—Rudra as Sky-god and Underworld-god—Rudra as Sky-prop—Later Rudra a Fusion of Deities—Rudra, Lono, and Ku, as Pig-gods—Different Treatments of same Gods throughout Polynesia—Local Specializations—Political Aspect of Pantheons—Asiatic Prototypes of Polynesian Gods—Living Forms of Gods—"God-bodies".

When Captain Cook arrived at the Hawaiian (Sandwich) Islands in January, 1778, it was believed that he was the god Lono. He cast anchor at Waimea on Kauai during the night, and when daylight came the wondering natives asked regarding his vessel, " what is that great thing with branches ", and some said, " It is a forest that has slid down into the sea." A native historian tells that others declared the vessel to be an Auwaalalua (" an animal that sails in the sea like a canoe—perhaps the whale). A priest named Kuohu, however, expressed the belief that the vessel was the temple of Lono, with the ladders and the steps to the altar. The first natives who ventured out thought the crew " were all women, because their heads were so like the women's heads of that period ". Kuohu the priest and two chiefs who went on

(26)

WOODEN FIGURE OF A GOD

From a sacred enclosure, Hawaiian Islands

The heads of these war-gods are frames of wickerwork made of the aerial roots of a kind of fig tree covered with string network to which the feathers are attached. The eyes are made of plates of pearl-shell.

The head of this figure is adorned with human hair and the eyes have large wooden pupils.

(25)

WAR GODS OF RED FEATHER WORK, HAWAIIAN ISLANDS

board ". saluted Cook by prostrating themselves and with prayer ". Some wished to seize the vessel because they saw so much iron on it. They had evidently a previous knowledge of iron. A warrior who seized iron and tried to escape with it was shot at and killed, and when darkness came on guns were fired and rockets displayed. The natives wished to avenge the warrior's death by attacking the ship, but Kuohu " dissuaded them from so perilous and reckless an adventure ".

Kuohu began to doubt if the visitors were gods, and came to the conclusion that they were merely *Haole* (foreigners), " but the young people and the majority looked upon Cook as the god Lono ".

S. M. Kamakau, the native historian, refers to an interesting native tradition regarding white men which had its effect in the Hawaiian attitude towards Captain Cook. An ancient chief, named Paumakua, had been a great explorer who " circumnavigated the world ", which means, as Fornander explains, that he had visited " all foreign lands outside of the Hawaiian group ". On his return from one of his voyages he was accompanied by two white men, said to be priests, " from whom several priestly families in after ages claimed their descent and authority ". The strangers were remembered as tall men with bright sparkling eyes, white skin and reddish faces.[1]

When a high priest, who did not see Cook and his men, was told of their arrival, he declared they were foreigners and added, " They are surely the people that will come and dwell in this land." Others referred to an ancient prophecy about the coming of white foreigners who would ride on the backs of dogs with long ears (horse.)[2] There was thus among the Hawaiians, as among the Aztecs, a tradition of a prophecy regarding the coming of white people. As we have seen, Cortez

---

[1] A. Fornander, *The Polynesian Race*, Vol. II, p. 25.
[2] A. Fornander, *op. cit.*, pp. 168–9.

and his Spanish soldiers were supposed by the Aztecs
to represent the white Quetzalcoatl race and were at
first regarded as " white gods ".

Cook left Niihau in February, 1778, to explore the
Behring Straits and the North-west Passage. In November he returned to the Hawaiian group, and in
December discovered the island of Hawaii. He anchored
his ships in the bay of Kealakeakua in the middle of
January. The explorer was regarded as no other than
the god Lono. Koa, a priest, had an impressive inter-
view with Cook. Captain King relates:

" Being led into the cabin, he approached Captain Cook with
great veneration, and threw over his shoulders a piece of red cloth,
which he had brought along with him. Then stepping a few paces
back, he made an offering of a small pig which he held in his hand,
while he pronounced a discourse that lasted for a considerable
time. This ceremony was frequently repeated during our stay
at Owhyhee, and appeared to us, from many circumstances, to be
a sort of religious adoration. Their idols we found always arrayed
in red cloth in the same manner as was done to Captain Cook and
a small pig was their usual offering to the *Eatooas* (divinities)."

When Captain Cook landed that afternoon he was
conducted by Koa, the priest, Palea, a chief, and others
to the sacred place of the god Lono. This was a *marae*,
which Captain King describes:

" It was a square solid pile of stone, about forty yards long,
twenty broad, and fourteen in height.[1] The top was flat and well
paved, and surrounded by a wooden rail, on which were fixed the
skulls of the captives sacrificed on the death of their chiefs. In the
centre of the area stood a ruinous old building of wood, connected
with the rail on each side by a stone wall, which divided the whole
space into two parts. On the side next the country were five
poles, upward of twenty feet high, supporting an irregular kind of
scaffold; on the opposite side towards the sea, stood two small
houses with a covered communication."

---

[1] " It was ", says Fornander, " one of the ancient *Heiaus* of a truncated pyramidal form,
that obtained before the southern migratory period."

On the top of the pile to which Cook and King were conducted, stood two wooden images and " a long piece of carved wood of a conical form inverted, rising from the top of their heads; the rest was without form, and wrapped round with red cloth ". This pole was evidently the symbol of Ku (Tu).

A tall young priest with a long beard presented Captain Cook to the images and then, chanting " a kind of hymn " in which Koa joined him, led the two captains to five poles fixed at the end of the *marae*. At the foot of these poles were five images in semicircular form and in front of the middle figure was a stand on which lay a putrid pig, and under it " pieces of sugar-cane, coconuts, bread-fruit, plantains and sweet potatoes ".

The putrid pig was formally presented to Captain Cook who could not help feeling disgusted. Then the scaffolding was ascended. Towards the *marae* came a procession of ten men carrying a live pig and a large piece of red cloth. The bearded priest accepted the offerings. He wrapped Captain Cook in the red cloth and formally presented the pig to him.

Then all descended to the place where the images were ranged in semicircular form while the two priests chanted their hymns. Then Koa led Captain Cook to the images, addressing each in a sneering tone and snapping his fingers as if to emphasize the supreme divinity of the white Lono who had arrived. He, however, prostrated himself before the central image and kissed it, and prevailed upon Captain Cook to do the same.

The visitors were next led to the lower part of the *marae*, and there Captain Cook was seated between two wooden idols.

A procession then approached Cook with an offering of a baked pig and vegetables, reciting a chant in which Lono was invoked.

A feast followed, but Cook, thinking of the putrid

pig, could not be prevailed upon to accept a morsel of the baked pork.

Captain Cook, having distributed some gifts of iron, &c., allowed himself to be conducted back to his boat. As he was led along the shore by men with wands, the spectators prostrated themselves.

The presents made to Cook were a tremendous drain on the resources of the natives, and when he returned after encountering a gale which damaged his ship, there was a perceptible waning in native enthusiasm and friendliness. The sailors had mixed freely with the women and caused bad feeling,[1] and some of them on their return assaulted a young chief who took revenge by stealing a boat which was broken up to obtain the nails. Captain Cook acted foolishly in going ashore with an armed party to seize the king until the boat was restored and in blockading the bay. A canoe from an adjoining district was fired upon by the blockaders and one of the two chiefs on board killed.

This tragic happening led to the murder of Captain Cook. He was interviewing the king when a warrior flourishing a spear rushed in, and approaching Cook said his brother had been slain by the white men and he would be revenged. Cook fired at him with his pistol. Another native flung a stone and Cook shot him dead, and then struck a chief with his sword.

" The chief instinctively seized Cook with a strong hand, designing merely to hold him, and not to take his life, for he supposed him to be a god, and that he could not die.

" Captain Cook struggled to free himself from the grasp, and as he was about to fall uttered a groan. The people immediately exclaimed, ' He groans—he is not a god,' and instantly slew him. Such was the melancholy death of Captain Cook." [2]

The death of Cook did not entirely dispel the illusion

---

[1] Especially as venereal disease was introduced, as was the case elsewhere.
[2] Sheldon Dibble, *History of the Sandwich Islands*, 1843, quoted by A. Fornander, *op. cit.*, Vol. II, pp. 191 *et seq.*

that he was a deity. Although some declared he was not
Lono, others insisted he was, "and expected he would
appear again ". Ellis tells how the latter revered Cook
after he had died:

" Some of his bones, his ribs and breastbone were considered
sacred, as part of Rono (Lono) and deposited in a *heiau* (temple)
dedicated to Rono, on the opposite side of the island. There
religious homage was paid to them, and from thence they were
annually carried in procession to several other *heiaus*, or borne by
priests round the island, to collect the offerings of the people, for
the support of the worship of the god Rono. The bones were
preserved in a small basket of wicker-work, completely covered
over with red feathers; which in those days were considered to be
the most valuable articles the natives possessed. . . . Part of
Captain Cook's bones were preserved by the priests and were
considered sacred by the people probably till the abolition of idolatry
in 1819."

After that date the relics were secretly concealed in
a cave.[1]

The myth of the god who has been expelled but is
expected to return is found, as we have seen, in the
mythology of pre-Columbian Mexico. Quetzalcoatl,
the Aztec "white god", was driven away or forced
to emigrate like Tangaloa from Mangaia and Lono
from Hawaii. It is improbable that similar historical
happenings in Mexico and in two widely-separated
groups of Polynesian islands were productive of similar
myths. A more reasonable view seems to be that the
original expulsion myth had been formulated either in
South-eastern Asia or in India and subsequently carried
to America on the one hand and Polynesia on the other
by groups of sea-farers. Perhaps it had to begin with
some connexion either with the struggle between the
Buddhists and the Brahmans, or had reference to the
displacement of Vedic by Brahmanic gods. It may be,
too, that in the myths there is a memory of the Tammuz

[1] W. Ellis, *Polynesian Researches* (Second Edition), Vol. IV, pp. 135-7.

myth—the departure of a god for a period to the under-world. In the World's Ages doctrine the god of a particular Age departed when a new Age began.

The displacement of a fair-haired deity by a dark-haired deity is to be traced in the complex myths associated with the Hindu god Rudra, whose original Vedic character was transformed by the cult-fusing Brahmans so that he ultimately became completely merged in Shiva (Siwa), whose trident symbol, as has been stated, was discovered by Fornander in Hawaii. The dark-haired Rongo of Mangaia and the fair-haired Lono of Hawaii may have been simply forms of the Hindu Rudra. In one of the Hindu *Vājasaneyi Samhitā* (XVI, 1 *et seq.*), Rudra is the lord of regions, "green-haired trees", roads, beasts and food, and he is "*yellow-haired*". But in the *Atharva-veda* (II, 27, 6) occurs the passage:

"Rudra, who hast healing remedies, who hast *dark locks*, who art the performer of works, destroy the food of him who seeks to take ours; make it savourless, O plant!" [1]

Rudra, Muir notes in his summary of the god's character, is found "presiding over medicinal plants and the removal of disease".[2] He is, withal, connected with the mouse.[3] "This is thy portion; thy victim is a mouse," says the *Vājasaneyi Samhitā* (III, 57). Like Mouse-Apollo in the Troad, he was the controller of disease. Being the cause of disease, which he shot as arrows from his bow, he was able to remove diseases.[4] That fact should be borne in mind by those who incline to regard the disease-curing god of Polynesia as a beneficent or peace-loving character, instead of a malignant and irascible deity like Rudra, who, however, could be flattered and propitiated.

[1] Muir's *Original Sanskrit Texts*, Vol. IV, pp. 327, 332.
[2] Muir, *op. cit.*, Vol. IV, p. 394.   [3] Muir, *op. cit.*, Vol. IV, p. 321.
[4] As in the *Iliad*, Book I, where he is sacrificed to so that a plague caused by him may cease.

Like the Mangaian Tangaloa and the Hawaiian Lono, Rudra could be prevailed upon to go away. In the *Samhitā* quoted above in which Rudra is " a medicine, a medicine for men " and " a source of ease to rams and ewes ", his worshippers declare, " We worship Tryambaka, the sweet scented, the increaser of prosperity . . . who bestows on us husbands."[1] Rudra is invoked to depart by those who wish to be freed from death and made immortals:

" This, Rudra, is thy provision; with it depart beyond the Mūjavat, with thy bow unbended, and concealed from view, clothed with a skin, without injuring us, gracious, cross over. . . . Thou art gracious (*Siva*) by name; the thunderbolt is thy father. Reverence be to thee: destroy us not." [2]

In a famous prayer, quoted from the *Mahābhárata*, occur the lines:

" Reverence, Rudra, to thy wrath and to thine arrow. . . . The arrow, O dweller in the mountains, which thou bearest in thy hand to discharge, make it, O lord of the mountains, auspicious; do not slay men and cattle. . . . May he who glides away, blue-necked and red-coloured . . . be gracious to us. . . . May the bow of the god with braided hair be stringless, and his quiver contain pointless shafts." [3]

When Rudra hears imprecations from worshippers who fear but flatter him, he " glides away " or " departs ". A native commentator says he is invoked as " wise and bountiful, &c.", because " he departs and directs his destroying arrows towards some other quarter. . . . The worshipper flatters him with fair words . . . to pacify his anger. . . . He is called a physician, and moreover is acquainted with healing herbs; but he carries also diseases and contagions themselves as arrows in his quiver, and slays therewith men and cattle."[4]

[1] This was spoken by virgins walking round a sacred fire.
[2] Muir, *op. cit.*, Vol. IV, pp. 322, 326, 382, 397.
[3] Muir's *Original Sanskrit Texts*, Vol. IV, pp. 322, 326.
[4] Quoted by Muir, *op. cit.*, Vol. IV, pp. 382 and 3.

Here we may have a clue to the contradictory character of the Hawaiian Kanaloa, who was sometimes referred to as a beneficent deity and sometimes as an evil-working deity.

The Polynesians, like the Hindus, flattered and propitiated the gods so that they might go away and cause trouble, if they so desired, elsewhere. They thought of their gods sometimes as sailing in canoes from island to island. Turner gives a prayer in which mention is made of an offering of intoxicating 'ava (kava):

"Here is 'ava for you, O gods! Look kindly towards this family; let it prosper and increase; and let us all be kept in health. Let our plantations be productive; let fruit grow; and may there be abundance of food for us, your creatures. . . . Here is 'ava for you, O sailing gods! Do not come on shore at this place; but be pleased to depart along the ocean to some other land."

A prayer addressed to a family god for whom a fire is lit says:

"Drive away from us sailing gods, lest they come and cause disease and death." [1]

A fire was lit to Tuialii, King of chiefs, a god whose incarnations were the sea-eel, the octopus, and mullet; he was also seen in the ends of banana leaves. In the prayer over the fire, the god was invoked to send other families to the "lower regions", but "give us life and health".[2]

In Scotland fairies were similarly flattered and propitiated so that they might do no harm.

The "arrows" of the Hindu god Rudra are not always arrows of disease, as is made evident in the following passages:

"Reverence to the Rudras who (live) in the sky, of whom rain is the arrows."

"Rudra's arrow, a celestial bolt, flies abroad; reverence be to

[1] G. Turner, *Samoa*, p. 116.   [2] *Ibid.*, pp. 75-6.

it in whatever direction from hence (it flies). . . . Let us not with our tongue offend Rudra, who rushes on, thousand-eyed, viewing all the world, who hurls his shafts in our presence. . . . Fierce god, betake thyself elsewhere; slay the offspring of the malignant. . . . Do not assail us, Rudra, with consumption, or with poison, or with celestial fire: cause the lightning to descend elsewhere than upon us." [1]

Rudra is in the *Atharvaveda* (XV, 5, 1) a god of the Underworld like Rongo of Mangaia; he is also a god of lightning and the sky like Lono of Hawaii:

" The gods made Rudra deliverer from the intermediate space of the lower region. . . .

" The gods made Mahādeva (Rudra) deliverer from the intermediate space of the upper region. . . ." [2]

Rudra raises and props the sky, he sends whirlwinds and causes other storms [3] like Lono (Rongo), he is a " resounder " or " loud-shouting lord ". Wilson,[4] referring to the *Satarudriya*, the " Rudra book ", sees in the later Rudra " the blending of the two destructive deities Storm and Fire ". Rudra had acquired certain of the attributes of the bolt-hurling Indra, of Vayu, the wind god, and Agni, the fire god. A text of considerable antiquity, after ascribing to Rudra " a martial character ", proceeds to refer to him in " the three-fold function of universal creator, preserver, and destroyer ".

In the Hawaiian trinity of Kane, Ku and Lono, the influence of the post-Vedic Rudra appears to have been deeply impressed. These deities were not sharply defined. Lono and Ku acquired some of the attributes of Kane as well as those of each other. Both Lono and Ku were war-gods. It may be said of either of them, as of the Hindu Rudra:

" His anger, ill-will and destructive shafts are deprecated. But

---

[1] Muir, *op. cit.*, Vol. IV, pp. 331 *et seq.*   [2] Muir, *op. cit.*, Vol. IV, p. 339.
[3] Muir, *op. cit.*, Vol. IV, pp. 329, 330.
[4] Introduction to *Rig Veda*, Vol. I, p. 394. The power to bring healing is ascribed to Vayu as to Rudra. Muir's *Original Sanskrit Texts*, Vol. V, p. 146.

he is also represented as benevolent, as mild and easily invoked, beneficent, gracious, as the cause or condition of health and prosperity to man and beast." [1]

Like Tane, both Lono and Ku were connected with the pig as Rudra was with the boar, which caused storms and brought fertilizing rain.

Those writers who attempt to draw up a religious system for Polynesia as a whole, appear to assume that the various deities were everywhere sharply defined. But such does not appear to have been the case. The political events in Polynesia are reflected in the treatment of individual deities. Here the Tangaloa cult is supreme and there the Tane cult. The cult which became politically influential in a particular area elevated its special deity or group of deities and relegated the supreme deity of another area to a subsidiary position, transferring certain of his attributes to their own supreme deity. We have seen how the treatment of Tangaloa differed not only in certain groups but in a single area. He was the Creator in Samoa and restricted to the sea in New Zealand; in Hawaii he and Kane were the twin deities of one cult, while another had Kanaloa specialized as an " evil spirit " connected with the underworld. According to others Ku (Tu) was the evil spirit.[2] Similarly Rongo was on one group the dark underworld deity and on another the fair sky god. The local specializations were made possible by the dual characters of the imported prototypes of the Polynesian deities.

These differences in the Polynesian treatment of deities were not apparently wholly due to local political changes, however. The various migrating bands who settled from time to time on the South Sea Islands appear to have imported new groupings of deities which had been effected in Asia. The influence of the Rudra cult

---

[1] Muir's *Original Sanskrit Texts*, Vol. IV, p. 400.

[2] A. Marcuse, *Die Hawaiischen Inseln*, pp. 97 et seq., and Sir J. G. Frazer, *The Belief in Immortality*, Vol. II, p. 393, No. 1.

must have had something to do, for instance, with the transformation of the dark Rongo of Mangaia into the fair Lono of Hawaii. As we have seen, the post-Vedic Rudra had become a highly complex deity before being " exported " from India. In the texts he is " sometimes said to be brown or tawny, but ", says Muir, " he is also said to be white complexioned ".[1]

It is evident that deities like Tangaloa, Tane, Tu and Rongo cannot be accounted for and fully explained by reference to the Polynesian evidence alone. Their history like that of their worshippers is rooted in Asia.

A point of special interest that may here be noted is that the Polynesians regarded it possible for a god to appear in human form. Captain Cook was in one area regarded as Tangaloa and in another as Lono. On Mangaia the priests were incarnations of deities. Kings were semi-divine during life, and, as in Samoa, became gods after they died. At the same time gods might assume the forms of sea-monsters, birds, fish, reptiles, &c., and they might use as temporary or permanent bodies, blocks of carved or uncarved stone, tree trunks, or wooden images, axes, ear-rings, and so on.

[1] *Original Sanskrit Texts*, Vol. IV, p. 395.

CHAPTER XXII

The Polynesian Adonis and Other Deities

Oro of the Feathers—Idol a Log of Wood—The Two Pomares—Destruction of Idols—Proposal to fuse Christianity and Paganism—Oro as a Sun-god—Connexion of God with Areoi Secret Society—Oro's Human Bride—Oro's Brother becomes a Pig—Degrees in Areoi Society—Moral Depravity of Areois—Religious Purpose of their Organization—Moaning for Oro and weeping for Tammuz-Adonis—Fertility Festivals in Egypt and Polynesia—Sun Cult and Megaliths—Pig Forms of Oro, Tammuz, Adonis, and Osiris—Hawaiian and Hindu Pig-gods—Hawaiian Kamapuaa, a Rain God and "Man Pig"—As Spouse and Enemy of Pele, Fire and Volcano Goddess—The Fish-pig—Maui as God and "Culture Hero"—Son of a Virgin Goddess—The Showers of Maui—Maui regulates the Sun and the Seasons—How Maui got Fire for Mankind—The Quest of Immortality—Hine Goddess of Death and the Moon—Whiro as God of Darkness and the Sea—Animal, Fish, and Reptile Forms of Deities.

When the missionaries who had gone to the South Sea Islands in the good ship *Duff* began their labours in the Society group, the god who was receiving most attention from the natives there was Oro. His idol was a block of wood stuck all over with red feathers. Human beings were sacrificed to him in time of war, and seasonal rites were performed to procure his aid as a god who promoted growth, ensured the food supply, and brought general prosperity. Gill was of opinion that Oro was identical with the god Rongo, but this view has been sharply questioned. Indeed, it is asserted that the Society Islands form of Rongo is not Oro but the god Roo, who corresponds to Ono of the Marquesas and Lono of Hawaii. Tregear and Hare Hongi connect Oro with the shadowy Maori god Koro who was the deity intimately associated, as was the Tahitian god, with dancing ceremonies and love-making. Craighill Handy, too, is of opinion that Oro and Roo were originally quite distinct, but that in late times Oro embodied the characteristics of Rongo. " It is permissible," he says, " to speak of Oro when he functioned in the capacity of a harvest god as corresponding to Rongo." [1]

Ellis found that in Tahitian mythology Oro was the eldest son of Taaroa (Tangaloa). Taaroa and his wife, Oro and his wife and their two sons constituted the chief deities in the Pantheon. Mr. Nott, however, informed Ellis of another god named Rumia who was, according to some, " superior to them all ", but Nott was unable to " meet with any of their priests or bards who knew anything about him ". [2] Raa or Ra, the sun-god and Tane were also known, and a son of Tane was " Temeharo, the tutelar deity of (King) Pomare's family ". [3]

When in 1815 King Pomare II, who had become a Christian, won a victory over the pagan army of Tahiti, the temple and altars of Oro were destroyed. " The Lord of hosts had been with them, the God of Jacob was their helper," wrote Ellis. [4] Oro had promised victory to the Pagans and he was discredited. No opposition was shown when Pomare's men entered the national temple to degrade Oro and the others.

" The priests and people stood around in silent expectation; even the soldiers paused a moment, and a scene was exhibited, probably strikingly analogous to that which was witnessed in the temple of Serapis in Alexandria, when the tutelar deity of that city was destroyed by Roman soldiers.

At length they brought out the idol, stripped him of his sacred coverings and highly-valued ornaments, and threw his body contemptuously on the ground. It was a rude, uncarved log of aito

---

[1] E. Tregear, *The Maori-Polynesian Comparative Dictionary*, pp. 170, 424; Hare Hongi, *The Journal of the Polynesian Society*, Vol. XXIX, p. 26; E. S. Craighill Handy, *Bernice P. Bishop Museum Bulletin*, 34, p. 110.

[2] *Polynesian Researches* (Second Edition), Vol. I, pp. 323-4.

[3] *Ibid.*, p. 325.

[4] *Polynesian Researches* (First Edition), Vol. I, p. 253.

wood (*casuarina equisatifolia*) about six feet long. The altars were then broken down, the temples demolished, and the sacred houses of the gods, together with their covering, ornaments, and all the appendages of their worship, committed to the flames. The temples, altars, and idols all round Tahiti were shortly after destroyed in the same way."

Unfortunately, from the point of view of the modern anthropologist, the scenes could not be photographed at that time, or the relics preserved. Ellis proceeds to tell:

"The log of wood, called by the natives the body of Oro, into which they imagined the god at times entered, and through which his influence was exerted, Pomare's party bore away on their shoulders, and, on returning to the camp, laid in triumph at their sovereign's feet. It was subsequently fixed up as a post in the King's kitchen, and used in a most contemptuous manner, by having baskets of food suspended from it; and, finally, it was riven up for fuel.

"This was the end of the principal idol of the Tahitians, on whom they had long been so deluded as to suppose their destinies depended; whose favour kings, and chiefs, and warriors had sought, whose anger all had deprecated and who had been the occasion of more bloody and desolating wars for the preceding thirty years than all other causes combined. Their more zealous devotees were in general now convinced of their delusion, and the people united in declaring that the gods had deceived them, were unworthy of their confidence, and should no longer be objects of respect or trust." [1]

A burning of idols had previously taken place on the island of Eimeo. There Mr. Nott converted a priest named Patii, who declared "he would bring out the idols under his care and publicly burn them". He was as good as his word. Near the large national *marae* in which Patii officiated he had a great quantity of fuel collected and set on fire. Then the gods were brought out.

"They were small carved wooden images, rude imitations

[1] *Polynesian Researches*, Vol. I (First Edition), pp. 256-7.

of the human figure, or shapeless logs of wood, covered with finely braided and curiously wrought cinet of coco-nut fibres and ornamented with red feathers."

The gods were stripped of " the sacred cloth in which they were enveloped ", and of their ornaments and cast into the fire.[1]

When the missionaries first expostulated with the people for worshipping Oro, " the god of feathers ", they propitiated him with, as Ellis tells, " pearls, or pigs, or other offerings." At Atehuru they beheld Pomare I and his men " at the great *marae*, where a number of ceremonies were performing in honour of Oro, the great national god ". Ellis writes:

" As they passed the *marae*, they saw a number of hogs on the altar and several human sacrifices placed in the trees around; and when they reached the spot where the chiefs were assembled, they found Pomare offering five or six large pigs to Oro on board a sacred canoe, in which the ark, or residence of the idol, was placed." [2]

Pomare wished, in response to an oracle, to have Oro conveyed from Atehuru to Tautira, but the local chiefs opposed him. Then Oro was taken by force, and Pomare had one of his servants sacrificed to the deity. War broke out over this forcible seizure of the god, and ultimately the Atehuruans recovered Oro. The possession of the idol would have greatly increased the power of the ambitious Pomare I who was originally only a district chief. His successes in war were due in no small measure to his having obtained firearms and ammunition from British vessels, as well as recruits from among British seamen. " To the favour of the gods," writes Ellis, " he considered himself indebted for the aggrandizement of his person and family; and if the missionaries would have allowed the claims of Oro or Tane to have received an equal degree of attention to that which they required

[1] *Polynesian Researches* (First Edition), Vol. I, pp. 209 *et seq.*
[2] *Polynesian Researches* (Second Edition), Vol. II, pp. 50-1.

for Jehovah, or Jesus Christ, Pomare would readily have admitted them." The King refused to "renounce his dependence upon the idols of his ancestors ".[1] His son Otu assumed his father's name and became Pomare II, and it was he who was converted and transformed into the destroyer of idols.

The readiness of Pomare I to recognize the religion of the Christian missionaries, if it were fused with his own, is an interesting modern instance of a process which must have been active at various periods in the history of Polynesia. As the missionaries of Buddhism and Mithraism incorporated in Asia and Europe the deities of other faiths, so apparently did the missionaries of more than one intruding cult on various groups of South Sea Islands. The supremacy of the Oro cult in the Society Islands apparently had a political significance.

According to Dr. W. H. R. Rivers the Oro cult was originally a sun cult. He draws attention to its intimate connexion with the secret Areoi organization.[2]

Ellis had much to tell about the Areois.[3] According to their belief, Oro, son of Taaroa, who lived in the sky, wished to have as his companion a human girl. Two of his brothers made search on the earth and found residing near the foot of " Red-ridged mountain " the excellent Vairaumati, a female " possessed of every charm ". Oro descended on the rainbow and took her as his wife. It then became his custom to descend on the rainbow every evening and return " by the same pathway on the following morning". The woman bore a son whom Oro named Hoa-tabu-i-te-rai ("Friend, sacred to the heavens ") and he became " a powerful ruler among men ".

The two younger brothers descended on the rainbow one evening to search for Oro. When, at length, they found Oro and his bride, they were ashamed to salute

---

[1] *Polynesian Researches* (Second Edition), Vol. II, pp. 66-8.
[2] *Sun-Cult and Megaliths in Oceania* (American Anthropologist, Vol. 17, No. 3, July–Sept., 1915, pp. 431 *et seq.*).
[3] *Polynesian Researches* (Second Edition), Vol. I, pp. 229 *et seq.*

them without offering gifts. One of the visitors, therefore, transformed himself into a pig and a bunch of *uru*
(red feathers). The other brother made the presentation;
but although the pig and feathers remained, the transformed brother afterwards resumed his former shape.

Oro considered it necessary to commemorate this
"mark of attention", and made the younger brothers
gods, constituting them Areois and founders of the
secret society.

Ellis tells that, in commemoration of this pig-and-
feathers incident, the Areois in their ceremonies " carried
a young pig to the temple, strangled it, bound it in the
ahu haio (a loose open kind of cloth) and placed it on
the altar. They also offered the red feathers, which they
called the *uru maru no te Areoi*, ' the shadowy *uru* of the
Areoi', or the red feathers of the party of the Areoi."

The brothers, as gods and kings of the Areois, lived
in celibacy, and their devotees were forbidden to have
offspring. Those who joined the Order, therefore, had
to consent to the murder of their children.

The Areois were strolling players and " privileged
libertines ". They went from island to island " exhibiting
their pantomimes and ", adds Ellis, " spreading a moral
contagion throughout society ". Captain Cook saw on
one occasion seventy canoes filled with Areois.

There were seven degrees in this secret society, each
being distinguished by a system of tatooing. When a
candidate was initiated he received a new name, and a
red belt, performed certain gesticulations and repeated
a " song or invocation ". His final act was to seize " the
cloth worn by the chief woman present ". At the festivals
members were raised to higher degrees with due ceremony, the marks of the degree being in each case tattoed
on the individual. The Areois were freed from all labour,
and had to be feasted by the " industrious husbandman ".
When members died they were privileged to go to
Paradise known as the " Perfumed " or " Fragrant

Rohutu ", situated in the aerial regions " near a lofty and stupendous mountain in Raiatea ". It appears, however, that admission to this Paradise was confined to those Areois whose friends could pay the high fees demanded by the priests. A life of constant pleasure, similar to that enjoyed in Hindu Paradises, was promised the Areois. Ellis says, " they (the souls) were supposed to be employed in a succession of amusements and indulgences similar to those to which they had been addicted on earth ".

Ellis could not see anything but moral depravity in the Areoi ceremonies. But Rivers, drawing upon the evidence of Moerenhout,[1] has shown that the features of the cult that usually occupy most attention are " superficial " and " perhaps only recent additions to a ritual which had a deep and truly religious purpose ". Although infanticide prevailed among the Areois in the Society Islands, it was unknown in the Marquesas and other groups. The licentious dances and certain other shocking practices were confined to " the lowest ranks of the societies ".

It appears that in some of the Society Islands and in the Marquesas, the Areois limited their festive proceedings to a portion of the year. They remained inactive when the sun was north of the equator. During this period the god Oro " was believed to go to Po, the obscure and dark home of the dead, and the members betook themselves to their *marae* or sacred enclosures to pray for the return of the god from this land of obscurity to *Rohoutou noanoa*, the home of light and life and the proper abode of the god ". From the end of April or May until the following October the Areois were in retreat.

" They suspended all their amusements and bemoaned the absence of the god until the time came to celebrate his return anew at the following equinox."

---

[1] *Voyages aux îles du grand Océan*, Paris, 1837.

Rivers was convinced that we have here " a ritual celebration of the annual death of the sun and of its coming to life again to bring abundance and fertility ". In the Gambier Islands the Areois had festivals in October and April " which show ", Rivers has emphasized, " that the societies must have had a purpose and meaning similar to those of the Marquesans ". In the Marquesas the place of Oro is taken by the god Mahui.

The moaning of the Polynesian Areois for the sun-god who had gone northward to Po recalls the Pagan " abominations " at Jerusalem which are referred to by Ezekiel:

" Then he brought me to the door of the gate of the Lord's house which was towards the north; and, behold, there sat women weeping for Tammuz.

" And he brought me into the inner court of the Lord's house; and, behold, at the door of the temple of the Lord, between the porch and the altar, were about five and twenty men, with their backs towards the temple of the Lord, and their faces towards the east; and they worshipped the sun towards the east." [1]

Tammuz-Adonis was mourned for during the period that he dwelt in Hades with the goddess of death and the underworld, Erish-ki-gal, the Babylonian Persephone. In the spring Ishtar descended to search for him.[2] Un-moral practices prevailed in connexion with the Baby-lonian Tammuz-Ishtar cult as among the Polynesian Areois.

In Egypt where, according to Herodotus (Book II, Chapter 164) the people were, like the Areois, divided into seven classes or castes, Osiris was mourned for as was Tammuz in Babylonia and Oro in the Society Islands. Once a year an assembly took place at Bubastis which resembled the assemblies of the Areois. " Men and women," says Herodotus,[3] " come sailing all to-gether, vast numbers in each boat, many of the women

---

[1] *Ezekiel*, Chapter viii, verses 14 and 16.
[2] My *Myths of Babylonia and Assyria*, pp. 95 et seq.   [3] Book II, Chapter 60.

with castanets, which they strike, while some of the men
pipe during the whole time of the voyage; the remainder
of the voyagers, male and female, sing the while, and
make a clapping with their hands." At each town the
women in the boats called to the females and "loaded
them with abuse", while others played or sang or danced
and some "uncovered themselves". At Bubastis a great
deal of wine was drunk.

On the day of the feast of Bacchus (Osiris), a pig
was sacrificed at every house door, and the Egyptians,
according to Herodotus (Book II, Chapter 48) behaved
as did the Greeks at a similar festival. " Instead of the
phalli," he says, " they have contrived certain figures of
about a cubit in length, some parts of which are made to
move. These the women carry about the streets and
villages, the indications of the sex being made almost
as large as the rest of the body; with these, and preceded
by a piper, they sing, in a long procession, the praises
of Bacchus (Osiris)." Herodotus says that the Egyptians
explained to him by " a sacred and mysterious reason "
their behaviour with the phalli.

The licentious character of the Polynesian ceremonies conducted by the Areois were similarly " mysteries ". Moerenhout was of opinion that their pantomimes and other mythological representations were
concerned with " the two principles of generation in
nature ". He recognized in the Areoi rites " ideas similar
to those the ancient Egyptians attached to the phallus
and the inhabitants of India to the lingam ".[1]

Craighill Handy discerns in the South Sea Islands
fertility festivals three dominant religious motives—" the
effort to stimulate nature directly through psychic
rapport, the desire to render thanks to the patrons of
fishing and agriculture and finally the honouring of the
spirits of relatives and ancestors in the other world ".[2]

[1] Quoted by Craighill Handy, *Bernice P. Bishop Museum Bulletin*, No. 34, p. 309.
[2] Craighill Handy, *op. cit.*, p. 310.

Rivers has drawn attention to " the similarity of the ritual of the secret societies of four different parts of Oceania "— Tahiti and the Marquesas, the Banks Islands, the Solomon Islands, and New Britain—and shown that " the ideas and practices found in these four parts of Oceania have a common source ". He points out, however, that the annual movements of the sun in the equatorial belt do not cause changes in luminosity and heat-giving " sufficiently great to suggest a simile with birth and death ", and comments:

" The representation of the sun's annual movements by the events of birth and death becomes much more easy to understand if the idea were brought to these tropical regions from a latitude where the representation would have a real meaning and be concordant with the behaviour of the sun. . . . There can be little question that such a latitude must be placed in the northern hemisphere for, if we except the southern part of South America and perhaps the south of New Zealand, there is no part of the southern hemisphere which could have been the home of such an idea."

Rivers found that the cult of the sun was in several places associated with the cult of dead ancestors as well as with the custom of erecting megalithic monuments. In the Society Islands and the Marquesas, the Areois held their celebrations at the *marae* enclosures with their pyramidal structures. Rivers traced in Melanesia connexions between ghost societies and megaliths. The remarkable correspondence between " the distribution of stone structures and secret societies in Oceania " suggests, in his opinion, that " the secret cult of the sun " erected the stone buildings " which form one of the chief mysteries of the islands of the Pacific ". There were, however, " two different streams of megalithic culture ".[1]

When John Turnbull visited Tahiti, the Areois were active and prominent. " It was now," he wrote,

[1] W. H. R. Rivers, *History of Melanesian Society*, Vol. II, p. 549; and the *American Anthropologist* (N.S.), Vol. 17, No. 3, July–Sept., 1915, pp. 431 *et seq.*

" a Bartholomew-fair-time at Otaheite; nothing but singing and drumming from morning till night." [1] Similar proceedings prevailed at Hawaii where, as we have seen, Lono, before his departure, instituted sports. The Hawaiian Hula dance organization was less elaborate than the Tahitian and Marquesan Areoi organization, but the significance of their rites appears to have been similar. Craighill Handy writes in this connexion:

" The hula troupes in their religious function served in the great festivals in the same way as did the Areoi in the southern islands, singing chants composed on mythical, historical, and eulogistic subjects during the seasonal rites and upon the occasion of the birth or marriage of a king or chief." [2]

Of special interest is Oro's connexion with the pig. Like Tammuz, Adonis, and Osiris he had a pig form. As we have seen, one of the younger brothers transformed himself into a pig as an offering to Oro, but not like the Set pig, the brother of Osiris, to do evil. Kane of Hawaii had a pig form as Kane-apuaa, *puaa* meaning " pig ". " Sometimes Ku or Lono would be substituted," says Westervelt,[3] who expresses the opinion that the word *puaa* " carried the idea of digging or uprooting the soil ". It is more probable that the pig god was imported from Asia, where he sometimes figures as a sky-god who causes thunder and sends rain, and fused with other deities there. In Polynesian stories the souls of the dead may appear in pig form and raid yam fields.

David Malo quotes the following from a Hawaiian religious composition:

" Life through the king: life through the gods,
    Behold the sacrifice—a pig.
    Sacred is the pig—it is there, O God.
    It is done.   We are saved."

[1] *A Voyage Round the World*, London, 1813, p. 285.
[2] *Bernice P. Bishop Museum Bulletin*, No. 34, p. 309.   [3] *Legends of Old Honolulu*, p. 34.

Other extracts are:

" Here is the pig, O Uli in the heavens.

.   .   .   .

Give us now the blood of swine,
Give us now the blood of dogs,
The blood of human sacrifice,
Provide, O Kea, swine and dogs in abundance for you, O Lono."

When a pig was offered to a Polynesian deity, the sacrificers gave him the head, retaining the body for themselves.

In Hawaii black pigs were preferred as offerings to deities, being considered sacred. Herman Melville, in his *Omoo*, informs us that black pigs were similarly invested with sanctity in the Marquesas. During a pig hunt, in which he took part, his friend " Shorty " wounded a pig and Melville killed it. None of the islanders could be induced to carry this pig, " some invincible super- stition being connected with its black colour ".[1] The pig which was offered to Captain Cook when he arrived at Hawaii, and was identified with the god Lono, was a black one.

Vishnu, the Hindu god, had a pig form—a human body with a boar's head. Rudra is, in the *Rig-veda* (I, 114, 5), called the *varaha* (boar). In the *Ramáyana* the god Brahma " becoming a boar, raised up the earth and created the whole world with the saints, his sons ". The god Trita, who in Zend (Persian) lore is the " water- bringer ", and is referred to in the *Rig-veda*, had a con- nexion with the pig. As Indra slays Vrittra, the serpent- dragon water-confiner, Trita slays the water-confining boar. It is interesting to find, in this connexion, Vedic references to the storm-clouds as " boars ".[2] As we have seen, the pig and the octopus were associated in Samoa. The shark-god and the pig-god were similarly associated in Hawaii.

---

[1] *Omoo* (Everyman's Edition), p. 229.
[2] Muir's *Original Sanskrit Texts*, Vol. IV, p. 396, note, 162.

The Hawaiian pig god Kamapuaa had quite a Hindu aspect, as Fornander has pointed out, when he figured with eight feet and eight eyes, and therefore with four faces or heads. Like a Hindu Nāga, he was able to change his shape, however, sometimes appearing as a small black pig or a gigantic pig monster and sometimes as a human being who had, however, to conceal " his pig-like deformities under a covering of Kapa cloth ". Similarly shark-men had a shark-mouth between their shoulders and dog-men a dog's jaws on their bodies. When Hindu Nāgas assumed human shape, serpents were either twined round their neck or concealed in their hair. The " water-horse " of Scotland, when in human shape, has sea-weed and sand in his hair.

In his pig and human shapes Kamapuaa exercised supernatural powers. He might make himself invisible and then fight against and put to rout large numbers of warriors; he might transform an enemy into stone, and he might prove so impervious to attack that great boulders thrown over a cliff were shattered as they struck him while he lay on the shore beneath and yet did not injure or even disturb him. He had, further, the power to increase his weight, and there are stories about him in this connexion which resemble those told regarding the Aztec god Tezcatlipoca who similarly made himself heavier when an endeavour was made to remove his gigantic and offensive body.

A Hawaiian myth tells that Kamapuaa, the pig-god, became the spouse of Pele, the fire-goddess, who had her home in the volcano. The pair had long been at enmity, and Kamapuaa " drove Pele from place to place " by pouring sea-water into her " pit ". The god Ku is referred to in some of the versions of the myth as an ancestor of the pig-god, Kamapuaa, who was capable of becoming a fish at will as he passed from island to island. In the end he confined Pele and her sisters to the southern part of Hawaii, ruling over the northern part himself.

He watered his part of the island with gentle showers
and sometimes caused fierce storms. For many centuries
the fields of the farmers were made fertile by Kamapuaa.
When Pele caused the earth to shake and sent lava,
Kamapuaa called for heavy rains to fall and cool the
lava.

Pele made peace with the handsome pig-god for a
time, appearing as a beautiful maid, while her sisters
danced. The pair were married and lived happily for a
time. But Pele was prone to outbursts of fiery rage, and
one day the couple quarrelled and parted for ever. Then
the volcano-goddess waged fierce war against the pig-
god, aided by the gods of Po, the dark Underworld.
Kamapuaa escaped to the sea and assumed the shape of
the fish named *humu-humu-nuku-nuku-a-puaa*, which has
a skin so thick that it can resist water when it is made to
boil by hot lava. This fish, when caught, usually makes
a noise " like the grunting of a small pig ". Westervelt
says that:

" Kamapuaa figured to the last days of Pele worship in the
sacrifices offered to the fire-goddess. The most acceptable sacrifice
to Pele was supposed to be *puaa* (a pig). If a pig could not be
secured when an offering was necessary, the priest would take the
fish *humu-humu-nuku-nuku-a-puaa* and throw it into the pit of
fire. If the pig and the fish both failed, the priest would offer any
of the things into which it was said in their traditions, Kamapuaa
could turn himself." [1]

Another Polynesian man-god was Maui. It is possible
that the original Maui was a great explorer who discovered many islands which he " fished up ", as told in
the folk stories.

The memory of Maui, however, was confused with
that of ancient deities. Like the Mesopotamian Oannes,
who came up from the Persian gulf and instructed the
people of Eridu in various arts and crafts and obtained
many necessary things for them, the Polynesian Maui

[1] *Legends of Old Honolulu*, pp. 246-77.

was what is usually called a " culture god " or " culture hero ". He not only " fished up " (discovered) islands, opening for mariners the " paths " of the sea, but obtained fire from the Underworld as did Prometheus from the sky-world, raised the sky and regulated the seasons by catching the sun in a noose of his rope, and controlled all the winds save the west one. He perished in his attempt to overcome the Death-goddess and make human beings immortals.

Maui in his god-form was reputed to be the son of a virgin goddess and to have had one eye like jade and another like an eel's eye. A Hawaiian sacred poem makes him the son of Hina-of-the-fire, who was the daughter of Mahuie, the fire-goddess. The Maoris, on the other hand, referred to the fire-goddess as Mahuika and regarded her, not as the grandmother, but the ancestress of Maui. Some regarded Mahuika as a male, not a female. Pele, the volcano- and fire-goddess, was in Rarotonga spoken of as a daughter of Mahuika. According to S. Percy Smith, the Maori fire-goddess was identical with Pele.[1]

Tregear, in his study of the Hawaiian " Creation Song ", quotes Hina, mother of Maui, as saying:

" I have no husband, yet a child is born."

The brothers of Hina fought against Maui who, in the poem, sends creative showers as the Egyptian deities weep " creative tears ", causing plants, &c., to spring up. The " Creation Song " tells of the struggle between the brothers of the virgin-goddess and her son:

" They fought hard with Maui, and were thrown;
And red water flowed freely from Maui's forehead—
This was the first shower by Maui.
They fetched from the sacred Awa bush of Kane and Kanaloa.
Then came the second shower by Maui.
The third shower was when the elbow of Awa was broken.

[1] Craighill Handy, *Bernice P. Bishop Museum Bulletin* 34, pp. 118-9; quoting authorities.

The fourth shower was the sacred bamboo of Kane and Kanaloa.
The fifth was the edge of the umu (oven).
The sixth shower was the first rise.
Maui sobbed and inquired for his father.
Hina denied that he had a father."

Hina sends Maui forth to find his line and hook,
" which catches land ", saying " go hence (to sea) to your
father ".

" When the hook catches land, 't will bring the old seas together,
Bring hither the large Alae (a bird) of Hina,
The sister bird.
Of the great fiery showers caused by Maui."

Like the pig-god Kamapuaa, Maui was in one of
his forms a god with eight eyes. Tregear explains the
reference by showing that the Maori bat-god had eight
eyes—the Maori " Pekapeka " and the Hawaiian " Pea-
pea ".

The Hawaiian poem refers as follows to Maui regu-
lating the seasons by " roping the sun " which was
moving too swiftly:

" Maui became restless and fought the sun
For the noose that Maui laid.
And Winter won the sun.
So Summer was won by Maui.
They drank of the yellow waters to the dregs
Of Kane and Kanaloa.
By strategy the war
Embraced Hawaii, encompassed Maui (the island),
Kanai, around Oahu.
At Kahalu was the afterbirth, at Waikane the navel.
It dropped at Hakipuu, at Kualo."

In the pedigree part of the Hawaiian " Creation
Song ", Maui is mentioned as a son of Kanaloa (Tangaloa)
and further on as the son of the *malo* (loin cloth) of
Kalana.[1]

---

[1] Tregear, *Journal of the Polynesian Society*, Vol. IX, pp. 38 *et seg.*

Gill found that in the Hervey group of islands Maui's mother was Buataranga, " guardian of the road to the invisible world ", and his father Ru, " the supporter of the heavens ". These two dwell in the Underworld (Avaiki), as did also the sun-god Ra and Mauike, god of fire. When Maui was very young he was made one of the guardians of the upper world in which dwell human beings. Everyone ate raw food, having no knowledge of how to produce, procure, or use fire.

Maui discovered one day that his mother had cooked food, and he resolved to follow her to the Underworld from which she had come to visit him. He heard her utter the " Open Sesame " which caused a black rock to split, revealing the entrance to Avaiki. Then he went to Tane and obtained from him a red pigeon. Entering this bird, he went to the black rock and recited the " Open Sesame " charm. The rock at once divided and he flew down to the Underworld. The pigeon perched on a bread-fruit tree and Maui came forth and revealed himself to his mother, making known that he wished to obtain fire. She directed him to the dwelling of Mauike, the fire-god, and after engaging in a conflict with that deity, Maui was instructed how to make fire by friction of fire-sticks. After returning to the upper world, Maui revealed to mankind the secret of how to produce and use fire and cook food.

A Maori version of the myth makes Maui obtain fire from Mafuike, the fire-goddess. There are other variants of the myth in Polynesia and Melanesia. In the Society Islands, however, Maui was scarcely known. The fire-goddess appears to have been peculiar to Maori mythology. Elsewhere the deity is a male.[1]

The story of Maui's attempt to obtain immortality for mankind is given at length in Maori sacred literature. He goes forth to search for the death-goddess Hine-

[1] W. W. Gill, *Myths and Songs from the South Pacific*, pp. 51 *et seq.*; R. B. Dixon, *Oceanic Mythology* (quoting authorities), pp. 41 *et seq.*

NATIVE CARVINGS, NEW ZEALAND

Face of upper figure carved to represent tattooing

Reproduced by permission from the Hunterian Museum, Glasgow

NATIVE CARVING, NEW ZEALAND

The left and central figures have pearl-shell (*Haliotis*) eyes

nui-te-po—(Great Mother of Hades) an old hag with
red eyes of jasper, teeth like obsidian, hair like seaweed,
a great mouth and a body like that of a man. When
Maui finds her in Po, she is fast asleep. He endeavours
to pass through her body, for if he can come out of her
mouth, she will die and there will be no more death.
But the old woman wakes up too soon and she kills
Maui. That is why the death-goddess continues to claim
her human victims.[1]

Writing of Hina, the moon, White says the Maori
referred to her as the " man consumer ". She was " a
source of death " and she caused night to be.

" Maui said to Hina, ' Let death be very short '—that is,
let man die and live again, and live on for ever. She replied, ' Let
death be very long, that man may sigh and sorrow '—that is, Let
man die and return to the world of darkness, and be the cause of
grief and wailing to his friends.

" Maui again said, ' Let man die and live again, as you, the
moon, die and live again ', but Hina said, ' No: let man die and
become like soil, and never rise to life again '."

In another version Hina says: " Let death be long,
and when man dies let him go into darkness, and become like earth, that those he leaves may weep and wail
and lament." It is added: " And so it was. This is why
men cry over their dead." [2]

All through Polynesia Hina " is ", Tregear says,
" connected with the moon ". In the Hawaiian " Creation
Song " she is referred to as " Hina the sprig taken
ashore and warmed by the fire ". This is a reference to
the Maori myth of Hina " the Fish of the Moon ".
Owing to the unkind treatment of Maui, she flung
herself into the sea where she floated for months, being
at length thrown up on the beach. She was restored to
consciousness by two men to whom she gave her name
as " Stranded-log-of-timber ".[3]

---

[1] Sir George Grey, *Polynesian Mythology*, Chapter II.
[2] J. White, *Ancient History of the Maori*, Vol. II, pp. 87, 90.
[3] E. Tregear, *Journal of the Polynesian Society*, Vol. IX, pp. 44 *et seq.*

There are in some of the legends several Mauis, the hero being usually the younger brother. " There have been very many Mauis in Polynesian history," says S. Percy Smith, " and in process of time the deeds of some ancient and mythical Maui have become confounded with those of men who lived in later ages." [1]

Among the greater deities may be classed Whiro, the god of tempests, who waged war against his brothers Tane, Tangaloa, Rongo, and Tu because they had separated Rangi and Papa, their parents. He departed to the Underworld and became a deity of darkness and death, or he was cast down from the sky by Tane as was Lucifer in Asia. As Iro or Hiro he was the god of thieves and a god of the sea.[2] Tane, as sky-god, and Whiro, as Underworld-god, are reminiscent of the ancient twin deities of light and darkness represented also by Tangaloa and Rongo in some of the myths.

The Maoris regarded Whiro as " the origin of evil in the world ". His representative was the lizard, " the harbinger of death ". Best says that " this explains the great dread that the Maori folk entertain for the lizard, and why seeing a lizard is deemed a very serious omen ". It is a Maori belief that when the gods decide to destroy a man " they do so by introducing a lizard into his body, and that creature devours his vitals and so causes death ".[3]

Other gods had likewise their animal, fish, and reptile forms. Craighill Handy, quoting Teuira Henry, shows that in Tahiti the *ata* (ghosts, reflections, or incarnations) of the gods were numerous. The boar was the *ata* of Oro, the dog the *ata* of Toahiti, the sea-gull was the *ata* of Tane. " Different kinds of lizards were the *ata* of various gods." The *ata* of the sea-gods was the turtle. " But Taaroa (Tangaloa), the creator, had the greatest variety of *ata*. The whale, tropic bird,

[1] *Hawaiki* (Fourth Edition), p. 158.
[2] Ellis, *Polynesian Researches* (Second Edition). Vol. I, p. 328.
[3] Elsdon Best, *The Maori*, Vol. I, pp. 107.

parrot, fish, and the albatross are all described as his *ata* and the ray-fish is spoken of as the " swimming temple of Taaroa ".   Sharks were incarnations or ghost-forms of certain chiefs of ancient times.   In Hawaii " the shark gods were most common and played the most important rôle in actual worship ".   These might at will assume human or shark forms.[1]   Ellis found that in the Society Islands the blue shark was the only kind " supposed to be engaged by the gods ".[2]

[1] E. Craighill Handy, *Bernice P. Bishop Museum Bulletin*, No. 34, pp. 127 128.
[2] *Polynesian Researches* (Second Edition), Vol. I, p. 329.

CHAPTER XXIII

The " Fire-walk " in Polynesia

Modern Records of Ancient Ceremony—Polynesian and Phœnician "Fire-walks" over Hot Stones—Asiatic "Fire-walks" over Glowing Charcoal—Europeans take part in Polynesian Ceremonies—Great Heat of Stones—Two Hundred "Fire-walkers"—Immunity from Burning Injuries—Society Islands "Fire-walkers"—New Zealand Memories of Ceremony—Tongan and Tahitian Ceremonies—Wonderful Fijian Performance—Theories as to Skin Protection—A Great Fiery Oven—Registering the Heat—A Sensational Performance—Doctor examines Feet of "Fire-walkers"—A Honolulu Exhibition—Not a "Fake"—The Bonds of Superstition.

The ceremonial " fire-walk ", which has a history rooted in antiquity, was known to and practised by groups of Polynesians. It was not perpetuated on many islands and may never have been practised on some. The available records of the ceremony are confined to the Society Islands, the Tonga or Friendly Islands, New Zealand, Fiji, and Hawaii. In New Zealand " fire-walking was remembered by the priesthood long after it had been discontinued. It has been practised, however, in modern times in the presence of reliable observers, under the direction of some hereditary fire-walkers of the Fijian and Society Islanders. From the latter group came the men who conducted the ceremonies in Rarotonga and Hawaii, which are described below. In the next chapter it is shown that there were similarly hereditary fire-walkers in Bulgaria and Spain.

As in Asia and Europe, the fire-walk in Polynesia was supposed to increase, or be a manifestation of, religious " merit " or power (*mana*), and it seems also to have been intimately connected with the seasonal expulsion of evil influences. It certainly increased the prestige of those who directed the ceremony and of the others who took part in it.

An interesting fact regarding the South Sea Islands "fire-walk" is that it was performed over heated stones and not as in India, China, and Japan over glowing charcoal. The Phœnicians appear to have had a ceremonial "fire-walk" similar to that of the Polynesians. As much is to be gathered from the evidence provided by *Ezekiel* (Chap. xxviii, verses 14, 16). In pronouncing judgment on Tyre, the Hebrew prophet says of that city, whose king impersonated the god Melkarth:

"Thou hast walked up and down in the midst of the stones of fire. . . . By the multitude of thy merchandise they have filled the midst of thee with violence, and thou hast sinned: therefore I will cast thee as profane out of the mountain of God: and I will destroy thee, O covering cherub, from the midst of the stones of fire."

Evidently the practice was essentially a religious one and as great an abomination to orthodox Hebrews as were the mouse feast, the sacrificial eating of swine, the "weeping for Tammuz", sun-worship, and so on.

Like the practice of mummification and the religious ideas connected with it, the "fire-walk" appears to have been imported into different areas and incorporated in various faiths. In India, as will be shown, it was observed by Dravidians and Hindus, and, in some instances, even by Moslems, in China by Taoists and Buddhists, in Japan by sects of the Shinto faith, in Anatolia and Italy by worshippers of a goddess, while in Bulgaria and Spain it survived into Christian times.

It may be that the diffusion in the East of the practice and the fundamental ideas connected with it, should be regarded as primarily due to Phœnician influence. The fact that it reached Polynesia indicates that it was diffused by sea-farers. Perhaps the Phœnicians perpetuated and developed a practice connected with a doctrine originated among another people. A Biblical reference to a Babylonian "fire-walk" is given below. The Egyptian evidence is also of interest.

Instances of the "fire-walk" in the South Sea Islands will first be dealt with.

Colonel Gudgeon, formerly British Resident, Rarotonga, relates how he had seen and gone through the Polynesian *Umu Ti*, or "Fire-walking Ceremony". He states that a large log-fire had been kindled to heat the stones. Two of the stones had been taken from a *marae* and a native asserted that they resisted the heat. Some branches of the large-leaved *Ti* (or *Dracæna*) were used in the ceremony. Colonel Gudgeon and his friends undertook to accompany the natives on their fire-walk and he relates:

"The *tohunga* (priest) and his *tauira* (pupil) walked each to the oven, and then halting, the prophet spoke a few words, and then each struck the edge of the oven with the *ti* branches. This was three times repeated, and then they walked slowly and deliberately over the two fathoms of hot stones. When this was done, the tohunga came to us and his disciple handed his *ti* branch to Mr. Goodwin, at whose place the ceremony came off, and they went through the ceremony. Then the *tohunga* said to Mr. Goodwin, 'I hand my *mana* (power) over to you; lead your friends across'.

"Now there were four Europeans—Dr. W. Craig, Dr. George Craig, Mr. Goodwin, and myself—and I can only say that we stepped out boldly. I got across unscathed, and only one of the party was badly burned; and he, it is said, was spoken to, but like Lot's wife looked behind him—a thing against all rules.

"I can hardly give you my sensations, but I can say this—that I knew quite well I was walking on red-hot stones and could feel the heat, yet I was not burned. I felt something resembling slight electric shocks, both at the time and afterwards, but that is all. I do not know that I should recommend everyone to try it. A man must have *mana* to do it; if he has not, it will be too late when he is on the hot stones of Tama-ahi-roa."

There can be no doubt about the reality of this "fire-walk " by white men.   Colonel Gudgeon goes into further details:

" To show you the heat of the stones, quite half an hour afterwards someone remarked to the priest that the stones would not be hot enough to cook the *ti*. His only answer was to throw his green branch on the oven, and in a quarter of a minute it was blazing. As I have eaten a fair share of the *ti* cooked in the oven, I am in a position to say it was hot enough to cook it well.

" I walked with bare feet, and after we had done so about 200 Maoris followed. No one, so far as I saw, went through with boots on. I did not walk quickly across the oven, but with deliberation, because I feared that I should tread on a sharp point of the stones and fall. My feet also were very tender. I did not mention the fact, but my impression as I crossed the oven was that the skin would all peel off my feet. Yet all I really felt when the task was accomplished was a tingling sensation not unlike slight electric shocks on the soles of my feet, and this continued for seven hours or more. The really funny thing is that, though the stones were hot enough an hour afterwards to burn up green branches of the *ti*, the very tender skin of my feet was not even hardened by the fire. Many of the Maoris thought they were burned, but they were not, at any rate not severely."

The *tohunga*, who directed the ceremony, was a young man of the Raiatea family " who are hereditary fire-walkers ".[1]   Apparently the fire-walking cult had long been perpetuated in the Society Islands whence, as we shall see, came also the fire-walker who performed at Hawaii.

The editors of the *Journal of the Polynesian Society*, when publishing Colonel Gudgeon's evidence, stated that the Maoris of New Zealand were acquainted with the fire-walking ceremony " which was performed by their ancestors. On reading Colonel Gudgeon's account to some old chiefs of the Urewera tribe, they expressed no surprise and said that their ancestors could also perform the ceremony, though it was long gone out of practice."

[1] *Journal of the Polynesian Society*, Vol. VIII, pp. 58–60.

Mr. Elsdon Best, writing of the fire-walk, says that its only purport in New Zealand, so far as he could ascertain, "was to add *mana*, prestige, force, renown, *éclat*, to ritual functions.

"In Polynesia it is called the *umu ti*, and is manipulated as a huge *umu* or steam oven. After the performance of the fire-walk, the oven is utilized for cooking a collection of roots of the *ti*, a species of *Cordyline*. It was this same *umu* that was utilized in New Zealand. The act was one, not of walking through fire, but of walking barefoot over extremely hot stones, heated for hours on a huge fire kindled in the pit." [1]

Miss Teuira Henry, who describes a "fire-walk" in Tonga, tells that her sister and niece walked with the natives over the red-hot stones and suffered no injury. A French naval officer photographed the ceremony. An interesting fact is that a native religious chant, in which there were many obsolete words, was recited by the priest. Another fire-walk was witnessed on the island of Raiatea, Society Islands, by Mr. Hastwell, San Francisco, who has recorded that the stones were heated to a "red and white heat", and that they were crossed several times in leisurely fashion by the "fire-walkers". [2]

A lengthy account of the Fiji "fire-walk" is given by Dr. T. M. Hocken in a paper read at Otago in May, 1898. [3] He says the ceremony is called by the natives *vilavilairevo*.

"A number of almost nude Fijians walk quickly and unharmed across and among white-hot stones, which form the pavement of a huge native oven—termed *lovo*—in which shortly afterwards are cooked the succulent sugary roots and pith of the *Cordyline terminalis*, one of the cabbage trees, known to the Maoris as the *ti* and to the Fijians as the *masawe*. This wonderful power of fire-walking is now not only very rarely exercised, but, at least as regards Fiji, is confined to a small clan or family—the *Na Ivilankata*—resident on Bega (= Mbenga), an island of the group, lying somewhat south of Suva, and twenty miles from that capital."

[1] *The Maori*, Vol. I, p. 270.   [2] *Journal of the Polynesian Society*, Vol. II, pp. 105 *et seq.*
[3] *Transactions and Proceedings of the New Zealand Institute*, Vol. XXXI.

When preparations were being made for the "fire-walk" Dr. Hocken set himself to collect whatever information or explanation the natives could provide, but "with no very satisfactory result". As he remarks, "the facts were undisputed, but the explanations quite insufficient". He goes on to say:

"Some thought that the chief actors rubbed their bodies with a secret preparation which rendered them fireproof; others that lifelong friction on the hard hot rocks, coral-reefs, and sands had so thickened and indurated the foot sole that it could defy fire; but all agreed as to the *bona-fides* of the exhibition."

The "fire-walk" described by Dr. Hocken took place on a day which was "blazingly hot and brilliant". A great crowd of natives had collected where the great oven was "pouring forth its torrents of heat from huge embers which were still burning fiercely on the underlying stones". The heat was very great. "These were indeed," says Dr. Hocken, "melting moments for the spectators. The pitiless noontide sun, and the no less pitiless oven-heat, both pent up in the deep well-like forest clearing, reduced us to a state of solution from which there was no escape."

The oven (*lovo*) was circular, "with a diameter of 25 feet or 30 feet; its greatest depth was perhaps 8 feet, its general shape that of a saucer, with sloping sides and a flattish bottom, the latter being filled with the white-hot stones. Near the margin of the oven, and on its windward side, the thermometer marked 114°."

Preparation for the ceremony was made by clearing away from the hot stones the smouldering logs. Mr. Vaughan of the Meteorological Department at Suva had a thermometer in "a strong japanned-tin casing", and he had it thrust out at the end of a pole and held over the centre of the hot stone pavement.

"But it had to be withdrawn almost immediately, as the solder began to melt and drop, and the instrument to be destroyed.

It, however, registered 282° F., and it is certain that had not this accident occurred, the range of 400° would have been exceeded, and the thermometer burst."

The "fire-walkers", the "descendants of Na Galita", numbering seven or eight, who had been concealed in the forest, then came forth, and the native spectators received them with "vociferous yells". They came forward towards the oven.

"The margin reached, they steadily descended the oven slope in single file, and walked, as I think, leisurely, but as others of our party think, quickly, across and around the stones, leaving the oven at the point of entrance. The leader, who was longest in the oven, was a second or two under half a minute therein."

Dr. Hocken examined one or two of the "fire-walkers" before the ceremony took place, and found that "the skin, legs, and feet were free from any apparent application. . . . The foot-soles were comparatively soft and flexible—by no means leathery and insensible." The two Suvan theories were thus disposed of. Dr. Hocken continues:

"This careful examination was repeated immediately after egress from the oven, and with the same result. To use the language of Scripture, 'No smell of fire had passed upon them'. No incantations or other religious ceremonial were observed. Though these were formerly practised, they have fallen into disuse since the introduction of Christianity."

One of the fire-walkers informed Mr. Walter Carew, when that gentleman was Resident Commissioner and Stipendiary Magistrate in Fiji, that he could not explain how he was able to perform the "fire-walk". Dr. Hocken gives his words as follows: "I can do it, but I do not know how it is done". He also said that he "does not experience" (during the "fire-walk") "any heat or other sensation". The natives asserted that "any person holding the hand of one of the fire-walkers could himself pass through the oven unharmed".

A fire-walk at Honolulu, Hawaii, is described by Mr. Gorten in the *Boston Evening Transcript* of 20th March, 1891:

"Papa Ita, a Tahitan, has given us exhibitions of the famous fire-walking which is still practised in the South Sea Islands and parts of Japan and India.

"On the vacant land swept a year ago by the Chinatown fire a great elliptical pit was dug and a large quantity of wood placed therein, on which were piled the lava rocks. All day the fire burned till the stones were of a white heat; then the white-haired native from Tahiti approached the fiery furnace dressed in a robe of white tapa, with a girdle and head-dress of the sacred ti-leaves and a bundle of leaves in his hand for a wand. Striking the ground with the ti-leaf wand, he uttered an incantation in his own language, which was a prayer to his gods to temper the heat and allow him to pass; then calmly and deliberately, with bare feet, he walked the length of the pit, bearing aloft the ti-leaf wand. Pausing a moment on the other side, he again struck the ground and returned over the same fiery path. This was several times repeated, and he even paused a few seconds when in the middle of the pit to allow his picture to be taken. The stones were undoubtedly hot and were turned by means of long poles just before the walking, to have the hottest side up, and from between the rocks the low flames were continually leaping up. The heat that radiated to the spectators was intense. . . .

"None but natives, of course, believe there is anything supernatural, but we cannot explain how he does it. It cannot be called a fake, for he really does what he claims to do, and none, so far, dare imitate him. The natives fall down before him, as a great Kapuna, and many interested in the welfare of the Hawaiians deplore these exhibitions, feeling it is bad for the natives, in that it strengthens their old bonds of superstition, to the undoing of much of the advancement they have made."

CHAPTER XXIV

The " Fire-walk " in Old and New Worlds

Chinese Fire-walk—Expulsion of Evil Influences—Priest in Conflict with Spectres—A Spring Ceremony—Government opposed to Ceremony—Fire-walk in Japan—Bathing Preparations—Men, Women, and Children tread Glowing Charcoal—Fire-walk in Southern India—A Goddess invoked—Draupadi and Sita—Fire-walking by Hindus and Moslems—As a Low Caste Ceremony—Brahmans ignore it—Government opposed to Ceremony—Flowers substituted for Fire—Fire-walk in the Mauritius—Babylonian Fire-walk—Shadrach, Meshach, and Abednego—Anatolian Priestesses Ceremony—Hereditary Bulgarian Fire-walkers—Fire-walk in Ancient Italy—Evidence of Strabo, Virgil, and Pliny—Spanish Fire-walkers—West African Fire Test—Fire-walking in Ancient Egyptian Otherworld—Fire-walks in Pre-Columbian America—European Fire-leaping Ceremonies—Origin of the Fire-walk.

The fire-walk has long been practised in China. De Groot[1] refers to it in his chapter on " Possessed Mediums, Exorcists and Seers " as a means " for the acquisition of immunity from evil", and therefore from the spectres. Like the ceremonial walking of the " bridge of swords ", it is supposed to secure annual purification of an area. The Chinese names for the ceremony are *táh hé* (" treading fire ") and *kiáng hé-lō* (" walking on a path of fire "). When it is to be performed a small layer of charcoal is spread out on the square in front of the temple, and it is gradually enlarged by the laity and those under the patronage of the temple god. The propitious hour is fixed by the oracle or indicated by " spirit writing " and then a priest places written charms on each side of the layer to ward off the

[1] *The Religious System of China*, Leyden, 1910, Vol. VI, pp. 1292.

spectres. These are, however, more thoroughly expelled by blowing a horn and ringing a handbell, and by spells, charm-water and rice and salt. Men ignite the charcoal and keep it glowing by waving fans.

Meanwhile young men with banners incite the spectres to attack, and a priest[1] furiously cleaves the air with a sword, the strokes being perpendicular. The demons are thus maimed or driven away. Then the priest " vehemently flogs the soil with his mat on the four sides of the fire, while uttering imperative spells— an exorcising purification final and radical!" Having completed this part of the anti-spectre ceremony he leads the fire-walk:

" With agility and quickness he pushes the roll (of mat) right through the glowing mass, virtually splitting it up into two halves, in this way ' opening a fire path ' (*Khui hè-lō*), which thus, while pushing, he is himself the first to tread. But the layer of fire is thin, so thin indeed that he might have opened the path with his shod feet; but his aim being to overawe the spectres, ostentation before these things is necessary. *Sai-Kong sak ch'ióh*, ' a *sai Kong* pushing a mat ', is a saying equivalent to our ' much ado about nothing."

De Groot's description continues:

" The fire-path laid open, the *Sai Kong* walks it a second time at a quick pace, now ringing his handbell and blowing his horn. He is followed by his younger colleagues who are officiating with him, after whom come the several *hoat tiuᵍ*,[2] brandishing their swords, the *lô iên sê*[3] with their rings, the children under patronage (of the temple god) and the general public many of whom wear paper charms on their dresses, cheering tumultuously, to the rousing noise of gongs, cymbals and drums. Many pass through the fire two, three, and many more times; and the palankeens containing the images of the temple gods are fetched and carried through it. And it is not until the glowing fire is dying out that the noisy crowd disperses from the spot to seek diversion elsewhere in the

---

[1] The *Sai Kong*, a " Wuist master ", or " master Wu ". This class of priest specialize in sacrificial work and exorcising magic.

[2] Youths possessed of divine influence—unofficial priests.   [3] Other possessed helpers.

square or in the temple, especially at the theatricals, which on great festivals are always performed almost uninterruptedly for the amusement of the gods and their beloved parishioners."

De Groot says that those who celebrate the fire-walk ceremony are supposed " to observe the vigil beforehand lest he might burn himself", but " probably nobody attends to this precaution because it is so troublesome ". People in mourning, and those whose birthday cyclical characters are in collision with the characters of the days or hours when the rite is celebrated, must keep at a distance lest they should suffer injury or disturb the propitious effect of the ceremony.

Sir James G. Frazer, quoting German writers,[1] says that in the Fo-Kien province of China the fire-walking festival falls in April on the 13th day of the 3rd month of the Chinese calendar. It is taken part in chiefly by the labouring class, who refrain from sexual intercourse for seven days and fast for three days before the ceremony. They receive, during the period of preparation, instruction in the temple how to discharge the duty laid upon them. The fire-walk is a more realistic and impressive one than that described by De Groot.

" On the eve of the festival an enormous brazier of charcoal, sometimes twenty feet wide, is prepared in front of the temple of the Great God, the protector of life. At sunrise next morning the brazier is lighted and kept burning by fresh supplies of fuel. A Taoist priest throws a mixture of salt and rice on the fire to conjure the flames and ensure an abundant year. Further, two exorcists, barefooted and followed by two peasants traverse the fire again and again till it is somewhat beaten down.

" Meantime the procession is forming in the temple. The image of the god is placed in a sedan chair, resplendent with red paint and gilding, and is carried forth by a score or more of barefooted peasants."

On the shafts of the " sedan chair " stands a priest who strikes blows at the invisible spectres with his sword.

---

[1] *The Golden Bough* (Third Edition), Part VII, Vol. II, pp. 3 *et seq.*

He has a dagger stuck through the upper part of an arm, the exorcising priests being given to self-torture. Sir James's summary of the German evidence continues:

" Wild music now strikes up, and under the excitement caused by its stirring strains the procession passes thrice across the furnace. At their third passage the performers are followed by other peasants carrying the utensils of the temple; and the rustic mob, electrified by the frenzied spectacle, falls in behind. Strange as it may seem, burns are comparatively rare. . . . The peasants carry off the charred embers from the furnace, pound them to ashes, and mix the ashes with the fodder of their cattle, believing that it fattens them."

The old Chinese Government disapproved of the ceremony, and on the following day many of those who had taken part in it were beaten by the police.

The *Field* gave in 1899 a vivid account by Mr. Andrew Haggard of a fire-walking ceremony in Tokio, Japan, on 9th April, 1899. It was held in connexion with the festival of the god of Ontaki mountain in a small Shinto temple in the Kanda quarter of the city. A large number of European ladies and gentlemen were permitted to attend. Those who were seated nearest to the enormous fire which had been kindled " literally scorched long before the walking on the fire began ". The Europeans present were not asked to take part in the ceremony.

Before the performance those who were to walk over the fire stripped themselves naked and squatted on the floor of an apartment beside big tubs containing cold water.

" Without a stitch of clothing they remained squatting on the cold flags, and alternately pouring bucket after bucket of cold water on their heads, and offering up long prayers and chants with the most wonderful gestures of the arms and hands, all of which gestures had some symbolical meaning. . . . During the bathing the worshippers also swung their bodies about and became quite excited in the operation, much like an Egyptian dervish dancing."

There was a large number of fire-walkers and they had to take turns at the washing ceremony. Meanwhile the fire awaited them.

"Upon arrival at the temple at 4.30 p.m. we saw a long blazing and smouldering heap of damp straw. Underneath this was a bed of lighted charcoal. By the time that the fire-walking began the straw had been consumed, and, as it was now almost dark, the lurid glow upon the faces of the white-robed worshippers and the crowds of Japanese against the surrounding railing was most weird."

The fire was beaten flat with long poles so that there was a level surface to walk upon.

All those who took part in the ceremony clothed themselves in loose white garments. Then they walked towards the fire which was being constantly fanned by huge fans and became hotter than ever. One leader sprinkled salt on the fire at each of the cardinal points;[1] another struck showers of sparks with his flint and steel. The salt was "an emblem of purification". When the company had walked round the fire, one of them stepped on some scattered grains of salt and then "deliberately walked through the fire from end to end". He accomplished this in seven paces.

"He did not seem to suffer from the fire in any way, and shortly after he walked through it again. Others now, but at first the men only, followed his example. Some of the old men hurried a little; but most of them, old or young, were very deliberate, stamping down each foot hard into the red-hot charcoal at every step.

"Old women, many young women, and one or two little children, now began to follow, walking through the fire from end to end. Many of the women walked through carrying their babies on their backs. One very tiny child there was a boy, who stood for some time crying on the edge of the fire, fearing the ordeal. One of the men spoke kindly to him, and walked through in front of him. Presently the little fellow plucked up his courage and walked

---

[1] The salt-sprinkling was also a feature of the Chinese ceremony.

straight through too. It was a most extraordinary sight. He could not have been more than six or seven years old. And not one of all these was hurt in the least. I examined their feet afterwards; they were quite soft, and not a trace of fire upon them."

According to Mr. Edgar Thurston, formerly superintendent of Ethnography in Madras, fire-walking is " widespread throughout Southern India ".[1] He says it is believed the ceremonial " secures to the villagers their cattle and crops and protection from dangers of all kinds. An individual who suffers from any chronic complaint makes a vow in the name of the goddess (Draupadi) that if he is cured he will walk over the fire." Those who invoke the goddess Draupadi worship her thrice daily for ten days and attend readings given by a priest of portions of the *Mahábhárata*. During the part of the preparatory period they are clad in saffron, and sleep in the temple at night. " The devotee," says Thurston, " observes a fast on the day of the fire-walking, and, early in the morning, goes to the temple and worships the goddess along with others who have taken similar vows. They then bathe in a tank to secure perfect cleanness of body."

The charcoal used for the fire-walk is obtained by burning about a ton of jungle wood in a shallow trench. The glowing embers are then spread over a permanent platform.

Thurston tells of a ceremony which began with a procession walking from the temple carrying images of Draupadi, Krishna, and Arjuna.

" The idols were placed in front of the platform, and, after worship had been offered, the priest, decked with garlands and clad in a yellow cloth, walked over the embers with measured steps and quite calmly. The other devotees then rushed on to the platform, and walked over the glowing cinders to the other side, where they cooled their feet in a puddle of water (the pāl-kuli, or milk pit). The glowing embers were loose, not beaten down or

---

[1] *Ethnographic Notes in Southern India*, Madras Government Press, 1906, pp. 471 *et seq.*
(D 917)

flattened in any way, and the feet of the fire-walkers, as they passed through, actually sank into the loose bed of fire. This was particularly noticeable in the case of the pūjāri (priest) during his calm and deliberate passage. Neither he nor the devotees lifted their feet high. They seemed rather to wade through the embers, as through shallow water. . . . An interesting feature of the ceremony was that a boy about eight years old walked over the embers, while a still smaller child was hurried over, hanging on to its father's hand. A few performers, too, carried children across on their shoulders. . . . Many of those assembled at the ceremony took away with them some of the sacred ashes to be used as a charm to drive away devils and demons." [1]

Draupadi, who was worshipped as a goddess, was an incarnation of Sree (Lakshmi, wife of Vishnu) and joint wife of the five Pandava brothers, who were incarnations of the god Indra. In the *Mahábhárata*, which celebrates the great war for supremacy between the Pandavas and the Kurus, Draupadi had origin in a sacrificial fire. At the conclusion of the war, in which the Pandavas were victors, Draupadi proved her chastity by walking through fire, and it was proclaimed at the ceremony that those who, trusting in her and having implicit faith in her powers, undertook to walk over fire, would get rid of any maladies they suffered from, and attain all objects of their desire.

According to Mr. H. K. Beauchamp, who in the *Madras Mail*, 1901, gave an account of a " fire-walk " at St. Thomas's Mount near Madras, Draupadi is worshipped at an annual festival in Allandur temple. The " fire - walk " is reputed to secure "to the villagers their cattle and crops, and protection from dangers of all sorts ". These dangers, of course, come from evil spirits which are waging constant war against mankind and always endeavouring to cause disorder in Nature.

The Badagas of the Nīlgiris celebrate the fire-walking ceremony " to propitiate the deity Jeddayaswāmi to whom vows are made. In token thereof, they grow one twist or plait of hair, which is finally cut off as an offering to Jeddayaswāmi." A coco-nut, camphor, incense, flowers, and a four-anna piece are also offered. Thurston quotes an eyewitness of the fire-walk of the Badagas who says, " I examined the feet of one of the men and one of the women who went through the ceremony, but beyond black impressions on the soles, there was no marked injury."[1]

The ceremony is an annual one at the village of Nuvagōde in Ganjam, and " the officiating priest sits on a seat of sharp thorns " while it is being performed.[2]

Mr. J. G. D. Partridge gives an elaborate description of a fire-walk at Nuvagōde. The ceremony is performed once a year, during the Dassara festival, by the priest of the temple of a village goddess, who was " dressed as a woman with rows of silver bells round his waist and a large head-dress covered with feathers "; in his right hand he carried " a bare sword ". He danced and darted about in quite a frenzied manner. Before walking over the glowing charcoal he dipped his feet in " a mixture of rice-water and milk ".[3]

Writing of a fire-walk in Travancore Mr. G. F. D'Penha says he asked a young man his reason for going through the ceremony. " He told me he had been ill, and had promised the god that he would go through this performance if he recovered. He got better, and so was carrying out his part of the contract. This was, he said, the third year that he had done it." [4]

Some Moslems as well as Hindus perpetuate the ancient ceremony. Mr. G. H. Bernays witnessed a fire-walk at Sivakāsi in the Tinnevelly district. An old priest walked over the glowing charcoal.

---

[1] *Ethnographic Notes*, pp. 476–7; and E. Thurston, *Omens and Superstitions of Southern India*, p. 141.
[2] *Omens and Superstitions*, p. 145; and *Ethnographic Notes*, pp. 475–6.
[3] Quoted in *Ethnographic Notes*, pp. 478 *et seq.*
[4] *Indian Antiquary*, XXXI, 1902.

" On arriving at the centre of the pit he halted, stooped down, and, gathering some of the ashes in his hands, threw them up in the air, and allowed them to fall in a red rain upon his naked body. He then walked slowly out at the other side. He was followed by several others. . . . After this ceremony the usual Mohurrum ' tamāsha ' took place." [1]

According to Mr. Francis, writing in the *Gazetteer of the Anantapur District*,[2] the Mohurrum at Gūgūdu " is, strange to relate, entirely managed by the Hindus of the village, the Muhammadans taking but a small part in it. Hindus, to the number of several thousands, also come in for the ceremony from the adjoining villages." When the bonfire is lit there are lamentations over the death of Hussain and Hasan. Then a regular fire-walk takes place. Mr. Francis writes regarding it:

" First the musicians, who are Mangalās (barbers) by caste, walk through the fire, and then follow all sorts and conditions of others, both Hindus and Muhammadans.

" The same thing on a smaller scale is done at the Mohurrum at Mālyavantam. The Muhammadan Pīrs at Gūgūdu are held in great veneration, and all castes, even Brāhmans it is said, make their vows to them and distribute sugar to the poor if they are successful in obtaining the object of their desires."

According to the 1854 records of the Madras Government, " the ceremony of walking through fire is only of partial occurrence, and can scarcely be called a religious observance, being performed for the most part in fulfilment of vows voluntarily made. The practice does not appear to be acceptable to the higher classes." At Ganjam it was found that " the Muhammadans, during the Mohurrum, are in the habit of passing through the fire ". Only some of the Sūdra [3] classes observed the ceremony at North Arcot. " The Brāhmans have no concern with them." At Salem Hindus and Moslems

---

[1] Quoted in *Ethnographic Notes* (1906), pp. 481-3.
[2] Quoted by E. Thurston, *Ethnographic Notes* (1906), p. 483.
[3] The lowest of the four great castes.

fire-walked in fulfilment of vows. In 1850, during the celebration of the Mohurrum at Tinnevelly " a Muhammadan fell accidentally into a fire-pit prepared for the ceremony of walking through, and died three days afterwards ". The ceremony was discontinued in consequence of this accident. At Godāvari fire-treading is regarded by the Lingadharloo as an efficacious ceremony " for recovering their sanctity if by any chance they lose their lingam (the symbol of Sīva, which they wear); but, even amongst them, it is not considered an essential ceremony ". At Kistna " the devotees run or hop over the coals as quickly as possible ", and "among the Muhammadans the ceremony is sometimes observed, at the Mohurrum, before the astanam or hall where the Pīrs are installed and exhibited ".[1]

Mr. Thurston, writing in 1906, says "the Government some years ago set its face against the ancient practice of fire-walking, and the Collector of Tanjore introduced a ' happy reform ', having prevailed upon the people to use flowers instead of fire". The flowers are consequently being trod upon "devoutly in honour of the goddess ".

Mr. Andrew Lang says that the fire-walking ceremony is performed yearly in the Mauritius. " The walkers are natives of Southern India who carry this rite also to Trinidad and the Straits Settlements. The process is religious and is usually undertaken in fulfilment of a vow." Mr. Lang proceeds:

" A shallow trench of about fourteen yards in length is dug and dry wood is piled on it to about four feet in height. This is kindled, and burns down to red embers. These are then raked smooth with long rakes, the heat being intense, so that the fire cannot be closely approached. A goat is then decapitated and carried round the pyre. A priest next enters, walks through the fire, and dances in the middle. He then stands by the edge and watches the others who walk through. Several seemed under the influence of drugs or strong excitement." [2]

The Biblical narrative of Shadrach, Meshach, and Abed-nego is suggestive of a fire-walking ceremony. Nebuchadnezzar, who had these men cast into the fire, exclaimed:

" Lo, I see four men loose, walking in the midst of the fire, and they have no hurt; and the form of the fourth is like the Son of God."

He went close to the fire and called out their names.

" Then Shadrach, Meshach, and Abed-nego came forth of the midst of the fire. And the princes, governors, and captains, and the king's counsellors, being gathered together, saw these men, upon whose bodies the fire had no power, nor was an hair of their head singed, neither were their coats changed, nor the smell of fire had passed on them." [1]

The goddess Perasia or Artemis Perasia of Hieropolis-Castabla in Cilicia, Asia Minor, appears to have been a deity similar to the Artemis of Cappadocia. According to Strabo (XII, 2, 7) the priestesses of the Cappadocian goddess were wont to walk barefooted over fire and they suffered no injury by so doing. They were supposed to be protected during the ordeal by the goddess. Sir James G. Frazer, referring to the rite, calls attention to the remarks of Jambilchus, the Syrian philosopher, who says of inspired persons that they " are not burned by fire, the fire not taking hold of them by reason of the divine inspiration; and many, though they are burned, perceive it not, because at the time they do not live an animal life. . . . They rush into fire, they pass through fire, they cross rivers, like the priestesses of Castabala."

Mr. Andrew Lang [2] provides interesting particulars regarding the Bulgarian rite:

" The fire-walkers in Bulgaria are called *Nistinares* and the faculty is regarded as hereditary. . . . They dance in the fire on May 21, the feast of SS. Helena and Constantine. Great fires of scores of cartloads of dry wood are made. On the embers of these

---

[1] *Daniel*, iii, 19-27.   [2] *Magic and Religion*, 285-6.

the Nistinares (who turn blue in the face) dance and utter prophecies, afterwards placing their feet in the muddy ground where libations of water have been poured forth. The report says nothing as to the state of their feet. The Nistinare begins to feel the effect of the fire after his face has resumed its wonted colour and expression."

In ancient Italy the " fire-walk " was performed by worshippers of the goddess Feronia. That deity had a sanctuary at the base of Mount Soracte, and there, according to Sir James G. Frazer:

" Once a year the men of certain families walked barefoot, but unscathed, over the glowing embers and ashes of a great fire of pinewood in presence of a vast multitude who had assembled from all the country round about to pay their devotions to the deity or to ply their business at the fair. The families from whom the performers of the rite were drawn went by the name of Hirpi Sorani, or ' Soranian wolves '; and in consideration of the services which they rendered the state by walking through the fire, they were exempted, by a special decree of the senate, from military service and all public burdens." [1]

According to Strabo, the fire-walkers were inspired and protected by the goddess Feronia, whose sanctuary was revered by the Latins and Sabines.

Virgil in the *Æneid* [2], describing the funeral of Pallas, makes Aruns say that the fire is fed and the fire-walk performed in the worship of Apollo, guardian of sacred Mount Soracte while " strong in faith we walk through the midst of the fire and press our footsteps in the glowing mass ".

Pliny [3] likewise connects the rite with the god of the mountain whose name is believed to have been Soranus. Varro, quoted in Servius's *Commentary*, expresses the opinion that the fire-walkers smeared some substance on the soles of their feet before entering the fire. From a reference to the custom in Silius Italicus (V, 175 *et seq.*)

---

[1] *The Golden Bough* (Third Edition), Part VII, Vol. II, pp. 14-5.
[2] Book XI.   [3] *Natural History*, VII, 19.

it seems that the " fire-walkers " passed thrice through the furnace holding the entrails of the sacrificial victims in their hands.

Mr. Andrew Lang, dealing with the Spanish " fire-walkers ", tells that in Inquisition times they were employed in extinguishing fires. He quotes as follows from the evidence provided by the last Earl Marischal of Scotland who visited Spain:

> " There is a family or caste in Spain, who, from father to son, have the power of going into the flames without being burned, and who, by dint of charms permitted by the Inquisition, can extinguish fires." [1]

A remarkable fire ceremony, resembling the " walk " is reported from West Africa by Mr. A. B. Ellis [2] who tells that to test their chastity the priests and priestesses of the Tshi-speaking peoples of the Gold Coast submit to the ordeal of standing one by one in a narrow circle of fire. This is " supposed to show whether they have remained pure and refrained from sexual intercourse during the period of retirement and so are worthy of inspiration by the gods. If they are pure they will receive no injury and suffer no pain from the fire."

There are no records in Ancient Egyptian literature of ceremonial " fire-walks " performed by the living. It would appear, however, that in the Otherworld the dead and even the gods had at times to brave the dangers of fire. Mr. Warren R. Dawson, whom I have consulted, informs me that there are obscure references in the Pyramid Texts to an " island of fire " which in later times became a " pool " or " lake of fire ". Among the Middle Kingdom coffin texts are funerary spells for immunity from fire. One is a " spell for entering into the Fire and coming forth from the Fire behind the sky ".

From the 18th Dynasty onwards there are references to and pictures of a rectangular fiery-red " pool " with

---

[1] *Magic and Religion*, p. 285.   [2] *The Tshi-speaking Peoples of the Gold Coast*, p. 138.

a brazier at each side and a baboon at each corner. This fiery pool was situated in the Otherworld. A spell (LXIII, A) in the *Book of the Dead* is " for not being burned with fire and for drinking water in the Netherworld ". Another spell, which is very corrupt, " apparently refers ", Mr. Warren R. Dawson says, " to Osiris coming unharmed through the Lake of Fire (or the Lake of the Fiery Ones) ". According to the *Book of the Gates*, the Duat was peopled with fiery serpents and had lakes of fire in it.[1] The walls of the chambers in the tombs of the kings at Thebes are covered with pictures of this mysterious region and of its inhabitants.

The *Book of the Gates* has many allusions to fire and the means whereby the god, and with him the dead, may turn its terrors into enjoyment. For the " pool of fire " had its inhabitants who, as the texts tell us, lived happily and fared well therein. These beings had magical immunity from fire; their pool was an abode, not of terror but of pleasure. The fire could not harm them; it consumed only the enemies of the sun-god.

The " fire-walk " was imported into pre-Columbian America by sea-farers, but apparently not from Polynesia, because the walk was over glowing charcoal, not heated stones. Sir James G. Frazer reproduces the evidence given by Diego de Landa.[2]

The ceremony was observed by the natives of Yucatan, the peninsula at the south-eastern extremity of Mexico which had a flourishing civilization prior to the Spanish conquest. In the ancient native Calendar the year marked by the sign of *cauac* was reputed to be particularly unlucky and it was believed that during it there would be a high death-rate, great loss of maize crops owing to extreme heat and swarms of devouring ants and birds.

[1] Warren R. Dawson, *Asiatic Review*, April, 1921, p. 348.
[2] *Relation des Choses de Yucatan* (Paris, 1864), pp. 231–3.

" To arrest these calamities they used to erect a great pyre of wood to which persons contributed a faggot. Having danced about it during the day, they set fire to it at nightfall, and when the flames had died down, they spread out the red embers and walked or ran barefoot over them, some of them escaping unsmirched by the flames, but others burning themselves more or less severely. In this way they hoped to conjure away the evils that threatened them, and to undo the sinister omens of the year." [1]

Dealing with the fire dances of the Navajos north of Mexico, which were observed in winter and were supposed to bring bountiful harvests and fertilizing rains, he says that during the night a great pile of timber was set on fire. When the flames die down the dancers perform a " fire-walk " or indulge in " fire-leaping ":

" During the dance they throw sparks, smoke and flames about their bodies; they leap through the last glowing embers; they seem bathed in fire. This also they can do without getting burnt, as the white coating, the daubing with earth, protects them from the flames." [2]

Discussing the meaning of the " fire-walk ", Sir James G. Frazer remarks that the customs observed in different parts of the world " present at least a superficial resemblance to the modern European practice of leaping over fires and driving cattle through them ". He does not favour the theory that the ceremonies were " sun charms ", but thinks they were " purifications ". But " purifications " entailed the conquest of evil influences which were supposed to interfere with the season-controlling heavenly bodies and therefore with the welfare of nature and mankind.

It may well be that the ancient belief in fiery lakes or pools in the Otherworld, which were created by evil beings to impede the progress of souls towards regions of bliss, may have given origin to the " fire-walk " and

---

[1] *The Golden Bough* (Third Edition, Balder Vols.), Vol. II, pp. 13-4.
[2] Leo Frobenius, *The Childhood of Man* (Translation by A. H. Keane), London, 1909, p. 406.

to " fire-leaping ". If the feat of " passing through the fire " could be accomplished upon this earth, it could, according to those who in their ceremonies imitated the progress of souls, be likewise accomplished in the Otherworld. Indeed, according to the ideas of the living mimics, the souls would be aided by the successful performance of a ceremonial " fire-walk " in the world of the living, while " fire-walkers " after death were expected to carry their " merit " or power to the next world and be as successful there as here in overcoming fire.

In the various instances of the wide-spread fire-walking ceremony given above we are afforded glimpses of the process of grafting imported doctrines and practices on to existing religious systems. We can also detect, as in the case of Moslem fire-walks in India, the retention of the practices of an ancient religion among those of an imported religion which has been established by force.

It may well be that the first fire-walkers adopted beliefs regarding the welfare of the soul which in the area of origin required only the provision of spells, and that, in accordance with their prevailing practice, they gave them expression in ceremonial acts so that participants might be equipped for the fire-walking ordeal in the next world or souls be stimulated to imitate the living. In the Egyptian evidence given above we find that souls actually lived in "pools of fire".

All religious or magico-religious ceremonies had origin in specific doctrines, but the original doctrines were not everywhere remembered by those who perpetuated the ceremonies. In the case of the " fire-walk ", however, we can detect in Polynesia, America, China, India, &c., the haunting belief that the ceremony increased *mana* (power) and therefore strengthened the individual in his conflict with supernatural enemies, and also the belief that the participants were supposed to assist in overcoming the forces of evil which were opposed to the smooth working of the laws of Nature. In Egypt the dwellers in the "pools of fire" were apparently sun-worshippers who lived in these manifestations of the season-controlling sun. They became "one with Nature".